REBELLIOUS FRASER'S

THE FRASERIANS.

REBELLIOUS FRASER'S

Nol Yorke's Magazine in the Days of Maginn, Thackeray, and Carlyle

BY
MIRIAM M. H. THRALL

AMS PRESS, INC.
NEW YORK
1966

Reprinted 1966
with permission of Columbia University Press

AMS PRESS, INC.
New York, N.Y. 10003

Manufactured in the United States of America

TO
E. C. J.

PREFACE

The present study of the early *Fraser's* is frankly incomplete, since any full recovery of the lost columns would involve material too varied for a single volume and bibliographical enigmas to which I have no clue. One of my reasons for publishing this work is, indeed, that it may be supplemented and corrected by others, for the importance of the magazine has so long been recognized that some breaking of ground should be attempted.

Fraser's contains the best of Carlyle's and Thackeray's early work and throws light on one of the most difficult decades of the nineteenth century. The young rebels of the 1830 staff, who were gathered around the arch rebel William Maginn, exposed the frailties and foibles of their generation with provocative comment rare at any period. In reassembling the wit, erudition, and common sense of these famous satirists, I have limited myself to the fields of politics and literature, considering especially their attack on the social misery accompanying economic experimentation and their war on sentimentality and on the system which they racily denounced as "Puff and Plunder." For reference on the staff itself I have included notices of its prominent wits and scholars. In more detail I have examined the extraordinary relation of Carlyle to the magazine and the evolution of Thackeray's work under the editor, William Maginn.

The final chapters attempt to recreate this powerful editor and full-flavored wit, emphasizing the controversial points regarding his reputation. Maginn has so long been a brilliant figure on the border of recognition that no apology is needed for including his life in a book on the magazine which he identified in an almost autobiographic sense with himself. In considering his literary work I have omitted all except the more important questions in regard to his bibliography. Maginn was the most prolific magazinist of his age, and his writing, though published chiefly in *Blackwood's* and *Fraser's,* was so widely scattered among other periodicals that to recapture the greater part of it would be an impossible task.

Identification of work in *Fraser's* is, however, too important to be overlooked. Of recent years my research has centered around Thackeray and Carlyle, and its results have been included in appendices. The material which I presented earlier, in two articles on Carlyle's bibliography, appearing respectively in *Publications of the Modern Language Association,* for September, 1924, and *Modern Language Notes,* for May, 1931, has not been repeated here in full but summarized. Bibliographical data on other members of the staff have been confined for the most part to appended tables. There has been no attempt to make these a complete record of research, and important items in consequence remain unmentioned, since unless evidence for identification seemed reasonably valid it has been omitted. *Fraser's* itself only occasionally affords data sufficient for accurate tracing of authorship. The magazine's archives are no longer in existence, Longmans Green, its last publishers, not having even stray records of its early years. A good deal of its writing was collaborative; indeed, the method under which some of the articles were produced raises the question whether in the rapid give and take of convivial work the writers themselves always had a clear idea as to their individual accomplishment.

In bringing the present volume to completion I wish to acknowledge the guidance of the late Professor Ashley H. Thorndike of Columbia University, who first suggested my study of the early *Fraser's.* Like hundreds of other students who have felt the incentive of this great teacher's sensitive and enriching criticism, I find any tribute to his memory inadequate to express the originality and creative force of his contribution. My work on Maginn has been made more authentic by information regarding his family life generously furnished by his granddaughter, Mrs. Michael Scott, and by his niece, Miss Elizabeth Maginn. Even greater is my obligation to the Reverend Charles Wm. Maginn, who has devoted years to close study of his uncle's works and to gathering material for a biography. This material he graciously placed at my disposal, supplementing it by oral accounts. I have also received valuable aid from Professor Emery Neff of Columbia University, whose advice, especially on the sections dealing with Carlyle, has opened new approaches. To Professor Charles S. Baldwin I am deeply indebted for criticism of the manuscript and suggestion as to its revision. Throughout its preparation for the press I have had the expert assistance of Emily Cooper Johnson, whose generous gift of time and skill I welcome this opportunity to acknowledge. Other friends who have patiently watched the growth of this work and have helped by their scholarship, taste, and encouragement are Professor Anne K. Tuell of Wellesley College, Professor Helen Griffith of Mount Holyoke College, and Lois L. Comings, Assistant Editor of Publications of the Metropolitan Museum of Art. I also wish to thank with especial warmth Miss Bertha Blakeley of the Mount Holyoke College Library, whose cordial coöperation has repeatedly facilitated my research. The officers of the British Museum Library and of the Widener Library at Harvard have been most considerate and resourceful. For the reproduction of *Fraser's* cover I am indebted to the Widener Library.

MIRIAM M. H. THRALL

MOUNT VERNON, NEW YORK
October, 1933

CONTENTS

Part One

THE ROUND TABLE

Part Two

REVOLT IN CRITICISM

Part Three

REVOLT IN POLITICS

Part Four

WILLIAM MAGINN

APPENDICES

ILLUSTRATIONS

PART ONE
THE ROUND TABLE

CHAPTER I

FRASER'S AND THE 1830'S

At a propitious moment in the beginning of the year 1830, Billy Maginn, Irish Doctor of Laws and seasoned magazinist, walked gayly into the publishing shop of James Fraser at 215 Regent Street. Fraser, who had by shrewd application grown prosperous in his business, was in an adventurous mood. For some time the thought had been gaining ground in his mind that he would like to start a magazine—popular, to be sure, but also scholarly and substantial—one in which he could take pride as well as find amusement. The *Foreign Review* and *Foreign Quarterly,* James Fraser felt, would supply his new organ with contributors, thus insuring from the start its repute for scholarship. What the ambitious Scotchman was still uncertain about was popularity. And then came to him Billy Maginn, the "Doctor" himself, otherwise known by his valiant pen name of Sir Morgan O'Doherty, Adjutant.

At the end of the first brief chat in the publisher's back parlor behind the spare little shop in Regent Street, the bargain was struck. Fraser was generous in his offer; Maginn quick in his acceptance. The small, shrewd publisher, with his keen eyes looking kindly from a thin angular face, had liked the genial and equally small man who sat before him. For the next six years they were to sit thus, opposite each other at the huge round table in the back parlor—little men both, but complete masters of the board.

Why William Maginn, or the "Doctor" as he was familiarly called, had turned up at a moment so particularly in accord with the secret ambition of James Fraser was a matter which intimately concerned the fortunes of that brilliant but variable Irishman. The redoubtable Sir Morgan O'Doherty, Adjutant, had in fact gone hunting a job in much the same spirit as that in which a small boy takes a dare. Indeed the Adjutant was always himself something of a small boy. During his troubled and often harassed life he had never taken time to grow up. He was too much of a wit and a practiced joker to take seriously either his own scholarly accomplishments or his own predicaments, and his nervous exuberance kept him from remaining long disaffected or inactive. Yet by the beginning of 1830 it had become evident even to one of his easy optimism that *Blackwood's,* the great Tory magazine to which he had earlier given so much of his time, no longer wished to accept the kind of articles he wanted to write. He was in short an unwelcome contributor. *Blackwood's* must be made to realize its mistake. And forthwith he determined to edit a Tory monthly after his own liking—a monthly which should rival *Blackwood's* itself.

A more cautious person than the impetuous Maginn might well have hesitated to undertake a task so little likely to succeed. *Blackwood's,* or the "Maga," was the most popular periodical of the time and its sway was both despotic and far-reaching. But the "Doctor" was never without boyish bravado or the wish to put his own powers to the test. As capital he had nothing except the twelve years of hard labor during which he had served the multiple needs of the English press; he had an expensive family to support, and a great variety of debts. Armed with a knowledge of these and a roll of manuscript he had started forth, as the story goes, with another literary man about town who bore the prophetic name of Fraser. As the two sauntered arm in arm down Regent Street, Maginn, noticing the sign over the door of the publisher at 215, jovially exclaimed, "Fraser! Here's a namesake of yours. Let's try him." Thus casually was the enterprise begun. James Fraser, it may be added, never acknowledged relationship, though Maginn's friend, Hugh Fraser, is said to have contributed occasionally to the magazine and liked frequently to visit the back parlor. Since he was one of the projectors who presumably assumed fairly heavy responsibility in financing the venture, the periodical was named after him rather than James Fraser; but his connection with it would seem to have been brief and none too clear.

The rôle of Maginn is less difficult to define. The statement made in the magazine itself to the effect that he was never really its editor sprang without doubt from his having no share in the reading of proof, a task which in those days was always associated with the position; but it is beyond question that he established the magazine's policy and was the recognized leader of the staff, whom he ruled with the capricious high spirits of a comedian and the infectious zest of a propagandist. He was repeatedly referred to by his associates and by others as the editor. Percival Banks, one of the earliest and most intimate members of the staff, mentions him by that title[1]; as does the powerful Fraserian, Father Prout,[2] who was his prime companion in roguery, and for a short time his successor in the position of editor.

In appearance the new Tory monthly was unpretentious, very like *Blackwood's* in format, with some hundred and twenty-five closely printed, double-columned pages within a brown jacket bearing the emblem of Scotch thistles and the unwieldy title *Fraser's Magazine for Town and Country*. The paper was of good quality, capable of withstanding the years, but what chiefly distinguished the magazine were the finely executed engravings forming its "gallery" of portraits, which appeared in each issue during practically the first seven years.

The magazine thus casually projected became at once the most popular and most daringly outspoken organ of the London press. Apart from its individual contributors, it was in itself famous, as waggish and disconcertingly wise a hybrid as ever won the admiration of the public. More remarkable is the light which it incidentally throws on the reputation of three great men of its century. Carlyle has suffered in the esteem of some critics from his lack of generosity in appraising Coleridge. Thackeray has recently been accused of insincerity and prudishness. Disraeli has from the first faced the charge of sophistry, of convincing Young England of Peel's misdeeds in order that he might the more easily usurp Peel's power. Each of these accusations seems ill-founded after a study of the shrewd and delineative monthly, itself so devout in its antagonisms, so earnest in its clownish raillery. William Maginn also is vindicated by a study of *Fraser's*—and rightly, since through its violence he made so many enemies that clumsy calumny has remained even to this day upon his name. Maginn should have been long since recognized as the greatest magazinist of the nineteenth century, one of its most clever satirists, and a scholar and critic of distinction. Could the monthly have at once risen from its grave on library shelves, it would have cried out his achievement and his innocence. He was a drunkard and a spendthrift, an eccentric and unaccountable genius; but he at no time sold his political opinions, nor did he seduce and blackmail the poet Letitia Landon. More important, the magazine holds the answer to the vexed question, so long a matter of heated controversy: What did Thackeray contribute to its early volumes? No partial study of its pages is adequate to unbare the secret; the full scope of the work is needed even to approximate a solution. Of more recent interest is the contention that Carlyle may have had a hand in a few of *Fraser's* unacknowledged essays. Here again, a general knowledge of the magazine, its aims and its contributors, is required, since local investigation leads to misapprehension.

Fraser's abrupt founding was in keeping with its vehement history. During the fifty-two years of its existence, from February, 1830, to December, 1882, it was to be one of the most important organs of progressive thought and open revolt in the Victorian age. With its first number *Fraser's* opened battle against the Utilitarians of its day, advancing upon *laissez-faire* measures with a fury which gave no quarter to Conservative, Liberal, or Radical. Nor did the magazine grow less formidable at the death of its belligerent founders, Maginn and Fraser. After a brief indecisive period it was taken over in 1847[3] by the no less stalwart leaders of the Broad Church movement, which in its intricate ramifications and influences was responsible for much of the vigorous rebellion against doctrines and traditions that were hampering scientific and theological, as well as social, development. During this later period the magazine fearlessly included in its pages Charles Kingsley's revolutionary novel *Yeast,* which followed its publication of his *Hypatia.* Even more boldly disruptive were John Stuart Mill's famous *Utilitarianism* and *Non-Intervention,* and Buckle's almost equally famous *Mill on Liberty* and *The Influence of Women on the Progress of Knowledge.* James Anthony Froude, for many years the monthly's brilliant editor and contributor, even persuaded Ruskin to make it the vehicle for his economic series later published as *Munera Pulveris.* The articles were too heterodox to be tolerated by the public and had to be discontinued, but the effort to produce them was characteristic of the magazine's restless rebellion.

It is not strange that so high-minded and courageous a policy should have attracted the attention of thoughtful men. Sir Leslie Stephen became one of *Fraser's* frequent correspondents, as did Max Müller,

John Tyndall, Richard Jefferies, George Henry Lewes, Sir Arthur Helps, Sir John Skelton (better known under his pen name of Shirley), Andrew Lang, Sir Aubrey de Vere. Carlyle, Ruskin, Frederic Harrison, James Spedding are from time to time represented, as well as Palgrave, Gosse, Richard Garnett, Coventry Patmore, the Tennysons.

Fraser's success was the more remarkable because throughout its life of fifty-two years, true to the rebellious notions of its founders, it never allied itself with the political policies of any government and therefore never gained political subsidy or endorsement. It was the only half-crown periodical—and one of the very few periodicals at any price—which in that day maintained its independence of party leaders. Although under Maginn it adhered staunchly to Tory principles, it was far too pugnacious to tolerate party men or methods or motives. Under the Broad Church influence, while it crossed to the Liberal side, it kept clear of party issues, at no time showing enthusiasm for the policies of any specific government and for the most part ignoring or opposing them. Even in its last years the monthly quotes with a proud sense of kinship from one of its earlier articles on the days of Maginn and Fraser. It will be seen, the Broad Church editor, Parker, comments in referring to Maginn's policy, "that we undertook to bolster up no faction; to pin our faith to no man, nor any set of men; to support to the best of our ability the established institutions of the country; and to deal with every public measure, as it came before us, strictly according to its merits."[4] Nor can the writer bring himself to judge harshly even the more raw pugilism of this first staff. He bids his readers remember that if there be good in a magazine, "it begins its career impetuously. Strong in its impulses, earnest in its views, it lashes out to the right and the left, wherever there may seem to be wrong which requires correction, or cant that demands exposure." This is a fair example of Fraserian assertion. Points of view might, and indeed did, change radically with the years. Yet in spite of antagonistic doctrines, a spirit of obstinate independence unites the various phases through which the magazine passed, giving to its volumes a community of aggression at times as binding as that of thought.

Nor was the magazine without a more tangible unifying purpose. The leaders of the Broad Church movement and other progressive writers for *Fraser's* were more or less directly under the influence of Coleridge. Charles Kingsley, Principal Tulloch, Sir Arthur Helps, Sir Leslie Stephen, John Stuart Mill, among the eminent students and interpreters of the mystic philosopher, were all closely associated with the magazine. In the earlier period, under the editorship of Maginn, the indebtedness was openly avowed.

Not without reason did *Fraser's* in its first numbers boast that it was written with "the counsel of Coleridge and the countenance of Scott," and quite rightly did Coleridge, "the old man eloquent," hold honored place in the famous cartoon of its staff. Not that he was responsible, presumably, for the appearance in the magazine of the few pieces of work bearing his signature. The satirical poems were printed, it is to be hoped, without his permission, and the monologues and notes arranged by Heraud were published after his death.[5] But he spoke of *Fraser's* with approval and characteristically regretted that he could not send it a series of articles. None the less, although doubtless without his own knowledge, he was constantly giving to its pages a contribution of a most real and pervasive nature. Heraud, for a while assistant editor, was his avowed disciple and would-be expounder; Edward Irving was one of his warmest and most intimate friends; and several of the other Fraserians had at some time attended his Thursday evenings at Highgate. Through them much of Coleridge's righteous self-confidence found its way into the magazine. His hatred of Liberalism, his mystical faith in the Established Church, his theological rendering of Schelling's metaphysics had without question their effect in emboldening and cultivating the work of the magazine. Maginn, it is true, did not need the admonition of Coleridge to convince him that in England's factories children were "bred up in cotton," and that England's so-called Liberalism was adverse to true reform. As has been said, he early took his own stand against the political economists and the philosophical reforms of Liberalism. But the constant presence, as it were, of Coleridge at his council table strengthened his position, and there can be no question that he gained something of his exalted self-assurance from the knowledge that his thoughts were being echoed in articles steeped in the high subjects of German metaphysics and English theology.

Since it is the purpose of the present book to study the early periodical, from 1830 to approximately 1840, it should be stated at the outset that the volumes which contained this lofty material in such abundance were so strangely conglomerate as to draw from Carlyle the disgusted comment of "dog's meat-tart of a periodical." *Fraser's* was reputed to have had the most brilliant staff of its time; probably it had the most brilliant of the century. It contained the greater part of Carlyle's early writing, including that Bible of the later Victorians, *Sartor Resartus,* the best of young Thackeray's narrative and critical essays, and no little popularized scholarship by such writers as the gayly erudite Father Prout and the learned Cambridge stripling, Thomas Wright. Yet it also had a reputation for tumultuous and wicked humor. The question arises, How did it become so paradoxical? The answer lies in its editor.

"Naught to do but be jocose, or with a pin impale our pigmy foes." Thus boasted William Maginn, according to his satiric custom; for *Fraser's Magazine* beneath its punch-bowl roistering was fearfully, even tempestuously, in earnest, and no wit of the day was more alarmingly serious than Sir Morgan O'Doherty, Adjutant.

For at least five years before Maginn began *Fraser's,* he had been storing up great rage against his time, and he relished to the full its noisy outburst in the early numbers of his magazine. Not a political leader of the day of whatever party escaped the indignant cudgel of the periodical; scarcely a popular writer was unscotched by its disapproval. Nor was the revolt against politics and literature less violent because often the weapon employed was ridicule. It was a matter of doubt whether *Fraser's* antagonisms were more to be dreaded when marshaled in grim array or when sported in raucous mirth.

In this impish and exuberant warfare the magazine foreshadowed in a more brutal and more focused form the pranks of the later *Punch,* that national panacea which it anticipated by some ten years. If *Punch* was in earnest most of the time, *Fraser's* was in earnest all the time. Its buffoonery might on occasion be coarse and its personalities indecent, but beneath its levity was dogged conviction. Like *Punch,* it had discovered that "when you practice virtue you must do it with a laugh." The quotation might, indeed, be amended to include politics among the virtues, or even personal spleen; but the intention was the same. "I find," writes the editor, "I am going to moralize, which is a horrid waste of time."

Nor must it be forgotten when mentioning *Fraser's* as a precursor of *Punch* that the wily and inveterate Maginn in the last months of his life was to become one of the charter contributors to that spritely periodical, or that his aide-de-camp Thackeray was afterwards to be for years a prominent member of its staff. At Maginn's death *Punch* claimed him as its own by donning for the first time in its as yet brief course the black border, which has ever since been famous as its symbol of mourning for the passing of those who have had the wit to make the world laugh at folly.

The magazine, thus established as a wit with an earnest purpose, became at once buffoon and scoffer, opportunist and casuist; it was earnestly polemical and righteously informative. Its methods were unpredictable, and its style was as multiple as its personality. And yet with all its protean changes, true to the fable, it managed to remain itself. Its reactions might be unexpected, but they were not uncharacteristic. Nefarious or generous, its sins and virtues were on its own head and its impulses were self-actuated. As long as Maginn controlled the policies of *Fraser's,* the monthly remained histrionic but definite in its policy.

Yet it would be wrong to identify the personality of the monthly with that of the editor. Rather, *Fraser's* was the result of Maginn at work with others in a close incorporation that took to itself a life not of any one person but rather a more generous and urgent transcension of the group. The very violence of *Fraser's* warfare on its age gave common cause to its staff, unquestionably quickening and intensifying their individual reactions. The slashing editor Maginn, the young student Carlyle, the dilettante Thackeray, the priest and Bohemian Prout, the anthropologist Croker, could scarcely have failed, however unconsciously, to urge one another on. Thus the magazine, boorish as it frequently was, came to look at the age with strangely disillusioned eyes, fashioning for its privileged staff an uncanny perspective and freedom, as if subsequent modes of thought and to some extent of style already lay open before them.

Coming at the beginning of the 1830's, the battle royal of the magazine's eminent staff has special significance. The decade of the thirties, full as it was of enigmas, has always been difficult to understand. It was sufficiently near the beginning of the century to feel the full force of the industrial revolution. The nation was devastated, but had yet gained no perspective on remedial measures. Thoughtful people knew that the sturdy peasantry had been made paupers, that children were herded into factories to turn out from machines work which from time immemorial had been done in the home by their elders. They were aware of upheaval in every rank of life and every department of government, but were without the wisdom to foresee the outcome or the scientific knowledge to direct it. England had produced no man in whose leadership it had faith. Reforms were at best of doubtful benefit and entailed immediate suffering without alleviation.

It is unfortunate that a decade of such sharp paradox and confusion of issues should have brought forth few spokesmen. Nearly every other decade in the nineteenth century had its great authors to interpret it; but that of the thirties, as is well recognized, was an interregnum between two periods of literary activity. The contemporaries of Shelley and Byron had either died in the twenties or had practically ceased to write; the contemporaries of Tennyson were to do their characteristic work in the forties or later.

Yet the thirties, for all their scarcity of spokesmen, were not without literary significance. They were, it will be remembered, the incubative years for the great Victorians, when the subsequent dictators of British thought were growing into manhood and forming their views on the dubious state of things around them. Five young giants were already beginning to publish. Dickens early started to make the daily papers a lucrative vehicle for his entertaining protest against the errors of the time. Browning, vainly trying to gain the attention of an unheeding public, was pouring forth gratuitously his autobiographic spirit. Tennyson shyly produced two small books of early poems before he withdrew into his wise silence of ten years. Carlyle and Thackeray, as has been said, were finding their main outlets within the pages of *Fraser's* itself; and also within those pages can be traced the influence of Coleridge, whose idealism was indescribably shaping the thought of the younger generation.

In a decade of this sort the ordinary run of work in any periodical has enhanced value. In the case of *Fraser's* this value is magnified by the brilliance of its staff, and the magazine, in consequence, becomes an important index. In its files daily occurrence revives and the period takes on circumstantial complexity.

The very informality of *Fraser's* style, in contrast to that of the more sedate reviews, increases this topical value. Even conventional writers liked the caper of their surroundings, and well-established authors were often metamorphosed, using a style alien to that of their previous work. Contributors from a distance fell into the monthly's easy raillery and swift, often flashy, retort, accepting as their own its special antipathies and jesting in terms of its favorite jests. Even so stout an individualist as Carlyle by no means escaped its journalistic caprice.

It is hardly worth while to inquire how the bulk of this writing would rank today. Its habitual assumption of infallibility is irritating to the modern reader. We are inclined to forget that to judge and to be judged was the customary repartee of the thirties, and that lack of the oracular in statement was considered lack of force. Personalities are no longer the *sine qua non* of rebuttal, and in these *Fraser's* was even in the indulgent eye of its own day a notable offender. On the other hand, although often coarse and cheap beyond endurance, the magazine was yet capable of dexterity in allusion and phrase. It was wholesomely opposed to the long-winded didacticism of its day, and its own approach was rapid and informal. Its staff tolerated neither the bombast nor the sentimentalism which was then in fashion. So they put their vigorous young minds and high spirits to the task of ridicule, with a gleeful savagery born of their own discernment.

Fraser's belongs to the trio of the first modern magazines. It was at once the follower and rival of *Blackwood's,* that great parent monthly within the pages of which were shaped the chief features of our magazines of today. Each of this first trio, *Blackwood's,* the *London Magazine,* and *Fraser's,* should receive more attention than has heretofore been accorded. Only scattered and fragmentary work has as yet appeared on either *Blackwood's* or the *London Magazine,* and none of any sort on *Fraser's*. Yet the importance of all three has long been recognized and their influence on subsequent periodicals and on literature in general is unquestioned.

FRASER'S

MAGAZINE

FOR

TOWN AND COUNTRY.

N° LXI.

JANUARY, 1835.

LONDON:

JAMES FRASER, 215 REGENT STREET;

WAUGH AND INNES, EDINBURGH; W. R. M'PHUN, GLASGOW; W. GRAPEL, LIVERPOOL; AND GRANT AND CO. DUBLIN.

SOLD ALSO BY ALL BOOKSELLERS AND NEWSMEN IN TOWN AND COUNTRY.

HALF-A-CROWN.

To edit a monthly was an even greater adventure in the twenties and thirties of the last century than it is at present. In those years the magazine in the modern sense was so near its beginning as to be amorphous, feeling its way to form, experimenting with its faculties. The three initial monthlies were attempting to be all types of organ at once: meddlesome journal in the affairs of the moment, political monitor, philosophical and critical review, and amusement supplement. They discussed national problems as freely as the well-established quarterlies, the *Edinburgh Review* and the *Quarterly Review,* and included the same type of informative article. On the other hand they early developed those departments which have since proved to be more particularly the magazine's own—fiction, biography, travel, and the creative, as opposed to the critical, essay. They tried the editor's easy chair squib, the personal anecdote, the character sketch, the burlesque episode, the burlesque story—even the serial novel.

In spite of this diversity of function the great trio of the twenties and thirties had a focus which is practically unknown today, and could at will turn their full strength towards promoting or decrying a cause or an individual. Almost an entire number of a magazine was then on occasion produced by a comparatively small group of men who were thinking in unison and writing very largely on clearly defined issues. Individual articles were of course sent in by a rather large body of contributors who were included in the staff, but much of the writing was in the hands of a few members intimate with the policies of the editor. Thus while the magazine might give the impression that it was drawing from the talent of the country at large, as indeed it was, none the less so much of it was frequently produced by several eminently versatile men that a whole number could be a unit of insufferable destruction.

The magazine of the twenties and thirties thus became one of the most powerful weapons of personal and political warfare that the press has devised. The system of anonymous writing made the task of disciplining it far from easy. It was reaching a constantly increasing reading public. It was less diffuse than the newspaper which came out every day, and yet it threw itself into politics as ardently as any of the dailies and coped with the minutiae of home and foreign policies with the same sense of divine right to arouse, instruct, and guide. In short, its longer interval of publication won for it at least apparent perspective, while its method of swift production secured for it immediacy. Luckily no monthly remained in this monarchical phase of development long enough to gather the national prestige of that great arbiter of public opinion, the London *Times*. The very ruthlessness of the magazine's method set its own time limit. If a few men appropriated undue control, they also had to expend undue effort. It needed no normal strength to write the larger part of a periodical in comparatively few days; and the tales that are told of the early Titans record travails of no unheroic nature.[6] Of Maginn, it is said that he could easily turn out at a sitting of from five to six hours some sixteen octavo pages of fine double-column print, or on an average of about twenty-five hundred words an hour.[7] It is scarcely to be wondered that subsequent staffs were unwilling to carry on a magazine by such gargantuan methods.

From the moment of its founding *Fraser's* was a financial success. Its growth was as rapid as the mushroom fame which the slanderous "Chaldee Manuscript" had earlier brought to *Blackwood's*. "Regina," as the new monthly at once regally nicknamed itself, soon had, it was said, as large a circulation as that of any half-crown periodical of the day. Even by the end of its first year it boasted of selling 8,700 copies—"a *bonâ fide* sale"; and added with a smack of satisfaction, "Consider, we are scarcely a year started."[8]

As it turned out, the two founders of the magazine, the long-headed publisher and the headlong editor, had chosen their time well. The day had by no means come when literary fight of the rough-and-tumble sort was eschewed. A man who would command attention must first attract it. The age was itself hard hitting, and those who would appoint themselves its mentors must show no favor. In this requirement *Fraser's* was not lacking. Its thrusts, if keen, were also strong; its laughter could be coarse and its punishments unsparing. In the name of Oliver Yorke, its fictitious editor, the country was alternately chastized and cherished; individuals were unhesitatingly denounced or lauded, public ceremonies satirized, and pretenders snubbed. In addition it had more amiable qualities; it was rarely pedantic; and it could poke fun at itself most handsomely and most egotistically. In a squib tucked in for full measure on the reverse of the table of contents for January, 1832, we find it not uncharacteristically describing itself as

> That Magazine most quizzical,
> Sublime and metaphysical;
> Conducted with sagacity,
> And wondrous perspicacity,
> By famous OLIVER YORKE, sir—
> Good at the knife and fork, sir.

There was indeed no periodical which quite so well met the demands of its time for bold thought and bolder expression as did that of the devil-may-care, brilliant Nol Yorke. Of the quarterly reviews, the *Edinburgh* had always, even in the first zeal of the youthful Jeffrey, Sydney Smith, and Brougham, been well aware of its own dignity as a public guide. The *Quarterly,* since the retirement of Giffard, had become far less sensational in its condemnations, and with John Lockhart, the son-in-law of Sir Walter Scott, as its new editor, was seeking gravity of manner as well as of matter; and the *Westminster* was devoted almost solely to propaganda. Of the magazines *Blackwood's* was becoming weary of its early literary carousal and was emulating the sobriety of the quarterlies; its rival, the *London Magazine* of Lamb and De Quincey fame, had after a brilliant but unequal fight of nearly a decade been discontinued in 1829; and the *New Monthly* was at this time too painstaking in method and uneven in merit to secure any real grip on the age. Not one of these, in short, was filling the place that *Blackwood's* had held in its boisterous days while Maginn was still one of the leading members of the staff. With the creation of Oliver Yorke in 1830 the public found the jubilant combination of fun and learning, of sage comment and outrageous personality, which won its immediate and devoted applause.

As a group of writers, the Fraserians have usually been evocative of accounts marked by gaiety and good spirits. Whether we read of them in Professor Lounsbury's evaluation of the criticism of the thirties, or in biographies, such as those of Ainsworth and Thackeray, we find extenuating comment. Even Mr. Michael Sadleir, who studies the Fraserians in their savage onslaught on Bulwer Lytton, speaks of "the first eight scintillating years" of the magazine's existence and refers to it as a "higher-powered *Blackwood's*."[9] It is, indeed, difficult to be hard on these care-free scholars, who laughed so heartily, and drank so deeply, and wrote so vehemently around their famous editorial table. For all their ferocity they maintained an offhand quality which was disarming. Their cruelty was premeditated; yet their sallies so mixed riotous fun with abuse as to have the effect of playful irresponsibility.

For a man with the reputation of being unassuming, Maginn had a prodigious instinct for self-advertisement. While he was still living he managed to become legendary. He was reported more clever than he reasonably could have been; his learning more fertile; his memory more apt. With mildness and cruelty thus magnified in wizard reputation, he became both terrible and endearing, a man of sharp lightnings and childlike allurements. In the same fashion, Maginn's prancing spirit surrounded the magazine which he controlled with a golden dust. Great as was the merit of *Fraser's* its prestige in its own day doubtless acquired an arrestive brilliance through the blithe audacity of its editor's advertisements.

Among Maginn's most engaging triumphs was that of employing the magazine's young artist, Daniel Maclise, to sketch the more prominent of the Fraserians seated about the round table at a staff dinner in the publisher's back parlor. The engraving[10] shows the editor in the act of rising to make a speech—"God knows about what," comments Maginn in his letterpress, "for the audience were by no means an auditory." At his right appears a faint, background figure of a Jack Tapster, emblematically drawing a cork, and sleeping soundly on his left shoulder is the equally faint outline of the inebriate Nol Yorke. Opposite Maginn sits the shrewd and alert little publisher, James Fraser, and between them, circling to the right and to the left are twenty-five contributors, including Carlyle, the Reverend Edward Irving, Coleridge, Thackeray, James Hogg, Southey, Allan Cunningham, Barry Cornwall, John Galt, Robert Gleig, Theodore Hook, Count D'Orsay, William Ainsworth, Sir Egerton Brydges, William Jerdan, John Lockhart, Father Prout.[11] Since at the time James Hogg and several others of the group were not in London, and neither Irving nor Coleridge was living, Maginn, with a wink towards the artist Dan Maclise, explains that violations of unity of time and place have been amended by unity of spirit. To which he waggishly adds:

> If you be a painter
> Or if you be a poet,
> You may sometimes try
> A lump of a lie,
> And nobody will blow it.

Perhaps because of this saucy admission the cartoon with its accompanying letterpress has been accepted as history—convivial in character but of unquestionable authenticity. It is still thought a mark of distinction that a writer is named by Maginn as among the original contributors and is to be seen in Maclise's drawing sitting next to Thackeray or Coleridge or Carlyle. Indeed, these first years of the magazine's proud popularity would probably be less heard of today had it not been for the quick pen strokes of its editor and illustrator. The cartoon is a record of actual dinners, and without this evidence the special sort of pungent reference which gives longevity might have been lacking. As it is, there is a peculiar liveliness about the reputation of the Fraserians. The element of time seems scarcely to matter, and they are still spoken of in much the same terms and with much the same freshness of appraisal as they were in their own age—as if posterity had agreed not to lose the zest of so goodly a company.

From the first Maginn had liked the Round Table. It had, he explained, literary association of high and ancient story, making for equality and fraternity, like its prototype in King Arthur's hall at Camelot. Above all, it was a big and hospitable board, around which any of the Fraserians who happened to be in London could sit at convivial ease till dawn streaked the east and even James Fraser's goodly supply of meat and drink ran low. For they were great trenchermen, this gay, brilliant staff of "Regina." And the best man among them was perhaps that famous concocter of whiskey punch, the blithering Irish editor, alias Sir Morgan O'Doherty, Adjutant—Billy Maginn, the "Doctor," himself.

"You'd betther teke anither twist o' the limon," admonished the Doctor; "it's a divilish dale too sweet."

And a willing Fraserian continued:

Accustomed, from our infancy, to obey the slightest hint of the Adjutant on all matters connected with taste, we had armed ourselves with the citric acid, and were about to squeeze the contents of the fragrant "limon" into our punch-bowl, when a knock of the most alarming character was heard at the door. "Who can that be?" exclaimed half a dozen of us, *unâ voce.*

"It's the divil cum boddering wid a conthrebution,"[12] answered Crofton Croker, the "five-foot-nothingness," who had become the first authority on Irish folklore.

Thus with sudden breaks into levity the *Fraser* fraters pricked their minds to almost superhuman efforts on the nights before the magazine went to press.

The scene as here presented recalls the earlier famous *Noctes Ambrosianæ,* which Maginn had started in *Blackwood's* and which Wilson was for many years to continue in the same magazine. In *Fraser's* levees Oliver Yorke, the fictitious editor, presided as mock heroic monarch much as Christopher North held the board at the Ambrose dinners depicted in *Blackwood's Noctes.*

The alacrity with which the device of a fictitious editor was appropriated by *Fraser's* shows how well it was adapted to the needs of the magazine in the 1820's and 1830's. For it is obvious that the good Oliver was more than a name recurrent to the pens of the Fraserians. Without the shield of a general pseudonym such calumnies as *Fraser's* dealt could not have been filliped with so light a hand. Neither Maginn nor any of his staff writing under an individual pen name could have been so brutally jovial or so capricious. But Oliver Yorke, the right ready, ingeniously sinning Oliver, gave corporate safety.

CHAPTER II

MAGAZINE MISCELLANIES

Among important symbols of Nol Yorke was his punch bowl; nor were his inebriate remarks confined merely to what he chose to call "ruminations" around its "remains." The hearty editor was frequently in his cups, and his punch was never without double significance.

> To laugh [write Maginn and Lockhart in brief anticipation of Max Beerbohm] is the privilege of man. It is beyond comparison the most valuable right that he can boast of. It is, moreover, peculiar to himself. No animal but he (for we do not admit our friend, the hyæna, to be an exception) can achieve a cachinnation.[1]

Some of the laughter in the magazine is far less potent today than it was, depending on a timeliness that has vanished; yet enough remains of its galling mirth to justify its reputation for slander as well as for more heart-easing qualities.

FRASER'S PORTRAIT GALLERY

The greater part of the magazine's timely thrusts are contained in its occasional writing. This is for the most part assembled in the famous biographical series, "The Gallery of Illustrious Literary Characters," and in the "Reports," "Ruminations," "Levees," "Coronations," "Symposiacs," and "*Fraser* Papers" of the fictitious editor, Nol Yorke, though they are also in burlesques under such suggestive captions as "Bubble and Squeak," "The Book of the Season," and "Poetry of the Sandwich Islands," as well as scattered among the more serious pages of the magazines. Most of this pugnacious wit will be reserved for a later discussion, but a word should be said here concerning the "Literary Characters."

The "Portrait Gallery," as *Fraser's* proudly termed the series, was an innovation, the first attempt which any English magazine had made to give informative, intimate accounts of the more prominent living men of letters. There were eighty-one sketches in all, including the three group pictures: "The Fraserians," "The Antiquaries," and "*Fraser's* Maids of Honour," the last a number of the prominent women writers of the time.

All of the "Gallery" was written by Maginn with the exception of five sketches. Carlyle contributed the portrait of Goethe, Lockhart that of Maginn, and Prout those of L. E. L., Béranger, and O'Brien. Among other famous folk whose portraits are in the "Gallery" are Carlyle and Lockhart themselves, Godwin, Cobbett, Harriet Martineau, Francis Place, Daniel O'Connell, Brougham, Isaac and Benjamin Disraeli, Sydney Smith, Theodore Hook and his fellow beau, Count D'Orsay, Bulwer Lytton, Harrison Ainsworth, Cruikshank, Scott, Washington Irving, Thomas Moore, Campbell, Coleridge, Lamb, Leigh Hunt, Wordsworth, and James Hogg.[2]

To this list another name should be added, that of Sir John Bowring, linguist, poet, anthropologist, editor of the *Westminster Review* and one of its chief contributors. *Fraser's* itself, after a few years had passed, evidently wished to overlook his connection with the "Gallery." In the preface to the magazine for January, 1840, when enumerating the originals of the portraits, it passed over the sketch entitled "Tydus-pooh-pooh, our Man of Genius" as "merely a joke, the point of which is now forgotten." But the "joke" is so characteristic of *Fraser's* absurdity that it should be elucidated. In studying the files of the magazine one finds that our Man of Genius is none other than Jack Churchill, who parodied the folk poetry of Dr. Bowring under the signature of Tydus-pooh-pooh. Maginn seized upon the notion of Churchill's representing the true Bowring and invented a meeting between the two men at one of Oliver Yorke's fictitious audiences.[3] On Bowring's recognizing his double he was made to withdraw at once in annoyance. It was about the time of this imaginary encounter that Maginn and Maclise fashioned the wickedly satiric "Gallery" sketch of Tydus, in which the nose ring suggested the anthropological nature of Bowring's poetry and the features were none other than those of Bowring himself. The remarks accompanying the sketch carried out the joke with lighthearted insolence.

As in the "Man of Genius," Maginn's letterpress accompanying the portraits is usually sharply disciplinary, a brisk wielding of the rod over the naked faults and frailties of his great contemporaries. Maclise's pen-and-ink drawings of the victims are scarcely less punitive. Although at the time a boy, and entirely unknown, the nimble satirist was already at the height of his power. Nowhere in his later work was he to show more delicacy and firmness than in these early drawings for *Fraser's*. Some of them, such as the clever sketches of Disraeli and Coleridge, have become well known through reprints in subsequent notices and biographies; and the whole "Gallery" was republished from *Fraser's*[4] with copious and carefully detailed notes by William Bates, professor in Queen's College, Birmingham. In the *Academy* for April 15, 1871, Dante Gabriel Rossetti wrote enthusiastically:

> I suppose no such series of the portraits of the celebrated of any epoch, produced by an eye and hand of so much insight and power, and realized with such a view to the actual impression of the sitter, exists anywhere. . . . Indeed, no happier instance could well be found of the unity for literary purpose of what may be justly termed "style," with an incisive and relishing realism.

In their own day the successive issues of the portraits were awaited with the greatest curiosity and no little apprehension, for it was impossible to predict the lengths to which the waggery of Maginn and his agile illustrator would go or who would next fall beneath their summary infliction. Shirley Brooks, the big *Punch* editor, who was growing up at the time, admits, according to his biographer, Mr. G. S. Layard, that it was the "good smart abuse in some of the Maginnery"[5] which first incited his own ambition to write.

Among the most skillful and on the whole flattering of the portraits is that of Henry Brougham, who as Lord Chancellor was in the full tide of his rapid career. In seeking, as was suspected, the position of prime minister, he had opened an insidious attack on Grey, who was then, Maginn remarks with reference to the politician's genius for placing his relatives in office, "nepotising at the head of the government." The skit gives a rapid review of the "Journalist-Chancellor":

> On the woolsack, leaping through cases, as Harlequin does through a hoop, without touching them, wonderful in agility and most dexterous in despatch, exciting the astonishment of the audience, and winning the tribute of a clap from the upper gallery of the press; in the House of Lords as droll as Punchinello, and about as dignified; in the *Edinburgh Review,* as airy as Jeffrey, and as deep as Mackintosh; in the *Times,* as oracular as a Stock Exchange reporter on the evening before settling day; at the Beefsteak Club as comical as he is in the House of

Lords—great over a bottle, over a case, over a debate, over an article, it is impossible to say in which he is greatest.

With a glance at Maclise's sketch Maginn turns to the question of the Chancellor's immediate employment:

When we look upon the eager eye, the relaxed wig, the flung-aside gown, the whole air full of grimace and grog, it strikes us that abuse of the venerable senior, as he calls him, who is now nepotising at the head of affairs, is the staple commodity which is flowing full and fast from his nimble and caustic pen.

Yet Maginn admits with that unexpected fairness which he occasionally displays towards his political enemies, that Broughman is no "rat," the inelegant term of the day for a person who deserts a cause in the rodent fashion of leaving a sinking ship:

Why should he not despise the imbecile congregation of idiots, on whose shoulders he pranced into Chancery, firmly holding the animals whose backs he bestrode by their elongated ears? They are his property —his own natural prey—and he is free to make *game* of them, especially since the new bill has put an end to the sin of poaching. We cannot conceive Brougham ratting. He may leave the set to whom he is now attached, but it will be much more in the character of a cat than a rat— he will not depart without shewing that he possesses talons, which can turn upon the hand that patted him, and under whose smoothing pressure he had so long purred in hypocritical murmurings. The time is, we imagine, not far distant, when his bounce is to be taken, and his colleagues find themselves unable to keep him by the tail.

Those who are familiar with the acrobatic achievements of "Bridlegoose Brougham," as Maginn, doffing hat to Rabelais, usually called the Chancellor, will realize that the above sketch is a remarkably concise and spirited picture. Nor should the personal comment at the end be omitted:

He has declared himself born in St. Andrew Square, in Edinburgh; others assign him an humbler birth-place in the Cowgate. To us, who consider all parts of Edinburgh perfectly equal in respectability, the controversy is of the smallest possible importance.

The beginning of the sketch, it will be noticed, is characteristic of the "Gallery's" rapid portraiture. Modern journalism has made us familiar with summarized caricature, but in the 1830's it was a novelty in magazine writing. The same quick penciling is seen in the following sketch of Maginn's fellow Fraserian, Theodore Hook, novelist, editor of the ultra-Tory *John Bull,* prince of wits and popular beau:

> He has just descended from the grand vestibule of the Athenæum, where he has been enjoying Praed's rhymes of the morning, a well-cayenned mutton-chop, and a glass of the Murchison sherry; forthwith he will glide round the corner, under the shade of the York pillar—not forgetting as he glides . . . O'Brien's doctrine as to the original design of the round towers of Ireland—and ensconce himself in the small oratory of the Carlton dining-room, there to refresh body and mind with another chop, another bumper, and another squib. Theodore will then be primed to shine in the Conservative circle above stairs, bright over all the other luminaries of the gang, until it be time for him to doff his knowing surtout and appear in finished grace, the full-figged swell of the eight o'clock board, whether in Piccadilly, in Palace Yard, or in Privy Gardens, or beneath some less stately roof, more worthy to ring with the trumpet-notes of honest laughter and the linked sweetness long drawn out of *"One cheer more!"*—the delighted and delighting guest of some huge-paunched alderman, red-gilled archdeacon, or gorgeous widow. . . . Peace and jollity go with him, where-ever he is this evening destined to pick his turbot-fin, lap down his magnum, exhibit the splendid *tabatière* of the Capitan-Pacha, and shower wit and fun and conundrum about him—like a fountain of Vauxhall fire, radiant but harmless! Peace be with the most unenvious of satirists, the kindest-hearted of libellers, the most sincere, steadfast, unflinching champion of the long cork, and the Alliance of Church and State!

Even toward *Fraser's* enemies the "Gallery" occasionally granted fair field, especially if the involuntary subject happened to win the personal approval of Maginn. Thomas Campbell, though harshly treated elsewhere in the magazine as a worn-out poet, one of the originators of the "College of all the Cockneys" (London University), and the editor of *Fraser's* hated Whig rival, the *New Monthly,* is honored with second place in the "Gallery" and a squib ending in fraternal censure.

> There's Tom Campbell in person, the poet of hope,
> Brimful of good liquor, as gay as the pope.
> His shirt collar's open, his wig is awry,
> There's his stock on the ground, there's a cock in his eye.
> Half gone his last tumbler—clean gone his last joke,
> And his pipe, like his college, is ending in smoke.

What he's saying who knows, but perhaps it may be
Something tender and soft of a bouncing ladye.

Maginn then adds that the song becomes scurrilous and that he suppresses, therefore, all the culpable verses to come to the last, which is panegyrical.

Well! though you are yoked to a dull Magazine,
Tom, I cannot forget it, what once you have been;
Though you wrote of Lord Byron an asinine letter;
Though your dinners are bad and your talk is no better;
Yet the song of the Baltic—Lochiel's proud lay—
The Seamen of England—and Linden's red day—
Must make up for the nonsense you write and you speak,
Did you talk it and write it seven days in the week!

Occasionally a portrait is so offensively personal as to make unpleasant reading. An illustration of the slanderous coarseness to which Maginn could descend is his treatment of the poet Samuel Rogers. Indeed the only excuse for reviving the sketch is that no account of *Fraser's* "Gallery" would be just which avoided a full portrayal of its vulgar iconoclasm; and the reputation of Rogers is too well established to suffer from what can today appear only as abusive and stupid distortion. According to his habit, Maginn was not intimidated by the power or popularity of his victim. Rogers had been from his youth a literary magnate of wide and influential connections. His *Pleasures of Memory* was still revered as a great work and his subsequent poetry was esteemed. As a prosperous banker, he could afford to act the beneficent host to the upper layer of resident and itinerant literati. His house, his breakfasts, his dinners, were equally famous. Moreover, he was himself reputed to have such a well-barbed tongue that apparently nobody had hitherto dreamed of offering him public affront. Maclise's sketch shows the potentate seated, gaunt and prematurely aged, beside a table on which are placed a watch to tick away the time and a pile of books, diminishing in size, to suggest the decreasing importance of his successive works. The first words of Maginn's letterpress, after an ominous *De Mortuis nil nisi bonum!* refer to the cadaverous portrait: "There is Sam Rogers, a mortal likeness—painted to the very death!" And from that moment, the fearless editor presses into compact form gossip he has collected on the untimely living-death of the poet. He speaks of the "French valet's announcement of him as M. le Mort," mistaking him for his friend Tom Moore; of Mackintosh's suggestion, when at election time no accommodations remained at any hotel in a country town, that Rogers "try snug lying in the church-yard"; of Theodore Hook's "friendly caution, when he saw him at Lord Byron's funeral, to keep out of sight of the undertaker, lest he should claim him as one of his old customers." Maginn then adds, "Independently of the persecution Sam suffers from being dead, a grievance which he has in a great measure outlived; he is an ill-used gentleman, in being made Pun-master-general to the United Kingdom." In newspapers from Hindustan to the Orkneys he is godfather "to all the bad jokes in existence." The very Negro and the Hindoo

father their calembourgs on Rogers. Quashee or Ramee-Samee, who know nothing of Sir Isaac Newton, John Milton, or *Fraser's Magazine,* grin from ear to ear at the name of the illustrious banker, and with gratified voice exclaim, "Him d—— funny, dat Sam."

With unmitigating scorn for the veteran's poetry, Maginn insists:

By this fame, Sam must be known, after he is allowed to be dead by the parish officers. For, after all, the literary glory of Sam will be one of the smallest. His verses are of the petty larceny school of poetry. When Wordsworth read in *Don Juan* the commandment that

"Thou shall not steal from Samuel Rogers,"

he remarked very properly that no theft would be more hazardous, because, not only Sam might reclaim the pilfered goods, but there would be no small danger of their being looked after by those from whom the said Sam had originally stolen them.

In conclusion, Maginn relentlessly sums up:

He has a pretty house, with pretty gewgaws in it—he gives tolerable dinners, and says very spiteful things—he is an ugly man, and his face is dead, and his jokes flat. His poetry is poor, and his banking-house rich—his verses, which he purloined, will be forgotten—his jests (which others made for him,) may be remembered. The Pleasures of Memory will go the way of all other Pleasures, but it is not impossible that his name may, like Joe Miller's, be perpetuated as the unwilling godfather of a book of conundrums. *Sic transit gloria Sammi.*

Daring as this attack appears today it must have seemed far more rash at the time it was published, when Wordsworth, Mackintosh, and Hook were all alive to contradict its statements had they been able to do so, and when Rogers himself had ample provocation to say "spiteful things." Yet Maginn's abuse was so abominable that nobody would have condescended to answer him—especially when London gossip had just been put into a state of high excitement by the publication of the squib.

One of the milder instances of Maginn's iconoclasm is the affectionately apologetic sketch of Coleridge, the magazine's tutelary saint whom it delighted to laugh at and to honor:

Procrastination, that thief of time—the quotation is old, though the author is Young—has beguiled him onward in comparative idleness; and his best ideas have been suffered so often to lie unused, that they have at last appeared as the property of others. . . .

But Coleridge cared for none of these things. On he went, holding the even tenour of his way, *conversing* with all and sundry. Many a critic deemed original has lived exclusively by sucking Coleridge's brains. The late William Hazlitt was one of the most conspicuous thieves. There was not an observation—not a line—in all Hazlitt's critical works, which was worth reading, or remembering, that did not emanate directly from our old friend the Platonist. . . .

Would that we could see him drinking everlasting glasses of brandy and water in coffee-houses various—or carousing potations pottle-deep, as of old, in the western world of Bristol—or making orations to barmaids and landladies, and holding them by his glittering eye and suasive tongue; and, above all, we most ardently hope to witness the publication of the conclusion of

The lovely Lady Christabel,
Finished by Coleridge hale and well!

THE STAFF AND ITS WORK

Among the functions of the "Gallery of Literary Characters" was its jaunty but very real assistance to Nol Yorke in unifying the strangely assorted contents of his magazine. Within its long line of "Portraits," already listed, appeared from time to time the better known members of the Fraserians themselves. Besides those of Hook and Coleridge, from which passages have just been quoted, thumb-nail sketches were given of James Hogg, John Galt, Robert Macnish, David Moir, John Lockhart, Francis Mahony, Crofton Croker, William Jerdan, and William Maginn. Finally there was a good-natured but gusty wigging of the on-coming Scotchman Thomas Carlyle.

The sketches in the "Gallery" form a saucy accompaniment to *Fraser's* more dignified work in biography. And here it should be remembered that most of Carlyle's abundant writing for the early volumes developed some phase of biographical theory. Merely to enumerate his articles reveals the extent of this contribution, ranging from the sketches of Edward Irving and Goethe, the reviews "Boswell's Life of Johnson" and "Schiller, Goethe, and Madame de Stael," the three essays on the relation of history and biography, "Thoughts on History," "Biography," and "Quæ Cogitavit," to the longer autobiographical *Sartor Resartus*. Both *Count Cagliostro* and *The Diamond Necklace* should also be included as biographical narratives, brilliant illustrations of Oliver Yorke's flair for invention. Maginn had from the first believed in literary exploration, the searching out of new fields and new methods of work; and it is to the credit of Carlyle that, deep as he was in German revolutionary thought and French revolutionary practice, he should have met *Fraser's* gay demand for variety with an important contribution to biographical method. *Count Cagliostro* enters that fine outer field where psychology, history, and biography meet in robust narrative. It may not be too much to say that the creative biography of Lytton Strachey and others finds its direct forbear in *Cagliostro*.

The work of four other biographers in the monthly should not be entirely overshadowed by the brilliance of Carlyle. Colonel Mitchell sketched his contemporaries under the caption "Reminiscences of Men and Things," and narrated the lives of eminent soldiers and scenes from the wars of Napoleon. John Mitchell had begun his career as a man of the world at the age of twelve when he went to Berlin with his father on a mission to the court of the new king, Frederick William III. Subsequently he was welcomed in many capitals, was a confidant of the Duke of Wellington, spoke fluently an astonishing number of languages, became famous for his *Life of Wellington* and his *Fall of Napoleon,* and worked indefatigably to correct abuses in the British army, in which he ultimately became a major general. It is not surprising, therefore, that his rambling essays for *Fraser's* show a wide experience, and, however diffuse and flippant, have a circumstantial base which makes them well worth the reading.

Although his "Reminiscences of Men and Things" could not be

openly acknowledged, as they took grotesque liberties with matters which were of recent occurrence, there can be little doubt that they are from the alert pen of the ranging Colonel. The material dovetails closely with his experiences and also with the rambling essays signed Bombardinio and Sabertash, which he himself republished and which, though often little more than jottings, are again of real value because circumstantial. Among the men whom he portrays in most detail are Lafayette, Louis Philippe, Metternich, Thiers, Chateaubriand, Victor Hugo, and Guizot.

Of equal worth is a brief series of recollections by Gibbons Merle, which came out anonymously under the caption "A Newspaper Editor's Reminiscences." As editor of the *Globe,* the ablest of the evening papers in the reign of George IV, Merle had been thrown with prominent political economists of the day, among them Jeremy Bentham. Since these recollections also were not republished, it is almost by accident that their identity can be established. In speaking of his early life the author mentions that at one time he edited a forgotten paper, *The White Dwarf.*[6] According to *The Times' Tercentenary Handlist* this paper ran for a short time in 1817 and 1818 and was edited by Merle. Among the accounts which are of most interest, in addition to those of Bentham, are "the editor's" impressions of Shelley, whom he had known as a boy.

More prolific was the biographical work of Robert Pearse Gillies. His *Recollections of Sir Walter Scott,* which first appeared in *Fraser's,* is the best known of his writings; but the anonymous series under the caption "Humours of the North" also deserves attention, as only a small portion of it was republished in Gillies' own autobiography. The sketches record impressions of the old Scotch lairds whom the gossipy author had known either personally or through local report.

Unlike its biography *Fraser's* work in narrative would seem to have been almost accidental, a haphazard offspring of the magazine for which nobody felt responsible. Carlyle submitted his deft "Cruthers and Jonson," which compares favorably with the best short stories of that day. There was the much discussed "Elizabeth Brownrigge," which burlesqued Bulwer's *Eugene Aram* so shrewdly as to tempt biographers into ascribing it to Thackeray. There were one or two brave historical tales by the energetic young scholar Thomas Wright, whose work has already been mentioned as a distinguishing feature of the monthly. But the best narratives of the early magazine were only apologetically mentioned by the staff. They rushed unrestrained and healthy from the pen of the Scotch peasant, James Hogg, famous as the Ettrick Shepherd. Hogg sent a good deal of poetry to *Fraser's,* but far more diverting are these short prose tales. Fashioned on the model of John Galt's *Ayrshire Legatees* and *Sir Andrew Wylie,* they show a robust side of country life rarely depicted with such untrammeled realism. On one occasion the rash "Shepherd" produced a story so purely naturalistic as to call forth the disgusted epithet "Hogg's last grunt."

John Galt[7] was also a steady contributor to *Fraser's,* who merits more attention than he has received. By the time the magazine was founded in 1830 he had nearly written through his early Scotch material and had turned to the field of the West Indies and Canada. His own life was singularly abounding, full of travel, high business projects, and bravely-met disappointments. When the Canadian Company, which he had been instrumental in founding, failed, he returned to London in 1834, broken in health and almost penniless but still unalterably industrious. Before his death, five years later, he had completed his sixtieth volume and written there is no telling how many uncollected articles and stories for magazines. One of the most astounding of literary hacks was John Galt—"a broad, gausic Greenock man, old-growing, lovable with pity," Scott calls him in 1832; "eats and drinks with a certain west-country gusto and research." At its best his writing has a forthright quality, a generosity of life that makes it unsurpassed in its line.

Galt's influence was felt not only by Hogg but by the talented young Scotchman, Andrew Picken, whose guileless romances, fresh and sturdy like his own heather, occasionally appear until his early death in 1833. Like other tale writers for *Fraser's,* he has been overlooked in the glamor that has surrounded the high-handed satirist, William Makepeace Thackeray.

Thackeray's informal narratives were in the beginning the outgrowth of his critical reviews. In *Yellowplush* and its rambling successors is expressed a young man's dissatisfaction with the literature popular in his own day, its style and even more its interpretation of life. As late as *Barry Lyndon* his work in *Fraser's* was to show distaste for prevailing manners and attitudes. The question of Thackeray's criticism is, however, too involved for discussion in the present brief survey and must be reserved for a later chapter. To enumerate here the wise work of Yellowplush, Titmarsh, and Ikey Solomons is scarcely necessary; nor need we add that it contributed to the stimulus which *Fraser's* narrative writing exerted on its period.

Yet however Thackeray may have won the approval of discerning readers, other folk in the magazine met with more immediate popularity than did the creator of the Shums, Deuceaces, and their shabby-genteel neighbors. Theodore Hook, fashionable romancer of fashionable life; L.E.L.,[8] sentimental novelist and poet; Harrison Ainsworth,[9] recorder of dashing adventures—all brought to the magazine at the moment of their brief glory far more fame than did the scornful young author of *Yellowplush*. Even Harriet Downing, as the Monthly Nurse, and the prolific Wightwick, as Blue Friars, were both prime favorites, as were Caroline Bowles in her wayside sketches by the charming Selwyn, Charles Apperley in his famous sporting news by the great Nimrod, and Percival Banks as Morgan Rattler. There were also the lightly authoritative essays of Bombardinio and Captain Orlando Sabertash, the fantastic pseudonyms of John Mitchell, already mentioned in connection with his biographical articles. Less entertaining but highly acceptable to their first readers was the work of two compatriots and close friends, David Moir, renowned as Delta, and Robert Macnish, almost equally popular as A Modern Pythagorean. Robert Gleig, later to be esteemed as Chaplain General of the Army and author of reminiscences of Wellington, was also a staunch and respected contributor, as was Theodore Martin, better known as the collaborator of Aytoun over the classic signature of Bon Gaultier. Even before the end of the magazine's first decade Martin was offering it an assortment of tales and burlesques.

The Fraserian who most completely won the affection of the public, however, was Maginn's boon companion, the Irish Catholic priest, Father Prout. Will-o'-the-wisp scholar and wit, Prout has piqued curiosity from the day his first essays lured readers to literary bypaths. On the *Fraser* staff he was powerful; for a while, we are given to understand, he even played the part of the good Nol Yorke himself and guided the magazine through the critical months following Maginn's withdrawal from the editorship.[10] Francis Sylvester Mahony, who wrote under the pen name Father Prout, the well-loved priest of Watergrasshill, Ireland, was a Jesuit by training, with a fine sense for the integrity of scholarship and a whimsical, nomadic pen that ran lightly over the learning of centuries. Expelled from his order for a foolish escapade in his youth, Prout maintained through his long life an honored place among the aristocracy of Bohemia. He was a warm friend of Thackeray and Browning,[11] who with others were attracted by his firm mind, his unexpected tongue and his curiously recondite lore. Toward the end of his life a pleasant comment shows him in his favorite Paris, a wisp of a black-cloaked figure, chatting with Thackeray across his customary table at the Café Riche on the boulevards.[12] Allingham, also, describes visiting him with Thackeray "in a narrow street at the back of the Palais Royal, in a large lowish room." The Father, "loosely arrayed, reclining in front of a book and a bottle of Burgundy," greeted them in a low voice. " 'Evening boys, there's a young chap asleep there in the corner,' "—and Prout pointed to "a young Paddy from Cork, or thereabouts, who had been on a lark in Paris and spent his money."[13] At this time the mellow old scholar had returned from a decade of idling in Greece, Asia Minor, Egypt, and Rome, and was a treasured correspondent for the London *Globe,* inducing it by the popularity of his articles to buy a font of Greek type for his classical quotations. Yet genial as this later work is, Prout was never to excel the dexterity of his earlier familiar writing in *Fraser's.* His learned confidences on the modern Latin poets, on Horace, on his favorite Béranger, his amazing polyglot translations, are among the pleasantest surprises which the worthy Nol Yorke offers. At its best there is in both his early and his later work a tartness. "It is a vulgar error of your countrymen," he admonishes the English, "to connect valour with roast beef, and courage with plum-pudding. There exists no such association; and I wonder this national mistake has not been noticed by Jeremy Bentham in his Book of Fallacies." Nor should it be forgotten that Prout wrote *The Shandon Bells,* and was as loyal an author of the

Emerald Isle as was ever haunted by Irish melody. To the end he was, in his own homely metaphor, "an Irish potato seasoned with Attic salt."

An excellent and amazingly dexterous hoax which the Father aimed at one of Maginn's old butts, Thomas Moore, was turning various of the famous "Irish Melodies" into Latin verse and then solemnly declaring that the Irish poems were translations.[14] Prout, like so many other witty scholars of the day, delighted to transpose well-known contemporary poems into Greek and Latin. Unlike others, however, his roguery was frequently not satisfied with juggling two languages. The polyglot Jesuit on occasion manipulated three or even four. Thus the English of Millikin's "Groves of Blarney" burgeons in the pages of *Fraser's* in Greek, Latin, French, and old Irish,[15] and afterwards in Italian. It was said that the Italians came to like their version so well that years later it was sung by Garibaldi's soldiers on the shores of Lake Como,[16] a culmination of the joke which would have pleased the original roisterer immensely.

Three Fraserians of more metropolitan fame were the editor of the *Literary Gazette,* William Jerdan, and two of London's famous beaux, Count D'Orsay and Theodore Hook. Jerdan was addressed at the famous staff dinner, January, 1835, as Mephistopheles, and was, therefore, possibly the author of a clever verse squib, "Mephistopheles Politicus," for December, 1833. Hook, who wrote his novels and edited the insolent *John Bull* in his stride to innumerable dinner engagements, has been mentioned as presumably contributing to the magazine's narratives. As Dr. M. F. Brightfield points out in his recent study of Hook,[17] although there is nothing in *Fraser's* that especially bears his imprint, yet it is probable that he wrote for the monthly edited by his friend Maginn. It may well be that he had a hand in the popular hoax, "The Miller Correspondence," for November, 1833, and in "April Fools," for April, 1835, as well as in verses, such as the songs attributed to him in the "Symposiac," for November, 1830, and in "The Fraserians," for January, 1835. He was a man of superabundant and easy wit, with a genius for improvising verse satire. When told that he was considered by Byron the only real English improvisator of that great poet's acquaintance, Hook, who was out of favor with the Tory government and in prison, turned aside the compliment with a querulous, "I don't know that I am an improvvisatore, but I'm sure I am an unlucky Tory."[18] Less robust than Hook, D'Orsay was the most exquisite beau of the day, the center of Lady Blessington's literary soirées at Gore House, and in the words of the Fraserians, "the beloved of all who knew him." As with Hook, it is impossible to say just what contributions this most popular and facile of young men made to the most popular and facile of magazines, but his presence at Round Table gatherings was presumably not unproductive to the monthly.

Prout probably took the place on the *Fraser* staff of John Abraham Heraud, already mentioned as Maginn's assistant in editing the magazine during its first three years, and as the conscientious follower of Coleridge. Heraud was a strange paradox, a metaphysical poet who had common sense enough to earn his living for half a century by writing for the periodical press. His interests ranged from the stage to philosophy, embracing mesmerism along the way. Twice he wrote a successful play; and from middle life to advanced age he was a conventional dramatic critic for the *Athenæum* and the *London Illustrated Magazine*. Yet philosophy was always more than a side interest with Heraud. He was an excellent German scholar and knew at first hand the romantic philosophers and poets who followed Kant. His two long religious poems, *The Descent into Hell* and *The Judgment of the Flood*, are full of metaphysical references; and his critical essays for *Fraser's* include a bewilderment of transcendental discussion. In conversation he is said to have had great zeal for dialectic and a flair for learned citations.

The position of Heraud in the magazine involves so many factors that it will be considered later in more detail. A word should be said here, however, in regard to that other probable transmitter of Coleridge's thought, the Reverend Edward Irving. When *Fraser's* was started in 1830, this stormy spiritualist had been in London for eight years. He had already changed the poverty-stricken church in Hatton Garden into an affluent parish with an imposing new edifice in Regent Square. Although his influence was obviously on the wane, he still held spellbound throngs from the fashionable world while his melodious threats of doom rolled into the second hour and often into and through the third. The closeness of his relation to the *Fraser* staff is shown by the devoted loyalty of the magazine. When Irving's fame was reversed, following the uncouth manifestation of the "tongues," the monthly allowed him to use its columns to explain the singular phases of his spiritualism. Somewhat earlier it had devoted several pages to his defense.[19] At the time of his death, although he had been driven from his church in disgrace and even expelled from the ministry by an act of the Scotch Presbyterian Board, *Fraser's* announced its complete faith in his integrity. Maginn staunchly affirmed that, however mistaken the Scotch minister might have been, there could be no question as to his sincerity. "Irving—alas! no more . . . the eloquent, the enthusiastic, the learned, the honest, the honourable, the upright, and the good . . . who in his own soul was true." "This panegyric comes from the heart."[20] In all, the Fraserians published three obituary notices[21] of their colleague, including the touching tribute by Carlyle. Subsequently affectionate reminiscences were informally introduced in their articles.

How much Irving actually contributed to the magazine is questionable. Father Prout, whose word in such a case must be considered final, speaks of him as "a frequent writer in Fraser, and frequenter of his sanctum, where 'oft of a stilly night' he quaffed glenlivat with the learned Editor."[22] A less secular relation to the staff is indicated by his signing a letter to James Fraser, "your faithful Friend and Pastor."[23] According to a statement made in the monthly itself[24] his individual work was limited to the explanations of his own faith, already mentioned, and to a narrative, "Recollections and Observations of a Scottish Clergyman," for May, 1830. Infrequently, also, he may have aided Maginn and Heraud in political and ecclesiastical articles. Yet however few of his sonorous jeremiads found place among the succinct periods of the monthly, there is no doubt that the leonine Scotch preacher lent earnestness to the staff's point of view. Lofty spiritualist, he was the confidential friend of Coleridge during the great mystic's later life, and his presence at the editorial table unquestionably strengthened the staff's relation with the Highgate seer.

Very different in type, but none the less influential, was John Lockhart, seasoned satirist, son-in-law and biographer of Scott, and editor of the *Quarterly Review.* A frequent member of the back-parlor group,[25] he was in the beginning so deep in its counsels as possibly to have had a hand in the editing. He was an old collaborator of Maginn in *Blackwood's* as well as presumably in the burlesque *Whitehall;* and in all probability he continued his collaboration in the political and critical reviews of *Fraser's,* which expand the complaints humorously presented in that novel. A long series of satirical poems signed Pierce Pungent bear especial evidence of his joint authorship with Maginn, the signature even being reminiscent of his well-known *Blackwood's* pseudonym, Scorpion. Critical essays on Hogg, Campbell, and Wordsworth,[26] also by Pierce Pungent, would seem to continue the survey of contemporaries started by Lockhart and Maginn in their joint *Noctes Ambrosianæ* for *Blackwood's,* July, 1829, and would thus contribute to the probable authenticity of all the Pierce Pungent work. Certainly Lockhart is frequently mentioned by name in the various symposia and levees of Oliver Yorke, and is presented as playing a pugnacious part at staff dinners.

Two other roisterers of the inner circle were Percival Weldon Banks and John Churchill. Although for nearly two decades Banks wrote articles for the magazine over his signatures Morgan Rattler and the Sergeant of the Law, he also played in the beginning a valiant part in the humorous levees and the general reveling of the monthly. He had a host of friends, belonged to a well-known Irish family, and was a scholar of some repute.[27] Churchill was, according to rumor, the most spectacular Bohemian of the group, a princely nomad with a rare preference for taking his night's lodging driving in cabs about the streets of London. At one time he was supposed to have been attached to the court of Ernest of Hanover, where, according to anecdote, "long he might have remained had it not been for inebriation and the sad spectacle of the pensioner unconscious in a wheelbarrow rolled before the royal window."[28] In his connection with *Fraser's* he was now amiable, now ruthless, a facile writer of burlesque, an all-round linguist, and an obedient hack. For the most part his identity is revealed only through some sly reference to our Man of Genius, a sobriquet which we have already had occasion to mention in connection with the "Portrait Gallery" sketch of Bowring.

The best kept secret in the magazine was the ownership of the swashbuckling pseudonym, Ensign Cornelius O'Donoghue. The gossipy letters and adventurous tales of the Irish Ensign for years filled the monthly's page with dare-devil fun and sound admonition. Yet in spite of the closeness with which the staff guarded this cherished contributor, there can be little doubt that the boastful Ensign was none other than diminutive Crofton Croker, the authority on Irish folklore. In the first place, O'Donoghue avowedly belonged to the inner circle of the Fraserians, yet he was not Maginn or Banks or Prout, the three Irishmen of the brotherhood. The pseudonym appeared long before Prout joined the Fraserians and continued after Maginn's death,[29] with no statement that it represented posthumous work. Furthermore, Banks in various of his garrulous articles mentioned that O'Donoghue left Ireland in early youth, that literature was not his main profession, and finally that he had given up writing to devote himself exclusively to pounds, shillings, and pence.[30] Now Croker was the only Fraserian to whom all of these three remarks applied. He left Ireland when he was twenty, devoted himself chiefly to his duties of clerk in the Admiralty, and in the early 1840's practically relinquished the pen for the pounds, shillings, and pence connected with this clerkship. Moreover, "Crofty" was by nature voluble and he had all the material for the O'Donoghue tales at his command. He is known to have had a hand in the stories of his friend Lynch,[31] a romantic officer who after Waterloo was placed on half pay and spent his time pacing the Killarney mountains, gun on shoulder, communing with the spirit of O'Donoghue. In addition, Croker had the stock of escapades inherited from his soldier father, who was a clever narrator. Finally he had, as he himself mentions, his own experiences: "sundry adventures with White boys, in caves and out of caves, upon hill-tops, with bootmakers and broguemakers, with smugglers and coastguard-men, with magistrates and murderers."[32]

The work of the jaunty O'Donoghue was, however, not the only writing which Crofton Croker contributed to *Fraser's*. As "Honourable member for Fairyland" and "Oberon of the Moderns," he had become too famous as a narrator of folk tales for him to leave his chosen field unrepresented in the magazine. From boyhood he had haunted the peasants' houses in primitive regions of Ireland, his ear pricked for the idiom of folk tales. The result was the first book on Irish anthropology, *Fairy Legends and Traditions of the South of Ireland.* It was immediately popular in England, commended at once by the Grimm brothers and translated into German, and later brought out in French. Continued interest in research made Croker one of the foremost authorities on Irish folklore and the earnest supporter of the Antiquarian Society, the Percy Society, and various other learned associations. His papers for *Fraser's* under the caption "Irish Minstrelsy" were either gathered into his book *Popular Songs of Ireland* or enlarged for the publications of the Percy Society.

Yet when all have been enumerated the most learned and popular writer for *Fraser's* remained its irascible Irish editor, William Maginn. The public was flattered by his scholarship, amused by his informality, and surprised by his wit. On the one hand, his satire heaped up enemies for himself, and, on the other, it heaped up sales for the magazine. In short, Maginn's reputation was both made and ruined by the periodical, and the discussion of his life becomes so complicated that it must be reserved for fuller treatment in a separate section. Our business here is rather to explain how the magazine came to spell the ruin of Maginn.

In a spirit of perennial infancy *Fraser's* sportively announces its own contents: "Politics, polemics, pastime, poetry, philosophy, promotion, pugnacity, pressography, personæ dramaticæ, personality, persiflage, perambulate our pages and perpetuate them to posterity." Obviously it is impossible to examine any great amount of this lively preamble. The poetry of Barry Cornwall and Hogg and Cunningham, the translations from Gothic and Persian, from Hebrew, Greek, Latin, and old French, and from more familiar languages, must be omitted, as must the serious articles, such as the anthropological reviews by Isaac Cullimore under the classical signature Hermogenes and the ecclesiastical discussions by the Reverend R. B. Seeley as the Layman of the Church of England. Even work of scholarly nature by Wright and Prout and Maginn can be only scantily mentioned in a later chapter since none of them contributed more than incidentally to the peculiar make-up of *Fraser's*. Three things, to summarize once more specifically, distinguished the magazine from its fellows: its politics, its criticism of contemporary writing, and its delirium of libelous and teasing fun. The first two will be considered in the succeeding chapters. The last becomes the rather ugly task immediately before us.

LAMPOONS

The magazine in a sprightly mood once spoke of itself as a "vigilant and pouncing periodical," and boasted "Many an attempt has been made to 'Bell the Cat,' but without success." There was indeed no escape from its penetration. Even the King was not immune. When it considered that George IV was submitting too readily to the Duke of Wellington, it cried ironically,

VIVAT REX.
Rex! Pish!—That's gone by—let us worship the new Dynasty—
VIVAT DUX![33]

and afterward Arthur, Duke of Wellington, is referred to as King Arthur.

Frequently the magazine's love of teasing broke out in pure boyish silliness. It delighted in the figure of the ass and playfully attached the long ears to various personages of the day, on one occasion remarking of a minor poet that he was "decidedly an ass of the very first ear." It impishly jeered at Brougham's interest in London University and also in the Diffusion of Knowledge: "Black Broom"

. . . may shut the avenues of knowledge,
By sweeping sense from Cockneydom's own College.[34]

Of the powerful Radical politician Francis Place, the tailor at Charing Cross, it remarked in 1832, the year of the parliamentary upheaval, that "in his capacity of breeches-maker, we suppose, [he] is a very busy man about the Westminster Rump." A little later, when the prime minister, Grey, began to create peerages with undue rapidity, it piped up: "There are my Lords Harrowby and Wharncliffe . . . they are the first number of a *Waverley* series." After Francis Jeffrey, the editor of the *Edinburgh Review,* was knighted, James Hogg, in a fictitious letter to the magazine, was made to write from Scotland:

A king may make a man a lord,
A belted knight and a' that;
But he can't make Jeff. a gentleman,
For a' that, and for a' that.[35]

THE EDITOR OF THE NEW MONTHLY

When Grey was being ridiculed for placing his relatives in office, Jeffrey shared in the censure for having in the expectation of advancement made promises which he did not keep:

Talk not of consistency—there we are deaf;
He must think not of that who is voting for Jeff.
'Tis the day of our profits—and who ever saw
A more liberal member than *Purse-in-the-paw?*

Grey Gaffer his kindred is placing, like Peel;
And yellow-faced Durham is Lord Privy Seal:
And the Treasury benches with Whiglings are stored—
And our own little Jeffrey's a neat legal Lord.[36]

Occasionally the Fraserians selected their verse form with care. Thus when Macaulay was sent to India, *Fraser's* appropriately celebrated his departure in mock classical lines sedately apostrophizing the ship on which he was to sail. One stanza on the "honourable Bab." or "Babble-tongue" will be sufficient:

Safe to the angry Cape of Hope,
  And safe to sainted Helen's namesake rock,
Unharmed in timber and in rope,
  Swift ship! conduct Reform's own bantam-cock.[37]

Among the best of the magazine's lampoons are those setting forth the madcap career of young Benjamin Disraeli, who, it will be remembered, had for the time being blocked his own fortunes by allowing himself to run as the Radical candidate for Wycombe, although he professed great devotion to the Conservative cause. True to *Fraser's* methods, Dizzy himself is made to utter the caricature, which to better the joke is in gay doggerel written as prose to suggest the singsong periods of the young man's own novels.

Appeal to Posterity

Oh ye, who yet unborn, cannot have felt the thorn that rankles in the breast of myself among the rest, of those who laughing, wailing, enjoying health or ailing, try on, though Tories lick 'em, to gain the day at Wycombe; remember, when you're living, the advice I now am giving.

If you be Whig, or Tory, or Radical, grown hoary, or youthful in sedition, yet yearning with ambition, I'll tell you how to fix your faith in politics. Choose first a clever tailor—then join each gay regaler—convince the fair you're witty, by lauding them as pretty—quiz every one not present, from highmost peer to peasant, especial care being taken of your peculiar bacon. When thus you've long disported, you'll find you're rather courted. . . . Leave off black velvet breeches and take to making speeches, which, on either side, may fit you, and never can commit you.

After a sharp rap at the *Wondrous Tale of Alroy,* and "the sad lament of Sal Roy," in which Dizzy had attempted an apology for his political eccentricities, the squib concludes with the sage remark that if the advice is taken, "half-listless, half-pomposity, you'll be a literary curiosity, like unfortunate Miss Baily, or Benjamin D'Israeli."[38]

The keen amusement which *Fraser's* took in this suggested addition to Isaac D'Israeli's *Literary Curiosities* is further shown in the opening stanza of a second elaborate burlesque on the impetuous career of son Benjamin.

The Torrent!

See, downward dashing to the Vale,
  The high-born Torrent goes!
And is it a voice of joy, or wail,
  From his swelling breast he throws?
Is there turbulent glee in his headlong course?
Or in fetterless rage hath he left the source
Of his peaceful birth for the realms of force?
Say, is it in sport or in scorn he mocks
The power of Fate, as his streaming locks
He flings to the winds, and laughs at the shocks
Of the flinty-hearted rocks?[39]

The squib it will be noticed bears an uneasy resemblance to Wordsworth's "Yarrow Visited," and thus like so much of *Fraser's* occasional verse offers a double burlesque. A more detailed instance of this divided fun is the lampoon on Bishop Phillpotts, whose biography is rendered after the fashion of *Peter Bell.*

TOBIAS PHILPOTTS [*sic*]

A LYRICAL BALLAD

Tobias Philpotts, fat and fair,
  Grew up a comely lad,
But yet a genius so obtuse,

As made his father say—Pho! goose!—
  And made his mother sad.

First to a tailor he was bound,
  But he was such a sot,
He ne'er could learn to know (poor soul!)
A button from a button-hole,
  Or breeches from a coat.

In their distress at his stupidity the parents ask advice of the squire, who proposes

Go, breed the nincoop for a priest,
  And he shall have a church!

The satirist then in full stride taunts Bishop Phillpotts with political apostasy:

First he was Anti-Catholic—
  And swore against the Pope;
And then he threatened George his King,
If he would e'er do any thing,
  But help him to a rope.

Then, turning right and round about,
  To shew with wit how cramm'd
He proved that four and five made seven—
St. Peter kept the keys to Heaven—
  And all without were damned.

The Duke and Peel, with friendly zeal,
  Took of the lad good care,
Gave all such patrons could confer,
And sent the Saint to Exeter,
  To be a Bishop there![40]

One of the liveliest lampoons in the magazine records the famous quarrel between Brougham as Lord Chancellor and the *Times*. Brougham is made to cry out angrily:

The devil take you all!
Ye wish for my fall?
Who was it praised me?
Who was it raised me,
  In prose and in rhymes,
From lawyer to baron,

And thence very far on
To th'administration
Of this changeable nation?
  The *Times!* O, the *Times!*

After several more stanzas of upbraiding, *Fraser's* saucily points to the progress which Brougham is making toward the premiership as an underlying reason for his neglect of the *Times*.

Hurrah for Lord B.!
What a talker's not he!
The eloquent scorner!
The witty suborner!
The Press is corrected,
The *Times* is neglected;
The Lords in the suds,
  The Commons obey;
The state-vessel scuds
  Most bravely away.
The fates no disaster
  For Brougham can prepare—
He knows not a master
  But the Prince of the Air.
Hurrah for Lord Brougham!
For the *Times* but a fig!
    Let it scold,
    Let it scold,
He will be the *first Whig*.[41]

The lampoons on Brougham are so full of spirit and evidently gave the magazine so much pleasure to concoct that it is a pity not to add the opening stanzas from

LORD CHANCELLOR DO-LITTLE

The Chancellor sat in his burley wig,
  And a burley Whig was he;
If he follow his nose, as it upward goes,
  He'll soon be of high degree:
And the devil will grieve to see him leave
  The Court of Chancery!

Idle, I ween, is that lawyer seen—
  He has little there to do;
With a wig in his fist, and a motion-list,

When the notices are few.
At *ten* begun—at *twelve all done*—
And the Chancellor GONE by two.

Gone, gone, gone,
(Like tables for taxes sold),
To tell the affair in Printing-house Square,
Where he went so often of old—
To be *blown* like a horn, when the people next morn
Their sheets of the *Times* unfold.[42]

Even affection did not interfere with the magazine's fun-making. Coleridge himself, venerated as he was by the staff, was pilloried in a fashion which must have surprised the "grand old man," both his rapt monologues and his inadvertent drinking being repeatedly burlesqued. On one occasion the poet is represented as rambling through promiscuous inanities to arrive at an insufferable insult to Hazlitt. Starting with Orpheus's determination "to open the way, as Milton has it, 'Smooth, easy, inoffensive down to hell,'" Coleridge unsteadily explains:

The wonder-working notes of the Orphean lyre drew after them beasts, and brutes, and savages, and trees, and stocks, and stones, dancing like Abyssinian maids, singing of Mount Abora; and by this is prefigured, that the soul of man, raised by high and holy emotions—I wish I had a glass of brandy and water— (*it appears in the hand of a plebeian—body unknown—Mr. Coleridge drinks*) —thank you, sir— high and holy emotions, to a participation with higher powers above, at last, rising by prescribed degrees, as in the notes of the gamut, ascends from harmony to harmony, until the transcendental philosophy of the ages of thought, soaring through the misty cloud of time, should envelope it by the music of nature, that

Divinest potency
Which, from the earth upsoaring to the heavens,
Fills the whole concave; and the angel clouds,
Dimming the north horizon to the south,
Spread radiance.

So that—I wish I had something to drink— (*the hand presents a glass of brandy and water—hand vanishes—so does the brandy and water.*) — So that—when I was editor of the *Morning Post,* and the Emperor Napoleon Buonaparte said that he declared war solely on my account, and I, like the illustrious John Dennis, was the sole excepted person from a party, of which the characters were— (*another glass of brandy and water*) —but I desist—for when, as Plato says, fact is reason, reason is not fact. I am dumb now—silent—because I know of old that my brains have been sucked for articles. I mention nobody but Pygmalion Hazlitt. However, when the sun arises to-morrow, and with its beam gladdens town and tree, and field and hill, and when the little birds, opening their cheerful bills, cry— (*another glass of brandy and water—supplied as before*) —open their cheerful bills, and cry forth their cheerful sounds indicative of spring, then do we think of music—the heavenly maid that was young when Collins, a very middling poet, because his books sold, wrote about her.[43]

Fully as grotesque are the magazine's lampoons of its own contributor Thomas Carlyle, whom it had common sense enough to look upon, none the less, as one of the great leaders of thought in its day. In reference to *Sartor Resartus,* which had earlier come out in *Fraser's* itself, the unfortunate philosopher is made to exclaim:

Thank Heaven! that mighty labour has been at last accomplished, though in a spirit of self-sacrifice, for an ungrateful world. But all effort must proceed from a Nothingness; and from this may an influence grow that shall, in the region of Something, create as it were an oasis in a desert—an islet, or even an isle, in the Ocean of the Infinite Void. In high estimation, as is known right well, I hold all poets and moral teachers, as a species of metaphorical Tailors, and, as their greatest Guild-brother, the never-enough-to-be-named-and written-about Goethe! With him, however, I dare opine, that the dynasty of Poetic Power terminates—with him it has ended! . . . For the era of Fable just completed, an age of Reality will commence; and what has been conceivable by Meditation, shall be realized by Action. For the Race of Literary Men has been, in all ages, a school of prophets; and the contributors of FRASER'S MAGAZINE are one and all, though the world know it not, and they know it not, Seers, albeit unacknowledged as such by others and by themselves. But this is as it should be; for *all* Consciousness is Disease, Unconsciousness is Health. Happy academy, this same Lyceum, No. 215 Regent Street! Happy master! Happy pupils!

At the conclusion of this overwrought wisdom John Lockhart is made to exclaim:

Humbug! A School of Prophets, indeed!—a School of Humbugs! To say nothing of the apparent irreverence of terming the *littérateurs* of this paltry generation of sciolists, or of any generation, even of Homer himself, prophets; it is enough for me that the notion is German.[44]

We have given a few of the sallies against prominent men to show the quality of the Fraserian thrust. First and last practically every man conspicuous at the moment in politics or literature felt the rapier or the bludgeon of the magazine's mirth. Even the host of small fry long since forgotten were cheerfully teased. Thus it wrote of the editor of its chief rival, the *New Monthly Magazine:*

From the pure author, Nature, came
  One article without a heading;
You stare—but I'll just prove that same—
  She manufactured Cyrus Redding!
    Witless Cyrus,
    Born to tire us,
  Cyrus, Cyrus, Cyrus Redding![45]

This was all innocent enough baiting. Though a little of it was written in bad grace, for the most part it was amusing rather than offensive. But nothing can be said in extenuation of the wanton insults of the magazine in its more vicious moods. Even toward personal friends and those to whom he was indebted Maginn was ruthless. His idea seems to have been: They have foibles and absurdities, they have erred; let them suffer.

In this frame of mind he occasionally turned against his patron the Right Honorable John Wilson Croker, stout Tory Secretary to the Navy. Croker's Cork brogue, of which he was ashamed, his lisp, and his redundancy are all pitifully evident when he is forced to lament in the pages of the magazine that a demonstration was made against him in his own Alma Mater, Trinity College, Dublin: "The young youths in Thwinithy, Twinity I mane, meen, waw going to thaws me in a blanket, which show'd their bad teest." His burst of indignation and self-pity is interrupted by a song in which as Member of Parliament for Hertford, he is coarsely reminded of a recent fray in the House.

The man that of Trinity College,
  Thought himself the sleek white-headed boy
Ev'n his friends, if he has such, acknowledge,
  Was well kick'd by bold Sergeant Lefroy.

Will his lisp now be frequent as ever,
  When he prates in the Parliament House?
Or will humbled John Wilson endeavour,
  In his seat to sneak in like a louse?

Yes, the days of his swaggering glory
Are set in the bottomless sea;
And what a sad end to his story,
To be Hertford's lickspittling M.P.![46]

No less crudely insulting was Maginn when Croker and his Tory colleagues lost office with the resignation of Wellington, whose refusal to concede parliamentary reform had incensed the rebellious Fraserians.

Say in the street: "The Duke's out," the answer is, "Delighted to hear it."
"So is Peel."
"Down with the rat!"
"And Lyndhurst."
"Poor devil!"
"And the Dundases."
"Thank God!"
"And Dawson."
"To be sure, the hound!"

With even more revolting detail Maginn in his own right rebukes his Tory friends:

The upsetting and overturning, the kicking out—oh, ye Gods! that the kicking had been literal—of these office-holders is, to my mind, pure delight. They, vagabonds as they are, talk, now-a-days, of going into opposition. Let them. The conspiracy of clerks is a grand affair. The recalcitration of the flunkies is fine. I cannot help thinking of a flock of geese, over-fed and fattened until they could scarce waddle, getting up an opposition to a pack of foxes.

Apologizing for changing his metaphor "as arbitrarily as the Duke used to kick out his ministers—honest and independent men!" Maginn adds:

I therefore compare Croker to another quadruped. (How glad he will be to find out *that* bull, and lisping over his display of teeth, maintain that a goose is no quadruped at all, but barely a biped—the wit of the turned off Secretary being remarkable and precise.) And the quadruped wherewith I liken Croker, is an ass. Every now and then, in a discontented drove, to which the costermonger in ordinary has not supplied provender in due abundance, you will occasionally see one who takes the lead in braying. This particular ass is always particularly important in his own eyes, but particularly intrusive in the eyes of all others. The cudgel falls upon his back in more than ordinary ratio, and if the bray be on the whole unsuccessful, even the remainder of the herd show their opinion of the impertinent uselessness of his obtrusive leadership, by treating him somewhat as the jackasses in Æsop are reported to have behaved when they clubbed to make a river.

Such an ass is Croker.

In regard to Brougham, the power behind the new minister, Maginn remarks:

It will take some time to make me and the Baron of Brougham and Vaux, and Lord High Chancellor of Great Britain, particular friends. But after all—Whig, Edinburgh Reviewer, Useless Knowledger, &c. that he is, I am glad to see him, or old Nick himself in power, in preference to a scurvy hack, who has been regularly bred in office, or kept angling after promotion, by kissing the ——— hand of every fellow that had any thing to bestow.[47]

Heavy belaboring of this sort is not humorous; it is incredibly boorish. As treatment of enemies it is preposterous; of friends, unforgivable. The same clumsy tousling recurs whenever Maginn particularly disapproves of his party. The burlesque of William Holmes, the Tory whip, or as then called, Whipper-in, is characteristic of the rough right and left with which the displeased editor indiscriminately delivered his blows. As a sign of the mute obedience of the Tory Members of Parliament, Holmes is made to brandish his whip and sing a song illustrative of his own practices as applied to prominent party men. One verse is enough to show its crudeness.

"Ho! whelps out of Ireland—Ho, hounds North of Tweed!
High, close to the cover—or else no more feed.
Hollo, Croker—Ho! Murr—Mangy Georgebob, Twiss, haw!
Bloody Jem, Scruffy Franky, whelp Tommy Macaw;
Keep up, keep ye up, steady there, Sturdy Bourne!"
So sings Old Bill Sligo to each in his turn.

In the speech which precedes this hunting song, Billy Holmes is made to characterize his pack:

To do them jeistice, for, God bless the dumb craturs! I'd scorn to wrong them, I have as purty a pack as ever snuffed up the scent of any thing worth running after. Then they come in, the dear bastes, with their noses down so close together that a handkerchief would cover 'em. It is a pleasure—a rale pleasure, to see 'em in full cry—a body can't help loving 'em as if they were a body's own child. It can't be doubted that they'll sometimes run wide; but that's when they havn't confidence in the gentleman that hunts 'em. If the poor brutes a'n't fed riglar too, who can think they've always the sperrit to run.

After a rather long account of the difficulties in handling his pack in the preceding session the worthy Holmes concludes:

As for politics, sure the likes of me knows nothing about them. Hoicks—hoicks—ya hip—ya hip—hilloo—in—in—tally ho—tally ho! An't hunting, hunting? And who cares who hunts the country, so the game's run down?[48]

Maginn's abuse was by no means confined to friends active in politics. Old comrades, such as the loyal and devoted Pearse Gillies, came beneath the satirical cudgel. His stuttering, his reiteration, his absent-mindedness, his gentle self-conceit, are disgustingly burlesqued. On one occasion immedately after losing his position of editor of the *Foreign Quarterly,* he is made to begin a public speech by forgetting the purpose for which he came to the platform and carrying on a private conversation with Coleridge.

Mr. Coleridge, I am glad to see you, and hope you are well. I have got a cold myself, and my lips are swollen, but you are looking superbly.

Brought to the point by his impatient audience, he continues:

This Magazine of Fraser's will never do—never—no, never. The writing is bad—yes, decidedly bad; slovenly—crude—indigested; slovenly! yes slovenly. It will never do; but I think I said that before. Yes, I did—did—did—before—before. . . . If the articles in Fraser's Magazine had been placed in my hands, I think—I am certain indeed of it—I could have wonderfully improved them; for Mr. Coleridge, you perceive, if I have any talent, and indeed it is nothing to boast of, I can improve whatever piece of writing has ever been composed by mortal man. It was I who gave Sir Walter his first idea of Ivanhoe. I had collected the German novels . . . from which my friend copied the incidents. Sir Walter wrote his novel, however, in too great a hurry. So did Wilson his Lights and Shadows, and Galt his Sir Andrew Wylie, and Lockhart his Adam Blair and Matthew Wald, and Hope his Anastasius. If they had severally advised with me on their labours, I should have counselled them, and said—yes—said—hem—hey—Yes, counselled—counselled—"Take time,"—and if they could not have taken time, then I would have rewritten his novel, for any one of these my friends;—Friends—yes—ay—yes—friends. . . . Gentlemen, I propose myself for the Editorship of Fraser's Magazine, because I know it is in want of an Editor, and I am in want of a situation. . . . I beg your pardon, Mr. William Fraser;[49] do not look so scowlingly upon me—hem—he—ha—hey—no offence—no, no offence; but you know I am not so gay as you are. Your gaiety ought to incapacitate you for writing for the Magazine, and I can supply your place—yes, yes, supply your place. I do not think anyone will say that I am either gay or a dandy—no, no, neither gay nor a dandy.

Maginn comments that Gillies thereupon turned himself slowly around to show all his quarters and points to the multitude.

Do not, gentlemen, I beg, laugh at me, for that will make me laugh, and this is a serious matter.—Ha—ha—he—ho—he—ho—ha—hi—hi!

Thereupon Gillies sat down "in the midst of shouts and laughter."[50]

In addition to writing burlesques of its own, *Fraser's* published for the first time one of the famous lampoons of literary history, Byron's "Verses on Sam Rogers." The outrageous burlesque, which the magazine announced it had received from a friend, would presumably never have come to light had it not been for the audacity of Maginn. Rogers was prominent as a "bard, beau, and banker" and had repeatedly spoken with gratification of his friendship for Byron. This attack, therefore, from the dead, set London gossip agape and incidentally sold outright the entire issue of the magazine which contained it. Since its printing reveals as nothing else can the brazen effrontery of *Fraser's,* a few lines are given here:

Eyes of lead-like hue, and gummy;
Carcass pick'd out from some mummy;
Bowels (but they were forgotten,
Save the liver, and that's rotten);
Skin all sallow, flesh all sodden,—
Form the devil would frighten God in.
Is't a corpse stuck up for show,
Galvanized at times to go?

. . .

Vampyre, ghost, or goul, what is it?
I would walk ten miles to miss it.

In Maginn's introduction to these shocking lines he explains that they were in Moore's hands when he wrote his biography of Byron for the publisher, John Murray. In regard to Murray himself, "in many respects one of the best fellows in the world," Maginn libelously explains that he has been "debauched" by the high Whigs of his acquaintance "into manifold sins of omission and commission, which must weigh heavy at last upon his bibliopolic soul." He should not, we are told, have given Moore the task of writing Byron's life because "it was morally certain that he would cut out, with unsparing hand, every thing in his lordship's correspondence which could in any way annoy the Whig gentle or noble folk, upon whose smiles or whose dinners it delights the little poet to live." Moore

"has sown the page with stars thick as a field," almost every star indicating that some great Whig name lies eclipsed by it. Poor Leigh Hunt is sacrificed without mercy, because he is poor;—but all the jokes on Lord and Lady Holland and their set, Cam Hobhouse and the other beasts after his kind, Douglas Kinnaird, Sam Rogers, &c. &c.—the whole blue devilry of Whiggism—are suppressed . . . and their omission is a signal specimen of literary dishonesty.[51]

These punch-bowl thrusts at Moore and Murray and incidentally at the "blue devilry of Whiggism," Cam Hobhouse and "the other beasts after his kind," were shortly afterward continued in the magazine's own burlesque on the erring biographer, Moore.

RECEIPT TO MAKE A WHIG POET

. . .

Some wreaths of flowers and curls and tangles;
No end of diamonds, pearls, and spangles;
Bright wine, that bubbles in the chalice,
To make the heart pour out its malice;
A benefactor—for a Nero;
An Irish rebel—for a hero;
A pig of Epicurus' sty—
For a romantic history;
A harp, piano, and a fiddle:
A bibliopole or two—to diddle;

. . .

A most emphatic veneration
For the Brag Administration;
Some glimpses of the moon and stars,
And of the land of olive-jars.[52]

A second skeleton which *Fraser's* dared to take from literary closets was the mock epitaph on James Mackintosh,[53] penned some twenty years earlier by its own staff "counselor," Coleridge. Maginn, who had sought out the long-forgotten verses from the *Morning Post* for December 4, 1800, did not publish them in *Fraser's* until after Mackintosh had died. Clever as the epitaph seems today, it had at the time of its appearance, shortly after the death of the philosopher, a reprehensible brilliance. The picture of the devil and his dam squatted on the newly dug grave while they watched for their victim's soul to arise was sufficiently gruesome to shock even callous readers; especially since Maginn, with his usual eye for dramatic effect, reserved until a subsequent issue of the magazine the extenuating explanation of the lapse of time between the penning and the printing of the verses.[54] The only editorial comment which accompanied the poem was to the effect that the magazine itself heartily concurred with the views expressed therein. For *Fraser's,* death adjured no decent quietus on ridicule.

The wanton venom of the Fraserians should by rights have involved the magazine in some dozens of lawsuits. Its comparative immunity reveals the poor manners of the day and the general lack of sensitiveness in a public which could lend support to such obvious slander. In all, James Fraser, the publisher, had to defend himself in court on only three occasions, one of which was due not to scurrility but to an unfortunate mistake on the part of a conscientious contributor. The legal defenses made for the magazine in both of the other libel suits are printed in full in *Fraser's* itself.[55] The first was brought by a minor poet and essayist of the day, Alaric A. Watts, whose predilection for harmless sentimentality had provoked Maginn and Lockhart to burden him with the martial name of Alaric Atilla. In comparison with others, Watts had met with fairly mild handling, but he very sensibly decided not to endure without protest. Although he was awarded only slight damages, he at least had the satisfaction of not allowing himself to be cowed.

The last suit followed a tragedy which brought the more rampant days of the magazine to an abrupt end. In August, 1836, Maginn, with customary insult, reviewed an autobiographic novel, *Berkeley Castle,* by Grantley Berkeley. The hot-headed young nobleman thereupon attacked James Fraser with a loaded riding whip, beating him nearly to death. The result was a duel between Maginn and Berkeley, a suit for assault brought by Fraser against Berkeley, and a counter-suit for libel brought by Berkeley against Fraser. The publisher was granted a hundred pounds damages; Berkeley's suit was withdrawn, each party paying his own costs. Since the occurrence was cataclysmic in the lives of Fraser, Maginn, and even Berkeley himself, it will be mentioned again later. Here we need comment only that the punishment, sordid as it was, held the quality of a Greek nemesis. Disaster ought indeed to have haunted the magazine from its first libelous number in 1830. That fate bided its time with classic temperance for nearly seven years, made it not less inevitable. In all reason *Fraser's* should not have escaped justice.

PART TWO
REVOLT IN CRITICISM

CHAPTER III

THACKERAY

The great enigma of *Fraser's Magazine* during its early years is William Makepeace Thackeray. Lewis Melville in his life of the satirist exclaims in exasperation, "The mention of *Fraser's* brings us face to face with the unsolved question that is the stumbling-block of the biographers and bibliographers of Thackeray: When did Thackeray begin to contribute to this magazine, in which appeared the best of his early work?"[1] Without trace of his apprenticeship, we suddenly find him among its full-fledged contributors. In Maclise's cartoon which appeared in *Fraser's* for January, 1835, Thackeray is to be seen with *pince-nez* raised in quizzical condescension, seated among the twenty-seven members of the staff who are banqueting in the publisher's back parlor, the most individualized figure in the group. That he was actually at the dinner is given on the authority of Gleig, who was also present.[2] Yet not until nearly three years later, in November, 1837, does his picturesque signature Yellowplush begin to foot the magazine's columns, nor has the most careful search of bibliographers brought to light anything of account which can be ascribed to him prior to that date. C. P. Johnson finds only one short ballad, "Il était un Roi d'Yvetot," in the "*Fraser* Papers" for May, 1834, that he is willing to pronounce indisputably Thackeray's. Other pieces for which he has collected evidence he considers of doubtful authenticity.[3] A few of these, Melville feels, are of sufficiently good standing to be admitted to Thackeray's bibliography. Yet even were all added, they would still remain paltry, giving little promise of the brilliance and maturity of *Yellowplush*.

Fortunately some slight information is to be gained concerning the early stages of Thackeray's acquaintance with *Fraser's* editor, William Maginn. The first source consists of jottings in Thackeray's diary for 1832. According to these he saw Maginn a number of times, went to dinner with him, was persuaded by him of the value of Greek, and even promised to read it daily. The second source is an account given by Francis Mahony, or to use his endearing pseudonym, Father Prout, to Blanchard Jerrold, who recorded it in full in his memoir of the Father. Mahony was not only a prominent member of the *Fraser* staff but an intimate friend of both Thackeray and Maginn. Jerrold was the son of Douglas Jerrold, the lively contributor to *Punch,* and warm friend of all three men. Since Blanchard Jerrold was himself a protégé of both Prout and Thackeray, he presumably gave the Father's narrative more accurate attention than would have been granted by the casual hearer. His talk with Prout, he tells us, took place possibly about the time Thackeray sailed for America, leaving his old friend, the Father, in a reminiscent mood.

Mahony's account, it is to be noticed, begins with a point blank statement:

"I introduced Thackeray to Maginn." He laughed as the vision passed before him. "Thackeray was a young buck in those days: wanted to make a figure in literature—*la belle affaire!* So he thought he must help himself to a magazine. It is an expensive toy. A magazine wanted —in those days, I know nothing about these—an editor. I recommended Billy Maginn. . . . Before Maginn could go into the matter he must have 500 *l.* for deck clearing. . . . This was a startling beginning; but Maginn was not to be had on any other terms. He was the only available man at the time. . . . Thackeray was obliged to come to Maginn's terms. Maginn got his first hundred; and where do you think I brought them together. . . . At the Crown Tavern, Vinegar Yard, Drury Lane! . . . It was a poor business, was the new magazine," the Father resumed, thinking leisurely over it. "It wasn't likely to get on." Then a chuckle. "They quarrelled. People always fall out over a failure. It's your fault, and its mine, and it's t'other man's over the way. Maginn wasn't the easiest man in the world to deal with. The magazine lasted about six months. Thackeray wanted to sell it; but Maginn had a share. Maginn conceived that he ought to be consulted. I brought them together: Maginn in a towering passion, but he was capital. In the course of the meeting—at the old place, the 'Crown'—he volunteered an Eastern story too, of two pashas, close friends, and how they divided their property in a manner which gave all of it to one of them. You will wonder, but Thackeray listened delighted to the end, and didn't see Billy Maginn's drift. The boys! the boys! All this was before ye was born!"[4]

Melville in his biography of Thackeray refers to the existence of this account, but states that nothing more seems to have been heard of the projected magazine and therefore presumably it was never undertaken.[5] On examination of the passage we find the definite statement that the joint venture was not only started but was carried on unsuccessfully for some six months and that Maginn received at least his first hundred pounds for "deck clearing." Prout had an excellent memory, and since he was at the time in London working on *Fraser's* hand in glove with Maginn, his testimony must be accepted as establishing beyond question the fact that Thackeray and "the Doctor" undertook the joint conduct of a magazine purchased by the younger man.

The only periodical of which Thackeray at this time attempted ownership was the short-lived *National Standard,* a weekly started by F. W. N. Bayley, January 5, 1833, taken over by Thackeray,[6] if we may judge from his opening editorial, with the issue of May 4, and given up at the commencement of the following year, with the issue of February 1, 1834.

These dates are not inconsistent with Prout's account of the transaction between Maginn and Thackeray, or, indeed, with Thackeray's own statements of his early meetings with Maginn. Even though all their desires were ripe for immediate action, Maginn and Thackeray might well have had to wait for some time before they discovered a periodical which could be financed by a person of moderate means and which was also sufficiently alive to be worth buying. Thackeray, of course, might have known Maginn socially before Prout "introduced" them for the purpose of their business conference at the "Crown"; but it is not necessary to suppose such an acquaintance. According to his own statement, in his diary, he met Maginn in 1832. It was the year during which Thackeray came into his patrimony, gave up all thought of law as a profession, and spent some months in Paris for the purpose of studying art. His interest throughout this period and, it would seem, for some years afterward, vacillated between art and literature. Apparently he was desirous of trying himself out in both fields, yet not wholly satisfied with his achievements in either. It is, therefore, possible that the first meeting at the "Crown," described by Mahony, took place before Thackeray went to France and was followed by subsequent interviews after his return in December; on the other hand it may not have occurred until December. In either event, the search for a suitable magazine and the preparations necessary for taking over its conduct would probably have consumed the intervening months before the May 4 issue of the *National Standard,* for which Thackeray wrote his juvenile editorial announcing the change in the weekly's management.

The only argument against the *National Standard* as a field for Maginn's activity is its immaturity. Yet except for some of the boyish efforts of Thackeray the weekly was certainly no worse than other publications of its type. It bears, indeed, no little resemblance to *Fraser's Literary Chronicle,* later the Tory *Carlton Chronicle,* which began in December, 1835. Both were weeklies; both kept a weather eye on *Fraser's Magazine,* commenting on the monthly's contributors and views and publishing supporting articles; both had much the same aim and manner. *Fraser's Literary Chronicle* was edited by Percival Banks with the assistance of his *Fraser* colleagues, Jack Churchill and Maginn, the latter contributing to it at least his long series, "Adversaria."[7] It may thus be that the *National Standard* offered an earlier outlet for Maginn's informal jottings.

With the case standing thus, Thackeray, on the strength of his approaching association with Maginn, may have made his first contribution to *Fraser's* as early as the summer of 1832; or, as is more probable, he may have waited until his hand became somewhat less inexpert. The question is after all relatively unimportant since there is nothing in the magazine for 1832 and practically nothing for 1833 of which Thackeray could have been the sole author. Furthermore, even for 1834 the work which could on any possible ground be ascribed to him individually is very limited.

What presumably happened is that Thackeray entered the *Fraser* staff as a collaborator of Maginn. It was a relation which the failure of the *National Standard* would almost have forced upon them. Although its jejune quality has been perhaps unduly emphasized, yet on the whole, the weekly was a perfunctory job for the brilliant editor of *Fraser's.* It bears some slight trace of his practiced hand; but to all appearances he would seem to have put comparatively little effort into its editing. Possibly he realized that better writing would not necessarily have meant better selling, and that the public which it attempted to serve might even have been repelled by any unwonted originality of thought or treatment. Without doubt, also, he was aware of the youthful nature of Thackeray's contribution towards keeping the weekly afloat. Perhaps he even felt that he was doing quite as much as he was paid for, though unfortunately there are no means of determining how much that was, beyond the initial £100. On the other hand, the jovial, big-hearted editor might have had some slight compunctions as to his handling of the joint enterprise and might have felt under obligation to the young man who had sought his aid. In either case he doubtless realized that in undertaking the *National Standard* Thackeray had definitely placed himself under tutelage for the purpose of learning to push a pen with vigor and neatness. When the magazine failed, Maginn would have been the last man to leave an ambitious and promising apprentice in the lurch. The two men had formed the habit of collaborating to some extent on the *National Standard,* and it would not have been unnatural for them to have continued their association in *Fraser's.*

Two things may not be gainsaid. According to Dr. R. Shelton Mackenzie, Thackeray was taken on the staff of *Fraser's* at the request of Maginn, who had been associated with him on an obscure and short-lived periodical.[8] And certainly, as has been pointed out, less than a year later the young satirist appears in the *Fraser* cartoon for January, 1835, seated conspicuously among the acknowledged members of the staff. Although he is not mentioned in the accompanying letterpress, his place between Maginn's special aides-de-camp, Percival Banks and Jack Churchill, may not be without bearing on his relation to the editor.

Furthermore, after the third number of *Yellowplush* we find Thackeray, in a letter to James Fraser, from Boulogne, striking for wages, to use his own words. The letter is dated February, and must have been written in 1838 as it mentions plans for the hundredth number of *Fraser's,* which appeared in April of that year. Thackeray's wording would indicate that he was a member of the regular staff and was expected to be punctual in his correspondence:

I have seen the doctor, who has given me his commands about the hundredth number. I shall send him my share from Paris in a day or two, and hope I shall do a good deal in the diligence to-morrow. . . .

Now comes another, and not very pleasant point, on which I must speak. I hereby give notice that I shall strike for wages. You pay more to others, I find, than to me: and so I intend to make some fresh conditions about Yellow-plush. I shall write no more of that gentleman's remarks except at the rate of twelve guineas a sheet, and with a drawing for each number in which his story appears—the drawing two guineas. Pray do not be angry at this decision on my part: it is simply a bargain, which it is my duty to make. Bad as he is Mr. Yellowplush is the most popular contributor to your magazine, and ought to be paid accordingly: if he does not deserve more than the monthly nurse or the Blue Friars, I am a Dutchman. I have been at work upon his adventures to-day, and will send them to you or not as you like, but in common regard for myself, I won't work under price.

Well, I dare say you will be very indignant, and swear I am the most mercenary of individuals. Not so. But I am a better workman than most of your crew and deserve a better price. You must not, I repeat, be angry, or because we differ as tradesmen, break off our connection as friends. Believe me, that whether I write for you or not, I shall always be glad of your friendship and anxious to have your good opinion.[9]

The whole tone of this remonstrance, as Lewis Melville well observes, is scarcely the sort which a contributor without anything to his credit in the magazine would adopt in writing to a publisher who is just beginning to accept his work. The letter is certainly not to be explained on the basis of one short translation and one book review, the total of Thackeray's pre-*Yellowplush* work for which there is any sort of external evidence. *Yellowplush* itself, moreover, bespeaks its author as an old contributor. Not only is it a long jump ahead of the immature *National Standard;* as Melville comments, it was contracted for in advance and written so to speak from hand to mouth—which was not an arrangement a publisher would have been likely to make with an untried correspondent.[10] Moreover its satire, as we shall shortly have occasion to notice, was bred of *Fraser* quarrels.

When everything has been taken into account—the testimony of Mahony and of Mackenzie, the presence of Thackeray in the cartoon of January, 1835, the mediocrity of the *National Standard* and the brilliance of *Yellowplush,* the month to month production of the series, the letter striking for wages—there seems no escaping the conclusion that Thackeray was a well-established contributor to the magazine before he published his famous "Fashnable Fax" in the autumn of 1837. It seems fairly safe, therefore, to accept Mackenzie's statement, just referred to, that he joined the staff as a result of his work with Maginn, that is, presumably between May, 1833, and the beginning of 1834. It is also probable, as has been said, that he continued his relation of collaborator with Maginn.

As such, he doubtless bore a hand in the various rollicking compilations which from time to time appeared in the magazine and for a few days pointed the gossip of London clubs and taverns. The most conspicuous of these were the "*Fraser* Papers"[11] and the long "Report of the Proceedings" of the magazine for January, 1836. Like the earlier "Ruminations round the Punch Bowl" and the "Symposiacs," they were a hurly-burly of caustic mirth and admonition directed chiefly against the politicians and the poets of the day, though they occasionally included translations and original poems, comic or serious, by the Fraserians themselves or by outside writers. In this last connection it will be remembered that Thackeray's adaptation "Il était un Roi" appeared in the "Papers" for May, 1834. It is by no means necessary, however, to conclude that his activities were confined to the contribution of ballads. The "Papers" were concocted in the publisher's back parlor by the more intimate wits of the staff on the nights before the magazine went to press, and if Thackeray was, under the cloak of his former collaborator of the *National Standard,* a member of the group, it is not to be supposed that he kept wholly clear of the deviltry and daring that animated the tongues and the pens of the agile aides. Although he presumably would not have been tempted to insert splenetic political or personal jocularity into work of which he was the sole author, yet he may easily have entered with no little zest into corporate fun-making for which others were responsible. Even the more brutal political onslaughts of the "Papers" may not always have repelled him. Although he himself did not in his acknowledged work write on politics, it is quite possible that he was not averse to abetting the sallies of others if they chanced to whet his own dissatisfaction with governmental procedures. Such incognito practice in satiric buffoonery would have been admirable training for the capers of "Polite

Annygoats" and would have gone far toward filling the literary hiatus between the adept *Yellowplush* and the inexpert *National Standard.*

More active, we may presume, was his share in "Poets of the Day" for June, September, and December, 1833, for September, 1834, and July, 1835; and in the less scattered reviews, "A Dozen Novels" for April, 1834; "A Quintette of Novels" for April, 1835; and "A Decade of Novels" for May, 1835. Nearly all of these show a decrease in political allusions over previous critical work in the magazine and are in keeping with Trackeray's acknowledged post-*Yellowplush* reviews. One might, indeed, almost be inclined to ascribe some of them to Thackeray as the sole author were it not that they are built too firmly upon Maginn's tenets for the older critic's name to be discarded without better reason than his failing to make the customary number of spritely comments on his erring contemporaries. The whole question of identifying criticism in the magazine, in cases where there is no external evidence, is complicated by the excellent standards which Maginn early established and by the readiness with which his followers accepted them.

Aside from this collaborative work, Thackeray would seem to have done comparatively little writing for *Fraser's* prior to November, 1837. He presumably was the sole author of not more than three of the items that have from time to time been placed on his pre-*Yellowplush* bibliography. The identification of his articles is, however, a task so enwrapped in controversial detail that it must be left for fuller discussion in a bibliographical appendix.

One item only, the satire "Elizabeth Brownrigge[*sic.*]," for August and September, 1832, has been the subject of such prolonged contention among bibliographers that it must be treated before we can proceed further. The tale was aimed at the more vulnerable spots of the subject matter and diction of Bulwer Lytton's *Eugene Aram,* burlesquing its scenes and characters with a ludicrous closeness which destroys its own literary value but makes it a sharp weapon against its victim. The plot centers about the murderer, Elizabeth Brownrigg, whose horrid crime of whipping to death her two young apprentices had already been recalled to public attention by the verse squibs of the *Anti-Jacobin.* The author of the *Fraser* tale, with a careful eye for the refinements of conscience and breeding displayed by Bulwer's criminal hero, represents the coarse Elizabeth as a beautiful and supersensitive maiden, interested in Godwinian theories of education and moral philosophy. Even Bulwer's cat does not escape notice, the merry satirist pointing to its canine nature and foiling it with a dog of feline instincts.

The entire "Brownrigge" controversy has been summed up by Lewis Melville. As he points out, the burlesque was republished by R. H. Shepherd in his edition of Thackeray's works. Dr. John Brown first suggested that the tale was from Thackeray's pen.[12] Swinburne felt so strongly on the question that he wrote, "Just before *Catherine,* appeared another burlesque and grotesque horror—'Elizabeth Brownrigge,' a story in two parts, which ought to be Thackeray's, for, if it is not, he stole the idea, and to some extent the style, of his parodies and novels of criminal life from this first sketch of the kind."[13] Both R. H. Shepherd and J. P. Anderson give the tale without question to Thackeray,[14] and Charles Whibley states that in his opinion there is little doubt of its source.[15] Johnson, however, feels that "Elizabeth Brownrigge" bears no evidence of Thackeray's workmanship,[16] and M. H. Spielmann goes so far as to suggest that it was written by Douglas Jerrold.[17] From this state of contention Melville extricates "Elizabeth Brownrigge," summing up the evidence against ascribing the tale to Thackeray.[18]

Before leaving the question it should perhaps be added that there is no evidence in favor of Douglas Jerrold as the author of the "Brownrigge" tale, and that the charge of plagiarism which Swinburne made against Thackeray need not be taken too seriously. Jerrold was a good friend of Maginn, but nothing indicates that he was in any way connected with *Fraser's* or ever contributed to it. On the other hand, there is strong probability that the tale was written by Maginn, possibly with the help of Lockhart. "Elizabeth Brownrigge" is a double-edged satire; ridiculing not only the choice and handling of historical material by Bulwer Lytton and Horace Smith, among the followers of Scott, but also the practice of introducing ill-digested treatises on philosophic and moral doctrines into grotesquely melodramatic scenes. It should be noted that five years before the tale appeared, Maginn had published, probably in collaboration with Lockhart, the novel *Whitehall, or the Days of George the Fourth,* which also satirized the imitators of Scott, ridiculing in particular the mixture of unsound moralizing with flamboyant romance. Although *Whitehall* covers a larger field than the "Brownrigge" tale, the parallel between the two burlesques is so close as to leave little doubt that the 1832 story is by the same author, or authors, as the 1827 novel. Both lampoon the tendency in the fiction of the day to ascribe refinements and sensibilities to a character in the underworld, without regard for either reality or common sense; both ridicule sentimentalized versions of torture, and satirize the processes of justice preceding an execution. Furthermore Maginn had led up to the publication of the "Brownrigge" satire by scathing comments on Bulwer's dabbling in sentimental crime, the first as early as Volume I of *Fraser's*.[19]

If Maginn, as is safe to assume, was the author, or one of the authors, of "Elizabeth Brownrigge," Thackeray would have been justified in adopting the tale as a model. Maginn liked burlesque and fostered its use among the contributors to the magazine. Certainly it became one of the forms of attack most frequently and most skillfully employed by the staff. Practically all the periodical's enemies and many of its friends were parodied in verse and in snatches of prose. Furthermore, the literary communism of the *Fraser* brotherhood left almost no excuse for property sense. Styles and phrasing were freely exchanged, Maginn himself being a prime source of invention. Thackeray, therefore, in *Catherine* was following well-established *Fraser* tradition. The chances are, however, that he worked without reference to any exact model. "Elizabeth Brownrigge" was published in 1832, probably before Thackeray had joined the Fraserians. His own novel did not appear till seven years later, in 1839, long after he had doubtless forgotten the "Brownrigge" tale, providing he had ever read it.

Although the earlier burlesque was not from the pen of Thackeray, the accuracy with which he perhaps unwittingly modeled *Catherine* upon it illustrates how close was the bond between William Maginn and his young collaborator.

Few writers have, indeed, been so completely an outgrowth of their literary environment as was Thackeray—and few have so completely transcended that environment. At the commencement of his work for

Fraser's he sedulously imitated William Maginn; at the end he had fashioned himself to the creation of *Vanity Fair.* It is interesting to note that in this development nothing was at any time relinquished; the satirist kept to the last unsparing and jealous vigil over the oncoming sentimentalist. Thackeray's work became humane only as he guardedly learned to express his natural sympathy for failures and frailties without disloyalty to his early training on the *Fraser* staff. However tender and roundabout his sympathies ultimately became, he was never able to revel spontaneously in sentiment as was Dickens. He had early developed too steady and apprehensive an eye for fallacies in himself and others to be caught off guard in any real abandonment of the heart. To the end he remained basically the critic whose understanding of situations and characters was in the first analysis unemotional.

This persistence of clear-sighted and unhoodwinked satire is more easily understood when we realize the rigors to which he submitted himself in the first years of his training under *Fraser's* editor. William Maginn was an astonishing impersonation of the comic spirit, untouched by pity or fear, his sins of savage brutality sitting as an easy crown upon a sunny brow. His critical tenets were absolute: a fine devotion to Fielding, Smollett, Sterne: a distaste for whatever was mawkish or pretentious; a liking for plain speaking, the unaltered detail, the easy, direct word.

The closeness with which Thackeray placed himself under tutelage is further revealed by a study of the files of the magazine. It is impossible to find in the early volumes articles characteristic of his workmanship. Indeed, if there is anything characteristic about his writing in this period it is his apparently intentional effort at self-concealment, his eagerness to step boldly forth in the jaunty disguise of William Maginn. So painstaking was his imitation that in work where the two men are known to have collaborated, it is impossible on the score of style to decide where the shift of hands occurs. From the point of view of subject matter much of Maginn's writing could not be attributed to his youthful assistant, but there is no passage of Thackeray's early work which could not be attributed to Maginn.

The field, of course, of Thackeray's antagonism was by no means so large as was Maginn's. He had, for instance, no quarrel with Robert Montgomery or Thomas Moore, with Sir James Mackintosh, Robert Peel, the Duke of Wellington, or any other economist or political leader. Yet at the points where he joined Maginn's wide battle front he gave no quarter. The keen edge which his criticism acquired is seen when we compare his scornful appraisal of the annuals, those elaborate gift books which decorated drawing-room tables at Christmas, with the reverent attitude of reviewers for other periodicals, and with the more indulgent amusement of *Fraser's* at an earlier date. The young satirist begins with a matter-of-fact enumeration:

> A parcel of the little gilded books, which generally make their appearance at this season, now lies before us. There are the *Friendship's Offering* embossed, and the *Forget Me Not* in morocco; *Jennings's Landscape* in dark green, and the *Christian Keepsake* in pea; . . . nothing can be more trumpery than the whole collection—as works of art, we mean. They tend to encourage bad taste in the public, bad engraving, and worse painting. As to their literary pretensions, they are such as they have been in former years. There have been, as we take it, since the first fashion for Annuals came up, some hundred and fifty volumes of the kind; and such a display of miserable mediocrity, such a collection of feeble verse, such a gathering of small wit, is hardly to be found in any other series.[20]

Not until Thackeray joined the staff in 1834 did Maginn find his equal in criticism. *Fraser's* staff, as has been shown, were easily obedient to the editor, echoing his preferences and antipathies, most of them more or less unconsciously using his achievements. Their work is often to be confused with his, whole passages or even articles showing close imitation; but it is also frequently distinct, involving individual tastes and manners. Thackeray alone identified himself with Maginn, bringing to the subservience a discrimination as fine as the editor's own, and more rigid and exacting. It is to the credit of both men that there is no evidence of hostility or even indulgent rivalry between them. Willingly, it would seem, Maginn made room for his counterpart, showing neither surprise nor irritation at the doubling of his own thought; sedulously Thackeray, in his turn, studied the projects of the older critic, bending his supercilious young mind to promote them.

For several years the two leaders of literary criticism thus abetted each other in shrewd insolence and castigating personalities. Poor Bulwer Lytton bitterly complains of their unyielding duarchy in *Fraser's*. "That magazine, under the auspices of Dr. Maginn and Mr. Thackeray, long continued to assail me, not in any form that can fairly be called criticism, but with a kind of ribald impertinence offered, so far as I can remember, to no other writer of my time."[21]

That Thackeray was no less insulting than Maginn becomes evident when he laments what "Neddy Bulwer" might have been "had he not thought fit to turn moralist, metaphysician, politician, poet, and be Edward Lytton Heaven-knows-what Bulwer, Esquire and M.P., a dandy, a philosopher, a spouter at Radical meetings." The brutal critic then itemizes:

> He has thrown away the better part of himself—his great inclination for the LOW, namely: if he would leave off scents for his handkerchief, and oil for his hair; if he would but confine himself to three clean shirts in a week, a couple of coats in a year, a beef-steak and onions for dinner . . . how much might be made of him even yet! An occasional pot of porter too much—a black eye, in a tap-room fight with a carman—a night in a watch-house—or a surfeit produced by Welsh rabbit and gin and beer, might, perhaps, redden his fair face and swell his slim waist; but the *mental* improvement which he would acquire under such treatment—the intellectual pluck and vigour which he would attain by the stout diet—the manly sports and conversation in which he would join at the Coal-Hole, or the Widow's, are far better for him than the feeble fribble of the Reform Club.[22]

In later years, as is well known, Thackeray repented this youthful savagery, and wrote an apology to Lytton in which he quoted from one of his prefaces that offered public amends for the early work in *Fraser's*.

> Why [he asks] were some of these little brats brought out of their obscurity? I own to a feeling of anything but pleasure in reviewing some of these juvenile, misshapen creatures, which the publisher has disinterred and resuscitated. There are two performances especially (among the critical and biographical works of the erudite Mr. Yellowplush) which I am very sorry to see reproduced, and I ask pardon of the author of *The Caxtons* for a lampoon which I know he himself has forgiven, and which I wish I could recall. I had never seen that eminent writer but once in public when this satire was penned, and wonder at the recklessness of the young man who could fancy such

satire was harmless jocularity, and never calculate that it might give pain.[23]

Yet however heartily Thackeray might apologize for his youthful insults, he never retracted them, and for that reason they are of special interest to his biographers today. Bulwer Lytton still has a place on library shelves in spite of the high-spirited cudgeling to which he was for a few years subjected. As for Thackeray, much in his later writing is accounted for by this revelation of hard vision in his early years.

Mr. Sadleir in his biography, *Bulwer and His Wife: a Panorama,* has expressed the opinion that the Fraserian attack on the popular novelist was due to personal animosity on the part of both Maginn and Thackeray. He sketches in some detail consecutive instances of rancorous animadversion and feels that such pursuit over a period of years must have been motivated by ill will.[24] He admits that Thackeray's participation in *Fraser's* early attacks might have been due to Maginn's influence on a young and unformed critic, but concludes that the revival of faultfinding and ridicule in his own right must have sprung from jealousy at Bulwer's popularity and eminence as a novelist.

This is perhaps a natural inference to draw unless one is acquainted with the entire hostile campaign of the magazine against the literature and politics of the day. Bulwer's ears unquestionably tingled and doubtless he felt, as he said, that he had been worse treated than any other author. But after all nowhere did he meet with the scurrilous contempt that was visited upon Rogers, upon Thomas Moore, Harriet Martineau, Macaulay, Peel, Wellington, or even John Wilson Croker, the patron of Maginn. He was tossed from the horns of the *Fraser* critics with much the same care-free impertinence as were the Ladies Blessington and Morgan, the former a very good friend indeed of both Maginn and Thackeray. Although the attack upon him was more protracted, it must be remembered that he wrote more books which were worth attacking. *Fraser's* seldom wasted effort on work which it considered harmless or negligible.

One cannot review the full tale of *Fraser's* criticism without coming to the conclusion that its chief critics had clearly defined standards and were judging the work of Bulwer Lytton according to them. Mr. Sadleir himself has given an account of Carlyle's attack on "fashionable novels" and his animadversions on Bulwer.[25] Those who remember the prolonged satire in the last book of *Sartor Resartus* and the briefer, though no less tart, references in "Characteristics," will appreciate the heat of the philosopher's disapproval. Since these strictures were printed in *Fraser's,* there can be no doubt of the great contributor's support of the editorial attitude. In *Sartor* Carlyle even quotes a long passage from the magazine's first harsh review of Bulwer. That he himself had thought of writing a hostile criticism of the popular novelist is revealed in his letter to Napier, editor of the *Edinburgh Review:*

> I once proposed to Mr. Jeffrey to make a sort of sally on *Fashionable Novels.* . . . The Pelham and Devereux manufacture is a sort of thing which ought to be extinguished in British literature.[26]

A person who is not familiar with the entire trend of *Fraser's,* and few indeed would acquire that familiarity, can scarcely realize the violence of its protest against ostentatious or elaborate style and overstressed sentimentality or emotion. Bulwer, however talented, is at times not free, in Mr. Sadleir's opinion, from "signs of sham solemnity and a tendency to august humbug." In some of his best work there is an espousal of the baroque and a love to "orchestrate in words," which though effective would have repelled the Fraserians.[27] Later we shall examine in some detail their sharp attack on pomposity and melodrama. The exacting staff reproved what it deemed false or pretentious even in its friends, subjecting them to ridicule almost as sharp as it meted out to its opponents. Discrepancies of creed along various lines naturally increased its asperity; and Bulwer was considered fairer game because he was a prominent Whig, the chief novelist to expound the hated doctrines of political economy,[28] and the editor for a time of the rival *New Monthly,* which hotly answered *Fraser's* attacks.

Mr. Sadleir has been admirably just in praising the Fraserians for their immediate recognition of Bulwer as the author of *Godolphin*[29] at a time when the rest of the London literary world was floundering among misapprehensions. He also gives fully Maginn's clever appraisal of *Eugene Aram* as "a good story overlaid with tinselled frippery, spun out into tedious dialogue and vapid declamation," and as unpleasant to a sound taste in writing "as is a glass of curaçoa diluted in a pint of water to an unvitiated palate." But he considers that objection to the novel on moral grounds, "coming from the editorial clique of *Fraser's Magazine,* was sheer cant."[30] Who, indeed, he implies, were the Fraserians to find fault with a murderer's being presented as the central figure of a novel, and made an appealing character with whose predicament the reader must sympathize! Who, indeed, were they to remonstrate against "habitual tampering with sacred subjects," a "constant hankering after profanity and blasphemy," the filling of three volumes with "objectionable sentiments," and the basing of "an ostensible labour to be didactic, philosophical and practically moral" upon an unsavoury foundation! Yet *Fraser's* critical tenets were profoundly based on just these objections, as will become evident. In fact, the magazine's motives for hostility could not have been given with greater precision than in this summary of fallacies. But Mr. Sadleir is justified in not being able to forgive the personal abuse which debases *Fraser's* judgments. In a day of preëminent rudeness the monthly was conspicuously rude. Yet its insults, however grossly personal in character, were too ubiquitous to be attributed to personal motives, and its critical tenets were too widely applied and too well reasoned to be charged to insincerity.

Thackeray himself, it is to be remembered, denied any personal animosity toward Lytton, for whose kindness to Laman Blanchard he expressed gratitude. When taken to task by Lady Blessington for his persistent criticism of the novelist, he replied in self-defense, "But there are sentiments in his writing which always anger me, big words which make me furious, and a premeditated fine writing against which I can't help rebelling."[31] This explanation may have been actuated, as Mr. Sadleir suggests, by his desire to win the forgiveness of Lady Blessington, but it sounds very much like the truth. Certainly if he had been trying to put in words the touchstone of *Fraser's* approach toward criticism, he could scarcely have hit upon more accurate phrasing.

The sincerity of Thackeray's remonstrances against Bulwer is seen in the continuation of his attack on the crime novel when it was still further sensationalized by Harrison Ainsworth. Thackeray was indeed so apt a pupil of Maginn that in the course of time he even outstripped the older man in severity, with a more fastidious eye for flaws in taste and execution. Work which Maginn was inclined to condone was not spared by the punctilious awareness of Thackeray. However insultingly the exacting critic had denounced the work of Bulwer, his disgust did not reach its height until it was vented upon the gay romances of the younger rival in popular esteem, Harrison Ainsworth. Bulwer was, in Thackeray's opinion, at least serious in the use of his material; Ainsworth, who modeled his tales on *Paul Clifford,* subtracted all purpose other than to amuse, and wantonly falsified in order to gain sensational effect.

Thackeray's attack on his friend Ainsworth was the more conspicuous because it was in defiance of his older colleagues and was carried on single-handed or with the possible assistance of Edward Kenealy, a young Irish scholar who had joined the staff in 1838. Although Maginn in "Elizabeth Brownrigge" and several hostile reviews had taken issue, as we have seen, against the sentimentalized treatment of crime in the novels of Bulwer Lytton, the appearance in 1834 of Ainsworth's *Rookwood* with its valiant scamp hero, Dick Turpin, had completely disarmed him. Ainsworth himself was a Fraserian and a popular member of the inner circle that gathered in the publisher's back parlor. Furthermore, Maginn would seem to have had no little personal relish for the dashing ballads sung by the gallant highwayman. Although the report that he helped Ainsworth with the foot-pad songs was untrue, his partiality for the artless work of his young colleague was evident. It is not surprising, therefore, that the magazine assumed a friendly attitude toward the famous exploits of Turpin. Jack Churchill, Maginn's special aide, published a flattering review, "High-Ways and Low-Ways," in *Fraser's* for June, 1834; and two years later, when the third edition of the novel appeared, Maginn wrote the even more gayly complimentary notice, "Another Caw from the Rookwood."[32] In the interval between them the loyal editor several times found opportunity to advertise in his own sportive fashion the merits of Ainsworth. At the staff dinner for instance, described in the *Fraser* "Gallery" for January, 1835, Maginn represented his young friend as singing an improvised Turpin ballad[33] to the tinkling of Fraserian glasses.

Not until the publication in serial form of his second novel on criminal life, *Jack Sheppard,* did Ainsworth meet with any except the most cordial treatment from *Fraser's Magazine.* No review of this fresh Newgate material appeared contemporaneously in the magazine, but shortly after the exploits of Sheppard began to fill the successive issues of *Bentley's* in 1839, Thackeray started his parody, *Catherine,* which came out anonymously in the parallel numbers of *Fraser's.* Nor was Thackeray's opposition confined to the chapters of *Catherine.* As Stewart Marsh Ellis, the biographer of Ainsworth, complains,[34] the exacting critic was responsible with John Forster of the *Athenæum* for the terrific hue and cry which arose against the demoralizing influences of criminal romance, and finally culminated in the satirical sketches of the early volumes of *Punch* and in Theodore Martin's burlesque ballads, *Flowers of Hemp: or the Newgate Garland.* Although Bulwer Lytton's crime novel *Paul Clifford* and Dickens's *Oliver Twist* also received their share of ridicule, the brunt of the censure fell on Ainsworth's *Jack Sheppard.* So strong was the feeling against it that objection was actually made to the election of Ainsworth to the Athenæum Club. When Lady Blessington wished to champion him, Ainsworth, according to Ellis, wrote to her: "I have been given to understand that I should meet with formidable opposition from a hostile party, whom I must term the Anti-Jack-Sheppardites; and have thought it better to let things take their course, and withdraw."[35]

The omission from *Fraser's* of any review of *Jack Sheppard* while it was appearing in *Bentley's* is significant of the power which Thackeray had at that time acquired on the staff. Percival Banks, previously mentioned as one of its first and most important members, had written to Ainsworth offering to review the novel in the magazine. "I am anxious," he concludes, "that it should succeed, and the more especially because I find certain of the dunces and blackguards are against you."[36] Evidently Thackeray's influence proved too strong for Banks, since not only did his critique fail to appear, but the burlesque novel *Catherine* clearly established the antagonistic attitude of the magazine. Thackeray's opposition became more pronounced when in the final chapter of *Catherine* he threw aside the mask of fiction and in his own person denounced the evil tendencies of Ainsworth's sentimentalized treatment of crime. In the same number of *Fraser's*, February, 1840, appeared a scathing review of *Jack Sheppard*, evidently written by Thackeray, referring to and supplementing the concluding remarks of *Catherine*.

Two other essays, which appeared at approximately the same time, support these sharp attacks on Ainsworth. The four works present a full development of the critical theory that a rugged holding to actual experience, even when crudely narrated, is more salutory and more effective as art than sentimentalized interpretation. The first of these essays, "Half-a-Crown's Worth of Cheap Knowledge," which Thackeray in his notebook speaks of as writing, was published in *Fraser's* for February, 1838, shortly before Ainsworth's *Jack Sheppard* began in *Bentley's Miscellany*. In this brief review of the penny press Thackeray attempted to convince the reader that unvarnished accounts of the lower classes by men who knew at first-hand the life they were depicting were more valuable as sources of information than the versions of that life found in the popular fiction of the day. The second essay, "Horæ Catnachianæ," for April, 1839, can also be definitely ascribed to Thackeray, as it opens with an explanation that it is the sequel of "Half-a-Crown's Worth of Cheap Knowledge." "Catnachianæ" has the same purpose as its predecessor: to prove that the popular Newgate-Calendar novels give a false picture of the lower classes and that therefore readers might well turn to sources which depict these classes at first-hand. The two articles closely parallel each other, "Cheap Knowledge" taking under consideration the penny journals written for the London masses, and "Catnachianæ" the ballad sheets hawked through the streets or circulated from shops like that of Catnach in Seven Dials.

In fact the interlacing of thought in these practically contemporaneous reviews is so close that passages could be transposed from one to the other without interfering with the argument. Thus in the concluding remarks of *Catherine* Thackeray showed that Fielding and Gay by keeping to sterner, more naturalistic details achieved at once better morality and better art than Ainsworth when he substituted refinements of sentiment and scene for the brutality and coarseness of actual existence. This idea is still further expanded in the *Jack Sheppard* review. Here Thackeray developed the thought that the rough facts of

Sheppard's life as given in the Newgate Calendar formed a more vigorous and instructive story than that which Ainsworth had fabricated.

> We cannot help thinking, that by keeping close to the true story, as he chose it at all, he might not only have pointed a better moral, but have more adorned his tale. Compare the parting of Jack Sheppard with his mother, in the apocryphal reading . . . with that of the true Codex Newgatorius.

Then follow parallel passages from the novel and the *Select Trials at the Old Bailey,* with Thackeray's comment,

> Alas! for the refinements of society, that will not allow us to call things by their right names, as in the days of more free-spoken grandfathers,—when we might call a spade a spade.

In conclusion:

> We back the reality against the romance,—the lady in her cups against the lady in her tears. Is not the whole history of the unfortunate lad's life told more graphically, and more truly, and therefore more poetically, by those three quarterns of brandy, than by a tub-full of maudlin pathos?[37]

Now this is a typical Thackeray reflection and might just as well have been found in the concluding chapters of *Catherine,* which also quote an unvarnished account for evidence of superiority to fiction, as in the *Sheppard* review—or, indeed, might just as well have been found eight months later in the article on Fielding which Thackeray wrote for the *Times* of September 2, 1840. In this last he again regrets that plain speaking is out of fashion, and that "later humorists dare not talk of what the elder discussed honestly."

> Vice [he explains] is never to be mistaken for virtue in Fielding's honest, downright books; it goes by its name, and invariably gets its punishment. . . . Ainsworth dared not paint his hero as the scoundrel he knew him to be; he must keep his brutalities in the background, else the public morals be outraged, and so he produces a book quite absurd and unreal, and infinitely more immoral than anything Fielding ever wrote.

How deeply Thackeray had the whole discussion at heart may be judged by his reopening it years later in his well-known lecture on Hogarth, Smollett, and Fielding, and again in his introduction to the works of Fielding.

"Horæ Catnachianæ" is particularly important because of the light which the review throws on its author's opinion of Charles Dickens. The generosity of Thackeray toward his great rival has been almost a phenomenon in literary criticism, persisting as it did in spite of the bitter personal quarrel of the two men and the hot rivalry of their followers which divided England into hostile camps. There was from the first an antagonism of aim and mode which admitted of no compromise. Thackeray's easy correctness and good breeding was by example a silent reprimand to the brilliant social and stylistic lapses of his rival. His grave insistence on truth, the need of presenting things as they were or in obviously satirical exaggeration, formed a natural cleavage with Dickens's spirited neglect of causes and consequences, while he bent himself to his own variety of realistic romance. That both novelists were aware of the gulf between them may be judged from Thackeray's remark: "He knows that my books are a protest against his—that if the one set are true, the other must be false." How completely Thackeray in the end understood Dickens and how warmly he appreciated the triumphs of his rival may be read in the commentaries scattered through his reviews and lectures. The early stage in the development of his estimate, when the faults of Dickens thrust themselves upon him so sharply that he had barely begun to recognize the excellence, is fully expressed in "Horæ Catnachianæ."

In its twin essay, "Cheap Knowledge," Thackeray had casually remarked that the admirable Boz, in contrast to the novelists of the time, gave a faithful account of the lower classes. The subsequent popularity, however, of Ainsworth's *Jack Sheppard,* with its contemporary presentations on eight London stages, made Thackeray peculiarly analytical of scenes dealing with criminal life. When he came to write "Horæ Catnachianæ" in April, 1839, he found Dickens as well as Ainsworth and Bulwer lacking in first-hand knowledge of roguery. The following passage contrasts their versions of crime with the raw accounts in the Catnach ballads and also with the work of Fielding. In reference to the ballads, he comments:

> There is more information about thieves, ruffians, swindlers of both sexes, more real vulgarity, more tremendous slang, more unconscious, honest, blackguard NATURE, in fact, than Mr. Dickens will ever give

to the public. There sits Blackguardism, calm, simple, at ease, uttering her own thoughts in her own language; not having a gentleman for a mouthpiece, not decked out with any artificial flowers of wit, nor trammelled by any notions of politeness or decorum. She has her own jokes, words, ways, as different from those that our popular writers choose to give her, as their habits are from hers: and when we say that neither Mr. Dickens, nor Mr. Ainsworth, nor Sir Lytton Bulwer, can write about what they know not, we presume that not one of those three gentlemen will be insulted at an imputation of ignorance on a subject where knowledge is not, after all, very desirable. Fielding, now, *had* some experience about such characters; and oh! with what a difference of humour and perception did he view and write about them. Dickens's Jew, Fagin, is one of the cleverest actors that ever appeared on the stage; but, like a favourite actor, the Jew is always making points to tickle the ears of the audience. We laugh at his jokes, because we are a party to them, as it were, and receive at every fresh epigram a knowing wink from the old man's eye; which lets us into the whole secret. Look, now, at Jonathan Wild the Great—the great, indeed. See how gravely he goes to work, how simply, how unconsciously. There is no leering and bandying with the galleries, to tell you that he is not what he seems; no joking and epigrams about his profession: he is in earnest, as the author was when he described him; as earnest as a great man would be with a great purpose.[38]

It has seemed best to give this passage in full because it throws so honest a light on Thackeray's estimate of Dickens. Failure to depict a gallows' hero was not, however, the gravest lack which the scrupulous critic found in the creator of *Pickwick* and *Oliver Twist.* Dickens's slang and general neglect of literary decorum annoyed him. Mr. Lilywick, Thackeray points out through an over-elaborate device of a German translation, is represented as a gentleman of some wealth and character, yet is given the manners of "a low buffoon, of coarse habits, ignorant of the very principles of grammar." Thackeray further comments:

The Kenwigs family are likewise described expressly as living elegantly; they occupy a floor in a hotel, as was the common fashion in London and Paris in those days. . . . Does *this* warrant the vulgarities of language which Bos's translator puts into the mouth of all his characters? Is bad grammar *elegant?* Is slang *elegant?*[39]

Yet even "Horæ Catnachianæ," which shows Thackeray's scruples at their height, admits:

All these opinions are, to be sure, delivered *ex cathedrá*, from the solemn critical chair; but when out of it, and in private, we humbly acknowledge that we have read every one of Mr. Dickens's tales with the most eager delight, that we watch for *Nicholas Nickleby* as the month comes around, and have the strongest curiosity and admiration for Mr. Ainsworth's new work, *Jack Sheppard*. Mr. Long Ned, Mr. Paul Clifford, Mr. William Sykes, Mr. Fagin, Mr. John Sheppard (just mentioned), and Mr. Richard Turpin, whose portraits are the most striking in the modern and fashionable Thief's Gallery, are gentlemen whom we must all admire. We could "hug the rogues and love them," and do—*in private*.[40]

This leniency was to develop toward Dickens, though not toward either Ainsworth or Bulwer, into as tender and as gallant an admiration as one man could pay the works of another. Improprieties of diction or early ignorance of thieves' dens counted not a whit against an author capable of producing the *Christmas Carol*.

Thackeray's generosity toward Dickens, though not extended in anything like the same degree to his other contemporaries, was none the less indicative of a general mellowing which began to take place in his work about 1840. Maginn's tutelage of his protégé had come to an end with *Yellowplush*. The observations of the astute butler consummated what the young author had learned from his work on the *Fraser* staff and at the same time added an element which did not spring from the hardy brotherhood, indeed was alien to their hail-fellow practice. How deeply *Yellowplush* had drawn from the tap of Nol Yorke may be seen when we examine not only the unfeeling and self-righteous mirth of the butler but the subjects upon which he expended it. The "notwice" for soup, and other affectations of the "fashionable novel," were old lampooning ground for the magazine, even the device of the butler himself having been satirically suggested by Maginn as a probable source of Bulwer Lytton's eavesdropping on fashionable life. What Thackeray did was to bring this old *Fraser* material to sudden fruition through his own social experience in the life which he was satirizing. For the first time in the history of the strapping periodical a well-bred though supercilious aloofness entered its pages. One looks in vain through the work of Maginn or his other followers for any sign of snobbery or delicate disgust. They were an unscrupulous lot in every sense of the word and quite too hearty to be aware of hairsplitting niceties or even decent refinements. With the act of creating a butler from his own world, Thackeray in a moment also created himself as distinct from William Maginn. To Charles Yellowplush a faint fastidiousness was as natural as was hard and unbending joviality. Nor was Thackeray's writing thereafter ever to be without this inbred condescension. Throughout his life, even as late as tender-hearted Philip, there was to remain a light admixture of scorn.

Two years after *Yellowplush* unfortunately came *Catherine*. From start to finish it is a crass, brutal burlesque, and in its self-explanatory last chapter Thackeray congratulates himself upon the success with which he has achieved its complete failure. It avoided, he boasts, arousing any more agreeable sensation than nausea.[41] Here then, is the magazine's hard, bright comedy, bemired, run amuck in a stupid welter of butchery. Thackeray was never to return to it; Maginn was not in a position to; and the other Fraserians, missing the glancing light of their leader, had already strayed to duller fields.

Yet bad as *Catherine* was, from its ruins emerged the completed personality of the sentimental satirist, William Makepeace Thackeray. He was convinced at last by its failure of the inadequacy of unrelieved satire. And with that conviction he accepted for his work a broader, more human basis. The desire to analyze appears in his writing and also the need to sympathize. How much of himself Thackeray had kept in reserve during his apprenticeship to Maginn is seen by the abruptness with which he closed the door on their literary intimacy. The sudden great calamity in his own private life doubtless hastened his growth in sympathetic analysis; yet it is also presumable that during the very period when he was most under the influence of Maginn's powerful personality, he had sufficient genius to achieve for himself a separate though unexpressed development.

In the small tract, "Going to See a Man Hanged," for August, 1840, for the first time Thackeray dropped the cold, metallic banter of the Fraserians and adopted a note of human interest and sympathy. The man who errs is not merely to be scoffed at but to be pitied. Not that his sins are to be condoned, or sentimentalized into brave deeds, or in any way made to appear other than they are; but the man himself, because of his sins as well as his virtues becomes a subject for intimate and kindly consideration. Nor is Thackeray's close scrutiny wholly confined to others. For the first time appears the spirit of the confessional. He analyzes the very pity and fear and disgust which he finds within himself, searching out obscure attachments that lie as a network at the bottom of the mind, rudimentary filaments of crudity and obscenity, mob ties and isolations. Something of modern psychology is implicit here, and in all of Thackeray's later work. There is a gossipy liking to moralize, but there is also care for the closer, less easy statement that gets nearer to the heart of things.

The change which came over Thackeray's writing is nowhere more evident in *Fraser's* than when we compare *Catherine* and *Barry Lyndon*. Both reprove the picaresque gallows' tale which Harrison Ainsworth brought into swift popularity. There is not a vestige, however, of human sympathy within the bestiality of *Catherine,* while *Barry Lyndon* is of Thackeray's new order, which mildly and gracefully tugs at the heartstrings. It has not a trace of *Catherine's* heavy-handed burlesque, but it is none the less after its own human fashion a satire. For Barry is not to be taken as a traditional picaresque hero, and surely not as a buffoon Jack Sheppard. He is from the first an engaging Irishman, endowed by nature with the gay irresponsibility of the picaresque, and affording inevitable satire upon all who are more seriously intentioned than himself. To the last page he never falls into the heavy ways of those he lightly ridicules, nor like Joseph Andrews does he wholly forget about them and step off in his own right. His chief business is kept well in mind: to show how clumsy more earnest heroes are and how easily he can run away with their hard-won tricks and make love to the reader into the bargain.

On the analogy of *Barry Lyndon's* sly dealings with desperado fiction, it is a temptation to trace Thackeray's talent for correcting his fellow craftsmen in the more intricate satire of *Vanity Fair*. Though the latter novel was not itself published in *Fraser's* it culminated the sequence of Thackeray's writing in the magazine, bringing to full power the qualities which had been slowly developing in his work. Narrowing the purpose of the great novel to discipline would of course be unwarrantable. Even more than *Barry Lyndon, Vanity Fair* transcends any set objective and creates for itself a life of wide and varied manifestations. Yet just as one of the initial impulses of *Lyndon* was presumably to throw light on the mendacity of "gallows" fiction, so it is possible that into the plan for *Vanity Fair* went a desire to expose the absurdities and falsehoods of that parent enemy, the older and more influential "fashionable novel." Thackeray had already through the biting remarks of Charles Yellowplush cut sharply at its ignorance and pretence. It would, therefore, not be strange if as one of the objectives of his second novel he had attempted a more detailed exposure of its sham punctilios and "silver-fork" refinements. Whether intentional or not, such a purpose is fulfilled even in minute detail by the book. Dobbin, Becky Sharpe, Amelia correct and humanize the typical heroes and heroines of Theodore Hook, Lady Blessington, and other "fashionable" faddists of the day, as the manners and customs of the Crawley household correct the sham proprieties and delicacies among which those heroes and heroines lived. Nor does this narrow satire supplant in any sense the broader satire on the social world itself, or lessen one whit the keenness of Thackeray's direct thrusts at its vices and incongruities. From every standpoint he was writing of the life he knew best, and true to the *Fraser* principle, he was writing of it as he knew it.

When we review the entire course of Thackeray's work from his first articles for *Fraser's* through the last of the "Roundabouts," we are impressed by how little his critical tenets altered. Once and for all he had accepted William Maginn's creed. Writing was to be robust, fine or rough according to its nature, but in any case without dissimulation or sensationalized warping. Yet in the application of this stiff rule Thackeray came to acquire a steadfast and disarming kindliness.

CHAPTER IV

THE CRITICAL WORKSHOP

The sincerity of *Fraser's* criticism becomes apparent only when we survey the whole field of its rebellion against the literary shortcomings of its day. Maginn believed that the magazine should support vigorous and full-blooded writing. With his own fine relish for Smollett, Fielding, and Sterne, he wished the public to know the denatured state of their contemporary literature in contrast to the wholesome products of the past. He objected to weak imitation wherever he met it, whether in poetry that echoed Byron, or in historical novels that exploited Scott, or in stories of criminal life which he felt diminished and sentimentalized their stalwart predecessors.

Again and again the magazine laments the bankrupt state of current writing. Oliver Yorke exclaims, "O let us not talk of our literature in the present day—we have none. It is true, we have a writing and a reading public; but the production of a work of art is neither expected by the one, nor attempted by the other."[1] Maginn, with reference presumably to Wordsworth and Coleridge, sadly writes, "We recollect who were they who once in our time gave us something worth reading, and we sorrowfully look for them or their like in vain. Has our poetry departed from us; and are we sunk to an age of criticism —an age which never affords any thing worthy of being criticized?"[2] When John Wilson, as Christopher North of *Blackwood's,* decries Sterne's *Tristram Shandy* and dubbs Uncle Toby and Trim fantastic shadows of Rabelais, Maginn answers, "Well! if they be, it would give us no small pleasure to find anybody now alive, writing any thing which might approach within the degree of a phantom of the kind-hearted captain, and the true-hearted corporal. A cartload of the sentimental novels since Sterne's time is not worth one *LeFevre.*"[3]

The *Fraser* reviewers were shrewd enough to realize that the authors who had the widest repute at the moment were imitative rather than original. The abundance of poetry and fiction being produced, they affirmed, was not a sign of wholesome activity; rather literary markets were glutted by ill-considered work. In analyzing the cause of the weakened state of literature they in no uncertain terms laid the blame upon rapidity of writing. Publishers were becoming manufacturers who sought the wholesale production and marketing of their goods; authors, like factory operatives, were enslaved to piecework, paid for quantity. Readers should be warned against such mercenary plants, which flooded the market with cheap writings, vitiated public taste by extolling these writings through organized "puff" reviewing, and corrupted authors by bribing them to produce the type of work considered most salable.

PUFF AND PLUNDER

The chief offender among publishers, *Fraser's* was glad to find, was its greatest rival, the firm of Colburn and Bentley, a properous West End house which owned the *New Monthly Magazine* as well as several journals and held shares in various other periodicals, including the powerful *Literary Gazette.* There would be good reason for placing *Fraser's* immoderate attack against Colburn and Bentley on the level of a commercial fray, had not Maginn previously established the sincerity of his own opinion in his anonymous novel *Whitehall,* which will be more fully discussed in connection with his political views. Since *Whitehall* was in the nature of a spitfire, flying in the face of Maginn's own party leaders as well as their opponents, of friends as well as of enemies, its ludicrous tableaux at least vindicate its author from the charge of hypocrisy. Among the best sustained of its scenes is a visit to the Burlington Street "factory" of Colburn and Bentley, during which one of the owners, armed with a lengthy ruler, demonstrates outlandish methods for speeding the operatives.[4]

At the establishment of *Fraser's* Maginn, with unlimited space for his ire, determined to fight these "West End" methods to the finish, and in consequence for several years there was scarcely an issue of the magazine that did not contain some slur against them. The following is among the more explicit:

> Indeed, writing now has, through the facilities afforded by the booksellers of the West End, become a matter of such ease, that in the items of income with many of Messrs. Colburn and Bentley's squad of scribblers it is no unusual thing to see placed—

To 1 Poem, 3 Novels
of 3 vols. each, 15
Magazine Articles,
37 Songs and pieces
of humorous and satirical Verses, and
2 Vols. of History . . . £425 15 7½

Quantity, and not quality, is the thing nearest to the author's heart; and the bookseller cares little what he publishes, since, from the present system of puffing, the vilest trash is sure of some sort of market.

Maginn called attention to the organized puffing of their wares carried on by Colburn and Bentley "with their *New Monthly Magazine,* their *Court Journal,* their *United Service Journal,* their *Sunday Times,* and puffs point-blank, oblique, inferential."[5] In another place he pointed out that of thirty-seven novels, eighteen were favorably reviewed in the *Court Journal* alone and eleven in the *Literary Gazette* of which Mr. Colburn owned a third.[6]

From the first numbers of *Fraser's* the dishonesty of the puff system was exposed.

The secret of success is involved in the right use of one grand, cabalistic word—PUFF; ay—PUFF—PUFF—PUFF. And as Gnatho gave his name to one sect, and Tartuffe to another; as pickpockets are known after their *maximus Alcides* Barrington, and philosophising jack-asses and howling materialists after their molten moon-calf of worship, old Jerry Bentham; so literary puffers and trumpeting booksellers should form themselves into a special guild, and choose Henry Colburn for their head—for he it is who has not only invented, but brought the present art and mystery of puff manufacture to its existing condition and consistence.

The tirade concludes: "Thou shalt live for ever, as Prince Paramount of Puffers and Quacks."[7]

In one of his more jocular moods Maginn described the joint booksellers in "buffoon's dress and cracked puff-trumpet of tin," drawing the crowd to their circus tent to see their menagerie of writers, including the popular novelists Theodore Hook, Bulwer Lytton, Horace Smith. "Valk up, ladies and gemmen," Bentley is supposed to cry, "and vitness all the monstrous and strange warieties of hanimals vich this here booth contains."[8] Thereupon follows a column of rapid lampooning: "Hook tyger, the Bulwer baboon, the Smith mocking bird, a hanimal remarkable for himitating the cry of better hanimals than himself, the Norton bird of Paradise"—the last, a saucy reference to the renowned beauty of the Honorable Mrs. Norton.

Absurd as this picture is, it would not seem overdrawn. Harriet Martineau in her autobiography, for instance, gives a detailed account of her series of annoying interviews with Colburn and Bentley, summing up her experience with the tart comment that

> it may be well to show how the degradation of literature comes about, in times when speculating publishers try to make grasping authors, and to convert the serious function of authorship into a gambling match. The way in which authors allowed themselves to be put up to auction, and publishers squabbled at the sale was a real and perpetual grief to me to witness. . . . I went to bed that night with a disgusted and offended feeling of having been offered bribes, all day long, with a confidence which was not a little insulting.[9]

Elsewhere in her autobiography Harriet Martineau records the shock with which she learned that she was expected to furnish Colburn and Bentley with the reviews of her own book; and when she indignantly refused to solicit her friends, she was made to feel that her unusual stand was causing inconvenience. In speaking of the immense power exercised by the *Literary Gazette* at this time, Samual Carter Hall, for some years the editor of the *New Monthly,* stated that a

> laudatory review was almost sure to sell an edition of a book, and an author's fame was established when he had obtained the praise of that journal. . . . The *Gazette* stood alone as the arbiter of fate.[10]

Its editor, William Jerdan, boasted that the morning after a review of *Crichton* had appeared in the *Gazette* Bentley offered Ainsworth £500 for a new novel.[11]

In explanation of this condition it is to be remembered that reviewing in the first quarter of the century was still under the thumb of politics. Periodicals lauded a book if the writer belonged to the proper party, and decried it if he belonged to the wrong one. And since the question was so perfunctory, it mattered little who wrote the reviews, whether critics hired by the publishers or the author's personal friends, or indeed the author himself. The practice was thoroughly indecent but accepted, and the shades of indecency were beyond the scope of the average conscience.

Against this prevalent state of corruption *Fraser's*, as we have seen, kept up a perpetual battle cry.[12] It deserves the credit of being the first periodical to denounce the dishonest practices of the day and to maintain a higher standard of reviewing within its own pages. A year later, it was to be followed in this stand by the *Athenæum* under the editorship of Charles Wentworth Dilke.

On the whole *Fraser's* lived up surprisingly well to its boast that its reviews were free from political manipulation and were not biased by consideration for publishers and authors. Now and again, it even hotly attacked books brought out by its own publisher, James Fraser,[13] and it was known to criticize unfavorably the work of its staunch contributors, such as Robert Gleig,[14] later Chaplain General of the Army, and Theodore Hook,[15] editor of *John Bull*, who were in addition both devoted Tories. On one occasion it took up the cudgels for Thomas Campbell, a Whig, as opposed to John Wilson Croker, the Tory Secretary to the Navy, the power behind the *Quarterly Review*, and the special patron of Maginn.[16]

Yet with the exception of Thackeray and Carlyle, the Fraserians never for a moment attempted to keep politics out of their reviews. Their hot-headed antagonism to the so-called political economists and their enraged disapproval of party leaders or of other prominent men were matters which they had on their conscience too persistently to recognize barriers in utterance. But their politics were interpolated, after their own peculiar and often none too coherent fashion, into their essays without affecting the surrounding subject matter. Thus even the mild review of Washington Irving's *Tour on the Prairies* reminds the reader that the prominent American is "as somnolent as Melbourne,"[17] and Father Prout starts an appreciation of Horace by being aware of "the ignoble doings of modern Whiggery, sneaking and dastardly in its proceedings at home, and not very dignified in its dealings abroad."[18] As for Maginn, his criticism is often so filled with extraneous political allusions that if he had been less clever, he would have found it difficult to make headway at all.

In consequence the majority of the Fraserians walked a fine line. They freely assailed the doctrines of a writer; but if, as in the case of Macaulay, his work showed literary power, they were careful to confine their attack to his doctrines only—or rather to doctrines plus the character of the man himself, for they admitted nothing sacred about personal reputation and early taught their foes to take whatever buffets they chose to give. On the other hand, when the work of an enemy showed symptoms of pretence, of overwrought sentimentality, of undue length or of otherwise faulty execution, their abuse became jubilant.

Those who were most roughly treated at these moments of ruthless hilarity were naturally the political economists and the writers who tended toward materialism in religion and philosophy. The staff viewed with such alarm any increase in the influence of rationalistic science and theology that they subjected even thoughtful work like that of Harriet Martineau to ribald scrutiny for being sacrilegious and immoral.[19] As for Bowring, the prolific editor of the *Westminster Review,* they considered him overblown and ripe for ridicule. His wide linguistic attainments they pronounced as dubious as his economic theories. When he published his version of Magyar poetry, they early suspected that "a shrewd fellow like himself might possibly be nineteenth-centurizing us, with this same knack of translating from all the tongues of Babel."[20] Not to be cozened, they produced their own rendering from the Magyar poets as a gauge for the scholarship of Dr. Bowring.

The Pious Maiden

Holy little Polly!
Love sought me, but I tricked him;
Polly, little holy!
You thought of me, "I've nicked him!"
Little holy Polly!
I'm not to be your victim.

Te Pikke Megge

Hogy, wogy, Pogy!
Xupumxé trtzááá bnikttm;
Pogy, wogy hogy!
Bsdnro plgvbz cttnsttm;
Wogy hogy Pogy!
Mlésrz vbquógp fvikttm.

The satire becomes bolder in depicting a drunken brawl among poets for the favors of a demi-mondaine. A sentimental note is added in the sudden reclaiming of a Magyar youth, suggestively named Quaffypunchovics, through his learning English and by accident coming across a volume written by a lady whose "intellectual fecundity has long been the theme of astonishment in her own country." On a deputation of his former associates waiting upon him, he exclaims,

(indignantly)
Blunder, bluster, botheration,
Bore and blast the boys of blame!

(tenderly)
Lighter, love's alliteration—
Matchless Mary Mitford's name!

And thereupon he expires. His friends, momentarily sobered by the blow which has deprived them of Quaffypunchovics, place on a tablet to his memory the words:

Here I lies,
To my own surprise!

After further juvenile merrymaking at the expense of Bowring, the Fraserians assure the learned Doctor that they will continue their attentions in ensuing numbers of the magazine:

Thy consonantal language, Magyar!
May puzzle some—to us it is but fun—
And, till our duty, self imposed, be done,
We stick to't fondly as adhesive tar.

Pleased with their own perspicacity, the iconoclastic staff draw the self-laudatory conclusion:

And when the fine spun web of fame we sever,
The effect is terrible and overpowering,
As may be testified by Dr. Bowring,
Whose Magyar pipe is now put out for ever!

Yet though the Fraserians' estimate of their enemies was harsh and not infrequently outrageously insulting, it was often shrewd, the reviewers being generally clever enough to recognize faults even if not generous enough to admit virtues. Almost the only instance, though a conspicuous one, in which their critical judgment was thrown hopelessly awry by political hostility was Maginn's scornful critique of Peacock's *Crotchet Castle*.[21] Even here the reviewer attempts to save himself by taking the ground that it is absurd to compare Peacock with Rabelais, who would not for a moment have tolerated the political economy of McCulloch, but "would have hitched the great doctor of absenteeism into an immortal chapter, as probably one of the consulting advisers of Panurge, 'when he had the flea in his ear,' and set forth his rugged ribaldry as a jest for ever." Nor is Maginn entirely without justification when he carps at the reputed scholarship of Peacock. After quoting various passages which he finds are "not learning, nor anything like it," he ends with the remark, "Ignorance manifested in ninety-nine pages is not to be palliated by bits of out-of-the-way Greek, scraped out of a lexicon, in the hundredth. Such was not the scholarship of Rabelais, whose learning breathes forth in every page, and who quotes it in none."

For the most part, however, the Fraserians pursued their slashing methods without running foul of genius. Fairly secure in their position, they took pleasure in widely announcing their own purity of motive, and in hurling anathema at the ignoble ways of the Colburn and Bentley periodicals.

CRITICAL THEORIES: CARLYLE, HERAUD, MAGINN

Probably *Fraser's* greatest service, sometimes too ostentatiously declared, was in the occasional introduction of esthetic theory into its reviews. Heraud, and even Maginn, who was little of the metaphysician and still less of the mystic, realized through their own reading of Lessing, Schlegel, Schiller, and Goethe, or through the reflections of Coleridge, that their individual judgments ought to be supported by philosophical principles. Thus the criticism of Maginn spasmodically strained itself for brief references to the creative imagination as concomitant to excellence, and to the functioning of the mind in the process of creation. More deeply read in German philosophy was Heraud, who now and then almost lost sight of the subject under immediate review in his earnest search for support from Coleridge and his predecessors in romantic idealism. Among other works he submitted Godwin's novels, Byron's *Cain,* Isaac Taylor's *Physical Theory of Another Life,* and the Bridgewater treatises to inspection from the cloudy summit of Coleridge's teaching.[22] All told, there were approximately eighty articles which show the influence, however distorted, of some phase of transcendental esthetics or metaphysics.

Few magazines of the day, as Carlyle was at pains to point out, entirely neglected German work. In *Fraser's* the emphasis given to it was exceptional. As is well known, much of the early writing of Carlyle himself, while he was most closely enrapt in German transcendentalism, was published in *Fraser's*. The whole question of his indebtedness to his German masters has in recent years been ably treated;[23] and we no longer need to be convinced that the great English master showed in *Sartor Resartus* and the rest of his *Fraser* work a sympathetic community with German thought if only by his departures from it. The articles of Heraud make direct reference to German philosophers, poets, and novelists, including Fichte, Klopstock, Novalis, Richter, Herder, Heine, as well as Schlegel, Goethe, and Schiller. He wrote three fairly careful studies of German poetry and one of German and French philosophy, and made various translations from the German poets. Nor were translations by other Fraserians lacking. In short, when we consider the range of German work and influence in *Fraser's,* we find that the magazine played an eminent part in the spread of German philosophy and literature which had been started by Coleridge at the commencement of the century.

It should not be forgotten in estimating *Fraser's* reviews, that the greatest critic publishing at the time was Carlyle, and that some of his analyses, including his famous essay on Boswell's *Johnson,* appeared in the magazine. His method, to climb upon the shoulders of an author, to study the man himself, his purposes and capabilities, and in the light thus gained to judge his accomplishment, was the day's most interesting development in criticism. It exerted a marked influence upon his fellow Fraserians. Though they were sometimes unable to appreciate the integrity of his inquiry, and too often paraded paraphernalia of judgment to which their obvious prejudice gave the lie, they immeasurably strengthened their criticism through the example of Carlyle, gaining a more thoughtful and conscientious approach.

Heraud especially came under the influence of Carlyle. Disciple though he was of Coleridge, his ear was none the less strained for the clearer accents of the younger idealist. With surprising assiduity he filled his own mind with the thought and phrasing of the great Scotchman's early critical essays, especially "Burns," "Goethe," "Novalis," "Richter." He finally appropriated Carlyle's interpretation of the hero as a great man capable of turning his genius to whatever work the exigencies of the moment required. A passage from "A Cambrian Colloquy on the Decline and Fall of Poetry," written as early as December, 1834, shows how fully he occasionally voiced Carlyle's thought. The dialogue continues a discussion of poetic genius which Heraud and, to a less extent, Maginn had been intermittently carrying on from the first number of the magazine. Coleridge's idea of genius as exceptional aptitude along one line in contrast to the full development of the perfect man does not appear in this essay, although it had been previously expounded by Heraud. Instead, the genius himself has become such a perfect man and is spoken of in terms startlingly prophetic of Carlyle's later *Hero as Poet*. "Supposing," one of the interlocutors of the dialogue is made to remark, "a real genius to arise in our day, and to 'feel the god within,' his first question must be with himself, *Cui bono?* What am I to do with my genius?" After elaboration of the theme, the comment is made:

> For my part, I don't believe a word of poetic genius being born with a man, but only genius—the convertible ductile ore which may receive any impress whatever at the hand of culture, and in the mint of whatever asylum chance may present for its final form and figure.
>
> Perhaps, had poetry and not arms been the vogue in Napoleon's youth, we should now be reading some sublime epic poem of the great Corsican poet Napoleon Buonaparte.

In still further detail, though with a shift of emphasis, the critic later carries the argument into a discussion of Milton's controversial writings:

> Read [we are told], what nobody reads, Milton's prose works, and you will find the genius of the poet of the lake of penal fire at work darkly, like a roaring underground volcano, yet as palpably as when painting the pains immortal of the blessed become damned. There is something terrible in his wrath and his outpourings are no less noisome and foul than the sooty and sulphureous breath of the eternal prison-house.[24]

The work of Heraud is occasionally so closely imitative as to suggest the possibility that Carlyle himself had some share in its composition. From the passage just quoted, for instance, we might conclude that he was the only author of the "Decline and Fall of Poetry" were it not that there are numerous details about the essay, in addition to its clumsy structure, which indicate that the major part was Heraud's.

Carlyle would have presumably concurred, for instance, with the article's censure of Byron's numerous imitators, but it is doubtful if he would have worded the censure in a form highly derogatory to the original poet.[25]

The problem of determining the authorship of these pseudo-philosophical essays in *Fraser's* is complicated by Heraud's disregard for all rights of literary property, his zeal to accept as his own the thought and phrasing of others. Reverberation of Carlyle's early work is not the only echo in his articles. They are filled with Coleridge's creative power of the imagination, the transcendental ego, its will to be, its missionary instinct to convert. Whether the argument is directed against Chalmers, or Taylor, or that most conscientious infidel William Godwin, we frequently find that God and the king of England are alike upheld by the precepts of Samuel Taylor Coleridge—although precepts so stated that the mystic of Highgate might have been puzzled to recognize them. Thus the strange meeting ground of Carlyle and Coleridge was John Abraham Heraud—and that is a good deal to say about a man, whether he was plagiarist or genius.

The question of authorship becomes even more involved because Heraud was also under the strong influence of his own editor, William Maginn, and conscientiously followed his opinions and manner. When writing in collaboration with Maginn or under Maginn's incentive, he acquired as by miracle a style that also approximated Carlyle's. In consequence the articles of Heraud are so full of astounding ventriloquous effects that the task of determining what is his own work and what is Carlyle's or Maginn's is peculiarly difficult.

It is only fair to state, also, that Carlyle in his turn would seem to have caught something of the journalistic manner of Maginn in the repetition of catchwords and phrases as well as in a more praiseworthy direct and personal approach. Certainly for one reason or another the informal element in Carlyle's style rapidly increased after he commenced contributing to the popular monthly.

Widely different as they were, Maginn, Heraud, and Carlyle had an astonishing amount in common. They were students of the Bible and had much the same literary background. They quoted many of the same authors, and to no small extent shared the same interests, as for instance their admiration of Milton and their dislike of utilitarianism and all its accompaniments in the advance of the mechanical age. Moreover, they also had in common as an immediate background the violent, indeed explosive, magazine in which they were publishing.

In the face of so many obvious sources of confusion it is impossible to state with any accuracy what writing in *Fraser's* can be accredited to Carlyle. None the less it is probable that among the magazine's unidentified articles bordering on philosophy or containing philosophical allusion, there is at least a little work from his hand. So conspicuous is the evidence of his authorship that Mr. J. A. S. Barrett, in the *Literary Supplement* of the London *Times* for January 20, 1927, and for April 26, 1928, pronounces three of the articles to be from his pen. Mr. Barrett bases his decision on the repeated use of characteristic words and phrases, on identity of allusion and on Carlyle's quotation in *Sartor Resartus* of a passage taken from one of the articles. A few years before Mr. Barrett published his evidence, the present author called attention to two other essays in the early *Fraser's* having such obvious marks of Carlyle's workmanship that their authenticity seemed unquestionable.[26] For one of these, a review of Cunningham's *Life of Burns,* April, 1834, the arguments are strong, since references to Scotland preclude attributing the work to Heraud, who was born and brought up in England. The author of the review in exposing the sturdy quality of Scotch peasantry includes reminiscences of his own Scotch peasant birth and boyhood. He also continues, in the true Carlylian vein, the discussion of the "new light," which Carlyle had introduced in his famous 1828 essay on Burns. Since there is no likelihood of finding on the *Fraser* staff a second imitator of Carlyle, and one with whom both the theological interests of the essay and the avowal of Scotch peasant parentage are to be associated, we may conclude that the review is Carlyle's. Proof of authenticity here as elsewhere is, however, too detailed for a chapter such as the present and must be reserved for a bibliographical appendix.

Elusive as is the identification of these pseudo-philosophical articles, one statement may be made with assurance. Whether or not Carlyle had any hand in the essays, there is no doubt that he knew about them and that presumably to some extent they determined the subsequent course of his own writing. The weakening of his interest in metaphysical speculation might well have been caused in part by surfeit of it in the work of Heraud, especially if he himself had been brought at any point into close contact with that work or had discussed phases of it with its pertinacious author. There is a monotony as well as a vagueness and confusion about Heraud's use of German material; and his repetitions and strange misunderstandings must have exasperated Carlyle. The use of German idealism to combat political enemies or to defend the Church against its assailants could scarcely have failed to intensify his scorn for Coleridge. Constant rehearsal in *Fraser's* pages of Coleridge's political and ecclesiastical application of philosophy set forth the mental processes of the Highgate seer in a prejudicial light. Heraud did not understand Coleridge, and though he can hardly be blamed,[27] it is unfortunate that he should have so frequently attempted to interpret him. What Carlyle says about Coleridge's throwing out "logical swimming bladders" and "transcendental life-preservers" is certainly just criticism if applied to Heraud's well-intentioned misrepresentations of his master.

Maginn and his more flippant aides were capable of poking broad fun at Heraud, and for that matter at Coleridge and Carlyle. At times the spread of Germanism over the magazine's pages aroused their amused exasperation. But none the less they were themselves, as we have said, influenced by the movement, their curiosity leading them to such remote reaches as Kant, whom they did not comprehend, but with whom they managed to stir their minds.

Only less interesting than this constant dipping into German esthetics and metaphysics, with its accompanying attempt to understand German literature, was the scholarly criticism of the Fraserians along other lines. There were Maginn's articles on the learning of Shakespeare and his few suggested textual emendations; there were Thomas Wright's reviews of editions of various early English texts; there were Prout's delightful and learned essays on Erasmus and the strangely assorted writers of Latin verse, Jerome Marco Girolamo Vida, Sarbiewski, Sannazar, Fracastor, Beza, Vanière, and the Scotchman George Buchanan.

To give an adequate idea of this scholarly work would be impossible in the present chapter. There is not opportunity here to trace with Prout Pope's indebtedness to Vida, for instance, or to point out the running fire of literary, historical, and biographical allusions by which the learned Jesuit reveals his scope of information and his whimsical turn of mind. Nor is such a study necessary to an understanding of *Fraser's* work in criticism. All magazines of the day contained articles on scholarly subjects and nearly all of them included reviews of foreign literature.

BURLESQUE AND REVIEW

What should be done, rather, is to give an account of the magazine's reviews of the contemporary literature. *Fraser's* scorn for the type of criticism then prevalent is shown in their burlesque of a "puff":

> What innumerable beauties sparkle in every line!—not strained conscious prettinesses, but spontaneous glances of loveliness—sparkles on the crest of imagination's wave—wild flowers which spring unlooked for from the ground. In one poetic word it is THE POTATOE!

The mixed, empty figures here at first thought seem to have overreached their mark, but when one returns to the burlesque fresh from reading some of the reviews in the Colburn and Bentley periodicals one is convinced of its occasional aptness. Defects in *Fraser's* criticism, however important to remember, seem venial in comparison with those of other periodicals. Good work can be found in all of the better magazines, but, as has been said, the general level of reviewing was low, and the group in James Fraser's back parlor were better informed than most of their contemporaries and more abundantly endowed with a sense of humor. Even the personal infatuation of Maginn and other Fraserians for the sentimental poetess L.E.L. did not wholly destroy insight. The following couplet reveals that these critics were capable of recognizing the falsetto when great affection ordinarily forced their praise.

> Golden violets!—who can smell
> Their bright hues but L.E.L.?[28]

In these brief lines is summarized what the world has ever since thought about L.E.L.—providing it has thought at all.

Less flippant in its prognostication was the essay on Wordsworth, written by Maginn, probably in collaboration with Lockhart, for the issue of June, 1831. It is chiefly interesting for its brief anticipation of the well-known lecture by Matthew Arnold. We feel on most familiar ground, for instance, when we read of the things which prevent full recognition of Wordsworth's greatness and learn that such recognition will come only when those poems which are unworthy of his genius have been barred from collections of his work. In no uncertain tones the authors speak of the "Hart Leap Well" as an "affected piece of maudlin mysticism." They doubt if the world will "ever be brought to relish the nursery-rhyme simplicity of his lyrical pieces, or to sympathize with his cant in reference to the feelings of his peasant characters, about happy thoughts, happy dreams, happy sounds." Yet their admiration is just as genuine and as generously expressed. The sentence in the essay perhaps most arresting is the one which reads: "We think that the gist of the whole argument regarding Wordsworth's poetical character is, *that he is an enthusiast,* and that of a bolder and more perfect kind than poets generally are." The wording here is pointed and memorable.

One of the most interesting features of the magazine's criticism was its stout championing of Wordsworth and Coleridge and its respect for Shelley. The latter is especially surprising since the exiled poet had professed his atheism and his faith in anarchy too frequently to be as yet generally admitted to English favor. Ordinarily, as we have found, *Fraser's* treatment of rebels from the nation's church and constitution was drastic. But Heraud recognized him as a philosopher, though a faulty one,[29] and joined Maginn in proclaiming him an obvious source, with Wordsworth, of one phase of Byron's work[30]—a point which doubtless gave satisfaction to the editor, who, as we shall discover, had small patience with the wide tribute paid to the famous Childe.

Fraser's championing of Coleridge was the natural outcome of his close intimacy with Irving and of the veneration in which he was held by the rest of the staff. The magazine's struggle to win public appreciation for his writing was long and valiant. Maginn and Heraud felt that a man with the personal influence of the seer of Highgate should not be underrated as an author because his work remained unread. They reminded the public that much in the essays of other men had been taken barefaced from Coleridge's writing.

It was always [Maginn insisted in his "Gallery" sketch of the poet, for July, 1833] worse done than if Coleridge had done it, and sometimes vilely perverted in spirit; but still the seed was good, and he has thus strongly acted upon the public mind of the day. We fear that his *Lay Sermons,* abounding as they do in brilliant and eloquent passages, have not found a very enlarged audience; but what he has spoken and suggested is now diffused throughout the literature of England, and forms part and parcel of every mind worth containing it in the country.

Maginn was one of the first to recognize that Coleridge's procrastination had diminished his own fame while adding to that of others. With clear-sighted loyalty the *Fraser* critic developed his theory:

His graceful *Christabel* is a flagrant instance of this. It remained twenty years unpublished, but not unknown; and when its example had reared the ballad epic, or poetical novel, to its highest and most magnificent state, it made its appearance, in the eyes of the reading public an imitation of its own progeny. We do not remember any worse luck in all literary history.[31]

Maginn's keen understanding of Coleridge's poetry is shown in his burlesque of its images. The lines of this verse critique are so finely delineative that they foreshadow modern appreciation of the poet, revealing both the directness of Coleridge's phrases and the prodigious indirectness of his thought. Coleridge is represented as making a speech from the balcony of Sir John Soane's house, which was famous for its works of art. An imaginary audience has come together for the purpose of "electing" the fictitious editor Oliver Yorke. Since the parody is one of the best that has been written on Coleridge, the opening lines are given here:

Ladies and Gentlemen,—It was a strange
Sensation that came o'er me, when at first,
From the broad sunshine, I stepped in and saw
The narrowing line of daylight that came running
In after me shut by the door outside.
All then around was dusky twilight dim,
Made out of shadows most fantastical,
The unsubstantial progeny of light
Shining on singularities of art.
There stood around, all in a circ'lar row,
Seven colossal statues—each a king
Upon a rich Corinthian capital.
Sceptres were in their hands, and on their heads
Were golden crowns, in shape similar

S. T. Coleridge

AUTHOR OF "CHRISTABEL."

To that small bonnet which adorned of yore
My dexter temple, when, the live-long day,
I delv'd the classics in that blue-coat school,
Fast by fam'd Newgate's jail.[32]

Probably the most brilliant instance of prognostic criticism in the magazine is the swift recognition of the then unknown boy, Robert Browning.[33] The critique of *Paracelsus* boldly begins, "All hail, Robert Browning! Verily, thou art a man after our own heart!" The reviewer admits that doubtless the versification of *Paracelsus* is imperfect, but insists: "There is, however, in its roughness, that which keeps the sense above the sound, and makes us attend to it whether we will or not." After a careful analysis of the poem he asserts defiantly that *Paracelsus* surpassed Henry Taylor's *Philip van Artevelde*. This remark was at the time heretical, *Artevelde* having been ten years in the making and been granted the place of highest honor among the more profound poems of the decade. Yet the *Fraser* writer without apology terms the famous *Artevelde* "a mechanic piece of work," in contrast to the poem of the unknown Robert Browning, which he finds "organic." In speaking of the latter, he writes:

> We see the thoughts growing up, and acquiring body and stature. . . . Defects there are in the work; but these belong to it because it is a moving, breathing thing. *Artevelde* is almost faultless; but only because it is made-up—a pattern article—to shew not life in itself, but skill in its maker.

One poem is termed original; the other, a derivative of German systems of transcendentalism and Lake School poetry.

Fraser's championing of *Paracelsus* must have been especially warming to the cockles of young Browning's heart because it was one of the few unreservedly enthusiastic and thoughtful reviews of his work during his early years of writing. John Forster's critique of *Paracelsus,* which came out in the *New Monthly* of the same issue as the *Fraser* article, was favorable but more conventional and cautious. As for the notices of *Pauline,* which had appeared three years earlier, their scorn would seem to have had no other purpose than to gratify a sense of the ludicrous. The Fraserians particularly had made merry over *Pauline,* declaring the young author as mad as Cassandra "without any of the power to prophesy like her, or to construct a connected sentence like any body else."[34] Their rapid change of front at the publication of *Paracelsus* was, therefore, the more honest and commendable.

The same hearty informality is found in *Fraser's* scholarly espousal of its own contributor Carlyle. From the first it had put trust in his genius, welcoming him to its pages as an esteemed correspondent when Teufeldröckh's wisdom was far from popular, and making cordial reference to his work so that the public might become aware that here was a man among men. Not that *Fraser's* was more slow to recognize Carlyle's absurdities than those of lesser writers, or to sharpen its wits upon them; but it insisted none the less on his transcendence. When *The French Revolution* was finally published, the magazine hailed it with flattering and fraternal parody:[35]

> The French Revolution? Well! By Thomas Carlyle? Better! Ay; better than the French Revolution by Itself—or the History its own Author! Why, this Book is itself, in a certain sense, a Revolution—and the Author its only Hero.

Today the truth of this statement has long been recognized, and we do not need the critic's detailed analysis of the book to be convinced that Carlyle is indeed the hero of his Revolution. In like fashion, a little further on in the same article the force of the following wording is equally evident:

> The most careless reader of Mr. Carlyle's writings can have scarcely failed to perceive, that what there is of the poetic in the system of transcendentalism has passed into his spirit and writings.

Carlyle was for the critic no stodgy interpreter of German thought.

> The whole cycle of occurrences [the essay goes on] passes before his mental vision, therefore, as a panorama—a stage-play show—an apocalypse. He is, as it were, in the spirit of the Lord's day, and instructed by a ministering angel to look upon the passing scenes with a prophet's eye; not in relation to time, and time-interests, and opinion, but in correlation to eternity.

Instances of heartfelt praise such as that of Browning, Carlyle, Wordsworth, and Coleridge are rare in the magazine. A passage, for example, on Thomas Hood stands out fully as much for its unwonted friendliness as for its deft discrimination.

> *A propos* of punning [Maginn and possibly Thackeray write]; Charles Lamb and Tom Hood had not only a genius for it, but for

something else. Hence their puns are always subsidiary, not principal. By means of a pun, they sometimes detect delicate analogies of thought; nay, sometimes the thought precedes and suggests the pun. Hence there is a mutual action and reaction between the sincerest thinking and the merriest word-catching, and from this contrast much of the reader's pleasure arises.[36]

That they even thus occasionally checked their rage is one of the saving graces of the Fraserians, for their strength lay in slashing criticism. They not only ruthlessly stigmatized many of their contemporaries as lacking in creative imagination and at best parasitic; they analyzed indebtedness to the past with a clarity which often proved wholesomely instructive. If the reviewers could not stimulate authors to work of first merit, they at least pricked the bubble of national complacency, making it no longer possible to consider inferior writing as either great or in any way distinctive.

Even in regard to the two chief sources of imitation, Scott's novels and Byron's poems, *Fraser's* by no means shared the blind adulation of its day. To Scott it was always loyal and affectionate, but it occasionally admitted, in spite of its admiration, that his novels were too hasty, too protracted, too monotonous, and too numerous. Byron the critics openly denounced. They acknowledged his genius, but they felt that he had been overrated and that it was high time his faults were frankly stated. Such a disciplinary attitude toward the famous rebel was conspicuous at a time when the Byron cult was at its height. In England and on the Continent he was ranked with the greatest poets of all time, and the almost fanatic element in the devotion to him was considered normal and justified by his preëminence.

Since Maginn's antagonism may have had no small share in bringing about the sudden reversal of opinion in regard to Byron which began about 1830, it may be well to give some idea of its sharpness. As early as the second number of the magazine, in two separate articles he subjects Byron to scrutiny. In both we find admission of the poet's strength but an unflattering insistence upon his weakness. After quoting Byron's theory in support of Pope, that imagination is relatively unimportant and that an "Irish peasant, with a little whisky in his head, will imagine and invent more than would furnish forth a whole poem," *Fraser's* editor turns sharply upon Byron himself:

> Say you so truly, my Lord Byron? Then quoth we, Most potent, grave, and worthy Signior, why did you not give evidence of what can be so easily attained? For the truth is, that every one of your characters is grounded on the same principle of construction; Harolds, Hugos, Laras, Corsairs, Alps, Manfreds, Juans, and Tassos; Mazeppas, Prisoners of Chillon, Dantes, Selims, and Giaours.[37]

The other article[38] contains the suggestion, afterward several times reiterated in the magazine with less tact, that Byron's success "was not altogether owing to his rare endowments. . . . Circumstances which, in the fate of other men, would have been deemed calamities . . . were contributary to the diffusion of his fame, and attractive to the merits of his genius." After this unflattering account of Byron's popularity, Maginn turns to a consideration of his poetry. "We do think, in the midst of all our admiration of his power and his originality, that there has been an artificial exaggeration of his genius, as well as that meretricious augmentation of his fame, which, it will be thought by many, we have treated too roughly." Even in a genial essay on the art of laughing, Maginn and presumably Lockhart find space for a passing fillip at the popular poet:

> Democritus, the laughing philosopher, was one of the wisest of men. He lived laughing for a hundred years, and then died unlamenting. What misanthrope or Megrim of modern times can do as much? Are all the grim affectations of *Childe Harold* worth an ounce of laughter? Not a grain! They do good to no one. They are "entertainment" neither "for man nor beast." They make us lean, stupid, ungrateful.[39]

Later, by 1836, remonstrance against the public's idol had so caught fire that we find one of the other Fraserians, probably Heraud, writing with animation,

> A noisy, declamatory style is a sure passport to success with the uninstructed; the recondite graces of the true minstrel escape their gross vision. Hence Byron bore away the palm from Wordsworth and Shelley, though his best thoughts were stolen from them; and his own chief merit lay in an ostentatious diction, which, again, was as pretty a piece of mosaic as one could wish to meet with in a summer's day.[40]

Against Byron's imitators the Fraserians' attacks were leveled with exuberant scorn. There is seriousness beneath their exaggeration when they affirm, "Perhaps Byron was the greatest foe to poetry and its reign in England that ever was." Through him the country has become "peopled with misanthropes, 'looking unutterable things'—in foolscap." The exasperated reviewers complain that the sacred "well-head of poesy" has been made "the head-quarters of pirates, murderers, and moping gentlemen, peeping through masks 'wonderous melancholy.' "[41]

One of the followers of Byron whom Maginn pursues in slashing style through the early volumes was Robert Montgomery, the author of *The Omnipresence of the Deity and of Satan.* The youthful homilist had been widely hailed by his fellow poets as a coming Milton, and the beauty and profundity of his work was already considered established. Maginn, however, had no more patience with those who augmented his fame than with the overpuffed boy himself. He complains of the great "bawling and braying of Arcadian nightingales, in praise of the sacred poetry of young Montgomery"—the "wonderful! and astonishing boy!" of "surpassing sanctity!" He ruthlessly turns to prose a passage from *Satan,* and asks if the reader can find in it "anything but false or imperfect imagery, monstrous tropes, ignorant use of language, empty rodomontade and prodigious bombast." "He has come forward," Maginn informs us, "a half-educated young man, and one, consequently, but crudely constructed in his mind, to speak to us, and instruct us in the high duties enjoined us by our religion."[42] And thereafter the magazine refers jocularly to Satan Montgomery, and on one occasion tells him squarely:

As to your *Satan,* 'tis the devil; and of your *Omnipresence of the Deity,* this is my

Opinion

God's omnipresence I believed,
And yet was wondrously deceived.
For, not long since, I chanced to look
In young Montgom'ry's maudlin book;
And can with confidence declare,
That not a trace of God is *there.*[43]

The same mirthful contempt is shown in the clever parody, "Holy Bob's Bardism," the last two stanzas of which reveal the bombast of *Satan's* philosophy.

And when the King of Terrors breathes his last,
  Infinity shall creep into her shell;
Cause and Effect shall from their thrones be cast,

And end their strife with suicidal yell.
And from their ashes, burnt with pomp of kings,
Mid incense floating to the vanished skies,
Nonentity, on circumambient wings,
An everlasting Phœnix, shall arise.[44]

Much of the poetry of the day *Fraser's* does not attempt to treat seriously, but passes by with a sly fillip as not meriting greater attention. The comment on *Autumnal Leaves* by Henrietta —— is merely, "Among these the sweet authoress disports like the kitten of Wordsworth."[45] *The Last Evening of Catanie* by one Spicer, is summed up with a mimicking eye for its hard-won rhymes, "So Catanie was shining radiant-ly in its own Sici-ly, under sunset as a cano-py."[46] Crofton Croker turns from a spurious Irish poem with the comment, "This is what we call in Ireland 'very fine oysters,' " and he questions if any true O'Donoghue was responsible for "all this taffeta talk."[47] Even in cases where more space is afforded, the treatment is often in the same bantering tone. The review of Lady Wortley's *London at Night,* for instance, is jocose from start to finish. Maginn begins with the suspiciously mild statement that he is predisposed in favor of the poetess as a member of a fine old Tory family, and then adds abruptly:

But what the deuce does Lady Emmeline Stuart Wortley know of *London at Night? London at Night!* Heaven help Lady Emmeline! The first notion she appears to entertain of that phenomenon is, that the "dread city is silent, since all strife is there forborne." . . . To what part of the town she can have got, we, who know it by heart from the Elephant and Castle to the Angel at Islington . . . have not a notion.

Later the critic, with a side nod toward the underworld, comments, "As for the crispy-wreathed smiles to be found on the Thames,–why such things there are; but not exactly as Lady Emmeline imagines. What say the poets of 'Wapping Old Stairs?' " Still in excellent humor, he ends, "By Cupid, the little God of Love, Lady Emmeline might as well have called her poem Nineveh at Noon as *London at Night.*[48]

Fully as flippant is Maginn's tone for *The Undying One* by the Honorable Mrs. Norton, whose personal beauty and social charm gave in her own lifetime an adventitious brilliance to her poetry and everything else connected with her. Maginn, who rarely grants any woman a fair field and no favor, points out that the conventional character of the Wandering Jew has in her poem been metamorphosed. "He is all for love. In Mrs. Norton's hands, indeed, it would be strange if anybody could be otherwise." The Wandering Jew of the original story, the critic amplifies, "is only a cobbler—but those who invented the tale lived before the time when *Childe Harold,* and the rest of that brotherhood, had framed the ideal of heroes. He is no cobbler here, but a Byronian of the purest pattern."[49]

Toward veteran offenders the magazine is more stern. Maginn's treatment, for instance, of the long established and popular poetess Felicia Hemans is relentless. He is disgusted by her sentimentalized imitation of Byron and the Lake School. More especially he is repelled by what would today be termed her sadism. "She is," he writes, " 'in sooth,' 'forsooth,' and 'by my troth' (to use the words of Mrs. Butler, the American bug-destroyer), a broth of a bardess. Not only does she adorn whatever she lays her hands upon, but the subject seems to grow and expand beneath that magic touch, till the gentle bloom of the opening line is forgotten in the fruitful beauties of the last." After which ominous opening follows one of the magazine's scathing parodies. "The Foot of the Mount" is too long to quote in full, but its opening and closing stanzas show that Maginn wished his readers to be aware of the cheapness of Mrs. Hemans's sensational appeal and of the ease with which lines like hers could be turned out. To sharpen his thrust he places the poem in quotation marks, solemnly stating it was written by her and dating it 1786.

"Rapt in the roaring of harmonious floods,
Inhaling wisdom from the vernal woods,
Watching the playful, ever-varying grace
Of Nature's ancient but renewing face,
I feel the flowing stream of sacred song
Hurry my soul with pleasing force along.
But, ah! while yearning for a brighter sphere,
The common cries of earth salute my ear:
'Tis a child's voice!—that cruel Widow Jenkin
Wallops away at her sweet babe like winking!

• • •

"Farewell, farewell, the healthful hills and vales
Of thy most ancient territory, Wales!
Farewell the mountain and the lonely glen,

Far from the humbug and the hum of men!
Farewell the murm'ring rill, the rushing stream,
And all that constitutes a poet's dream—
All, all farewell! my soul is overpowered,
Life's bowl of daily buttermilk is soured,
Because, alas! that cruel Widow Jenkin
Wallops away at her sweet babe like winking!"[50]

The parodies of Robert Montgomery and Mrs. Hemans just quoted are more than skillful raillery; they give in compact illustration two of the magazine's most strict critical tenets: dislike of the high and hollow word and distrust of the sentimentalized, altered detail. Fully as caustic is *Fraser's* objection to saccharine writing. The following lampoon of Thomas Moore is a deft and succinct statement of its disapproval.

Syllabub syllables sweetly strung,
Seeming so sillily smooth to be sung,
Sicken some singular sinners, they say,
Scorning soft sentiment's silvery sway![51]

Maginn's warfare against Thomas Moore was an old one, dating back to *Blackwood's* days, when he had soundly rated the popular poet for what he considered misrepresentation of the Irish spirit and an absurd indulgence in mellifluous effects. That Maginn felt Moore could on occasion sink to unrelieved vapidity is indicated in a burlesque which in his most provoking fashion he puts into his victim's own mouth at a mock recital of coronation odes in honor of William IV. The amorous poem begins with the stanzas:

Dear Kitty, from slumber awaking,
  Those beautiful eyelids unclose;
The morn, dearest Kitty, is breaking—
  Can it break, love, and thou in repose?
Nay, frown not; a strange gratulation,
  Dear Kate, for thy lover to-day!
Bring smiles to the gay coronation,
  And join we the gallant array.

Where's Cupid? Go seek him, dear Kitty,
  And we'll have *our* pageant too;
Bring hither the urchin so pretty,
  All beaming with roseate hue:

Your arms for a throne shall embrace him,
And there shall our homage be paid;
A wreath of sweet kisses shall grace him,
Which we, dearest Kitty, will braid.[52]

Maginn's contempt for "soft sentiment's silvery sway," especially as Moore applied it to bacchanalian poetry, is shown in the rousing burlesque, "A Grand Crowning," in which Sir Morgan O'Doherty sets forth his own views of a suitable coronation:

I suppose all was right that Will Howley has done,
That for oiling the King he has warrant divine;
But when I am the primate, as sure as a gun,
I shall hallow my King with a flagon of wine.
And let nobody think that a drop of the drink
On head or on bosom away I shall fling;
No! be-mitred I'll stand, with a pot in my hand,
And cry, "Here, you lubbers! three cheers for the King!"[53]

Objection to the labored sentiment of the conventional coronation ode is further developed in some six or eight lampoons of other prominent poets. The best of these is a long, empty, and resounding poem put into the mouth of Robert Southey, who was not only at the time poet laureate, but a distinguished Tory, a prime friend of the Fraserians, and one of the original contributors to the magazine. The vacuous stanzas begin with an invocation to Westminster Abbey:

Cathedral old! wherein Religion shrines
Bards, sages, heroes, in marmoreal pomp,
What rite preparest thou,
What solemn rite this day?
Can aught exalt the glory, hovering here
O'er shrines of memory to the good and great,
The learned, the eloquent?
Sublime in dust they sleep![54]

Light as this criticism is, it has a cunning which strikes at the individual faults of those whom it admonishes. We find good advice, for instance, in Oliver Yorke's reply to the Rev. Thomas Dale, Professor of English Literature at Cambridge, whose pompous sentimentality both annoyed and amused the Fraserians.

My reverend friend! why dole out rhyme,
And drawl, and sigh, and blubber the sublime?

Sweet bard of bliss to sympathetic souls,
Didst ever try a rasher on the coals,
And wash it down with Barclay's bottled ale?
Do this and flourish, cultivated Dale![55]

All told, there is in *Fraser's* fund of gay comment no little sage advice to various sentimental faddists of the day. By pointed neglect of the boudoir poets, for instance, the staff achieves a note of mirthful discipline. It nowhere condescends to review seriously the popular Thomas Haynes Bayly, in whose artificial verse the so-called boudoir school reached its highest point of inanity. Thus in the *Lays of the Twaddle School* "Butterfly Bayly" is set, with a fine eye for incongruity, against the serious-minded "Satan Montgomery." A few speeches from this instructive "Pastoral Duett" reveal its disciplinary trend:

R. M. Satan saintly I sang, with meek Maw-worm mummery,
And old Beelzebub's bard was young Robert Montgomery.
T. H. B. Satins and silks I sang gravely and gaily,
And the bard of the *boudoir* was Thomas Haynes Bayly.
R. M. To my genius and muse nothing earthly could come awry,
Such a devil of a poet was Robert Montgomery.
T. H. B. With my butterflies, buttercups, butter flow'rs daily,
I buttered my bread—heigh, for Thomas Haynes Bayly.[56]

Probably the most minutely detailed parody in *Fraser's* is that of the long Byronic highland poem entitled *Unimore* published in *Blackwood's Magazine*. It was by none other than the editor himself, John Wilson, long since identified with his famous nom de guerre Christopher North. *Unimore* covered some fifty pages of *Blackwood's,* and had been received with vast admiration. Maginn's burlesque has a line-for-line dexterity which permitted the two poems to be daringly printed on opposite pages of *Fraser's* for the more ready enjoyment of the reader. The swelling descriptions of *Unimore* are thus abruptly dashed against the solid realism of the burlesque, "Barney Moore, a Vision of Covent Garden and St. Giles's." In no other place except perhaps in his thieves'-cant verses does Maginn give such unrestricted play to his own fine sense for unsmoothed detail. He starts in the manner of Gay, though not on the scale; but in his zest over an Irish fight and night life in the slums of London, he outstrips in realism the less avid master. The tough, factual surface of the poem has a naturalistic quality which makes it seem out of place in its own decade.

THE AUTHOR OF "LALLA ROOKH"

Published by James Fraser 215 Regent Street

Muggy, and moist, and slob, and slippery!
It wants an hour of sunrise; and the rain
Pours down in torrents, and in splashing showers
Fills every gutter, steaming with perfume,
Rank and indelicate confoundedly.

. . .

Alive is every potatory tap,
Wine-vaults or cellar, with their pewter pots
And ruin azure-hued; while blandly smiles,
Hearing the coppers on the counter roll,
The trim-capped bar-maid; and the coves, enwreathed
With ladies of the night, brimful of gin,
Stagger along in lushy state, and fill
The air with odours, from the shortened pipe
Puffed frequently; and many a wandering bird,
'Neath the piazzas whispers words of love
To knight or squire, in blissful drunkenness.[57]

To give anything like a complete account of the magazine's parodies would be impossible. Burlesque was one of the Fraserians' chief methods of criticism, as well as its most searching. It often afforded a compact revelation of merits and demerits, summarizing the critic's estimate with a sharpness not easily gained by other means. Thus even Wordsworth, whom the staff venerated more than any other poet living at the time, was subjected again and again to the cutting scrutiny of parody, while the magazine's enemies were regulaarly rolled to the guillotine in the tumbrils of verse lampoon.

Although the brunt of its burlesques fell upon pocts, *Fraser's* expended no little of its slashing wit upon novelists whom it deemed in need of correction. In the earlier discussion of its attack on the publishers Colburn and Bentley we had occasion to mention the magazine's objection to overproduction as the cause of the hastily composed and imitative writing of the day. Among the worst forms of this "book making," in *Fraser's* opinion, was the three-volume novel on the pattern of Sir Walter Scott; and hot was the pursuit, as we have seen, of Bulwer Lytton and Horace Smith, the two chief historical novelists who elaborated upon *Waverley's* already ample pattern. Even the host of smaller folk who crowded around Bulwer did not escape castigation. When, for instance, *Sea-Kings in England* appeared, Maginn exclaims:

Now, Edwin Atherstone, this is not the way to write historical novels. It is not enough to take a historical name or two, to twaddle over old stories familiar as household words, to introduce eating friars and fighting warriors, and a double tier of gentlemen, one high born and haughty, the other of low degree, (a nobleman, however, in the end, "no waiter but a Knight Templar,") valiant as Amadis of Gaul, and as handsome as Adonis; another double set of ladies to match, one dark, the other fair . . . all these fine persons, mixed and kneaded up with some antiquarian lore about dresses, and dinners, and weapons, and buildings . . . to say nothing of the Babyonish [sic] dialect put here into the mouths of Kentwina, Elf, &c., a dialect neither resembling the English of the present day, nor the Saxon of any day; will not, we say, invest the dry bones of antiquity with life. All may be correct, (in the *Sea-Kings in England* scarcely any thing is so,) but it is stone dead.[58]

Insistence on reality, the need of writing from experience, we have found characteristic of *Fraser's* reviews. In speaking, for instance, of Dalton's *Chartley,* Maginn comments:

Novels of this kind appear to us more improbable than regular ghost stories. Admit the theory that ghosts do revisit the glimpses of the moon, and a tale may be framed, of perfect probability; but what theory can you frame which will make all the actions of every-day men and women completely at variance with what we see in the world?

After various instances of improbability, Maginn concludes:

Sir Walter Scott, we are sorry to say, has invested some of the strange characters of his novels—Meg Merrilies, for instance—with unbounded ubiquity, and authority over all persons within their reach; but even his example is not sufficient to make it a canon in the novel-writing world, that the outcasts of society should be the most important and authoritative agents in the most delicate transactions of life.[59]

When the three-volume novel which Scott had brought into such unprecedented popularity was directed not toward historical subjects but toward criminal life of its own day, and often fashionable life as well, the magazine's ire was doubly aroused. It found these interminable and hastily built stories full of incongruities and improbabilities. So discouraged does *Fraser's* become over the fiction of the day that on one occasion Maginn and Thackeray sadly exclaim, "It is a good novel in which the amount of readable pages arises to a dozen." Even the work of its own contributor Theodore Hook, high Tory editor of the high Tory *Bull,* it finds no better than the rest. Several times in the magazine Hook himself is delightfully sketched in his burly rôle of metropolitan jester, but at no point do the wily critics of the Round Table show enthusiasm for his novels. In regard to one of them, *The Parson's Daughter,* the same castigating critics write:

> The story is nothing. There is a rather uninteresting hero, in love with a wholly uninteresting heroine; and after the usual evolutions, which are now-a-days as well known as the kickings and caperings of Harlequin and Columbine, they are married, as a matter of course, with some hundreds of thousands a-year, and peerages, &c. &c. to match. Hook always finishes like a fairy tale—either a clap of thunder or a general ballet.

After this truthful summary of their friend's work, the two dictators of Round Table criticism admonish him whom they style "the wittiest man in this country, or in any other we happen to know of," to sit down seriously and write what he knows!

> A novel from Hook [they explain], with Sheridan, for instance, as a hero . . . and with Hook's own compotators and companions for characters, and the adventures of Hook himself and friends for incidents, would be a work that would bring us back to the days of *Tom Jones* and *Humphry Clinker.* There should be [they specify with a scornful thrust at the "silver-fork" punctilios of fashionable novels] no fine persons in the book: people might eat with any kind of forks they could get—Russell Square and Bloomsbury should be intimately known—porter, cheese, port wine, and other contraband things, duly distributed among the hungry and thirsty multitude—in plain words . . . Hook should write what Hook has seen. Let him consign to meaner hands the task of doing butler's duty, and setting tables in order.[60]

In the same fashion Thomas Hood, whose puns have already been noticed as meeting Maginn's approval, fared not at all well at the hands of the magazine. Although he was held in great affection by the Fraserians, several of whom, including Maginn, contributed to his famous *Comic Annual,* when he came to write his three-volume novels he was hotly attacked by his friends. *Tylney Hall,* the reviewers, who were again Maginn and presumably Thackeray pronounce "twaddling" and "perfectly worthy of being dedicated to the Duke of Devonshire." When Hood "makes his hero shoot his brother in a fine summer's evening," they comment: "Why, the sketches of Cockney sporting in the picture-shop windows supply nothing so absurd as this." As for Indiana Thurot, they find her "one of the most nonsensical imitations of Meg Merrilies ever attempted."[61]

We have earlier spoken at some length of *Fraser's* condemnation of Bulwer Lytton. An example of the treatment to which he was early subjected is a letter addressed to him in the magazine by Maginn, who has become particularly exuberant over what he considers Bulwer's "bitter bad writing" in the *New Monthly:*

Nobody knows better than yourself, that, to make a fashionable novel, all that is required is a tolerable acquaintance with footmen and butlers, which can be easily picked up by any ingenious gentleman who will feed these functionaries with a few pots of ale, reinforced by an occasional half-crown. This will supply the high life, the silver fork, the no-twice for soup, the ignorance of Bloomsbury Square, the antipathy to cheese and port, and all the other nice *minutiæ* which mark the exquisite knowledge of fashionable existence in these excellent volumes. . . . A preparation of five weeks would enable an operative to do *High Life,* or *Pelham,* or *Almacks,* or any of the other jobs of work of the same kind, in the most approved pattern; and, by judicious advertising, they might be all got off hand in the season. For works in the sentimental line, pilfer the indecency from Faublas, the reflections from Rochefoucauld, and the incidents from Harriet Wilson—and you have a *Falkland,* &c. &c. off hand. The meanness of the characters introduced you may draw from yourself.[62]

Even more insulting as well as more keen in its remonstrance against pattern work, is the following ironic comparison:

We stand up for Anne of Swansea. Perish the other novelists, from Cervantes to Sir Walter, but the lady's fame we must uphold. She, at least, is worthy of being compared with the author of *Pelham.* Her plots are more original, her delineation of character as striking, her reflections as profound, her historical lore as *recherché.* We shall probably some day compare, with all requisite minuteness, the *chefs d'œuvre* of these great authors, and, by a most searching and impartial analysis, endeavour to award with unbiassed judgment the relative rank, in romantic lore, of the fair author of *Secrets in every Mansion* and the "highly intellectual as well as handsome" gentleman to whom the town is obliged for *Pelham.*[63]

For the women writers, indeed, even the better of them, who crowd the ranks of "fashionable novelists," the magazine has a far from flattering condescension. It maintains: "Nothing can compensate in the novel for want of experience. And therefore is it, that the attempt of ladies generally to write of 'many-figured life,' is so utterly cold, incapable, and ridiculous." It feels that the feminine followers of Lister and Bulwer have little notion of what they are trying to do. " 'What *are* you after, Listonia Bulweria Wigetta?' exclaims the reader to the mocking-bird she-novelist." As the magazine itself states, most of the popular writers of the day were women, and the majority of them were not untouched by the fad of the fashionable novel, from the time-honored Jane Porter and Maria Edgeworth, to Lady Blessington, Mrs. Jameson, Mrs. Gore, Lady Morgan. The Fraserians, therefore, had their hands full in turning out lightly ironical and admonitory criticism. For the work of Mary Mitford they had persistent and unqualified praise, while they admitted that Mrs. Shelley was fully capable of doing what she set out to do. Maria Edgeworth they usually admired, though Maginn had the strange notion that her jovial Irish heroes were turned out by her father.[64] But writers like Mrs. Gore they found a sad problem, and, as for Lady Morgan, they were incapable of speaking of her seriously. The absurd exaggeration and empty pretense of her work were well lampooned in a burlesque "The Castle of Munderlungs," and the poor lady herself was so insultingly derided[65] that she wrote a letter of remonstrance to the critics. Concerning the moral of Mrs. Gore's *Pin-Money,* "that all heiresses, no matter whom they may marry, ought to be entirely dependent on their husbands for all their pecuniary supplies," the magazine remarks, "We think the females of the land will not swallow such blarney." After mentioning the "disjointed scenes, and drawling, insipid characters," and "language driven into convolutions," the reviewer sums up:

> Mrs. Gore can write very well, if she pleases to throw off a factitious levity of tone and sentiment, and verbiage—stick to her pure and native Saxon—leave off attempting to startle by the clap-trap effect of her composition—trust to her own genuine feeling—describe life in its real nature, and not in its artificial scenes—discard the notion that she can spin out with effect a novel into three volumes, even though it be to indulge the cupidity of her booksellers.[66]

Lady Blessington, whose house on Gore Street was one of the literary centers of the day, and who was a friend of many of the Fraserians, among them Maginn and Thackeray, fared scarcely better. Their condescension toward women writers is nowhere more entertainingly shown than in their light preamble on the "she-novel," adapted from Byron's theme, "The earth has nothing like a she-epistle." Such a novel, the reviewers, who were again probably Thackeray and Maginn, find "positively delicious," in "moments of mental lassitude":

> A genuine she-novel . . . trickles over and suffuses your passive brain, without occasioning you the least annoyance. You have no trouble, past, present, or to come. You will never be stimulated to recall, by an effort of Will, that of which you possess an habitual knowledge, to enable you to understand and appreciate some pregnant allusion, some fine, yet deep jest, as of a Shakespeare or a Rabelais. You never have to pause an instant about meaning or no-meaning; be it which it may, it lies upon the surface. You will never be moved from a state of the most Mohammedan or stoical indifference by any one of the multitudinous "battles, murders, and sudden deaths," or other things vehemently prayed against in our liturgy. . . . An inexorable Jupiter presides over all these compositions. A mighty event, the immolation of some tender virgin or virgins upon the rude altar of Hymen, is to be accomplished, and this by the especial instrumentality of some particular agent or agents;—it *must* be done. . . . A character who ventures to become troublesome has his brains extracted in a time which, under other circumstances, and in another place, would be considered awfully quick. And, sooth to say, moreover, a conspiracy and combination of numbers is of no avail; the authoress never for a moment loses her self-possession or natural powers, and is consequently enabled to toss them off by the dozen. For example, in the volumes before us, the Countess of Blessington has disposed summarily of about nine-tenths of the people she has introduced to the reader's notice.[67]

From this merry piece of butchery, as from those cited earlier, it becomes evident that *Fraser's* remonstrance against the novelists of its day was, like its remonstrance against the poets, cruel but apart from personal insults fairly sound. Certain of the more talented authors, such as Bulwer Lytton, were presented only in shadow; yet after all they shared in the faults of their time, and *Fraser's,* as we have seen, was seldom in a mood to illuminate merits.

Yet it will not do to leave this brilliant group of critics with a higher reputation than they deserve. They were without question unsystematic and desultory, and they were not free from mistakes. They seem to have had, for instance, a genuine admiration for the long-winded religious poetry of their colleague, John Abraham Heraud, and they were unduly partial to the versatile sentimentality of L.E.L., possibly because three of them at least were in love with the lovely Letitia. On one occasion also a recalcitrant member broke from the ranks to applaud Mrs. Hemans, whom it was the settled policy of the magazine to denounce. Nor was the range of their sympathy wide. Although they gave a good deal of space to foreign literature, they reviewed only what appealed to them. Thus Prout wrote enthusiastically about Victor Hugo, but neither he nor anyone else had a word to say about Balzac, who published some of his greatest works before 1834, including *Eugénie Grandet.* In the same fashion they erratically neglected Dickens in their own country, recognizing his power, but not taking him seriously as a craftsman, and carping against his romantic prevarication and his misuse of English idiom. Furthermore, for all their interest in the Elizabethan stage, they paid no attention to the spirited revival by Beddoes, either having neglected to read his plays or having failed to appreciate their imaginative appeal, despite their flaws. Hartley Coleridge, also writing at the time, they joined with the rest of the world in overlooking, unaware of the delicacy of his images. Nor did they pay any greater attention to Tennyson, though his stillborn volumes appeared at the beginning of the thirties. Two notes only are given to the author who was to hold the British world of poetry rapt for half a century. One refers to "Timbuctoo,"[68] and the other mentions with approval the "powerful" ballad of "The Sisters."[69] This neglect is the stranger since Thackeray was a personal friend and admirer of Tennyson. Had the chief *Fraser* critics, Maginn, Thackeray, and Prout, been as fine at all moments as they were at some, they would have seized upon this early work, pointing out to the unobservant public the richness of its promise. With shortcomings of this sort it is presumable that in an age of greater literary talent and range of production the limitations of the reviewers would have been even more apparent. In this connection it is to be noticed that Heraud, at least on one occasion, spoke slightingly of Keats.

If the Fraserians had been less brutal objectors, it is possible they would have found time and ability for more scholarly refinements and enthusiasms. One should not overlook the importance of their attack on corrupt reviewing and on shoddy "book-making"—on the system, to use their own words, of "puff and plunder." Nor should one overlook their salutary remonstrance against what they termed "the present universality of pseudo-fame, the present tame content in mellifluous sentences, and maudlin pathos." Yet persistent rage is limiting, and it is to be regretted that the magazine's critics so infrequently sought balm for their harassed spirits.

PART THREE

REVOLT IN POLITICS

CHAPTER V

FOUR LEADERS

The whole political stand of *Fraser's* under its first powerful editor bears sharply on the views of both Carlyle and Disraeli, the two mightiest foes of Liberalism that England produced. Maginn's insistence that the Tory party should adopt a reform program was destined to be forgotten, yet at the moment of its utterance it was not without wide influence. The popularity of the magazine and its large sale show that he created an audience who found his policies acceptable. Some of his articles against the Economic Radicals and the Whigs and in favor of reconstructing the Tory party were reprinted as separate pamphlets and sold, the magazine stated, by the tens of thousands, one of them reaching a sixth edition and another an eighth. It can thus scarcely be doubted that his attempt to create a conservative group devoted to practical reform helped to prepare a sympathetic audience for the later arguments of Disraeli.

At the time Maginn was penning his vehement protests against Peel and other party leaders, he could scarcely have realized, however, that a subsequent champion of his cause was to arise in the person of the excited young dandy who was dashing debonairly into literature and politics. No sooner had the Whigs won the Reform Bill of 1832 than, under the vigorous slogans of Daniel O'Connell, Disraeli ran as a candidate of the Radical party. "I start on the high Radical interest and take down strong recommendatory epistles from O'Connell, Hume, Burdett, and *hoc genus*. Toryism is worn out, and I cannot condescend to be a Whig."[1]

The early efforts of Disraeli to join the Radical party have never been considered as anything except a boy's very troublesome blunder, which not only postponed his political leadership but made his first steps toward that leadership unintelligible to friend and foe and apparently on occasion none too intelligible to himself. His hope of persuading the Radicals to pull on the discarded slippers of the Tories and run to the protection of the established institutions of the country was as fantastic a daydream as ever befogged the brain of ambitious young idealist, for Dizzy had not yet learned to build air castles of the solid and remunerative structure later so much to England's liking.

Three times the erratic boy ran as a Radical for Member of Parliament, and during each of the three unsuccessful campaigns he loudly espoused the party's principles. It was not until the autumn of 1834 that he considered the Tories had revived sufficiently for him to trust himself to their ranks. Nor was his decision even then forthright and definite; as late as November he wrote requesting Durham to recommend him as a Radical candidate. In the course of the letter he exclaimed:

> What do you think of the Tories! at a moment when decision and energy would be pearls and diamonds to them, they have formed a provisional Government! "The voice of one crying in the wilderness, prepare ye the way of the–Lords." Such is Wellington's solitary cry; a Baptist worthy of such a Messiah as–Peel.[2]

With a record of this sort, however well Disraeli might have known in his own heart that all along he loved a Tory, he found it difficult to persuade others of his devotion to the party. He had from the first written with scorching vindictiveness against the Whig dominion of the House of Commons, pointing out that it was founded on cruel self-seeking and laying bare its machinations to subvert the power of the king and the lords and to make itself permanent. But at the time, the ties which existed between Whigs and Radicals were extremely close. Since the Reform Bill the old-time Radicals with philanthropic aims had become almost extinct and the Economic Radicals had gained control of the party policies. With these Disraeli had so little in common that he might well have been considerably bothered to explain to his own satisfaction how he could tolerate *laissez-faire* doctrines in a Radical when he found them abhorrent in a Whig. To be a Tory and to advocate reform, according to Maginn's plan, was too much of an innovation to be very well understood in the thirties; but to be a Radical and to expect Tory support was beyond the pale of the possible. Although in Disraeli's early speeches traces can be found, as Monypenny points out,[3] of his later doctrine of democratic Toryism, they are bemired in the schemes of opposing parties and the overstatements of personal ambition.

Under the circumstances it is not surprising that there was more difference than resemblance between the political writings of Maginn and those of Disraeli. Yet on the points which they held in common the parallelism is arresting, and of all the more interest because it is not necessary to infer indebtedness on the part of the younger man. Maginn, it is true, had the advantage of priority in statement; but Disraeli had too ebullient originality to require or tolerate guidance. Furthermore, in spite of their dissimilarity of temperament and literary style, the two men were not unlike in habit of mind. Both were formidable antagonists, at once good-natured and merciless, conquering by variety as well as by keenness of rebuttal, and by indomitable volubility. What is more important, both were uninfluenced by those around them, of extraordinary restlessness, and extraordinary intuition and mental impetus. It was not, therefore, strange that their reactions should have frequently been similar.

The resemblance was at first confined to attacks on the Whigs. Later, as Disraeli developed the Tory issues of his policy, we find his thought taking a direction increasingly like that of Maginn, until in his open antagonism to Peel in 1843 and 1844 and his repudiation of Tory lack of aggression, he had covered many of the points which had so long been urged by the older writer. In other words, Maginn's doctrine was a pronouncement by which the government's conscience could be tested in successive public crises; Disraeli's, on the other hand, was an evolvement, a movement from within the Tory party which came to self-realization through political exigencies.

One doctrine did not attain its full utterance until seven years after the other had ceased to be proclaimed. And yet Maginn's writing is not an uninteresting commentary on Disraeli's more conspicuous achievement. When a man is in political life, his contemporaries and posterity are not infrequently troubled to know which of his acts spring from conviction and which from opportunism, and it becomes far from easy to discriminate between patriotism and party politics. The most severe criticism that has been made of Disraeli is that of lack of integrity in his opinions. He is often considered to have been too busy blazing his own path to glory to have cared whose reputation he slashed or what facts his o'erleaping logic disregarded. It has been questioned if he was sincere in his championship of the masses, or adopted the policy only as a melodramatic expedient; if he really thought Whig procedure monstrous, or if it merely suited his party purposes to claim it so; if principle led him to denounce Peel, or simply personal ambition. On these points the parallelism to Maginn's work is not without bearing. For six years in the pages of *Fraser's Magazine* the earlier prophet had warned the country that between Whig appropriations and Tory neglect the duties of a government to guard the interests of its people were left unfulfilled. He was not under Disraeli's disadvantage of having to wait until he had gained personal prestige before he could condemn the Tory leaders; nor did the success of his attack, as in the case of the great parliamentarian, depend upon his individual advancement. He could say what he wanted to, when he wanted to; his defiance of the Tories could be simultaneous with that of the Whigs and the Radicals. In consequence, he was free from all suspicion of timeserving. Political preference is not gained by wholesale animadversion.

Behind the journalistic outbursts of Maginn and his more politically-bent supporters were the philosophic meditations of the great protagonists against Liberalism, Coleridge and Carlyle. It is strange thus to juxtapose these names, separated as the two men were by differences of nature and habits of thought: by Coleridge's failure to clarify and complete his work; by Carlyle's neglect properly to recognize Coleridge as predecessor and fellow laborer, and by his strictures against "profitless" nebulosity. It is stranger still to find these men associated in *Fraser's,* whose turgid flow offered so unfit an element for their thought. Yet they were equally powerful in the magazine.

We have already mentioned Coleridge's protest against Liberalism as it was expressed through Heraud and other members of the staff familiar with *Aids to Reflection* and *Church and State,* and influenced by the misty theology of his Thursday talks. *Fraser's* devoted unconscionable space to valorous support of the established religion as the bulwark of England's social and political institutions. The argument that the legal church of the land was threatened and its prestige diminished by materialistic economists and Nonconformists sprang in part from Coleridge. Religion as an outgrowth of an *a priori* moral law must be safeguarded and authorized by the laws of the land, and must, of its own nature, in return safeguard those laws and the happiness of the people who lived under them. Even though Coleridge did not himself contribute to the monthly, his hatred of Liberalism as a menace to the well-being of the country[4] was in great measure responsible for *Fraser's* mingling of metaphysical speculation with discussion of church and state affairs. Certainly the singular admission of politics to the high walks of philosophy lends self-righteousness to the magazine's stand.

Carlyle's contribution to *Fraser's* warfare on Liberalism was made in his own right. A year before the founding of the monthly, the great symbolist, brooding in the fastnesses of Craigenputtock, had sounded forth in *Signs of the Time* his alarm against materialism. He bade England notice that the distance between rich and poor had increased, that machinery was strengthening its control of politics and was influencing education to ignore individual talent, that the nation, fed on the philosophy of Bentham, was worshiping the material; and that religion had become a matter of expediency and utility. When he came to publish in *Fraser's,* he continued this protest against utilitarian doctrines, their failure to provide for the spiritual or the idealistic side of man, their attempt to subvert religion by atheism and to conquer the planet by machinery while nine-tenths of the population fought against famine. The whole question of his remonstrance has been so pointedly discussed by Professor Neff in his *Carlyle and Mill* and in his more recent *Carlyle*[5] that treatment here is needless. Professor Neff throws new light upon Carlyle's relation to the Saint-Simonians, who from a different angle were carrying on in France much the same heroic rebellion against materialistic philosophy. He points out that the closeness with which the Scotch idealist studied their work shows how seriously he was taking to heart the ills of his own nation. In the third book of *Sartor Resartus,* especially, Carlyle analyzed the inadequacy of Benthamite Radicalism either to relieve the poor or to guide the rich. In his eyes, the Reform Bill had left the problem of reform still to be solved; *laissez-faire* had encouraged brigandage in the name of peace; helots opposed dandies on the scales of social depravity.

Maginn's remonstrance, unlike that of Carlyle, was a purely topical study of politics in their daily bearing upon state, church, and people. Among those who gave it attention was Carlyle himself. The philosopher was aware that England was sick; *Fraser's* provided him with statistics in regard to her symptoms. It is surprising in looking over his writing to find how many times he mentions the belligerent Nol Yorke and how frequently he was conscious of that despot's prejudices. Although the irascible contributor heaped abuse upon the magazine in his *Note Books,* terming it a "scavenger-cart of a magazine" and a "chaotic, fermenting, dung-hill heap of compost," he felt that beneath its scurrility it had more substance than the weighty organ of the political economists, the *Westminster Review.* The latter he described in a letter to Emerson as made of sand, in contrast to *Fraser's,* which he pronounced of the firmer consistency of mud, and therefore, in a literal and flattering sense, a "mud magazine." Certainly there is no escaping the conclusion that he devoted a good deal of time to thinking about *Fraser's* denunciations of evils, and in his own work for the monthly he was at pains to word his remonstrance against the age to indicate common cause with Nol Yorke. When in *Chartism* he gave for the first time a detailed diagnosis of the economic condition of English workers, he showed close sympathy with earlier *Fraser* material. No more than Disraeli was he indebted to Maginn. He knew his own mind before *Fraser's* came into existence and he reiterated his stand especially in *Characteristics* and *Sartor Resartus;* but the magazine provided him with the raw material for creative thinking, factual matrix for his images, evidence for his theories. Indeed, Maginn's political diatribes recurrently suggest Carlyle's later work. From the publication of *Chartism* in 1839, the great Victorian's grievances were to cascade over the course previously cut by the far-sighted editor. Until these mighty remonstrances of Carlyle, Maginn's articles against utilitarian policies were unparalleled in audacity.

From 1830 to 1835 was the period of Maginn's greatest volubility. *Fraser's,* as we have already stated, was to be throughout its history fearless in its attitude toward public movements; but in these early years speech was urgent upon it. Maginn was as sure as Carlyle him-

Yours faithfully,
T. Carlyle

self was to be by the middle of the century that the country was riding headlong to perdition. He was as fully convinced as Ruskin was to be in the sixties that England needed more practical economic reform and less *a priori* economic theory. He anticipated Matthew Arnold in denouncing the appalling lack of social and political enlightenment and questioned with him the efficacy of the remedial measures adopted by the Society for the Diffusion of Knowledge. In serious articles and squibs he lashed at the promulgators of Useful Knowledge, denouncing their tracts and scoring their National Schools for teaching utilitarian doctrines, and for teaching little else.[6] In short, *Fraser's* rebellion was a forerunner of the various phases of the great Victorians' protest against Liberalism. So insistent was its hatred of *laissez-faire* principles and of the political and social application of those principles that it became the habit of contributors writing on almost any subject to insert attacks on the ubiquitous foe. The monthly with its rash variety of style and ostentatious variety of interests was in reality a continuous polemic.

This attack was the more exceptional because it was contemporaneous with the events which it analyzed and it lacked the advantage of even short perspective. Maginn's opposition to *laissez-faire* nostrums was made at the very moment when they were reaching the height of their power. The passage of the Reform Bill in 1832 marked a triumph for the doctrines of Bentham, Ricardo, and Malthus, which was to establish for years their dominance over British home and foreign policies. Most of the Radical party made the principles of political economy the basis of their program, thereby gaining the name of Economic Radicals; the Whigs often lent the theories enthusiastic support, and even the Tories under Peel were inclined to concede many of them. Only the old-fashioned members of each party held aloof, and these were too few and too scattered to make their opposition effective.

Benthamite philosophy, it will be remembered, aimed at the political equality of classes and individuals. No class, according to its tenets, should be discriminated against by law; all individuals should have the right to self-expression in the government. This theory, Maginn vociferously pointed out, the Whigs by skillful manipulation used to build up what he felt threatened to be a powerful oligarchy. He bade his readers reflect that the Whigs assisted to the utmost in diminishing the prestige and privilege of the time-honored aristocracy. The rotten boroughs, which gave the nobility undue power in the House of Commons, they abolished through the Reform Bill and redistributed the seats among the manufacturing and mining towns. This much change in England's electoral system Maginn scornfully asserted they held necessary, but any further change, based upon that other half of the doctrine by which the Economic Radicals hoped to extend privileges to the lower classes, they repudiated.

In the same fashion, Maginn showed that the Whigs upheld only those tenets of Ricardian political economy which were to their own advantage. According to Ricardo's theory, or more accurately group of theories, all government protections and restrictions of industry were to be swept away; the law was neither to help nor to hinder but was to allow unregulated struggle between one industry and another, between home manufacture and foreign manufacture, between producer and consumer, between employer and employee. Under political manipulation this doctrine of *laissez-faire,* or nonintervention, Maginn indignantly reiterated, became a powerful instrument of class discrimination. The industrial aristocracy, he explained, used it in arguing that no new laws should be passed to protect labor, but had no thought of repealing the laws by which labor was at the time already oppressed. When in the course of the struggle the poorer class became destitute, the Whig capitalists, he showed, were willing to look upon that destitution as normal and necessary, and to cite Malthus's famous theory that the population of a country constantly tended to outstrip subsistence and to bring about a shortage of food and employment. Poverty, they were ready to agree, was the result of fecundity and its cure was to be found in its own hardships, which would not only decrease the number of people but eliminate those who were least fit. Any policy to strip the poor of government protection or to prevent government intervention in their behalf was, therefore, Maginn informed his readers, supported not only by Economic Radicals who had sponsored it but by capitalists who were ready to profit from it.

It was against this doctrine of *laissez-faire* that the artillery of the magazine was especially leveled. Maginn took it upon himself to show that all legislative changes should not be controlled by the followers of political economy, who, he said, were experimenting with life and liberty in the interest of abstract theories; nor by capitalists, who in advocating those theories were advancing themselves at the cost of suffering to others. He now and then even went so far as to imply that the Whigs, by repudiating the more humane aspects of the doctrines which were not to their advantage, were exploiting not only the masses of the people but the political economists themselves; and at least on one occasion he suggested that Bentham was doubtless innocent of evil intent and not responsible for the havoc which the misuse of his ideas was producing.

Nor did the Conservatives escape the fire of Maginn's rebuke. Staunch Tory as he himself was, he maintained that his party was weakly acquiescing in the exploitation of the masses and was thus turning coward and betraying its own cause. In a period of swift industrial change, political reconstruction was a necessary corollary to material development. Drastic reforms were needed; yet the Tories were allowing the formulation of laws to pass into the hands of others. They should themselves, he pointed out, have adopted an aggressive policy. They should have seen that the electoral system of the House of Commons was reconstructed, that labor was protected from capital, that the courts and prisons were purged; in short that the practical reforms on which the well-being of the country depended were carried through. In other words, the Tories should have been loyal to their tradition of conserving the institutions of the land by making the changes necessary to bring those institutions into harmony with the altered conditions of the time. Instead, Maginn complained, they let the opportunity of leadership pass from them, and permitted themselves to be placed in a subordinate position where they were forced to concede changes which were of immediate benefit only to the Whig capitalists.

In its sharp condemnation of Conservative chiefs *Fraser's* was alone among the Tory periodicals. *Blackwood's* objected now and then to the party's tactics; but it was milder, more dignified, and more sympathetic. Neither Wilson nor Blackwood was by nature unduly analytical. The *Quarterly* was the authorized mouthpiece of the party, through which, in the writings of John Wilson Croker, official pronouncements were made. *Fraser's* itself more than once regrets the tendency of the Tory press to countenance Tory inactivity. "It has been too much the custom of late years," we find stated in the preface for January, 1833, "for works of the same *avowed* principles as ours, to truckle to the enemy, to surrender point after point of their political creed, and, by an unmanly spirit of compromise, to throw themselves at the feet of their antagonists. Whatever errors REGINA may have committed, *she,* at least, has avoided this meanness." How little Maginn had in common with the reactionary Tories under the Duke of Wellington or with those who, like Peel, leaned toward Whig Liberalism—or, indeed, with the Whigs themselves, or with the Radicals, is shown in his pugnacious assertion:

> Are we Saints—are we Revolutionists—are we Whigs—are we Infidels? We are neither; but plain, downright, uncompromising disciples of that political system which would uphold the religion, the honour, and the institutions of our father-land. From our commencement, we have never flinched from that cause in which our armour was first buckled on. . . . Neither the hollow pretensions of Whiggery, the violence of Radicalism, nor the disgraceful pusillanimity and desertion by the Tories of their own principles, have been able to drive us from the position we at first took up, and on which we now stand. Faithful to our cause—like Abdiel,
>
> "Among the faithless only faithful found."

Yet in spite of this boldness of speech, at first thought one is tempted to doubt Maginn's sincerity. In his latter days, certainly, he was a drunkard, and at best a ne'er-do-well scholar and hack for the daily press. His political writing for *Fraser's* has a swashbuckling quality which repels. At its worst it smacks of the tavern and the drunken braggart, and is incredibly coarse in personalities. Furthermore, Maginn had a fashion of opposing a reform of the Whigs which was possible by suggesting a more sweeping reform which was impossible. For example, he was against removing the tax on bread, but wanted tariff on everything; he was against the ten-pound restriction but wanted universal suffrage. This espousal of reform might have been sincere, but as Tory freebooting it was open to suspicion. Certainly there was no doubt as to Maginn's being a freebooter. He was avowedly an ardent Tory who was avowedly opposing Whig reforms by recommending that his own party adopt a reform base. The question is whether he believed in his proposed reforms or merely set them up as obstacles to the opponents. Or did he vacillate between the two attitudes, at one time bending to honest support, at another to casuistry?

To arrive at an answer is of course impossible. Maginn was a practiced satirist and the line between satire and sophistry is never easy to draw. More especially he was an Irishman with an Irishman's enthusiasm as the solid base of his character. But in any event it will be noticed that his Hibernian zeal for Tory reform in no way affected the vehemence of his attack on *laissez-faire* philosophy. Maginn might or might not at all moments have been sincere in his proposals as to what reforms the Tories should undertake, but he was beyond dispute at all moments convinced as to what reforms they should never countenance. Rarely has a party been so stigmatized from within as was the Tory when it lent its support to measures based on the political economy of the day. The violence of Maginn's attack on Conservative leaders becomes, by a paradox, the best proof of his hatred of Liberalism.

Maginn also showed his deep-seated antagonism by not confining his remonstrances to *Fraser's*. In 1827, only three years after his arrival from Ireland, Gillies in describing his friend's conversation spoke of "his disposition to make sarcastic remarks on leading characters of the day, sparing neither Tory nor Whig."[7] The same irritable attack on prominent men, without respect to their political parties, is seen in Maginn's *Whitehall, or the Days of George IV*. This satirical novel is so uncontrolled in venomous hilarity that it becomes tedious; but nothing reveals more clearly the flamboyant sincerity of its hot-headed author. The grotesque savagery of the tale leaves not a shadow of doubt that Maginn was aware of the bitter injustices and miseries of his day; nor is it to be doubted that he traced these injustices and miseries to the cupidity of the nation's leaders and to what he considered their purblind faith in the doctrines of *laissez-faire* philosophy.

In estimating Maginn's sincerity it should be remembered that his numerous articles supporting the Church show a devotion not to be interpreted as sophistry. From the first, defense of established religion was the core of his political creed, since he felt that church and state were inseparably connected, and that neither could be threatened without involving the other. He was a sound Orangeman, as his father had been before him, and he brought from Ireland an emotional outlook on religious controversy. Early in life he had prepared himself for the Church, and although he never took orders, he retained his interest in theological questions and was a close student of the Bible. Those whom he deemed enemies of the Church, even if in high positions within its own employ, were therefore frequently exposed to as undignified derision as is to be found in the magazine.[8]

In short, the turbulence of Maginn's rebellion against Liberalism argues for the sincerity of his whole political program, unifying its various phases. It offers explanation for his reactionary policies on the one hand and his freebooting practices on the other. After *Fraser's* had been running for more than eight years, one of the staff in reviewing its struggle against "the evil spirit, LIBERALISM," writes that its "political career has been little else than one continuous effort, however feeble, to unmask the subtle deceits of that crafty foe, and to awaken the people of England to a just sense of the dangers attending its insidious manœuvres."[9]

CHAPTER VI

DENUNCIATION OF POLITICAL ECONOMISTS

Of *Fraser's* numerous articles and burlesques voicing its protest against the materialism of the political economists only the work of Carlyle has been republished in any permanent form, and in consequence one of the first and most daring phases of nineteenth-century revolt against Liberalism is almost entirely hidden in the files of the magazine. Yet Maginn's political stand is important and should be made available for study, the more so as he did not take it with his eyes shut. He was ignorant neither of the magnitude of his task nor of the rapidity with which it was raising enemies against himself. In combatting the economists[1] he was aware that he was challenging the whole political line-up of the kingdom, since politics and economics were interchangeable terms, and social and economic theories had become political practice. The leading men in politics, he explains, are not to be influenced "by investigation and proof."

Party notice, reputation, office, and seats in parliament, can only be gained, and the hostility of the press escaped, through belief in what is called political economy; and it naturally follows that public men are generally devout believers. . . . The matter to be thought of is not to discover and advocate truth, but to obey and echo the doctrines.[2]

In exasperation he cries against this tyranny:

Abstract doctrines of democracy and political economy are endowed with the sole control of public affairs, to the exclusion of all interference on the part of national conviction and desire. Institutions and laws—property and subsistence—trade, currency, and finance—religion and morals—are placed under rules as arbitrary as those of arithmetic and geometry. Here the great end of a free government is reversed: a nation is to have one that it may be strictly restrained from governing itself; from intermeddling with the management of its affairs; from making the least use of freedom—beyond electing rulers to keep it in all the essentials of slavery.[3]

Maginn's hatred of political economy is briefly formulated: "We despise those political economists who swallow the jargon of Malthus or Macculloch with good faith, and pure ignorance of the consequences of the doctrines they preach . . . we hate, as the enemies of the human race, all those who promulgate such doctrines with a knowledge of what must be their results."[4] In the second number he summarizes his reasons for this hatred in words that foreshadow Carlyle and Matthew Arnold:

The political economists teach their disciples to think of nothing but the *"wealth"* of nations; to look at the balance-sheet of the imports and exports, and to judge from that of the prosperity of a country; to examine the quantity of goods produced, without bestowing a thought upon the producer; and to think that the strength of a nation consists not in well-affected hearts and valiant hands, but in the figures which tell that so much cotton was imported, so much iron exported, so many power-looms erected, so many small farms devastated to be thrown into large ones. These ideas blot from the mind all exalting thoughts—all stirring sentiments. Wherever they prevail, patriotism is at an end. A shilling saved is sufficient reason for consigning our fellow-citizens to beggary. On the shores of the Baltic, labour is cheaper than on those of the Thames; let the labourer on the banks of the Thames, therefore, perish. A calculation of the expenses of the poor laws leads to the dreadful conclusion, that Nature's table is full, and that, in consequence, the new-born child of a pauper should be starved. This is the doctrine—almost the words—of Malthus. Every thing, in short, is by this school reduced to money—nothing else is worthy of consideration. Honour, bravery, religion, virtue, high spirit, proud feelings, are all matter of that frigid and detestable jesting which resembles what a morbid imagination might liken to a leering grin upon a skull.[5]

In this general denunciation of political economy Maginn declared an early war on the Malthusian theory of population.[6] The country, it will be remembered, was feeling the brunt of the industrial revolution, and distress was both widespread and acute.

The common people [Maginn writes] are steeped in wretchedness to the very lips. England may have been, as Napoleon averred, a nation of shopkeepers; now it is a land of beggars. Nearly 10 millions of poor rates are levied annually to support, at the rate of from two shillings to five shillings per week, the infirm, the unemployed, and the destitute. . . . The great mass of the people are unable, by their utmost exertions, to earn wages sufficient to render them more comfortable, or more than one or two degrees more respectable or independent, than the actual pauper.[7]

Yet in the face of these deplorable conditions, Maginn pointed out, the economists suggested no measures but emigration and the hard-headed and cold-hearted attempt to reduce the number of unemployed by abolishing even the scanty relief afforded by the poor laws.

> The grand fundamental principle with the "political economists" is, that the people are too numerous, and that it is an inherent vice or misfortune of the species to increase beyond the means of subsistence. Their plans, therefore, for the amelioration of the condition of the poor, always begin with some scheme for keeping down the numbers of the people; for preventing their increase; for limiting the growth of the population. The favourite notion with them is, that the poor-laws act as "a premium on population;" and that, consequently, the first and most imperative duty upon the legislature is to provide for their repeal.[8]

He angrily denounced as inhuman the proposals of the Martineaus, Chalmers, and other Malthusians to abolish all poorhouses, charity hospitals, outside aid of the poor, and to discourage private almsgiving. Even a popular treatment of the subject, such as Harriet Martineau's *Cousin Marshall,* called forth the censure, "a book written by a *woman* against the *poor*—a book written by a *young woman* against *marriage!*"

> The truth is [Maginn indignantly comments] that there is nothing here but a very old story. The feelings of these political economists towards the people, are just the same as those entertained three thousand years ago by Pharaoh towards the children of Israel. The cry is just the same: "Come now, let us deal *wisely* with the people, *lest they multiply upon us.*" And there are those among ourselves, who, if they dare, would gladly employ the same means with those adopted by Pharaoh.[9]

With common-sense bluntness Maginn asserted that the growth of population cannot be checked by adopting harsh methods of dealing with the poor. "The notion," he writes, "of starving people into a slow rate of increase is about the most absurd fancy that could possibly enter into a human brain."

> Speaking generally [he amplifies], a population always increases the more or less rapidly in proportion to the larger or smaller amount of poverty that exists amongst it. This fact thrusts itself upon our notice wherever we turn our view. The Irish cottager . . . is a well-known instance of it: he is poor enough, we suppose, for Miss M[artineau]

herself; indeed, except the English cottager is to be actually starved, we do not see how he can well be made poorer; and yet the Irish cottager's prolificness is too proverbial for us to dwell upon.[10]

Before England applies the economists' "preventive check" and sweeps away almshouses and infirmaries as "encouragements to the increase of population," Maginn suggests that it would be well for the nation to notice that Scotland, which has had no poor laws, has increased practically as rapidly as has England, and that Ireland, which also has had no poor laws, has increased far more rapidly—and both in spite of the fact that Scottish and Irish emigrants have settled in no inconsiderable numbers in England.

Maginn was ahead of his time in stoutly opposing the recommendation that no aid should be given the poor who had not yet been reduced to entering an almshouse. He considered that "a little timely help in illness or lack of employment often saved a family from becoming a permanent burden upon the public." In other words he advocated helping the poor man to help himself, and boosting him if possible into respectable citizenship again.[11]

The same common-sense humanity is shown in his leniency toward the mothers of illegitimate children and his denunciation of the repressive measures urged by the economists as both futile and heartless.

> The remedy here [he writes] is, that the mother of an illegitimate child shall support it solely; the father is to contribute nothing, and is only to be liable to her action for damages. A girl without a shilling is not likely to institute an action for damages in any case, and particularly against a man who can pay none; therefore in general he will be free from all liability.

With some heat Maginn continues:

> If both mother and father commit guilt, they ought to be equally punished; if both incur obligation, they ought to fulfil it alike. If the mother have a right to damages, her sole means of obtaining them should not be taken away. This unmanly and outrageous remedy offends as much against equity as wisdom.[12]

After showing that the "remedy will not diminish the force of passion or cause the promise of marriage or maintenance to be less relied on" and therefore will not lessen illegitimacy, Maginn points out that a woman of the lower classes can seldom support a child without resorting to prostitution, the very evil which the law is endeavoring to check.

In its detailed treatment of poverty and crime *Fraser's* was conspicuous among the magazines of the time. Periodicals of the thirties, with the exception of the *Westminster,* were not given to sociological study. Expression of the popular demand for reform was confined almost exclusively to the daily press, such as the *Leed's Mercury,* through which poured the turbulence of the followers of Cobbett, as well as the cooler pronouncements of men like Fielden. *Fraser's* alone among the magazines printed unsparing records of suffering and degradation. In addition to separate articles, several series of vehement protests against abuses ran through its numbers, setting forth the shocking cruelties perpetrated upon workers and the injustices accorded to criminals.

The sincerity of Maginn's interest is shown in *Fraser's* consistent support of the policies advocated by Michael Sadler, whose tireless efforts on behalf of the oppressed classes met elsewhere with scanty recognition. Sadler's humane studies of conditions in Ireland, of the fallacies of the Malthusian theory, and of the wretched state of the child operative in factories were given publicity in the magazine's columns. One of the most sympathetic tributes in *Fraser's* is Maginn's "Gallery" sketch of Sadler, September, 1835, written shortly after the death of the great reformer, the "poor man's friend."

Maginn's own interest in the laboring classes led him to acquaint himself at first hand with the dens of thieves and other law breakers in the back slums of both London and Paris.[13] His genius for chance acquaintance won for him admission as an equal to haunts where no amount of police protection could have procured him safe conduct. From these visits he formed the opinion that the majority of criminals were more sinned against than sinning, and that if conditions among the working classes were not remedied there could be no cessation of the constantly increasing wave of crime that was then sweeping the country. Crime, he states, is more the offspring of reduced circumstances than of sustained poverty.

For instance [he explains, in words which anticipate Carlyle], a Scotch highlander, accustomed to a scanty fare, is far from being demoralized in the ratio of his sustenance or his poverty. The *lord* of an

Irish cabin, who lives solely upon potatoes, sometimes with, and sometimes without salt, is not naturally a thief. It is only . . . when increased industry has to contend with decreasing remuneration . . . when the peasant considers himself oppressed, and the artisan robbed . . . that crime marches hand in hand with privation, and an increase of suffering produces an increase of guilt.[14]

Maginn adds that he has sufficient examples of this point to "fill the whole of this number of Regina, together with an appendix—twice the size of the *Quarterly Review,* advertisements included."[15] For instance, the rioting and burning in Kent during the administration of Wellington, he traces to poverty, affirming that it is useless for the political economists and the reactionists alike to seek elsewhere for the cause, or to think that the evil can be lessened by the unduly harsh punishments of hanging and transportation.[16] In the article, "Poverty, Crime, and Emigration," he answers various theorists, including the Bishop of London, who ascribed the rapid increase of crime "to the profanation of the Sabbath," and a Mr. Dunlop, who felt that it was the "effect of the malt and beer monopolies." With an angry exclamation Maginn restates his own position: "THE CAUSE! Need we conceal it? Need we shelter cant and oppression at the expense of justice? The source of crime, the fountainhead of pauperism and its consequences—is POVERTY!"[17]

With this point of view, it is not surprising that *Fraser's* directed some of its most heated protests against the debtors' prison and capital punishment. In exposing the injustice and stupidity of the debtors' laws the magazine pointed to their lack of logic, their expense to the nation, their pernicious effect on family life and on the individual, and boasted that it was the first to show that imprisonment for debt was against the constitution as well as the common sense of the country. The death penalty inflamed the Fraserians by its brutality and inexpediency.[18] They whole-heartedly supported Basil Montagu, a man who, they informed their readers, had worked for thirty years "quietly but effectively preparing the way for more humane laws." Thackeray, it will be remembered, in describing his own experience of going to see a man hanged, condemned executions as demoralizing and humiliating to the onlookers and explained that he was himself forced to avert his eyes.[19]

Perhaps the most interesting series in the magazine is that advocating the establishment of a court of appeals to examine the unjust verdicts given in the Old Bailey. Of the need of this court the writer of the series, who had evidently been associated for some years with Thomas Wontner, the Governor of Newgate, was amply convinced from his own observation. His articles, which later appeared in book form, rank among the documents of prison experience which are most outspoken in their exposure of the corruption and caprice of courts.[20] In turning over the pages of the Old Bailey session papers, he writes:

> The impression a perusal of these papers made on my mind, was as if all the business had been done by lottery; and my observation during twenty-two sessions . . . has tended to convince me, that a distribution of justice from that wheel of chance could not present a more incongruous and confused record of convictions and punishments. In no case (always excepting the capitals) can any person, however acute and experienced, form the slightest opinion of what the judgment of the court will be. Of this the London thieves are fully aware.[21]

He gives instances to show that the hardened criminal is no more likely to receive a heavy sentence than is one who has offended for the first time. Among the numerous unfair sentences which he cites is that of a lad under thirteen transported for life because he had stolen his companion's hat at a puppet show. The Old Bailey court sentences boys in the same proportion as men to transportation for fourteen years or life.[22] What makes the whole system, he reiterates, peculiarly oppressive is the impossibility of appeal from an unjust verdict. The secretary of state whose business it is to consider complaints is so guarded by subordinates, each requiring a fee, that redress is out of the question for the man who has not wealth or influence. A court of appeals, he sums up, is therefore an urgent necessity.[23]

A little later the same writer contributed papers on the hideous abuse of apprentices,[24] exposing the insanitary surroundings to which many of them were subjected, the degrading nature of their employment, their terrifically long hours, and their often cramped position. Even more violent were Maginn's attacks on the employment of children in factories. His articles[25] in support of Michael Sadler's factory reform bill,[26] then meeting its fiercest opposition in Parliament, set forth in unsparing detail the intolerable suffering of the little "white slaves."

No franker statement is to be found in Richard Oastler's well-known *Slavery in Yorkshire Letters.* Maginn writes that common terms of horror and indignation "are inadequate to the expression of the feelings excited by this dreadful picture. We must therefore leave the poor creatures to tell their own story in their own words."[27] Then follow some nine pages of fine print filled with grim citations from Sadler's report of children who had been tortured and maimed while being forced to labor daily on an average of from fourteen to sixteen hours, and in exceptional instances, nineteen.

Benjamin Gummersall is asked:
"Were you perfectly strong before you entered upon this labour?" "Yes."—"Can you now stand at all without crutches?" "Not without crutches or a stick, or something to lean against."—"Can you walk at all?" "No."—"Can you get up stairs?" "Perhaps I might creep up."—"Must it be upon your hands and knees?" "Yes, or backwards way."—"Do you get up stairs backwards way?" "Yes, every night."
Matthew Crabtree is directed to:
"State the condition of the children towards the latter part of the day, who have thus to keep up with the machinery." "It is as much as they can do when they are not very much fatigued to keep up with their work; and towards the close of the day, when they come to be more fatigued, they cannot keep up with it very well, and the consequence is that they are beaten to spur them on."—"What were you beaten with principally?" "A strap."—"Anything else?" "Yes, a stick sometimes; and there is a kind of roller which runs on the top of the machine called a billy, perhaps two or three yards in length, and perhaps an inch and a half, or more, in diameter; the circumference would be four or five inches; I cannot speak exactly."—"Were you beaten with that instrument?" "Yes."—"Have you yourself been beaten, and have you seen other children struck severely with that roller?" "I have been struck severely with it myself, so much so as to knock me down; and I have seen other children have their heads broken with it."
Jonathan Downe is asked:
". . . In addition to the beating, have you known any other methods of punishment resorted to for presumed offences?" ". . . There is a stool fixed up at one end of the room; the boy who offends is put to stand on this stool, sometimes on both legs, and sometimes on one of his legs, with the other up, and he has a lever to bear in his arms, thus [*here the witness exhibited the position, by elevating his arms above his head*]: and there he is to stand for ten minutes, or a quarter

of an hour, or half an hour, just according as the overlooker chooses; and provided he should lower his arms, and it is a great weight to bear for a quarter of an hour, I have seen the overlooker come this way, and say, 'Hold up;' and sometimes the boy will strive to hold it up, and not have strength to raise it; and the overlooker has a stick or strap, and cuts him till he does actually get it up; and the tears will run down his face, when he is there standing. I have seen it there frequently, and it is the regular practice."

In summing up this gruesome evidence, which is today too familiar to need further citation, Maginn indignantly exclaims:

It is *child-murder* which we are discussing,—and not, be it remembered, murder by strangulation, or poison, or drowning, or the knife, or any other mild and merciful infliction,—but *murder by slowly-protracted torments!* It is the dragging infants out of their beds hours before daylight; immuring them in impure atmosphere till a late hour at night, while their limbs bend into frightful distortion, their lungs become stuffed with poisonous dust, and their flesh is blackened with continual blows. It is the witnessing the death of four out of five before the age of twenty, under these torments; and the utter ruin, soul and body, of the survivors, from deformity, premature decrepitude, and destructive vices. It is this system which now awaits its verdict before a British public and a British parliament; and fearful will be the responsibility of that man who votes for its continuance, or would retard its condemnation.

When the best features of Sadler's bill were defeated Maginn was again fired to angry remonstrance. In regard to protection against machinery he writes:

No security whatever would be conceded by the mill-owners; nor would Lord Althorp, though earnestly entreated, demand any from them. And yet within the last three or four weeks, since the passing of the bill, we have seen in the public prints inquest after inquest, held in the manufacturing districts, on the remains of children who had been torn in pieces by the machinery of the factories. Doubtless, for every life absolutely lost we may calculate upon ten arms, or legs, or fingers, torn off. But what care the mill-owners, or what care the people at the Board of Trade, about the arms or the lives of a parcel of little children?[28]

In his violence Maginn did not overlook the wider political aspects of the situation. Regarding the relation of child workers to the problem of unemployment, he indignantly protests that surplus of labor is not caused, as the Malthusians would tell us, by God and nature,—but by the ungodly and unnatural proceedings of the mill-owners themselves. Their beasts are better used: no manufacturer would put his yearling colt into the shafts of his waggon, or task him with daily labour; and yet he crowds infants of six years old into his mill, confines them there, and keeps them on their feet for fifteen hours daily; while he turns their parents out of employment; and then complains of the poor-rates, and joins in the chorus of lamentation about our "surplus population."[29]

Maginn also realized that a second cause for the pitiful state of labor was England's neglect of Ireland. Of the condition of Ireland he has much to say. Like Carlyle and Matthew Arnold, he reminds his readers that her starving populace is not only a disgrace to England and an instance of her oppression but also a menace to her own laboring class.[30] There will be an apparent surplus of population, he writes emphatically, until measures are taken to relieve the suffering in the neighboring state and thus prevent the immigration of "large bodies of half-starved labourers from Ireland, who not only throw out of occupation an equal number of English labourers, but also reduce, by their competition, the wages of those who are still able to retain employment."[31] Since the Irishman has been accustomed to a pittance, he will lower the standards of living in England until the English laborer is reduced to his own level. With his eye on the object, Maginn writes:

> A potatoe excavator, two yards in length, with half a shirt and no shoes, who out of 9 *d.* a day could save 4 *d.* and yet live more sumptuously than his father, grandfather, or great-grandfather ever did, is landed free, and enters into competition with the free-born work-householder of Kent.[32]

The only way, Maginn concludes, to lessen this evil is to establish poor laws in Ireland by which the starving, assisted at home, may no longer flock to England to receive aid.

Important as it was to ameliorate the condition of the poor, Maginn realized that taxes levied upon the English landowners for this purpose were already disproportionately high. He therefore contended that the rates should be extended among businesses; that is, a business itself should be taxed according to its income and not merely according to the amount of land which it happened to occupy. On this point he writes:

Money employed in business ought certainly to have no exemption, though it might be more difficult to deal with than other money. Men of little capital might fairly claim exemption . . . but fairness renders it essential for the tax to reach men of great capital. A manufacturer has 50,000 *l.* afloat in his business, employs a great number of workmen . . . yet [because his plant covers only a small area] he contributes little more to the rates than the middling tradesman. Two shopkeepers live next door to each other, the one has 10,000 *l.* capital and saves some thousands yearly, while the other has 1000 *l.* and can scarcely live; yet both pay the same amount to the poor-rates. To remove crying injustice in these cases, it is necessary to tax capital. Though the exact amount of the latter could not be got, an approximation easily made would produce comparative equality. A tax of a quarter per cent on capitals exceeding 500 *l.* would be little felt; small capitalists would gain from it, in relief from poor-rates.[33]

Maginn especially regretted, and in this he was again far ahead of his time, that machinery was entirely free from taxation.

The steam-loom [he writes] and the steam-engine, although they supersede manual labour, and displace human hands, and turn the miserable mechanic, who is in derision still called a "free-born Englishman," into the streets or the workhouse, are subject to no domiciliary visits from the exciseman. These substitutes for manual labour pay no taxes. Even the export of coals is taxed, that they may work more profitably.[34]

More radical was his stand that stockholders, holders of the national funds, and all other money lenders ought not to be exempt from taxation. In making this proposal he realized that he was going against established opinion. Of stockholders, he writes: "Speak of extending to them the smallest part of the taxation which presses on the rest of his majesty's subjects, and you are declaimed against as though you advocated sacrilege."[35] Maginn feels that it "is the most vicious policy conceivable to give money lent at interest . . . advantages over other property." "If a tax of five per cent were imposed on the interest of stock, for the relief of the poor," the government would avoid the injustice of discriminating in favor of any special class. "We have thrown," he continues, "on agriculture and general trade all public burdens as far as possible, and then stripped them of profit by laws all favouring the owners of money."

In short, *Fraser's* contended that the whole labor problem with its allied question of the poor rates had been mishandled. By permitting constant increase of cheap labor through the employment of children and the immigration of half-starved Irishmen, the laws had favored the mill owners. Because the rates had not been reapportioned, land on the one hand had been overtaxed and inadequate provision on the other had been made for the great masses of the unemployed. "The trouble is not [Maginn states plainly in summing up the situation] that England is paying too much money for the support of her poor. The land owners may be paying too much for their own good and for the good of the consumer; but the country as a whole is paying comparatively little." The poor rate, he finds, had since its establishment constantly grown smaller in proportion to the national income; to grumble against it, therefore, was nothing more than shirking responsibility. Regarding the political economists' clamor for repressive measures, he writes:

> It requires a strong belief in the infatuation of these people, to prevent our charging them with downright effrontery. . . . To represent the poor as perpetually encroaching on the property of the rich, and as encroaching at so rapid a rate as to threaten the entire annihilation of all capital; and to state these things with their eyes open, and with the power of comparing and judging of things around them, is certainly one of the most astounding attempts that has ever been made, upon the credulity of the public. . . . Now what is the fact? . . . If there be any one thing clearer than another, it is this, that for many years past the rich have been growing richer, and the poor growing poorer; and both in a ratio quite inconsistent with the peace and happiness of the community.[36]

Maginn's contentions in regard to the labor problem were closely connected with his broader imperial policy.[37] Here, once again, he found himself at swords' points with the doctrines of political economy which were influencing men of all parties. In opposition to the leading statesmen of his day, he maintained that England should promote the interests of her colonies and bind them by ties of mutual protection ever more closely to herself. His exasperation at finding himself alone and unheeded in his desire for imperial conservation was as great as Disraeli's was at a later date.[38] The question, he feels, is remote whether any proper impression will be made on the minds of public men touching the immense and inexhaustible mine of wealth which the colonies of England form. . . . It is one of the calamities which rest on our unhappy country, that such men are on both sides [Whig and Tory] pledged to the prevailing policy.

"The present most intelligent and philosophical generation," he scoffs, "has discovered that colonies are huge and mischievous encumbrances; from this discovery it decides that government is bound by duty to vouchsafe them only injury and oppression." The economists' policy of placing imports from foreign countries and the colonies on an equal basis either by abolishing all duties or by raising those on colonial goods he considered a wanton neglect of the interests of the empire, and one which was in good part responsible for the widespread suffering and dissatisfaction.

In the name of common reason [he exclaims], what does the state of the empire call for? . . . Will trade flourish when American timber shall pay as much duty as Baltic, and want cease when Cape wine shall be exterminated by its foreign rivals?

If the kingdom, he adds, continues to "grind to powder its colonial, as well as native population, for the sake of ruinous competition with, and surrenders to, other countries—most richly will it deserve to suffer, as it assuredly will do, far more than the bitter evils by which it has been so long scourged."

It was also to Maginn only common sense that practical freedom of trade should be established between England and her colonies and that the closest economic interdependence should be maintained. The industry of the empire should, as a matter of course, be protected from competition from without and not sacrificed to the promotion of foreign interests and the payment of foreign workmen. The empire, he felt, was sufficiently large to be independent of outside support if it fostered colonial commerce and took as its main objective the furtherance of its own solidarity.

The means [he writes] which England possesses, beyond what any other country ever possessed, for acquiring wealth, and keeping her population in prosperity and abundance, are beyond calculation. Her immense colonies vary so much in the character of their productions, that each serves without clashing with the others. . . . Every thing they all produce is wanted by the population at home. As a field for the investment of surplus capital, the employment of redundant population, the sale of manufactures and whatever she has to dispose of, and the production of every thing she wants to buy—they may be enlarged to almost any extent.

In carrying out his imperial policy, Maginn would allow sufficient bounties to the colonies to restore and maintain their prosperity. Such liberality would, he believed, not only add to the national strength of England but go far to solve her labor problems.

The empire [he states] wants protection for capital and the means of investing it, profits, and employment at good wages for its labouring orders. . . . It is self-evident that, by the sacrifice of a few hundreds of thousands . . . the capital of the West India and other colonies might be preserved from farther waste—the colonies generally might be put in receipt of good profits—the means of investing capital in them might be much enlarged—the gigantic market they supply for our goods might be materially widened—an important impulse might be given to manufactures, &c.—and the market they furnish might be regularly extended with the growth of our population.

In accordance with his colonial policy Maginn was violently opposed to remission of duties except within the empire. Free trade with other countries stood to him as one of the projects of the political economists which were responsible for the widespread suffering among the laboring class. Indeed, in his eyes, the supreme cause of poverty, and of apparent surplusage of labor, was the reduction of wages under the tyranny of free trade.[39] As an example, he refers to goods manufactured in Lyons and other continental cities.

The poor creatures employed in those places are now working . . . at six-pence or seven-pence a day. Obviously, therefore, those goods cannot be rivalled, at equal prices, in our own markets, if our English weavers are to be paid three or four shillings a-day. The master manufacturers seeing this, immediately reduce the wages of their workmen. The workmen being paid by the piece, struggle to make up their loss by doing more work . . . and very soon the natural effect is felt in a glut of the commodity; a large number of the hands are thrown out of work, and a fresh outcry is raised about *surplus population*.[40]

The result of competition with Lyons, Maginn specifies, "has been to spread the most complete ruin, and the greatest possible amount of misery and wretchedness, over a population of more than half a million souls."[41] In answering articles in the *Westminster Review,* he cites reports made to the Silk Committee of the House of Commons, that in the spring of 1826 there were 167 manufacturers in Spitalfields, and in the spring of 1832 there were only 79. Those who continued in business remained because their capital was invested and they could not recover it. Maginn pointed out that the situation was even worse for the workmen than for the manufacturers, and cited instance after instance from the reports, to show that the majority of the former silk laborers had been thrown on their respective parishes, in one parish the number having jumped from 655 in 1821 to 7,378 in 1832. The workmen, he continued, quoting from one of the witnesses, "are now reduced to a state of destitution, hundreds of them without a change of clothes, and in many instances without any thing like a bed left in their cottage, sleeping on straw, covered with the clothes worn during the day, and huddled together for the sake of warmth." Yet these men, Maginn comments

> are wholly innocent of having had the least share in producing the sufferings which they endure; but are the mere helpless victims of a series of wanton experiments, made by men who consider the starvation of tens of thousands of their industrious countrymen a small matter, if it may but conduce to the success of a darling theory.

Nor does Maginn consider that a reduction of the price of silk for the consumer offers any real justification of free trade.

> Granted [he writes] our wealthy ladies may save, perhaps, five pounds each per annum in the prices of their silk habiliments; granted, that our farmers' daughters, and even our cooks and housemaids, may now clothe themselves in sarsnet and *gros de Naples,*—still we seek in vain to discover any real advantage in all this change.

Maginn does not neglect corollaries of the discussion, such as currency, but for the most part he focuses his scorn on the principle of free trade itself and on its advocates.

> The game [he writes] may be very profitable to Messrs. Todd and Morrison, very interesting to Dr. Bowring, and very amusing to Col. Thompson; but the poor silk-weavers may well say, "what is sport to you, gentlemen, is death to us." Messrs. Todd and Morrison, and Messrs. Leaf, may well drive a roaring trade, if silks can be afforded

at 3*s.* per yard, instead of 5*s.*, 6*s.*, or 7*s.*; and they may strenuously resist any attempt to stop this ruinous competition–ruinous to the manufacturer, but gainful to them;–but the workman who is obliged to work at a shilling a-day, because the Lyons weaver, to undersell him, is made to work at ten-pence, may very naturally grow tired of the whole system.

In pointing out the protracted evil resulting from free trade, Maginn asks:

What has been the result, after seven years' trial? Can the *Westminster Review* point us to a single branch of trade or manufacture which has been benefited by their nostrums? Can they point out any branch which has suffered under their infliction without great and serious injury?

As is to be expected from his opposition to free trade, Maginn could see no adequate reason for remitting the duties on corn. To repeal the corn law, he reiterated, would mean to sacrifice the agricultural interests of England, to ruin the farmers, to leave English land uncultivated while the people paid for the cultivation of that in foreign countries. For instance, in October, 1832, he writes:

If a *free* trade in corn with all the world should be allowed, then indeed will the competition destroy, not the colonial trade alone, but the entire agricultural property of the empire. How, may it be asked, is it possible for our highly taxed countrymen to compete against untaxed Russia, or for our clothed freemen to produce at the same rate as the almost naked serf?[42]

Maginn's colonial policy found further expression in his attitude toward West Indian slavery. He felt that the political economists, and the chief men of both Whigs and Tories who supported them, were in their promulgation of antislavery destroying the prosperity of one of the most valuable of English colonies.[43] His antagonism to the antislavery movement was not lessened by his belief that it was for the most part being carried on under false pretences. Its ostensible humanitarianism[44] was merely a bait to catch popular favor and the support of religious fanatics, who would trumpet the cause from one end of the kingdom to the other. The real object of the Whig mill owners was to draw public attention from their own brutality by expatiating upon that of the plantation owners. The wrongs of the black slaves in the

West Indies were thus made a screen for the wrongs of the white slaves in England.

> What impudence is it in us [Maginn writes] . . . to whine and cant over the oppression of West India slaves, and in the same breath to give up, without remorse, entire provinces of little children to a state of labour wholly destructive of health and morals.[45]

In condemning the cupidity, heartlessness, and the hypocrisy of those political economists who were smirched by the child slavery of the factories, Maginn was as unsparing as Carlyle was later in his *Nigger Question*. An instance of the kind of slur to which they were subjected in the magazine is the last stanza of a sensational poem describing the death from overwork and cruel treatment of a child operative in the factories:

> That night a chariot passed her,
> While on the ground she lay;
> The daughters of her master
> An evening visit pay;
> Their tender hearts were sighing
> As negro wrongs were told,
> While the white slave was dying
> Who gained their father's gold![46]

Maginn did not wish it thought that he favored the institution of slavery because he opposed emancipation propaganda. The question in the abstract, he said he was not concerned with. His sole contention was that the economists and their supporters by their policies of free trade and antislavery were striking at the prosperity of the colonies, weakening the ties which bound them to England, and in consequence operating to the detriment of the empire.

Promotion of the empire determined Maginn's position on foreign as well as on home affairs. Throughout the period under discussion his foreign policy did not change. In the first number of *Fraser's* he writes emphatically:

> Our business, then, in this our Magazine shall be to preach the necessity of peace, the absolute duty of non-interference in foreign politics, whether to assist distressed princes and disconsolate princesses on the one hand, or runaway patriots and craven constitutionalists on other. Let the nations of the continent arrange their internal affairs

as they please; provided they do not bear upon us, we need not intermeddle.[47]

Briskly he drove his point home:

There are people daily and hourly writing and speaking here about the eternal disgrace which England suffers, because Don Pedro's brother, and not Don Pedro's daughter, is sovereign of Portugal. . . . Others lament that Ferdinand the Seventh continues to play leap-frog with his attendants, to break various oaths . . . and to marry at least half as many wives as Henry the Eighth. Bad taste and bad conscience, perhaps; but

To Spain be all the woes of Spain,
While we, in Britain's happier reign,
Live undisturbed in peace.

He boasts that

by the mastery of the sea, won in many a glorious fight, from the days of Elizabeth and the Armada to those of Nelson and Trafalgar,—we have obtained that truest safeguard of national independence—the perfect certainty, on the part of our enemies, that any attempt to insult us is such an experiment as "drawing a tooth from an angry lion." . . . and as we need not go to war to prove that we know how to fight, we cannot conceive that there is any other necessity pressing upon us just at present.

To sum up: in the teeth of the political economists Maginn was determined to support and rectify the old foundations of English society and to rebuild them into an expanding empire. To this end, he taught that the landed interests of the country should be protected; England and her colonies should be self-supporting and independent of other nations for their supplies; a period of peace and freedom from foreign embroilments should be secured. The first duties of the government should be to restore prosperity to the laboring classes, to develop the colonies and right their grievances, to increase on the one hand the influence of the Church at home and on the other the fear of the Navy abroad. This summary of creed, practically every item of which was unpopular with the leading political factions of his day and antagonistic to the widespread doctrines and practice of political economy, shows the constructive basis of Maginn's attack on Liberalism.

CHAPTER VII

PROGRESSIVE TORYISM

Hatred of political economy under the name of Liberalism, we have shown, made Maginn, like Disraeli in the next decade, wish to reconstruct the Tory party. Each man realized that the industrial revolution had precipitated the need for legislative changes, yet that all parties were too much under the influence of political economy to be trusted with the government. Each man, in consequence, hurled himself against the Tories with a zeal born of the desire for reform.

CASTIGATION OF TORIES

From first to last, there was not a Conservative leader whom Maginn did not expose to vituperation and derision. The Tories under Peel he found were overconciliatory to the theories of the political economists; while those under the Duke of Wellington were reactionary and opposed to making reforms which should be coincident with England's industrial development.

Maginn lost no time in attacking both Wellington and Peel.[1] In his statement of "creed" in the opening number of the magazine he forebodingly remarks of Wellington's cabinet: "We shall . . . sedulously watch whether they attempt to do all the mischief which they desire." From that moment until their resignation in 1831 the relentless editor pursued them with a virulence astounding in an avowed Tory. He informed his readers that the Whig cabinet had displaced an administration, which "by its follies, fallacies, tergiversations, and utter incompetency, and we may add, its dishonesty, had rendered itself generally odious." With more specific insult he continues:

> They had succeeded a ministry whose maxims were Machiavelian [sic], whose policy was pernicious, and whose characters were worthless. They had come in to clear the lumber rooms of Downing-street of the accumulated filth of the Peels, Dawsons, Goulburns, Crokers, and Twisses; and in the serious task they had undertaken, we were willing to cheer them on, and bid them "God speed!"[2]

In regard to the Tory record in connection with the emancipation of the Catholics in 1829, Maginn had much to say. It is only fair, however, to state that his opposition to the Catholics was purely political. His attitude toward them personally was one of the greatest cordiality. If anything, he rather prided himself on the catholicity, in the narrow as well as the broad sense of the word, of his acquaintance; and one of the most active contributors to *Fraser's,* it will be remembered, was Francis Mahony, a priest and by training a Jesuit.

Maginn's dislike of the act of emancipation was the consequence of his belief that the Catholics as a political party would be antagonistic to the Established Church and therefore would be lined with those who were hostile to established institutions. The Church, as has been said, was to him the bulwark of English law and order, as well as of English monarchy. He was convinced that two churches, both with political aspirations, could not coexist in harmony. No rancor, he writes, "is of so deadly, immitigable a kind, as that which emanates from religious exacerbation."[3]

> The Roman Catholics will endeavour to insure their existence by every possible accession of political influence; and for a party so constituted the surest mode of accomplishing this, will be by spreading in every direction the tenets of their own faith. Religious converts are the most effective instruments for the designs of political leaders.[4]

Maginn, therefore, watched with apprehension every accretion of power of their leader, Daniel O'Connell. He was among the first to point out the tremendous strength which O'Connell finally gained when by shifting his party's support from the Economic Radicals to the Whigs he was able to decree who should form the government. That the prime minister of England should thus be determined by an Irish demagogue seemed to Maginn a menace. With equal alarm he noted that O'Connell managed to keep England and Ireland in constant fermentation.

On this latter point the editor had much to say. Ireland, Maginn felt, had been granted just enough power to tantalize her into wishing to gain more. She had much, he realized, to be discontented about and to strive for—so much, he insisted, that England would never be able to satisfy her except by granting her complete freedom. In his opinion,

AUTHOR OF "VIVIAN GREY."

therefore, unless England was prepared to repeal the Catholic Emancipation Bill, the sooner the separation of Ireland and England came, the better it would be for both countries. If the ministers, he writes, "think they can coerce Ireland, intimidate O'Connell, overawe the priests, restore tranquillity, and enforce a just obedience to the laws, with the assistance of the Protestants, they are mightily mistaken."[5] He then showed in detail the difficulties which England would have to overcome before she could satisfy Ireland, summarizing them in a paragraph which in the light of nineteenth and twentieth century developments is startling in its prophecy.

> No minced meat [he writes]—no bolus—no conserve of Whiggery—no juggle to delude—no snare to entrap, will have any good effect, or succeed in allaying the storm which the Wellington administration raised against themselves and the peace of the country. Military law and proscription cannot be enforced for ever. We may repel one wave, but another would come. We may crush O'Connell, but twenty O'Connells would start from the earth, armed against us, to avenge his fall. We may issue proclamations till we exhaust the Treasury, cover the walls with paper, and line the streets with soldiers, but all in vain. There is but one sovereign specific, and that we have named.

Maginn realized, moreover, Orangeman though he was, that England's procedure in the matter should not be governed merely by her own advantage. The question, he states squarely, "is not whether England would be weakened by her separation from Ireland; or whether she would lose a corn country and a cloth market . . . but whether, by leaving Ireland to her own internal government, the payment of her own debt, and her own system of commerce and manufactures, *her* [Ireland's] rank would not be elevated in the scale of nations, and the moral condition of her people improved."[6] That Ireland had not in the past received fair treatment, Maginn frankly admitted. The English laws had "for ages paralyzed their energies, overwhelmed them with pauperism, and placed them far beyond the landmarks of European civilization."[7] Under the Wellington administration, he writes, with a vehemence that anticipates Carlyle:

> The people of Ireland might emigrate, starve, or die—no matter, provided the price of the English funds could be maintained. Their silk trade is consequently destroyed; their linen manufactures are strug-

gling with annihilation; the Germans have obtained what is tantamount to a preference in our colonial markets [thus putting Ireland at disadvantage], and the kelp trade of Connaught is transferred to our devoted allies, the boors of Russia.

In short, the Tories have, in Maginn's opinion, done their utmost to help O'Connell ferment rebellion in Ireland.

If it had been the secret object of those who, for the last few years, have been entrusted with the government of this country, to make the people of England the dupes of Ireland, or encourage a sanguinary rebellion in the latter country, they could not have adopted measures more calculated to promote this object. The system which has been pursued, has been dictated either by imbecility or dishonesty—either by a disregard for the mutual interests of the two countries, or by an insidious desire to promote their separation.

In its open censure of the Tory government this comment is characteristic of Maginn's attack. Throughout the first five years of the magazine's existence Maginn followed Wellington and Peel and the more conspicuous members of the party with an almost venomous pertinacity. More than once he referred to the contention of 1829 as the period in which the country was "Peeled," and later he could not forget that the act which gave the deciding vote in English politics to Daniel O'Connell was immediately due to the Tory leader. All told, we find more acrid denunciation of Peel than of anyone else, not excluding Whig, Economic Radical, Dissenter, or Catholic. When, for instance, in June, 1833, Maginn thinks that a dissolution of Parliament is imminent, he writes with pointed warning:

But one thing we know, that the Tory party, or the Whig party, or any party, will be ruined by the contact of one man—of the man who has betrayed and deceived every body—of the man who at this moment is meditating some new stroke of political treachery—of the man whose whole career has been a career of duplicity and deceit—of the man whose only talent is cunning, and a knowledge of the paltry common-places that will sway a paltry assembly.

Who is he?

PEEL![8]

Almost as virulent as Maginn's attack on Peel was his relentless exposure of the Duke of Wellington. The Duke was condemned because he was opposed to reform, because he was himself despotic and his government unenlightened and corrupt. In pointing to his despotism Maginn writes: "His way is to force the inclination of men; to make them bend to his wishes,—either to urge them by the appliance of, as it were, brute force, to become the servants of government, or buy them heart and soul by the golden dispensation of ministerial patronage."[9] Maginn points out the arbitrary quality of the Duke's mandates, which recall the military discipline of a camp. His political supporters Maginn frequently refers to as his "household troops" who are bound by "the consciousness of weakness and fear." "Louis the Fourteenth," he continues, "entered his chamber of parliament with a whip. His Grace of Wellington, in language, and looks, and gait, insults men who are his equals in birth, rank, riches, influence, and amiable qualities of heart."[10] Elsewhere Maginn, in invective which Carlyle apparently was later to remember, denounces the Wellington block in the House of Commons as "men who are powerless, brainless, irregularly dined, wearing collars like Gurth the swine-herd, summoned to roost like his own bipeds by sound of horn, and otherwise loaded with the irons of some imperious feudal lord or borough proprietor!"[11] "Such men," he remarks, "should be relieved from the responsibility of enacting laws, the effects of which it is obvious they are incapable of perceiving."

From the first number of *Fraser's* Maginn denounced the Duke's reactionary policies, his indifference to obvious abuses and to the widespread suffering of the people.

> For two years [he writes, in a retrospective survey of the Duke's administration], the tables of both Houses of Parliament had literally groaned with the weight of the petitions of the people, complaining of distress. . . . They came from the agricultural labourer, reduced to rags and pauperism—from the fathers and brothers of those whom long suffering and despair had driven to crime and spoliation, to rioting, pillaging, and burning. They came from the starving artisan; from thousands of weavers, whose utmost exertions could not earn more than five shillings per week; from miners and spinners, whom the currency bill of Sir Robert Peel had reduced to live like slaves upon truck, and whose miserable pittance of wages, instead of being paid in the king's coin, or the current money of the realm, were paid in the rancid bacon and stale cheese of their employers. To these petitions . . . which spoke the sentiments of not less than twelve millions of the

population, it had pleased the Wellington ministry to turn a deaf ear, and treat with the utmost arrogance and disdain.[12]

Maginn's ire was especially aroused by Wellington's indifference to the growing demand for parliamentary reform.[13] In consequence *Fraser's* became a staunch supporter of the movement for reform which was to culminate in the defeat of the Tory government, in 1831, and in the passage under the Whigs of the great Reform Bill of 1832. Article after article, from the beginning of the magazine, urged the ousting of Wellington and redistribution of seats. In January, 1831, Maginn writes:

We are as firm as any of the most sturdy of our sect for Church and King, and therefore our opinions within the last two years, have come round decidedly in favour of Reform in Parliament, as the only means left of securing both from the assaults of discontent on the part of the populace, and the undermining of treachery on the part of the borough-mongers and their allies. The Parliament as at present constituted is not one on which any person, who wishes well to the institutions of the country, can rely. All that that body seeks is to perpetuate the power of those who mainly constitute it—to increase their influence—to load them with honours, and places, and pay, perfectly careless whether in so doing they sacrifice the interest of every other person in the state.[14]

At another moment he scathingly comments:

A more servile or contemptible body can never again assemble within the walls of St. Stephen's, but we have, nevertheless, to thank it for having gone to such a depth of degradation. It has convinced the most dull and careless that an alteration must take place; it has made the most intrepid defenders of the present system quail. What stronger argument for reform could be exhibited than that displayed in the person of Sir Robert Peel himself, standing up to resist it?[15]

ONSLAUGHT AGAINST WHIGS

When the Whigs under Grey were finally admitted to office in 1831, Maginn, Tory though he stoutly proclaimed himself, hailed their advent as the beginning of a better day. Even when a reform bill was framed which he felt would not justly represent landed interest, he still recommended that it be passed.

We may question . . . the sweeping nature of the change contemplated; but certainly we neither have good grounds for impeaching the sincerity or the patriotism of Earl Grey. Reform was indispensable —he came into office pledged to carry it—the people expected it—the Sovereign was favourable to it—and now we have the bill upon our table, and see it making its way in the Commons in the face of one of the most formidable oppositions ever formed against a cabinet measure.[16]

The article ends with the exhortation, "Under all circumstances . . . as some Reform is much better than no Reform, let the bill be passed."

Fraser's favorable attitude ended when Maginn became convinced that the Whigs had taken advantage of the widespread desire for reform to promote their own ends. No balance of powers, he realized, had been obtained; the tyranny of Tory dominion had merely been exchanged for the tyranny of Whig dominion, and the Whig dominion was even more dangerous since it was inimical to monarchy. Of the Reform Act itself he finally writes: The "real character of that artfully concocted scheme was nothing else, as we have already said, than a vast system of boroughmongering in disguise."[17] "The ten pound note rascality" threw the majority of the electors of the country into the ranks of the Whig middle class. At one stroke it deprived both the Tories of the vote of many of the agricultural laborers and the Radicals of the vote of the proletariat.

From 1832 on Maginn subjected the Whigs to as close an analysis of what he considered their rascality as he did the Tories for what he considered their weakness. Not infrequently an attack on one of the parties was begun with an oblique shot at the other. In discussing political corruption, for instance, Maginn writes:

The Whigs are now jogging along in the saddle of the Tories, and find it prudent to imitate their predecessors in every thing relating to place and pension. . . . Lord Brougham, with a laudable contempt for cash, has got his salary fixed at 14,000*l.* a-year, and his retiring pension 5000*l.*; the latter being only 1000*l.* more than that of Lyndhurst, or the money-loving, long-serving, much-doubting octogenarian Tory-chancellor Eldon. Grey, whose *amor patriæ* no one will dispute, any more than his *amor familiæ,* is satisfied with 120,000*l.* annually for self and relations.[18]

In the same spirit he exclaims, "What is more horrid in the whole history of Nepotism than the proceedings of Lord Grey, with his fifteen relatives foisted on the public?"[19] His despondency at the bankrupt condition of English statesmanship is expressed in an article for

June, 1832. "No one," he writes, "can look at the conduct which has been for some time displayed by Whig and Tory, ministry and opposition, ruler and subject, without seriously inquiring whether there be any conceivable shame or calamity which is not on the eve of falling on this unhappy empire."[20]

The neglect of the working classes to which the nation had objected in the Wellington administration Maginn found was as conspicuous in the Whig, in spite of the fact that Grey and the cabinet members had, previous to the formation of the ministry, ardently espoused the cause of the people. In regard to the harshness of the ministers, he writes:

Did they attempt to relieve those sufferings which they, while in opposition, only a few moons previously, had so sensitively, if not hypocritically deplored? Not they—honest, consistent, patriotic statesmen! They sent judges, armed with extraordinary powers, and legions of sergeants at law, and sharp barristers, headed by the Attorney General, to punish, not to soothe—to erect a gallows in every county, not to give the poor bread—to banish and imprison, not to administer alms or give employment to starving families.[21]

After the Whig suppression of trade unions Maginn dubs Grey "the mob-begotten minister, who, reversing the atrocity of Saturn, eats his parent. Later he remarks, addressing the working classes:

How beautiful is the benignant rule of Whiggery and the *juste milieu!* Good people of the Trades' Unions! do you not now feel how completely you have been humbugged? When you bellowed for a reform which could not, by any possible chance, be of the slightest advantage to you, you were honoured and cherished as the "people of England;" when you venture to beg for the remission of a harsh punishment of your own brethren, you are flung forth as something too filthy to be touched; and if you dare to growl, you are threatened with the dragoon's sabre or the policeman's bludgeon.[22]

When the Whigs succeeded in gaining the support not only of many of the Radicals, but of the great body of Dissenters and finally, as has been said, of the Catholics under O'Connell, Maginn became thoroughly alarmed for the safety of the monarchy. "The Dissenters, Catholic and Protestant," he writes, "are perfectly disciplined by their respective religions into one vast political party"[23] which is opposed to the Church and therefore opposed to those conservative institutions, including monarchy itself, which support the Church. The Dissenters, he repeats, "ever act with the party which is the most hostile to the Church and the most friendly to republicanism." In short, he became so convinced of the helplessness of the country in the grip of Liberalism that he felt the Whigs might at any time become avowed usurpers and in spite of the disinclination of the country, overthrow the monarchy itself. "We are numbered," he writes in 1835, "with those who conscientiously believe the monarchy to be in extreme danger; and we deem this danger to be inseparable from another, which to our infinite regret receives less attention than it merits. In our eyes, it is certain that the fall of the monarchy must dash to pieces the empire."[24]

RESTATEMENT OF FREEBOOTING

In the face of such danger, Maginn, in 1833, redoubled his efforts to urge upon the Tories a progressive program which should win the confidence of the nation by advocating the rights of the common people. The Liberals, he states, "labour to pull down wages with property, the servant with the master, and the peasant with the noble; and they are the most determined opponents of every measure for gratifying the wishes and bettering the circumstances of the working orders."[25] It was, he felt, imperative that the two classes, the highest and the lowest, recognize their common interests and their common cause against the Liberals. He reminded the Tories that the magazine had from the first steadily advocated practical reforms; he referred to its early sweeping demand for reorganization of Parliament, and recalled its continuous efforts in the face of the political economists to alleviate the condition of the working classes. He appealed to the Tories to realize that such reform along constitutional lines was not averse to their principles.

> Reform [he writes] is continually needful, and a free government exists in no small degree to make it. Abuse and defect, like weeds, spring spontaneously, and thrive from neglect wherever the ground is sufficiently fertile for better productions. . . . There may sometimes be destruction in reform, but without it there can be no conservation: those who wish to preserve must at least repair.[26]

More specifically, he explains:

> Toryism ought to be the *protective* system, as the system of the Radicals is the *destructive* one. It ought to protect the agricultural labourer

from the farmer, the factory-child from the mill-tyrant, the Spitalfields weaver from the competition of the men of Lyons; it ought to enlarge circulation; lessen in every way the surplus-labour which presses down the market; and never rest till general employment and fair wages were universal.[27]

In recommending this "protective" reform, Maginn urged the Tory party to repudiate the measures advocated by the "Bowrings and Thompsons, and Roebucks and Humes" of the *Westminster Review* and support those advanced by Michael Sadler.

The perfect incarnation [he writes] or every thing absurd, senseless, and atrocious, in the eyes of a Westminster Reviewer, is found in the person and in the plans of Mr. Sadler. The reason is not far to seek. If the schemes and propositions propounded by that truly enlightened man were once fairly embraced and put into operation by a Tory administration, a Radical would soon become a very rare animal. Well, therefore, may the Westminster Reviewers hate him. But in proportion as he is hated and feared by the Radicals and Economists, ought he to be admired and supported by all sound Tories.

In the present crisis, he pointed out that the whole political situation forced a progressive stand upon Tories. If they ever hoped to reinstate themselves, they must, he asserted, come forward with a reform program of their own and must stop conceding the measures of their opponents. For ten years, he writes, they have practiced concession "with a fidelity beyond what might be expected from fallible man: and what is the issue? Where are the Tories? . . . Not a Tory remains to say,—I, though but one man, have escaped the slaughter."[28] Even for those who call themselves Conservatives, there has been "unbroken calamity and disgrace," till "the state of the church is almost hopeless, and the peril of the monarchy is extreme."

The mistake against which he especially warned the Tories was their failure to distinguish between the desires of the people and the desires of the Radicals. The people, he claimed, if their wishes were forwarded, would soon learn to support those who offered them substantial help. Because the Tory party had never tested them it did not realize how distinct they were from the Radicals and how much the Radicals had misrepresented and exploited them.

We speak and act [he writes] as though the middle and lower ranks could not be divided into parties and influenced by party motives. If the Whig or Tory part of the population advocate anything, we say,—Oh, this is a party measure; but if the Radicals set up a demand, we reverently ejaculate,—This comes from the people.

As a matter of fact, he found that it did not come from any such source.

The voice of the real people can be always easily distinguished from that of party; while the one never seeks more than the correction of practical grievance or some general good, the other never seeks any thing but separate political profit. Yet [Maginn complains] petitions to parliament obviously and confessedly unconnected with party politics, are never treated as flowing from the people, and they seldom obtain the least attention; those which speak only such politics . . . are alone held to contain the sentiments of the people.[29]

In exasperation he asks:

Are we to flounder for ever in this miserable error? Is Mr. O'Connell, or Mr. Hume, or any other Radical leader, less a party man than Sir R. Peel or Lord J. Russell? Is the Radical press free from party spirit and interest? Do the Radicals and Dissenters display less of party discipline, violence, and cupidity, than other men? We call that division of society the people, which on every ground is far more a party or faction than any other.[30]

With apprehension he continues:

They speak not of equality; in all matters they boldly demand the lion's share—the sovereignty; and we are to comply, because, forsooth! they usurp the name of the people—the name of those whom they attempt to despoil and enslave in every quarter.

What the Conservatives must do, Maginn asserts, is to draw

the line boldly and vividly between wholesale and special reforms—[between] the reforms craved by the people for the correction of practical grievance and those demanded by party to subvert the balance of power—[between] the reforms to perfect institutions according to their constitutional uses, and those to alter them for separate party benefit. . . . The Conservative leaders [he adds] say, they consent against conviction and on expediency to many things of party origin and very dangerous nature. Why cannot they do this to the real people in things not dangerous?[31]

Maginn's attitude toward the political and social situation is summarized under the satiric caption,

The Prophecy of Plenty for the Year M.DCCC.XXXIII

. . .

Plenty of nostrums that never were tried,
Plenty of liberty, all one side.
Plenty to overturn, few to uphold;
Plenty of poverty, great lack of gold!
Plenty of promise, and nothing in hand;
Plenty of paupers all gaping for land;
Plenty of dupes to a handful of knaves,
Plenty of freemen fast verging to slaves.
Plenty of Atheists scoffing at God,
Plenty of faction at home and abroad;
Plenty of Colonies cutting adrift,
Plenty of demagogues lending a lift;
Plenty of newspapers springing the mine,
Plenty of readers to think it all fine.

. . .

Plenty of rogues with it all their own way,
Plenty of honest men skulking away;
Plenty of Whigs to send England to ruin,
Plenty of Tories to let them be doing.

Plenty of meddling without a pretence,
Plenty of war that is all for "offence;"
Plenty of mitres that tottering sit,
Plenty of churches with notice to quit.
Plenty of ancestry, just to disown,
Plenty of rats undermining the throne;
Plenty to-day to work mischief and sorrow,
Plenty to vote a republic to-morrow.[32]

PART FOUR

WILLIAM MAGINN

CHAPTER VIII

THE GROWTH OF AN EDITOR

Maginn accumulated so many enemies through *Fraser's* that after his death no attempt was made for thirteen years to collect his essays and verse; even then America was thought a safer place for the venture than England. Since his writing had been as prolific as Daniel Defoe's and far more dispersed, peppering the periodicals and several of the newspapers, there was at that late date no chance of getting it adequately before the public. The once famous wit and editor, who had lashed practically every prominent man of his time, thus became, in the apt phrasing of Mr. Michael Sadleir, a pungent marginal note to the biographies of other men. The personality of *Fraser's* was so completely a projection of the personality of Maginn that a book devoted to the contentions of the belligerent and powerful monthly cannot leave its chief protagonist with scanty notice or neglect to clear him of the ill repute resulting from the magazine's turbulent course. Recently fresh clouds have gathered upon his already darkened name. Before attempting to dispel them it will be well to supplement the fragmentary and often mistaken accounts of him by a biography which will let him more nearly step forth in his own right. What manner of man was he who in an age of sentimentality remained satiric and in an age of transition became determined?

SCHOLAR WIT

William Maginn was a misfit in the respectable, self-seeking nineteenth century. He understood his time altogether too well to be at ease in it, and should have been born back in the Middle Ages among care-free scholar wits irreverently forgathered about some legendary Golias, or possibly later, around even Rabelais himself. It is indeed a mistake to judge him apart from these vagabond kings of satire who were busy showing the world its sins without making any effort to hide their own. They took their ease in their own inns, but it did not occur to them to cultivate their gardens. Viewed as a man of affairs

Maginn is preposterous—unbusinesslike, full of impish vagaries and enigmatical assaults on friends as well as enemies. Viewed as a Rabelaisian scholar who chose to write himself down in the periodicals of his day, he becomes plausible and distinctive.

Bohemians, classicists—learned, improvident, satiric—such were the scholar wits of the ages, and such was William Maginn. It is significant that he was among the last of the Latinists, in the strict sense of the term. The Latin language for him was not to be displayed but to be thought in. He spoke it and made jests in it as if it were a living tongue. It is also significant that Maginn had prodigious information which he used only casually, seldom for its own end. The results of his occasional delicate and scholarly research were seldom given directly, as of intrinsic value in themselves; but were summarized under the caption of "*adversaria*" or crowded into articles like those against Dr. Richard Farmer, whose great essays scarcely deserved such insulting erudition. True scholar of the Middle Ages, Maginn seems to have thought in terms of dialectic, his mind going forward through argument and reaching its conclusions by means of dissent. Detailed as his work occasionally is, one has the feeling that much material was omitted from it because there chanced to be no statement of his opponent to call it forth.

True also to the tradition of scholar wits, Maginn was both wise enough and foolish enough to laugh at the things that were not supposed to be laughed at. He was consistently observant of the inconsistencies of life. Hypocrisies, foibles, sentimentalities, he hailed with the smack of the small boy. Was he too immature to take life seriously, or was he too profoundly mature? In either case he freed himself from ordinary obligations and became keenly jovial, ingenuously lovable, and highly dangerous.

Rabelaisian scholar that he was, he had no conviction of the inferiority of those below him, and no veneration for the mediocre accomplishments of those above him. He never had a patron whom he did not outrageously lampoon. He never favored a political leader one moment whom he did not ridicule the next. Ordinary party affiliations and machine loyalties meant little to him. He entered the political field, as it were, on the oblique, and pointed out the weaknesses of his own party from the angle of a truth-loving outsider. Frequently he did estimable work for the Conservative leaders, but it would have been foolhardy for them to reward him by appointment to office because at any moment he was likely to become far more harmful than an avowed enemy.

Not even Maginn's staunchest friends could help him to any great degree of respectability.[1] With the quick sympathy of a Goldsmith he gave away his coat when his own family was in need, and he went surety for an acquaintance when he had borrowed money himself. Much of the time he received an extraordinarily large salary for an editor, yet he always managed to be in debt. He drove a shrewd bargain one month but squandered his profit the next. His home was constantly the center for young Irish writers with high hopes and empty stomachs. On more than one occasion he tramped the length of London to find a job for an Irish workingman when he had to sit up all night not to neglect his own. Nor had he the least conception of how preposterous he was. He could insult a man most shamefully in print and be heartily disappointed not to meet him at dinner.[2]

In every way Maginn's wit was adverse to his own profit and his sympathies were vagrant and impolitic. He enjoyed sitting at the table of a lord, and was occasionally for a week or so at a time the guest at an estate. But he rarely confined his jokes to his host's enemies, and brought into ill repute the cherished foibles and conceits of the elect with an even-handed stroke that was as irresistible as it was leveling. On one occasion at a political dinner John Wilson Croker, who for many years was Secretary to the Admiralty and the chief writer for the *Quarterly Review,* stated with a shade too much gravity that his family came from Lyneham (he pronounced it Line-ham) and that if he were ennobled he would have himself gazetted not as Lord Croker but as Lord Lyneham. Whereupon Maginn, with an easy adjustment of values, remarked to his friend and patron, "Don't do that, Mr. Croker, for you'd then have to be re-gazetted Lord *Penny-a-line 'em.*"[3]

The ill-timed "Doctor" even failed to recognize ordinary class boundaries and proprieties. He had a flattering way of giving a chance acquaintance complete attention; could draw out a man's confidences and fill his mind with a rare elation, but was known to spend himself as freely and gayly for a street gamin as for a parliamentarian. On reaching a town he had the custom of searching out the foulest slums and maintaining equality with their vagrants. He habitually made friends with the priests and rabbis of the poor. In London and Paris he could act as guide among the cellars and alleys. Bermondsey, "The Mint," "The Rookery" admitted him to dens which were unsafe for the police; the quartier St. Denis, the rue du Temple, even welcomed him when a password was needed. In both cities he became an authority on thieves' slang and talked the patter with what in a less versatile man would have been incriminating accuracy.[4]

Maginn's intimate knowledge of the poor and the outcast adds import to his comment that the working of the poor-law system on English society "would form one of the most remarkable chapters in that great work yet to be written, 'The History of the *Lowest* Order from the earliest times,'—a work of far more importance, of deeper philosophy, and more picturesque romance, than all the chronicles of what are called the great events of the earth."[5] Maginn, as we have shown, was skeptical of values and creeds. It was a skepticism which was to become more common as the century advanced, with the quickened protest again materialism. Firm as was his devotion to the old institutions of the country and the Established Church, he had no faith in the dogma of religion. He would pore over the Bible for hours, reading it aloud and discussing it with his friends, keeping it in his pocket along with his Homer or Rabelais or Shakespeare; but his views, according to his friend Kenealy, conformed to no creed.[6] "Je vais chercher un grand *peut-être,*" he quoted from Rabelais. Less poetically he expressed his doubt in his "Song of a Sceptic," written for *Fraser's* of July, 1831, and later included in his *Magazine Miscellanies.*

The sky is dark behind, Jack,
  The sky is dark before;
And we drive along in a current strong,
  Without helm, sail, or oar.

We know not whither we wend, Jack,
  And we know not whence we come;
We are sure that our voyage must end, Jack,
  But where is the haven-home?

No star in the sky to guide, Jack,
  But all is dark, dark, dark;
And still colder runs the tide, Jack,
  The longer floats our bark.

IRISH PRODIGY

Billy Maginn's choice of his native land was one of his few acts of propriety. He was born in Cork on July 10, 1794,[7] and he found himself on the whole so happily placed that, in spite of congenital vagabondage, he remained there to his thirtieth year, a highly respected and by no means conspicuously unconventional resident. So great a miracle can excellent parents accomplish. Maginn's family sprang from the good old Irish sept or clan of Maguinness, sometimes abbreviated to Guinness or Maginn, and in the Scotch branches written as MacInnes or Innes. He himself never referred to this ancient line or to his family crest included in books on heraldry. For him it was enough, gloriously enough, to be an Irishman, with a broad Irish brogue rolling grandly on his tongue. He looked with fine scorn upon compatriots who sought to bolster up their Irish birth with lineage. Almost any Irishman, he would say, could spring from a king if he felt the need.

But of his own immediate family Maginn was complacently proud. It was big and genial and hospitable, intent on its own principles and accomplishments but also interested in those of others. Down to its youngest member it met strangers with a forthgoing charm that amounted to a genius for spontaneous intimacy. Besides Billy, there were two younger boys and two pretty little girls with quick bright eyes and quicker tongues.[8] The mother, Anne Eccles, was a woman of humor as well as of judgment. She belonged to an old Scotch family still living in Ecclesville, the town in county Tyrone which was named for it. Her three sons were graduated with high honors from Dublin University and later studied for the ministry. Billy, as we have already had occasion to mention, was never ordained,[9] presumably discovering early his own grave ineptitudes; the other two, John and Charles, were successively cherished by the parishioners of Castletown Roche. Charles lived to be an old man, and long after his death was still honored in the diocese. As one rough countryman put it, "He was the most conversable man goin' the roads"[10]—a remark equally applicable to the rest of the family.

While his family was still growing up, the father, John Maginn, for many years a teacher, opened a school on Marlboro Street. It soon proved to be the best in the county, and to it flocked Protestants and Catholics alike, for the old gentleman had a high reputation as a scholar, had written a Latin grammar for no less a school than Eton, and was himself a thorough and original teacher. The methods of the elder Maginn sound today astonishingly individual for the first decade of the nineteenth century. It is said that if a pupil liked mathematics and disliked Latin, he might follow his bias—"because the acquisition of one description of knowledge prepared and even led the mind to understand and master another." Even more modern was the requirement that the most advanced class report on the speeches of the best lawyers at the Cork assizes. Each boy was expected to attend some trial of special interest and to draw up his brief without assistance. The aim of his teaching, the master explained, was to make the pupils think, and he was highly displeased, to use his own words, with the boy who "crawled like a snail over the facts."

The effect of these vigorous ideas was seen in his eldest son. Billy was a genial prodigy born of a genial pedagogue. He learned the alphabet before he could talk,[11] lisped Latin in babyhood, and was fluent in Hebrew at the age of ten. He made up nonsense rhymes to divert his younger brothers and sisters, and he acquired facts to divert his father. At the beginning of January, 1806,[12] the proud parent took the boy to Trinity College, Dublin. The university, as is well known, had a formidably rigid standard, but the elder Maginn was also rigid. When informed that William should be returned to the nursery since applicants for the entrance examinations were supposed to be at least sixteen, he pointed to his diminutive offspring of eleven, saying laconically, "Try him." Young William passed, entered with honors, and proceeded on his university course with a thoroughness which won the heart of his straight-laced tutor, Dr. Kyle. Afterward, when Kyle became a bishop of the Irish Church, he did not forget the round-eyed lad who had sat profitably under his instruction. Throughout Maginn's life, even during his most erratic days, the Bishop remained loyal, taking an adoptive interest in the whole Maginn family, and appointing the two younger brothers successively to the rectorate of Castletown Roche in his own diocese.

Kyle was not the only person at Dublin with whom the eleven-year-old boy set up an immediate friendship. There was on the Trinity faculty a forbidding professor of Hebrew, a certain Dr. Barrett, famous for his astonishing greeting of "Do you see me now?" or if he chanced to feel like talking Latin, "Videsneme nunc?" Maginn met him on his second day at the university. The lad, we are told by Dr. R. S. Mackenzie, one of his early biographers and a friend of the family, was even more childlike in appearance than in years. He had on a small leather cap, and was dressed in a "short jacket, with large linen collar and frill turned over," and a student's gown "which had received several tucks to reduce it to wearable length." Barrett, supposing that he was a schoolboy masquerading to raise a laugh, sternly asked him,

> Do ye see me now? Who are you, little boy, and where are you going in that gown?

Billy's reply was characteristically explicit.

> Maginn, of Cork; I got tenth place at entrance, yesterday; I am going now to find Dr. Barrett, that I may get the Hebrew premium.

Barrett is said to have then remembered hearing the lad spoken of at the Fellows' table the night before. He reached down from his height, patted the boy on the head, explaining,

> D'ye see me now? I am Dr. Barrett, and if I had to look for you t'would be long ere I could find you, you are so small. Come along, and let me hear whether you know the Hebrew alphabet.[13]

Maginn, it is recorded, was actually given the first prize. Later, in his third year, he took up Sanskrit and Assyrian under this same Dr. Barrett.

It was thus while he was still at the university that Maginn laid the foundation for his interest in languages. With the classics he was always on intimate terms, readily making Greek dance an Irish jig, as Andrew Lang wittily remarked. The first third of the nineteenth century was one of the rare intervals when the Anglo-Saxon race broke from its monolinguistic self-sufficiency, and an occasional scholar knew as many as fifteen tongues. It became one of Maginn's favorite pastimes to trace words back to the Aramaic and to work out obscure philological relations. We find him studying Russian, and translating Basque, Turkish, and various Magyar tongues, as well as keeping up his interest in Hebrew, Sanskrit, and Assyrian. Old Irish, or Gaelic, he had learned in boyhood. Swedish, Portuguese, and modern Greek he picked up in the course of wide and peripatetic acquaintance with foreigners marooned in England. German he read extensively, and Anglo-Saxon followed from his knowledge of Scandinavian. With Spanish literature he was moderately familiar. For Italian he had a fine-spun attachment woven of more delicate fibres than he ordinarily liked to admit. With French he was as much at home as with English, having a peculiar flair for its vernacular and an exciting and fluent acquaintance with its thieves' slang.

In 1813, two years after Maginn had received the degree of A.B. from Dublin[14] and was well established as a teacher in the Cork school, a tragedy occurred in his family which placed undue responsibility on his shoulders. His father had always been aware of the high calling of pedagogue. As he was a strict disciplinarian in practice and also a stout Orangeman in politics, he one day felt justified in reproving the servants of a public official when their reckless driving endangered his personal safety. What he failed to recognize was that the ancient and honorable rights of pedestrian, pedagogue, and Orangeman were not universally recognized in Cork. He was promptly knocked down with such vigor that he took to his bed, nor did he ever again rise from it. Thus it happened that William Maginn at the age of nineteen became in his turn head of the school in Marlboro Street.

From the start he had much against him. He was short, slight, with a quizzical innocence in his round, boyish face, which we are told could readily be impish but not dignified.

> Solemn and steady [one of his intimate biographers assures us], he could never become, and although one of our best English parodists with his pen, he was a very bad mimic in his conduct. The idea of assuming a virtue, or anything else, which he had not, never entered his mind. He was one of those men who, if the fate of worlds depended on it, could not play the hypocrite for five minutes.[15]

Even qualities which were honestly his he did not turn to advantage. A pedagogue in those days was supposed to show a decent amount of learning whether he had it or not. People expected him to pronounce Latin distichs with suitable decorum. Maginn knew enough of the classics to please the most exacting parent, but he did not want to quote them. Like a small boy he was not averse to boasting, but he wished to choose what he was going to boast about, and Latin distichs did not seem to him desirable. He disliked information of any sort when it was didactic, and self-importance when seriously displayed he found annoying. In short, Maginn did not know the first principle of making erudition pompous.

But with his pupils he was on firmer ground. He had a great liking for all young people and was at his best with them. To the end of his life they flocked about him. Wherever he went, the children of the place found him out, vying with one another to keep up with his mind, studying their lessons to please him, hanging on his jokes and explanations. He was known to spend hours at a time giving them brilliant attention, as if their interests were all that very much mattered.[16] Like his father Maginn gave boys a sense of excitement in the use of their own minds. In his school there was fine scorn for what the Irish call a "cog." A boy who attempted to bolster up his own work by using a translation was a subject for public concern. We are told that a high tone of honorable and manly feeling pervaded the whole body of his pupils "and that even among themselves one of the heaviest offences was violation of the truth"—as it was "one of the rarest also." A zest for mental integrity left no place for an assumption of knowledge beyond what was honestly come by.

For ten years Maginn ran the school in Marlboro Street. They were busy years. In the beginning he was preparing himself for the ministry, and later, in 1819, he received his LL.B. and LL.D., from Dublin.[17] The doctorate in those days was comparatively seldom given by the University, and its requirements were high. As he was barely twenty-five at the time and looked still in his teens, he was jocularly dubbed the "Doctor" by his amused and admiring friends. It was said that Dublin had never before conferred the degree of LL.D. on so young a man. Nor was Maginn without social occupation. The city of Cork at the time had two literary societies or rather two branches of one society, and great was the rivalry between them. So fervid was the strife after the arts that Cork was called the "Athens of Ireland" in emulation of Edinburgh's title, "the Athens of the North." Maginn hurled himself into the ranks of the more radical of the two societies, "leveling his shafts," we are told, "at such of his associates as were most prominent in absurdity, priggishness, or pretension." Unfortunately for him, many of his missiles fell sharply on the cherished punctilios of the opposing leader, Samuel Carter Hall. So heavy was the fusillade that Hall left Ireland—glad, as he wrote in his *Retrospect of a Long Life,*[18] to escape from a contest which had won him enemies. He was subsequently to become Maginn's rival in London and to take full vengeance, in his published commentaries, on his early foe.

Meanwhile the defeat of Hall had by no means exhausted the rapacious satire of the youthful pedagogue. Maginn was finding out that he had much to say that he could not place in two local papers, the *Advertiser* and the *Freeholder,* which limited their attacks to the more vulnerable spots of the "beautiful City of Cork." Early in 1819 he began to fling himself through page after page of unrestrained and jubilant composition. This he sent first to the *Literary Gazette,* the best and most influential of the London weeklies, and a few months later, when the current of his production was too strong and swift for issue in a single periodical, to *Blackwood's* as well.

Both the English and the Scotch editors seem to have looked upon this gay gratuity from an unknown correspondent in the light of inexplicable treasure-trove and to have given bewildered and heart-felt thanks for the bounty. In those days William Jerdan of the *Gazette* was an important man in the literary circles, and was accustomed to receive tribute rather than to pay it, but for his Irish correspondent, C. J. Crossman, as Maginn chose to sign himself, he had an almost fatuous gratitude. Even after years had passed, when he came to write his autobiography, the once powerful editor exclaims: "Of Maginn, the precocious, the prolific, the humourous, the eccentric, the erratic, the versatile, the learned, the wonderfully endowed, the Irish,—how shall I attempt to convey any idea?" Jerdan recalls the great variety of Maginn's work, which came in a "perfect shower": "poetry, feeling or burlesque; classic paraphrases; anecdotes; illustrations of famous ancient authors (displaying a vast acquaintance with, and fine appreciation of, them)." He frankly acknowledges how much help to him these contributions were. "In short," he concludes, "Mr. Crossman's proper hand on the address of a letter, and the postmark 'Cork' were about the most welcome sight that could meet my editorial eye and relieve my editorial anxieties."[19]

Maginn's advent to the *Blackwood's* group was even more keenly appreciated. "The Maga," as the magazine was endearingly dubbed, was in the thick of its bitter quarrel with the so-called "Cockney School," of the *London Magazine,* which a few years later was to end so fatally for young John Scott. At once the "Big Three" of the *Blackwood* brotherhood, Wilson, Lockhart, and the publisher himself, recognized in their new Irish ally a subtle roisterer of their own order. He was worthy, they felt, to be admitted to their closest council, and they gladly watched him fill the pages of "Maga" with rich reverberation against their enemies. On one occasion Lockhart exclaims in a letter to the publisher, "How that *demon* has entered into the very core of Ambrose's"[20]—the tavern where the more fell designs of the brotherhood found birth.

Blackwood's own letters to Maginn are full of an intimate enthusiasm which shows how close was the relation between the two men.

I received all your parcels of the 8th, 9th, and 10th. Both your songs are capital; and I weary excessively for the introduction which you are to prefix. Captain Hamilton [a friend of Sir Walter Scott and one of "Maga's" most pleasant contributors] was like to die of laughing when he read them; particularly St. Patrick. Any one but yourself, he says, would mar the melodies.[21]

How much Blackwood came to depend on his Irish correspondent may be judged from the following letter written in 1820, at the time of the coronation of George IV.

I feel [he confides] prodigious anxiety about my next number; it is so much consequence that it should be very good as well as very lively. I entreat of you, as the greatest favour you can ever do me, to make the utmost exertions that your limited leisure will permit you. It would have an admirable effect if you could send me an article full of the true loyal Irish feeling which is at present sweeping all before it in your Green Isle. None but an Irishman can do this. At the same time, this is not to prevent there being plenty of the humorous and droll turn of communication. . . . The ode and the song everyone is delighted with; and a great deal more of the same kind is expected in our next number. Δ [Moir, another of the early contributors] writes me that he never almost read anything so good; and Wilson and Hamilton were quite delighted with them.[22]

Maginn's work for *Blackwood's* finally reached such proportions that according to Mrs. Oliphant, who has written the only authoritative and detailed study of the magazine, the Irish correspondent was at one time producing half the articles and nearly half the verse that appeared in the enterprising monthly.[23] Occasionally Lockhart and Maginn, or the "Doctor," as he was generally called, seem to have brought forth a number of "Maga" unassisted by the more temperamental member of the trio, John Wilson. Writing for Wilson, Mrs. Oliphant informs us, came spasmodically, in great gushes, and only after enormous convulsions of the entire man. When no convulsions occurred, the Professor sulked in gloomy immobility. "Let the Doctor do all kinds of clever things for Maga this time," he sighs on one occasion. "There should be a new, striking, delightful and conclusive preface, which M. and L. can do very well without W."[24] Luckily both "M" and "L" were rapid, and were used to informal, jaunty collaboration in which each understood the language of the other. "I think," Lockhart writes in answer to an appeal from Blackwood, "I may venture to promise you one way or other two sheets [thirty-two pages] but I shall not begin till I know what Maginn is likely to be at."[25]

From the first there was ready admiration between these two fluent colleagues. In acknowledging a number of "Maga," Lockhart enthusiastically writes the publisher, "Maginn is easily detected, and is as brilliant as ever."[26] A little later he speaks of a contribution by the Doctor which had kept him "laughing for hours," and adds, "Sir Walter Scott, Sir Humphrey Davy, and Mr. Stewart Rose all sat bursting their sides" over it.[27] More earnest appreciation of his Irish friend is expressed in his advice to Blackwood: "Do persuade him to give you more of his mind, and his beautiful scholarship."[28]

For some time Blackwood was unable to induce Maginn to accept payment for his voluminous contributions to the magazine, and was therefore obliged to bait the elusive Irishman with what substitutes he could invent. Once we find him writing:

I hope you will like this number of Maga, which I think one of our standard ones. I need not say how much it owes to you, and I cannot say how much *I* owe you for your most effectual assistance. Your contributions have now been so numerous and so valuable, in the truest sense of the word, that I trust you will allow me to return you some acknowledgment, for I cannot repay you for the kind and valuable aid you have given me. If you will not accept money, I trust you will allow me to send you books, and you would do me a singular favour if you would send me a list of those that would be acceptable to you. It is very awkward of me to ask you to do this; but ignorant as I am of what passes, or what you would most prize, I would not like to send you works you did not want.[29]

The difficulty of paying Maginn was increased by the fact that he did not reveal his identity to Blackwood until two years after he had become an intimate correspondent of the magazine. For some time indeed he signed even his letters to the publisher merely by the initials R.T.S.; nor did he help his bewildered friend by substituting on request a fuller signature, Ralph Tucket Scott. When Blackwood sent him a check payable to that unsubstantial gentleman, Maginn jestingly replied with a discouraging account of the difficulties which he had met in getting it cashed.

All told Maginn would seem to have approached his work for *Blackwood's* and the *Literary Gazette* in much the same mood as a truant from school springs for his fishing rod. His superabundant high spirits evidently grew restive under academic restraint, and he felt the need of mental leg-stretching, the sense of flinging himself through column after column of exuberant composition.

To acknowledge this work as his own would under the circumstances have been foolhardy. In his position as head of the Cork school not even so bold a man as the defiant young doctor of Dublin would have dared avow the extent or the character of his contributions to *Blackwood's* and the *Literary Gazette,* and the secret of his great progeny of pseudonyms, Sir Morgan O'Doherty, Adjutant, among them, was closely kept. It must not be forgotten that at this time in the nineteenth century the arts were still looked upon as a sad business for men of serious affairs to be mixed up with, betokening flippancy and effeminacy ill suited to positions of trust and responsibility. Even after a banker or lawyer had become well established and his reliability proved by half a lifetime of work, it was not an idle precaution that led him to cling to the secrecy of a pseudonym.[30] The only compositions of which Maginn spoke openly were the Latin paraphrases such as the racy rendering of the old ballad, *Chevy Chase*. These, one of his pupils says, he sometimes wrote during school hours, now and then stopping the study to call for a rhyme. "Luctus?" Maginn would question. "Fructus," a boy would answer. And the pleased pedagogue would nod "bene," as the room resumed work. There was nothing indiscreet about owning classical productions even of a lighter vein. Sir Morgan as Latinist was much less of a reprobate than Sir Morgan the jester. Many of the remarks of the latter gentleman could not with impunity have been made from the teacher's rostrum.

Yet the extent to which Maginn carried his magazine incognito was of course pure tomfoolery. Mrs. Oliphant in her study of *Blackwood's* bluntly terms it silly. Maginn doubtless found it silly also and enjoyed it accordingly, considering silliness an inevitable diversion for an intelligent person. Like his famous friend, Theodore Hook, he had a relish for the true finesse of a prank, and a great sense for the high calling of a good joke. They were among the most popular tavern men of their day, one suspects, because in their private lives both were natural, and at times presumably unconscious, comedians.

From the point of view of ludicrous silliness, for instance, there is much which is effective in Maginn's introduction of himself to Blackwood. The publisher had several times without effect asked his Irish correspondent to visit him, possibly with the notion of eventually breaking down his incognito. Finally in the summer of 1821 Maginn suddenly took the Scotchman at his word and arrived in Edinburgh without the slightest warning. In his own account of the affair, told later to a number of his friends, Maginn represented himself as first prowling all around Blackwood's house, back and front, carefully looking in at the windows. Without giving his name, he was admitted to the publisher's private office and began the interview with a "rather formal bow" and a "touch of the Cork brogue."

"Ye'r Misther Blackwood I presume, sir."

"Yes, sir. At your service."

"Be gor, sir, if you were only at my service a week ago, you'd have saved me a journey, but, be my conscience, as I'm here, I'm very glad entirely that you *are* at my service at last."

The supposedly irate visitor then complained that there was a man in Cork who was abusing him in the "old thrump of a Magazine" and demanded the offender's name. When Blackwood naturally replied that a request of such a nature could not be granted "without delay, and consideration," Maginn roused himself to fine rage:

> "Consideration, indeed; aren't you after writen to one Scott there? Maybe it's going to deny what you wrote, you are, maybe you'll deny this, and this, and this!"

and with the words he smacked upon the table letter after letter addressed to Scott in Blackwood's own handwriting.

> "Maybe you'll say they're not to the man that writes for you, and maybe you'll say that I'm not the man himself."[31]

The scene might have been taken from a modern Irish play. There is a rich Hibernian roll to the sentence "And maybe you'll say that I'm not the man himself." Maginn had more than an Irish brogue on his tongue; he had an infallible brogue of the mind.

ADVENTURER IN LONDON

Maginn's youthful exuberance was not without its effect on English and Scotch audiences. The braggart Sir Morgan became for the time one of the most popular names in magazines. Even Byron repeated passages from O'Doherty with admiration,[32] and on the occasion when he found himself the hero of one of the Irishman's famous *Noctes Ambrosianæ* was heard to exclaim, "By Jupiter, the fellow has me down regularly in black and white." Finally Maginn in his prosperous school in Cork was faced by such a growing demand for his writing that he found he had two almost equally insistent jobs; one by which he supported himself and his family and the other by which he kept himself amused.

By the autumn of 1823 he had already made fairly careful plans to leave the safer and more lucrative work and set forth on the friendly but precarious highroad of literary adventure. He had been head of the Cork school for ten years. His brother John, who had for some time been assisting him, was old enough to assume entire responsibility.

In the summer of 1821 and again in that of 1823 Maginn had visited London, making great strides in friendship with William Jerdan, the powerful editor of the *Literary Gazette*. Through Jerdan he was introduced to the three Johns, each of whom seems to have wanted to try his hand at making the young man's fortune: John Murray, best of publishers; John Wilson Croker, Secretary to the Admiralty and political potentate of the august *Quarterly;* and "John Bull," otherwise that prince of wits and most fearsome of editors, Theodore Hook. All three Johns early became aware of the versatile Irishman's usefulness.

Maginn's letters during this transitional period are full of elation and show the easy footing which he had secured not only in the *John Bull* but also in the *Quarterly*. In describing an interview with John Wilson Croker, he writes to Blackwood of the long-standing Murray-Blackwood quarrel:

> His [Croker's] opinion of "Maga" is high; but he is absurdly sore about the abuse of the "Quarterly" and of Murray. "If *you* knew him," said he, "you would not speak of him as you do." I assured him *I* had nothing to do with abusing Murray, but spoke openly about what I thought was the pitiful conduct of this "Quarterly" towards "Maga." He made no reply whatever. I asked him why L's ballads [Lockhart's *Spanish Ballads*] had not been reviewed according to promise to Sir W. S. [Sir Walter Scott]. He said that he never heard of any such promise, but would speak to Murray about it. In fact, he added, he did not know anybody who was *au fait* enough at Spanish literature to give a suitable review. That, I told him, could be easily remedied, for I would venture to do one myself. To this I got no answer. Now, I have not the knowledge to do a fit review, but do you get me a learned one, discursive on Spanish literature, antiquities, &c., and I shall send it in my own handwriting right ahead to C. with a proper letter. The devil is in the dice if he can get out of that. Would L. have any objection to do it himself? I assure him on honour I should do it if I had the knowledge, but I have not—I mean knowledge enough to make a good appearance in the "Quarterly."[33]

This is a boyishly unethical proposal, which, however, was quite in accord with the practice of the day. It was by no means an unusual occurrence in the first quarter of the century for an author to write his own reviews. In this connection it will be remembered and forgiven that Sir Walter Scott himself penned an excellent "puff" of *Old*

Mortality. Maginn's suggested hoax upon Croker was a bit of individual waggishness which showed not only his love of the practical joke but his very real concern for whatever affected the welfare of Lockhart.

Even more high-handed was he at a meeting with Croly, another influential Tory writer and man of affairs. The conversation turned to the "Z" letters, a series of attacks which Lockhart and others had published in "Maga" against the "Cockney School" of the *London Magazine,* and which included the brutal criticism of Keats.

I dined [Maginn writes to Blackwood] with him in company with an unspeakable wretch of the name of ——, who knows everything of "Maga" that Croly knows, and who boasts of enjoying the confidence of L. [Lockhart]. . . . I hope this is impossible, for the creature conducts some unheard-of paper in London, and is one of the press gang. He told me many other things, that he knew L. to be Z., for he had it from his own lips. Surely L. could not be such a spoony. I denied it flatly, saying that I had good reason to know that the gentleman who wrote Z. is now in Germany. He knew something about me, picked up among the pressmen, particularly my rumpus with Conway. The man is a cursed bore. I put your friends on their guard against him. He speaks of Scott as if they had been pickpockets together at Calder Fair.[34]

Maginn had a fine flair for the lie direct, telling it with an aplomb which dazzled if it did not actually confound his listeners. A third letter to Blackwood, dated June 25, 1823, and therefore written during the second summer vacation from his Cork school, gives a humorous account of his meeting with Colburn, the prosperous publisher, who wished to secure his support for the *New Monthly,* one of "Maga's" chief rivals.

I saw Colburn [he writes with a characteristic plunge into his subject]. He attended on me at his shop—spoke of the weather—the news—the newspapers—the periodicals—the "New Monthly"—"Blackwood's Mag." —Blackwood himself (very kindly) —his being in town—at the Somerset: was not I at the Somerset? I knew Blackwood?—his contributors? —his Irish contributors?—and in the end, after about an hour's conversation, he took me into his sanctum under pretence of showing me some old books, and making me a low bow, said he was happy to see Mr. O'Doherty in person. I laughed at him—said it was fudge—that he was bammed by somebody, &c. But he stuck to it. Complained of *my* ill treatment of him, particularly in accusing him of employing old Dictionary Watkins to draw up a life of Lord Byron—that he did no such thing, but bought the book honestly, without knowing anything about it. By Jupiter! this is odd, for it *was* I who wrote the article, out of Alaric's [Alaric A. Watts] notes. I of course denied everything plump. Never wrote anything for anybody. Would be sorry to abuse so respectable a person as Mr. C., or so valuable a book as the "New M." But I was talking to an incredulous auditor. He asked me to dine with him for to-morrow, which I declined: he shook hands at parting, quite cordial, and he whispered to me as I went away, "Thirty guineas a sheet." I laughed at him, and drove off.[35]

In spite of his close connections with London magazines and publishers Maginn remained in his Cork school until at the beginning of the new year, February, 1824, circumstances made his presence in London particularly desirable, almost necessary. Theodore Hook, popular man about town, huge, beaf-eating Beau Brummel, wit, wag, and improvisor, had been thrown into prison—and through no great fault of his own. He had been holding the honorary position of governor to a post in Africa which was being covered by a deputy. When a shortage occurred in the accounts of the deputy, the government, unreasonably suspicious, decided to hold their whilom favorite responsible for the full amount. Lockhart's description of Hook's arrest reveals both the plight of *John Bull's* editor and the faithful service of Maginn.

On his arrest under the Exchequer writ (August, 1823), he was taken to the dwelling and spunging house of the sheriff's officer. . . . his accommodations were mean, and the situation about the worst in London . . . a vile, squalid place, noisy and noxious, apparently almost inaccessible either to air or light, swarming with a population of thief-catchers, gin-sellers, and worse. . . . It was while shut up in Shire Lane that he made acquaintance with a man hardly—if at all—less remarkable than himself for natural talents, and infinitely his superior in all the knowledge that can be acquired from books—the late Dr. William Maginn. The doctor, by several years his junior, had then recently come over from Ireland to take his chance as a literary adventurer in the great city. He seems to have soon undertaken some share, we know not what, in the affair of the "John Bull." The editor's confinement must have made such assistance indispensable; and he might have searched Europe over without finding another spirit more congenial to his own. Dr. Maginn is mentioned as a daily, or rather a nightly, visitor throughout Hook's Diary, for a long series of months.

Subsequently they were separated by circumstances; but their mutual kindness seems never to have been disturbed.[36]

When Maginn came to London, in February, 1824, he was twenty-nine years old. On January 31, a few days before he sailed, he had married Ellen Bullen,[37] the daughter of an Irish rector, connected on her mother's side with the gentry of County Cork. Although their finances were precarious (Maginn received, according to Barham, the biographer of Hook, twenty pounds a month for assisting with the *Bull* and editing its milder companion, *Sachell's Weekly*), the young people left Ireland with high hopes. Lockhart, who was in London at the time, writes to his Edinburgh friends of Maginn's prospects:

My belief is, that he has come over by Croker's advice to assist Theodore in *Bull,* and to do all sorts of by jobs. I also believe that Croker thinks he himself will have a place in the cabinet in case of the Duke of York's being King, and of course M. looks forward to being snugly set somewhere in that event. It is obvious that Hook, Maginn, and all this set hate Canning; and indeed a powerful party of high *ton* (Duke of York at head thereof) *is* forming itself against his over-conciliation system.[38]

However high Maginn's expectations of political preferment might have been when he first reached London, in 1824, he was not to realize them. Canning was to remain powerful until his death nearly four years later. Meanwhile the ambitious Hook and his Hibernian assistant were to live a brilliant, hand-to-mouth life. Lockhart, who always kept a watchful eye over his friend, early noted Maginn's tendency to eke out his income by writing for the dailies, and regretted the association. On one occasion, after talking with Sir John Stoddart, the editor of the *New Times,* he writes to one of the *Blackwood* group:

I saw Old Slop, and introduced Maginn to him. What the Doctor and he might afterward agree about I can't say, but I do hope there may be a permanent connection between them, as among newspeople there is no doubt Stoddart is by far the most respectable man, and there is every reason to fear M.'s propensities tending more frequently to the inferior orders of the *Plume.*[39]

A frank comment on Maginn's lack of responsibility in connection with the *John Bull,* in spite of his assistance to its editor, is made by Barham.

His scholarship and education were infinitely superior to those of his friend Hook, for such he soon became, but unfortunately he possessed the same excitable, and erratic temperament only exaggerated, hibernized to a degree, that rendered it somewhat unsafe to rely upon him in a matter demanding the prudence and punctuality to be observed in the conduct of a weekly paper. So far as "John Bull" was concerned the idea of retaining his services was speedily abandoned.[40]

Yet Maginn was, after his own fashion, making his way. There is no better evidence of the esteem in which he was held than that Murray turned to him first as the man best qualified to write his great life of Byron. It will be remembered that, when the poet died in 1824, he left to Murray his notes, diary, and letters with the understanding that they were to be used as the basis of a biography. The papers were known to be in the publisher's possession and great was the excitement with which the public awaited the promised volume. In the course of his brief, erratic life, Byron had acquired Napoleonic fame, and during the years of his voluntary exile in Italy had exerted much the same imaginative appeal as did the involuntary exile of St. Helena. At the time of his tragic death his personality had assumed almost fabulous proportions. That Murray should have chosen Maginn to write the authenticated life of the poet was therefore as high a compliment as could have been paid to the young scholar.

For some months, while the entire Byron correspondence was in Maginn's hands, a hot discussion waged as to how much of the material should be given to the public and how much suppressed in order to shield the reputation of prominent persons involved. According to Kenealy, Maginn, whose sense for the value of complete exposure rivaled that of biographers today, recommended that Murray "publish the letters entire, with libels, sneers, satires, sarcasms, epigrams, confessions, and intrigues, unmutilated and unasterisked, and merely prefix to the work such information as was absolutely indispensable." Maginn was little inclined to follow his own time in its almost servile praise of Byron's poetry, feeling that as an artist the apostle of liberty had been overvalued. But he recognized that the poet's letters and diary were of more genuine stuff, and was convinced that this important biographical material should not be kept from the public because of its personal and political references. In

1825 he wrote in *Blackwood's Noctes,* Number XV: "His memoirs and letters are the only things of his that I have ever seen, that gave me, in the least degree, the notion of a fine creature, enjoying the full and unrestrained swing of his faculties." Murray finally became alarmed at Maginn's radical plans for the biography and turned the task over to the more gentle and gentlemanly Thomas Moore, who gave the world the emasculated volume that has until recent years been the chief available source for the poet's life. At the completion of the work much of Byron's manuscript was burned to remove forever the fear of its being published. This act of sacrilege aroused Maginn's anger, and for years he could not refrain from commenting on the pusillanimity of the biography in contrast with the full avowal of the man himself.

Further evidence of the rapidity with which the daring Irishman made a place for himself is that he was early on informal and confidential terms with the prominent men of the press, including the great editor of *The Times,* Barnes. Toward the close of 1825, when the vast plans for Murray's newspaper, the *Representative,* were under way, Maginn was one of the men whose aid it was considered imperative to secure. Benjamin Disraeli, the ardent young scapegrace who originally persuaded Murray to the huge venture, writes to Lockhart that his interview with the "prosopopœia" of the public press, as he characteristically calls Maginn, is "most important," because "really, after all, it is becoming acquainted, as it were, with the private opinion of Barnes, *etc.*" Maginn had been in London at this time less than two years, yet according to Disraeli's account he had already gained a position where he could command his own price:

Much, my dear Lockhart, has happened since we parted, I think of importance. In the first place *Maginn is engaged.* I called upon the Dr. shortly after your departure. It is impossible for me to give you any adequate idea of our interesting interview: to present you with a few of the leading features, you must know that M. speedily came to the point and told me that £300 to £350 per ann. was the regular salary for the services we required, but that it would not suit his views to go [to Paris, as foreign correspondent] for a less income than £500 per ann., *but that he felt bound in honor and candor to tell us that he did not conceive that our paper could afford or justify such an expenditure.* He then went on *backing Barnes against us,* ridiculing the attempt generally, swearing there was only one way to conduct a newspaper, that a newspaper *was* a newspaper, and other of these sage truisms. He "ventured to predict that with all our system, in six months' time we should be doing the same thing as the old *Times*"; that he was *"the most experienced man as regards newspapers in London,"* that he knew what the system was capable of, etc., etc.[41]

This shows a good deal of shrewdness on the part of Maginn, in spite of the boasting. His better judgment was, however, soon to be overridden. Disraeli continues in his highly colored style:

> As I did conceive him to be decently honorable, and as I felt the importance of arguing the question with a man who might fairly be considered a very prosopopœia of the public press, I thought the experiment might be hazarded of giving him a slight and indefinite sketch of our intentions. This I did with great caution, and mentioning no names. To give you an idea of the effect which I produced is utterly impossible. The Dr. started from his chair like Giovanni in the banquet scene, and seemed as astounded—as *attonitus*—as Porsenna when Scævola missed him. A new world seemed opened to him, and this sneering scribe, this man of most experience, who had so smiled at our first mentioning of the business, ended by saying that as to the success of the affair doubt could not exist, and that a year could not elapse without our being the very first paper going. . . . In brief, the Dr. goes to Paris.

It is interesting as a further instance of Maginn's newly acquired business instinct that Disraeli adds his salary of £500 was to begin from the time of their interview, early in November, 1825, and not nearly two months later at the date of his actual departure from England. Maginn thus taught those who would solicit his services that if they wished to secure the refusal of his time they must pay well for it.

There seems to be some doubt as to how Maginn conducted himself on this Paris trip. Lockhart, who had been most anxious that he should accept the position, appears to have been not wholly free from misgivings as to the outcome. He himself had arrived in London shortly before Maginn left for France. In December he writes to Wilson, "Maginn is off for Paris, where I hope he will behave himself. He has an opportunity of retrieving much, if he will use it."[42]

Samuel Carter Hall, Maginn's old enemy in Cork who first and last says a good many unpleasant things about his rival, does not mention the Paris sojourn, as he himself was in London at the time, acting as parliamentary reporter for the *Representative*. In regard to Maginn's general connection with the paper, however, he states bluntly that he "contributed his share to ruin it—during the seven months of its existence," and adds that he "was 'nothing if not intoxicated,' and he was worse than nothing then."[43]

To offset these rather dubious remarks, it is clear that Murray, who was a shrewd business man although caught in a bad predicament with the *Representative,* valued Maginn's services highly. When he felt that the editorial work of the London office was not pleasing the public, he recalled the Doctor from Paris to start a lighter section in the paper. At the same time he increased the Irishman's salary to an almost unheard of figure for the type of service he desired. The original £500 which he paid Maginn was unusually high. That he now offered the Doctor an additional £200 besides providing him with a house in which to live, shows how essential he thought him for the supplementary editorial job. Probably, therefore, Maginn's work was no worse than that of others connected with the ill-fated daily. Sir Walter Scott's description of his articles as "genteel-blackguard, touch and go" suggests they were at least readable, a quality in which the paper as a whole was deficient.

EDITOR

A year after the failure of the *Representative,* with the founding of the *Standard* newspaper in 1827, Maginn's days of literary adventuring were over. He had been away from Cork for three years. During that time he had been in Paris for over a year, had worked at Hebrew in the Bibliothèque Nationale, and planned his novel *Whitehall,* which he finished probably in collaboration with Lockhart. Besides his connection with the *John Bull* and the *Representative,* he had continued writing for the *Quarterly* and the *Literary Gazette,* and added the scholarly *Foreign Review* and *Foreign Quarterly,* and several of the popular annuals which came out in a silken flutter at Christmas.

In these three years Maginn had, in short, raised himself to a conspicuous position on the London press. In 1827, when he was appointed editor of the *Standard* newspaper with Stanley Lees Giffard, he was placed financially on what should have been a firm basis. The daily soon became through the stability of Giffard and the brilliance of Maginn the leading conservative paper, and the ebullient Doctor remained assistant editor for nine consecutive years, at a salary variously stated as £400 and £600. Yet though the lively O'Doherty continued to dip into the dispersed ink of the London press, he was not satisfied with so random an outlet for his activity, and must needs at the beginning of 1830 start a new organ for his own particular use. It was with his usual gay momentum that, as we have seen, he sought James Fraser's publishing house and brought out the first number of the magazine which he was to edit for the subsequent six years.

Thus casually, William Maginn stepped into his moment of fame. Without *Fraser's* to his credit he would have remained a brilliant adventurer in magazine writing, the inventor of *Blackwood's Noctes Ambrosianæ,* the creator of whole-hearted Irish songs and half a dozen admirable tales. With *Fraser's* he takes his place among great editors. He came to his office with his political and social views formulated, the wrongs of the time sharply impressed on his mind and to some extent the remedies. He was the center of a prominent group of writers. Even Maginn's enemy, Samuel Carter Hall, the editor at this time of the rival magazine, the *New Monthly,* writes in looking back years afterward at the youthful *Fraser* staff: "It was then different from what it is now. It was very brilliant; its writers were the most renowned 'wits' of the metropolis." Hall, to be sure, never able to forgive the personalities and indecencies of *Fraser's,* adds that it imitated "the worse features of *Blackwood's;* and if it gave the world much that was valuable, it contributed largely to the worst passions that are public and private afflictions."[44]

Maginn's need for his own periodical would seem to have been intellectual as much as financial, and possibly emotional as much as either. The Doctor found himself capable of using an indefinite amount of money and quite incapable of limiting his remarks to the conventional requirements of the *Standard* or yet to the decorum of more cautious magazines. Blackwood, as has been said, complained that the articles

William Maginn

Maginn sent him frequently lacked restraint and were so wantonly censorious of influential men that they could not be published. Even one of his light-hearted *Noctes* was so abusive that Blackwood commented to Wilson, "I have written him that it really will not do to run a-muck in this kind of way."[45] The Dublin Doctor had, indeed, since coming to London grown increasingly caustic in regard to public affairs. We have already had occasion to mention in the discussion of politics that Gillies noticed in Maginn's conversation as early as 1827 a "disposition to make sarcastic remarks on leading characters of the day, sparing neither Tory nor Whig." His picaresque acquaintance with all classes of society made him at once catholic and aculeate. In the great incognito of the penniless, to whom Maginn was always affiliated no matter how recently he had drawn his salary, his recognitions were swift. He became not bitter but thoroughly aware. From the moment he started *Fraser's* his scorn and amusement and rage broke tumultuously over its pages. Exultantly he branded himself as a powerful paradox: an ardent Tory who liked neither the men nor the measures of his party and an enthusiastic patriot who approved of almost nothing in his country.

Unfortunately *Fraser's* magazine, however it may have answered Maginn's intellectual needs, had less effect upon his finances than might have been expected. Even though his income from the *Standard* was augmented by at least an additional £600 from the monthly, the unaccountable Irishman still managed to keep in debt. It is true, he had his wife and three children to support, but £1,000 was in those days an adequate income for even a fairly indulgent father of a family. Furthermore, as has been said, Maginn's writing was at no time confined to the periodicals with which he was most intimately connected, and the wandering pen of O'Doherty was constantly augmenting the evanescent budget. Yet Maginn, true Bohemian that he was, royally spent his last shilling and borrowed his next. Destitution in others, as we have seen, he could not witness without trying to relieve. The relief might involve the doubtful ethics of giving bread when he was in debt to his baker; but for Maginn the baker's privation was a matter of the future and therefore a less poignant evil. Even his own family finally gave up the task of trying to restrain his irresponsible expenditure.

When he was himself hundreds of pounds in debt, he lent money promiscuously out of his recently paid salary, signed notes with indulgence, and lavishly entertained his friends on credit. On one occasion, Douglas Jerrold, who was among Maginn's guests at his favorite tavern, the Scalopian, came to his host's rescue to the amount of £10, the cost of the dinner. While the meal was in progress he had overheard in an adjoining room a noisy altercation between the care-free patron and the long-suffering proprietor, who was refusing to extend credit to cover the viands then being consumed before his enraged eyes. Realizing doubtless that the innkeeper, if not the persuasive Irishman, was in need of help, Jerrold tactfully settled the account,[46] probably to Maginn's regret. For Jerrold eventually was repaid, and it is doubtful if the innkeeper would have fared as well.

In 1833, after he had been receiving for three years the salaries from two full-sized jobs, the finances of the irresponsible Irishman remained a problem to his friends. "I don't suppose," Lockhart writes to Blackwood, "he has taken any step to wipe out his debt to you any more than to myself, and fear next Xmas we shall hear again of his being as bad as ever in money affairs."[47] About this time Maginn, as we have seen, received an additional sum, not less than £100 and possibly as much as £500, for helping Thackeray edit his short-lived *National Standard*.[48] Yet Lockhart's prediction was speedily to prove correct. In 1834 Maginn was in a garret on Wych Street, in the London slums, hiding from the vigilance of sheriff's officers. Later in the year he was thrown into a sponging house. Lockhart and various other friends became so alarmed at his condition that they started a subscription to pay off the more urgent of his creditors. Maginn was hurried off to Belgium till the amount of nearly £1,000 was raised, with which, as Lockhart himself writes, about £3,000 or £4,000 of debt were paid.[49] It was in Maginn's behalf that John Wilson Croker wrote in January, 1835, to Robert Peel, who was then prime minister.

There is a man, whom I am far from recommending for respectability, or even trustworthiness, one Doctor Maginn, but he is a powerful, and has been a useful, partisan writer, though I believe he has libelled both you and me. He is a zealous Conservative. He has been lately, and I fear long, in prison for debt, and was released by a subscription of some of his friends. I could not advise you to do anything

> *ostensible* for him, but 50 *l.* or 100 *l.* given by a third and safe hand—Lockhart, for instance, who managed the subscription that released him—would be well laid out. He is a powerful writer, and has, I think, some claim to be warmed by the sunshine, short and wintry as it may be, that now exhilarates his party.[50]

We learn that Peel, under a request for secrecy, at once sent the £100 to assist the man who had vehemently attacked him for the previous five years.[51]

Dips into slum life and debtors' prison, and a wide and varied acquaintance in the modern Babylon, as London was called, in no way lessened either Maginn's popularity or his prestige. His health suffered seriously,[52] but his reputation would seem, if anything, to have increased. In 1836 when Charles Dickens started *Bentley's Miscellany* the actinic Maginn was still at the height of his power. He was looked upon as so incontestably the leading periodical writer of the day that he was asked to furnish the opening editorial of the new venture. Comments on Maginn by his contemporaries during these years record his unusual mental alacrity and vigor. Thackeray speaks of a morning with Maginn as

> one of the pleasantest I ever passed. Maginn read Homer to me, and he made me admire it as I had never done before. . . . His remarks were extraordinarily intelligent and beautiful, mingled with much learning, a great deal of wit, and no ordinary poetical feeling.[53]

Carlyle also writes of him in his notebook after the first evening in his company:

> A rattling Irishman, full of quizzicality and drollery, without ill-nature, without earnestness, certainty of conviction or purpose in regard to *any* subject, except this one: *Punch* is *Punch*. A shortish thick-set man (looks upwards of forty) with a fine (almost genial) gray eye; wears a wig. Is the proper Palinurus and originator of *Fraser's Magazine;* wherein and in the *Standard* Newspaper, he finds his chief threshing-floor at present. I understand he "works mostly for the *dead horse* [the Tory party]."[54]

The lenity of this comment is the more conspicuous because with the lighter side of life Carlyle usually had little patience. Momentarily tempted by curiosity he had recently ventured to attend one of the Fraserian Round-Table dinners, and had come away heartily disgusted by the conversation, which was, he writes his brother, "about the basest I ever assisted in."[55] In regard to the same unfortunate dinner he sets down in his notebook: "Two objects would reduce me to gravity had I the spirits of a Merry Andrew: a Death's Head and a modern London Wit."[56]

More analytical is Lockhart's playfully exaggerated account of his friend's reputation, which was contributed to the famous "Portrait Gallery" of "Regina," as *Fraser's Magazine* was playfully called. With his eye on the subject, he writes that Maginn left "no moment absolutely idle," and that he allowed "no sense, however just, of superiority" to influence conduct or demeanor. Following this comment is the staggering summary of the Doctor's scholarly and literary achievement:

> Be a Bentley, if you can, but omit the brutality—rival Parr, eschewing all pomposity—outlinguist old Magliabecchi, and yet be a man of the world—emulate Swift in satire, but suffer not one squeeze of his *sæva indignatio* to eat your own heart. Be and do all this, and THE DOCTOR will no longer be unique.

Lockhart comes to the end of his Hibernian flattery with a brief review of Maginn's life:

> Whether shining a precocious gem, in Trinity College, Dublin . . . or sustaining the power and glory of Blackwood—or now co-editing the grand, unrivaled, staunch, sturdy organ of orthodoxy, the *Standard* – (we say nothing of a casual contribution to *Regina*) the redoubted O'DOHERTY has always been, is, and ever will be, the jovial also, the simple-hearted, the careless, and the benignant. FLOREAT DOCTOR!—Long may he continue at once the star of our erudition, our philosophy, and our dialectics, and, in his own immortal words,
>
> "A randy, bandy, brandy, no Dandy,
> Rollicking jig of an Irishman!"[57]

A description of Maginn at work among the Fraserians in the publisher's back parlor on the nights before the magazine went to press gives some idea of the power which lay behind the sportive and beguiling manner of the editor. He wrote, one of the Fraserians tells us, without pausing over his paper for words or ideas, seldom revising or altering what he had once penned, "or caring to look over his draft before sending it to the printer." His articles were full of allusion, frequently rather closely drawn analogies or direct quotations; yet Maginn was never known to look up a reference or appeal to a friend for a point or a phrase that eluded him. The tales that were told of his feats of memory are astounding. It was said that after a lapse of years he could recall a passage on some obscure matter which he had had no occasion to think of in the interim; and he could regularly be depended on to give the details of an event which was months old with as much fullness and accuracy as if he had just read the accounts of it in the morning papers of the day. Kenealy, who was himself one of the best informed members of the magazine's staff, says of the editor:

> Often when in want of some scholastic illustration for our own writing, have we applied to him, and never did we ask in vain. Quotations the most apposite: episodes the most befitting; obscure points of literary history, an elucidation of which we had ineffectually hunted for; sketches of minor literary men of other lands, the difficulty of finding which those conversant with such studies alone can appreciate; stray lines and sentences from authors read only once in a lifetime, and quoted but as curiosities; parallel passages in Greek and Latin and Italian and German authors; all these he could refer to without a moment's deliberation, as easily as if they had formed the business of his whole life.[58]

Since coming to London Maginn had in his own inevitable way fashioned for himself a biddable audience among magazine readers and a close following of literary men. Mrs. Thomson, a chatty essayist and novelist of that day, describes him on one occasion surrounded by his coterie.

> I made my way into the very thick of the throng. . . . All were standing, all were listening to some one who sat in the middle of a group; a low-seated man, short in stature, was uttering pleasantries, and scattering witticism about him, with the careless glee of his country—this was Maginn. His articulation was impeded by a stutter, yet the sentences which he stammered forth were brilliant repartees, uttered without sharpness, and edged rather with humour than with satire. His countenance was rather agreeable than striking; its expression sweet, rather than bright. The grey hair, coming straight over his forehead, gave a singular appearance to a face still bearing the attributes of youth. [She adds] I looked on for a moment, as the crew of authors, reviewers, playwrights, and novel-weavers paid homage to Dr. Maginn.[59]

The Doctor was indeed one of those men around whom literary anecdote rapidly accumulates. Typically the lovable, daring Bohemian scholar, he was already growing into a tradition. For gratuitous brilliance, he could, like his friend Theodore Hook, be depended upon, giving a natural attention to the repartee of life which needed no external stimulus. He was seldom alone. His encyclopedic information was never disconcerting. Groups grew intimate and loyal in his presence. A shrewd teasing became current, and men told jokes on one another and themselves, unashamed in a company which knew the virtue of human weaknesses. Thus at a dinner, Lockhart swiftly composed the clever one-rhyme epitaph on Maginn[60] which regaled the congenial company and was honored by shouts of laughter from the Doctor himself. The squib, with presumably the addition of the last seven lines, which were too grimly true for forecast, was later privately printed by Lockhart for circulation among friends.

Here, early to bed, lies kind William Maginn,
Who, with genius, wit, learning, life's trophies to win,
Had neither great lord nor rich cit of his kin,
Nor discretion to set himself up as to tin;
So his portion soon spent, like the poor heir of Lynn,
He turned author while yet was no beard on his chin;
And whoever was out, or whoever was in,
For the Tories his fine Irish brains he would spin,
Who received prose and rhyme with a promising grin,
"Go ahead, you queer fish, and more power to your fin,"
But to save from starvation stirred never a pin.
Light for long was his heart, though his breeches were thin,
Else his acting for certain was equal to Quin;
But at last he was beat and sought help from the bin,
(All the same to the Doctor, from claret to gin),
Which led swiftly to gaol with consumption therein.
It was much when the bones rattled loose in his skin,
He got leave to die here out of Babylon's din.
Barring drink and the girls, I ne'er heard of a sin—
Many worse, better few, than bright, broken Maginn!

Occasionally during these years in London glimpses are caught of Maginn's private life. Robert Pearse Gillies describes a walk in spring which he took with Maginn to Wimbleton where Lockhart was living in the hope, only too forlorn, of restoring health to the little son of whom he was so fond. One of the bonds between Lockhart and his friend may well have been the devotion which each of these caustic satirists had to children; and it is not difficult to picture the joy which the visit of the playful Irishman must have brought to the small invalid. Nor was this the only time when Maginn was at Lockhart's home. One of Lockhart's letters to Blackwood mentions that the Doctor had been with him and had given him a "most rich" account of improvising in collaboration with Wordsworth a lyrical ballad, "Betty Martin." The ill-assorted authors had composed and recited in alternation the verses of the poem, much to the amusement, it may be fancied, of the company gathered at Lord Lowther's to help with the Westmoreland elections. We learn, too, that Maginn used to spend whole evenings reading Italian with his own two bright little girls, or helping various of his small friends with their Greek, or playing games, and asking questions on history. We find him, too, a frequent guest at the soirées of Lady Blessington in Gore House, and with his friend, Theodore Hook, playing an increasingly conspicuous part in the literary Bohemia of the taverns. As an improvisator he was reported almost as skillful as the renowned editor of the *Bull*.

Various stories are told of Maginn at this time, some of which are presumably apocryphal. We learn from Jerdan that he used to run home from the tavern at a little dogtrot, his head full of whisky punch and the good counters of a friendly evening, his legs too unsteady to walk, but able to keep a fairly straight course at the quicker pace. We have also the pleasant but unfortunately more doubtful account of Maginn's eluding a bailiff who was trying to arrest him for debt. Dodging down an alley in swift flight to the River Thames, the wisp of an Irish waif seized the only boat in sight, rowed to midstream where he climbed on board a huge barge waiting for the tide and fell into talk with the men who were drinking and smoking in the moment of leisure. In a burst of fine enthusiasm he speedily brought them to such a high pitch of loyalty for the glorious institutions of England that, when he explained he himself was a martyr in defense of those institutions, they emptied their pockets for him to pay off the bailiff who was still pacing the shore.

No better account of Maginn's brilliant roguery is to be found than in the mocking verse of one of his prime enemies, Alaric A. Watts, who was eventually so exasperated by the pranks of the Irishman that he brought the action for libel to which we have already referred in connection with *Fraser's* quarrels. After due mention of the "drunken deevilries" and "pothouse jokes" of "Pat" Maginn and his fellow roisterers, including Crofton Croker, Watts concludes:

> Give him a glass or two of whisky,
> And in a trice he grows so frisky,
> So full of frolic, fun, and satire,
> So ready dirt around to scatter,
> And so impartial in his blows
> They fall alike on friends and foes.
> Nay, rather than his humour balk,
> His mother's son he'd tomahawk!
> And so he can but set once more
> His boon companions "in a roar"
> Will scruple not, good-natured elf,
> To libel his illustrious self!—
> A task so difficult, I own,
> It can be done by him alone.[61]

CHAPTER IX

THE STORY OF L.E.L.

Quite suddenly, in 1836, while Maginn was still a powerful and pampered literary dictator with the habit of punishing and praising whom he pleased, he separated himself from the staffs of both *Fraser's* and the *Standard,* relinquishing his authority as erratically and completely as he had gained it. At this time Maginn had been in London for twelve years, for the first three rising precariously but rapidly to a position of preëminence in the English press, and for the succeeding nine maintaining that position. But the moment had arrived when he was to plunge with apparent determination into adversity. Neither his friends nor his three children, to whom he was deeply attached, could check him; nor yet his own fine scholarship, which was never more alert than during these years of his swift decline.

To understand this last period of Maginn's life it is necessary to go back to the summer of 1821. When the aspiring young Doctor made his first visit to London, he formed what was to be a lifelong attachment for Letitia Elizabeth Landon, famous as L.E.L. Half the literary men in London were already in love with her or were about to be in love with her, for Letitia was witty and feminine. More than that, gossip had hummed about her even in her teens, although her only indiscretion would seem to have been that she was unconventional and had the misfortune to become the most popular poetess of England and the chief reviewer for William Jerdan's *Literary Gazette.*

Today it seems clear that the relation of L.E.L. both to Jerdan and to Maginn sprang from the underestimated bond of quick brains and ready tongues and not as rumor had it from a mercenary desire on her part to gain editorial support in publishing her books. To begin with her poems were immediately popular and stood in no need of "puffing," being facile and sentimental, and prized by the publishers and the public. Unquestionably also she gave to Jerdan, who was middle-aged and inclined to be indolent, far more help than she received, not only saving him the task of writing book reviews for his periodical, but constantly aiding him in its editing. Although Maginn was supposed to have assisted her with her own annual, *Fisher's Drawing Room Scrap Book,*[1] which came out in the silken array of Christmas gift books, such generosity, providing it existed, would have argued little from one of his disbursive temperament.

It is not strange, however, that rumors multiplied about her. No woman could at that time have held her position on the *Gazette* without becoming the center of scandal—and scandal moreover of a peculiarly envenomed nature. An adverse review in the *Gazette,* as Hall records in his *Memories,* ordinarily in the 1830's resulted in the failure of the book[2] and frequently in the enmity of the author. Literary hostilities were still looked upon as involving personal honor, and were occasionally settled by the sword or pistol. Since L.E.L. had no relatives who could protect her she was particularly open to more insidious forms of attack, which eventually culminated in anonymous letters warning her suitors of the circulated slanders.

According to her friends, the reports and letters tortured her almost beyond endurance.[3] Although spontaneous and unconventional, she was as sensitive to criticism as the most sheltered woman in that day of sheltered womanhood, and was as subject to overwrought emotions, self-pity, despondency, even to the "spasms" which afflicted so many of her sex. In her anxiety to protect her reputation she lived with two straight-laced spinster schoolmarms, the Misses Lance of Hans Place, submitting herself to their rigid rules, her friend Mrs. Hall informs us, as dutifully as if she were their youngest pupil.[4] Here in the little room at the top of the house she did her writing; here she gathered around her a close circle of women friends, loyal and devoted to her. Even the servants were said to be attached to her,[5] so easily did she transmit her mood to others. Miss Emma Roberts, one of her housemates, affirms that her whole life was spent in a domestic circle of her own sex, who were cognizant of her actions and among whom "no cloud ever arose."[6]

L.E.L.'s coquettish unconventionality may be seen in Anna Maria Hall's description of her first call upon the spritely little poetess, who at the moment chanced to be making a huge, beribboned cap for her grandmother. On failing to please the old lady, the girl of twenty-three set it on her own pretty head and curtsied gayly from the room, quite as if she had always known her visitor and had not been meeting her for the first time. The scene entranced the Irish novelist, who looked upon L.E.L. as a bewitching and brilliant child, although she herself was not more than twenty-five—barely two years older. The famous poetess was, she writes,

a bright-eyed, sparkling, restless little girl, in a pink gingham frock, grafting clever things on commonplace nothings, frolicking from subject to subject with the playfulness of a spoiled child, her dark hair put back from her low, yet broad forehead. . . . Her movements were as rapid as those of a squirrel; I wondered how any one so quick could be so graceful.

Then quite gravely Mrs. Hall adds:

I do not think that during the long intimacy that followed that child-like meeting, extending from the year 1825 to her leaving England in 1837, during which time I saw her nearly every day, and certainly every week—I do not think she ever loved me as I loved her; how could she? But I was proud of the confidence and regard she bestowed on me, and would have given half my own happiness to have sheltered her from the envy and evil that embittered the spring and summer-time of her blighted life. It always seemed to me impossible not to love her, not to cherish her. . . . she rendered you completely oblivious of what she had done, by the irresistible charm of what she was. You forgot all about her books; you only felt the intense delight of life with her.[7]

Another aspect of L.E.L. is given by Macready. After visiting John Forster, who was supposed to be engaged to the poetess, the famous actor makes the following entry in his diary under November, 1835:

Called on Forster, and stayed some time listening to a tale of wretched abandonment to passion that surprised and depressed me. He told me that he had been on the point of marriage with Miss L———, but that rumours and stories pressed in such number and frightful quality upon him that he was forced to demand explanation from one of the reported narrators or circulators, Mr. A. A. Watts[8]—that his denial was positive and circumstantial, but that it was arranged between themselves and their mutual friends that the marriage should be broken off. A short time after Forster discovered that Miss L——— made an abrupt and passionate declaration of love to Maclise, and on a subsequent occasion repeated it! It has lately come to light that she has been carrying on an intrigue with Dr. Maginn, a person whom I never saw, but whom all accounts unite in describing as a beastly biped; he is married and has four children. Two letters of hers and one of his were found by Mrs. Maginn in his portrait [portfolio?], filled with the most puerile and nauseating terms of endearment and declarations of attachment! I left quite concerned that a woman of such splendid genius and such agreeable manners should be so depraved in taste and so lost to a sense of what was due to her high reputation. She is fallen![9]

The letters to which Macready here refers Mrs. Maginn had in a moment of angry jealousy carried to John Forster, who in his turn had indignantly carried them to L.E.L. herself. Later both Forster and Mrs. Maginn realized their innocence. Forster tried to make amends, but Letitia wrote definitely ending her engagement to him. Her letter, like so much about her, is spirited, generous, and emotionally overwrought:

Again I repeat, that I will not allow you to consider yourself bound to me by any possible tie. To any friend to whom you may have stated our engagement, I cannot object to your stating the truth. Do every justice to your own kind and generous conduct. I am placed in a most cruel and difficult position. Give me the satisfaction of, as far as rests with myself, having nothing to reproach myself with. The more I think, the more I feel I ought not—I cannot—allow you—to unite yourself with one accused of—I cannot write it. The mere suspicion is dreadful as death.[10]

This rejection of the renewed advances of John Forster leads a modern commentator, Mr. D. E. Enfield, in his biographical study, *L.E.L.: a Mystery of the Thirties,* to conclude that the romantic poetess and tale writer had herself never really known love. He considers that her heavily sentimental stories with their abandonment to the ecstasies of love, adventure, and death were but temporary and unsatisfactory outlets of her own desire and need for the emotion which she herself had not been able to experience.[11] Certainly L.E.L.'s friends, even the most staunch, admitted that she went beyond the proprieties of that day in her informal behavior toward men, and were convinced that her spontaneous expression of whatever feeling chanced to be uppermost sprang from her sense of her own innocence and her childlike inability to attach serious significance to her acts. L.E.L. seems to have been an effervescent little creature, equally attractive to men and women, herself as yet emotionally untouched, an eager and awaiting child. The tension of this state of arrested development, however, would have peculiarly ill fitted L.E.L. to sustain the constant criticism and invidious persecution of anonymous letters to which her position on the *Literary Gazette* subjected her. For this reason the jealous act of Mrs. Maginn which brought to an abrupt close her prospects of marriage to Forster was especially disastrous.

Harmful as the act unquestionably was to the fortunes of L.E.L., it is only fair to consider that it might have been the culmination of years of jealousy on Mrs. Maginn's part. Although her husband had the reputation of being what is commonly called a family man, assiduously attentive to his wife and children, he never lost his idolatrous devotion to L.E.L. His most loyal biographers admit the warmth of his friendship for the little editor of the *Literary Gazette* and the *Drawing Room Scrap Book,* one of them remarking that for years it formed an attraction outside of his home. When *Fraser's* was established, L.E.L. became a member of its staff, contributing, according to the statement of the magazine itself, tales as well as poetry to its volumes. The bond thus offered, in addition to informal affiliation on the *Scrap Book,* might easily have caused Mrs. Maginn to suspect that an intellectual comradeship existed between her husband and the poetess which lay beyond her own power to share or comprehend. Edward Kenealy, staunch friend of Maginn's later years, in commenting on the connubial life of the witty editor, reveals a nervous disability in Mrs. Maginn which today one cannot help feeling might have resulted from a sense of frustration. On one occasion he describes waiting till a rather noisy altercation on the other side of a thin partition terminated in Maginn's being forced into a clean shirt.[12] Elsewhere he gives a shrewish picture of Mrs. Maginn in his brief extenuation of her husband's drunkenness: "Let us remember also that he had the misfortune to render applicable to him the bitterest part of the Epigram of Phillipides."[13] Then follow the lines on the mean, though rich, wife, with the comment that in Maginn's case there had been no consolation of riches. Although Kenealy felt only antagonism toward Mrs. Maginn, we cannot wholly overlook the possibility here presented of an unsatisfied emotional life.

The consequences of Mrs. Maginn's submitting the letters to Forster were disastrous to herself and her husband, as well as to the poetess.

In spite of Maginn's generosity and extravagance, it is doubtful if his family had up to this time suffered any real privation. With Mrs. Maginn's jealous action, however, came a sharp change. While continuing to some extent to support his family, Maginn was frequently away from home during the better part of two years, completely estranged from his wife by her act. In those days when a betrothal was almost as sacred as marriage, its breaking was nearly as harmful to a woman's reputation as a divorce. In the case of L.E.L. it doubtless gave color in the opinion of many of her contemporaries to the reports which were current about her. Maginn was unable to forgive his wife for the suffering which she had caused Letitia and for the disaster which she had brought into the poetess's life. Nor was he able to forgive himself as the indirect cause. Drawing his books and his friends closely around him, he drank deeply and satiated himself with study and the great diversion of talk. More and more hopelessly he sank into debt, living in the foulest slums to escape the vigilance of sheriffs. In his fear of arrest, he absented himself from the office of the *Standard* and from Fraser's shop in Regent Street, and within a short time ceased to be connected in any regular way with either the paper or the magazine, although he still continued desultory contributions to both. The shift in the editorship of *Fraser's* is whimsically recorded in the issue of October 1, 1836, of the *Carlton Chronicle,* directed by Maginn's friend, Percival Weldon Banks, himself a prominent Fraserian. Banks, who regretted the substitution of Father Prout for Maginn, comments on the fictitious Nol Yorke: "Of late he might be generally described as Proutian; but look on him for any length of time, and you will find that he is Protean."

Maginn's desertion of the periodical which he had founded might indicate that his wife's action was but one factor in a sudden general disintegration of his character were it not that his mental life seemed if anything to quicken, as if receiving a fuller allowance of his time and energy. It was at this period that he did his most scholarly and detailed work on Shakespeare and Homer, apparently finding patience for research when other fields of expression had been closed to him. He would seem also at this time to have been concerned about paying his debts to personal friends. In a letter to James Fraser, February, 1838, Thackeray explains in regard to Maginn:

He reiterates his determination to write monthly for you, and to deliver over the proceeds to me. Will you, therefore, have the goodness to give the bearer a check (in my wife's name) for the amount of his contributions for the last two months?[14]

According to this statement, Maginn had already for two months been contributing articles to the magazine in order that payment might be made to Thackeray. Evidently the publisher, not fully understanding his intention, was still holding the money till Maginn himself should call for it. This commendable effort to pay Thackeray called forth some of Maginn's best work. His famous "Homeric Ballads" were apparently undertaken with this purpose in mind, since they began with his contributions for January, the proceeds of which were to go to Thackeray. Among other thoughtful writing which immediately followed were the long and erudite ferreting out of Southey's secret, "The Doctor," for February and March, the clever "Murphy, the Meteorological Quack," for March, and the excellent article, "Mitchell's *Life of Wallenstein*," for April.

Maginn's editorship of *Fraser's* would have terminated less unhappily had he not in August, 1836, published a review of a novel by the Honorable Grantley Berkeley which we have mentioned in connection with *Fraser's* suits for libel.[15] The author was so infuriated that he made a personal assault on the publisher which was of incredible brutality and barely escaped being fatal.[16] On hearing of the outrage, Maginn at once acknowledged the authorship of the article and accepted the challenge of Berkeley. It would scarcely be possible to make the account of the beating of Fraser too lurid; even as staid a paper as the *Times* gave space in two successive issues, August 4 and 5, to its revolting details and censured the young noblemen, Grantley Berkeley and his brother Craven, for their cowardly attack on a defenseless man who was physically small and frail. Maginn was everywhere blamed for the review, though it was admitted to be a lively bit of writing, and was praised out of all proportion for his conduct during the duel.

From the first he seems to have been indifferent as to the outcome, paying so little attention to his aim that his first shot struck the ground a short distance from his own foot. Asked if he wished to fire another in its place, he replied casually that it might as well stand. Later in the duel he was questioned as to whether or not he wished the shooting to continue and remarked, "Blaze away, by God! a barrel of powder!" When Maginn's second interfered after the third round of shots, Berkeley left the field in bad blood, as the saying goes. He informs us in his memoirs, that had he been using the type of pistol to which he was accustomed he could have hit every button on his adversary's coat.[17]

Maginn's listlessness in the face of death, for Berkeley was one of the famous shots of his time and was supposed to be infallible, was indicative of his attitude in regard to everything that concerned himself at this time. According to Mrs. Thomson, he writhed at reference to the excruciating suffering of Fraser; yet he could be got to pay not the slightest attention either to his own health, which was alarmingly poor, or to his fortune.

In 1838, news reached London that L.E.L. had died under painful circumstances. For the two older men who had loved her the blow was heavy. Jerdan writes in his memoirs that he fell down insensate; Maginn was said to have been almost out of his senses for two days, and shortly before his own death in 1842, he felt, according to Kenealy, that he saw Letitia sitting reproachfully by his side. Nor was their sorrow without great cause. After a grim and mysterious marriage with a taciturn Captain Maclean, L.E.L. went with her husband to his isolated post on the wild coast of West Africa. Here two months later, October 15, 1838, sho was found in her bedroom dead from an overdose of prussic acid. The fate of the poetess caused consternation in England. Not only the newspapers at the time but diaries and letters for years afterward expressed grief at her mysterious end and revealed the wide affection in which she was held. Nor was the consternation lessened when it was learned that although her death might have been accidental, resulting from an overdose of the acid which according to the testimony of her husband and servant at the inquest she had occasionally taken to ward off spasms,[18] there was reason to think that the poison might have been forced upon her or that she might have taken it intentionally.

Madden, an English commissioner who a few months after the tragedy had visited Cape Coast Castle, as the post's fort was called, exclaimed in amazement:

How far the principles of medical jurisprudence are consonant with the practice at Cape Coast Castle in a case like this, of a lady alive and well between the hours of eight and nine in the morning, suddenly carried off by poison—a corpse before noon—the subject of a Coroner's inquest without a post mortem examination, coffined before sunset, and buried in a courtyard of a house she had been a living, healthful inmate of, within less than twelve hours of that burial,—is a question which must be determined wholly and solely on its own merits.[19]

It developed that the two chief witnesses had made contradictory statements at the hurried inquest,[20] and that one of these witnesses, L.E.L.'s servant, had apparently been detained in Africa for over a year, although she had been scheduled to return to England. Later it was discovered that letters written by L.E.L. on the night before she died had been withheld,[21] and there were various sinister rumors connected with a Negro mistress who had been hurried from the post at the approach of the English bride.[22]

Yet Madden was far from convinced that L.E.L. had not committed suicide,[23] a doubt which he maintained in spite of his belief that the Maclean servants had attempted to poison himself and that Maclean's "apathy was invincible." Letitia's exaggerated praise of the fort and the scenery, although both he described as dismal in the extreme, together with the reports of her high spirits at the dinners attended by the English in the wretched town of Cape Coast, led him to feel that she had attempted to buoy herself up till, no longer able to sustain the part she was playing, she had taken her own life.

In support of this view were passing references in her letters to not being permitted to enter her husband's room during the day and to being obliged to do work usually assigned to menials; and there was the longer description of her despondence at the approaching departure of her own servant, the only other white woman in the entire post.[24] Her friends also recalled the strange behavior of Maclean before the marriage; his sneering remarks about poetry and poets, especially women; his estrangement from her for months after he had heard the slanders, although he professed scorn for them,[25] and his insistence on a secret ceremony. They had at the time felt that the witty poetess, who was not without an undercurrent of melancholy in spite of her gay sociability, had small chance of happiness with her silent, and as it appeared, reluctant husband, and was ill adapted to a life of utter loneliness at the desolate West African post.

At the same time the testimony given at the inquest by Brodie Cruikshank, the young English officer who had been the guest of the Macleans, indicated that L.E.L.'s death had been accidental, and that her relation to her husband while at Cape Coast Castle had been happy and unstrained.[26] Mrs. Thomson, her confidential friend, reported that Letitia before her marriage had affirmed her love for Maclean.[27] Amid conflicting detail the British authorities made no attempt to pronounce on the cause of death, or even to complete an investigation[28]—and for years the public was to ponder over the poetess's alien grave beneath the pavement of the bare, sun-baked courtyard where the soldiers of the fort were put through their daily drill.

Maginn survived L.E.L. by only a few years. To the end he retained his character of Bohemian wit, growing ever more feeble in health and more shabby in appearance, but retaining his keen mind and alert scholarship. Toward the end one of Blackwood's sons, who had known the Irishman as a gay young visitor in the Edinburgh home, describes meeting him in London and being shocked by his emaciation and his cough. The Doctor, he adds, had given his address as the office of the *Age*,[29] the least reputable of the dailies to which the once ubiquitous pressman and magazinist contributed.

No less forlorn is the account of Maginn's drinking and playing to the last his rôle of practical joker. One of his oldest friends, Quinton Kennedy, narrated that at the end of a day which he himself had devoted to keeping the Doctor sober in order that he might meet a newspaper projector in need of an editor, the ungrateful Irishman suddenly eluded his guard. Stopping before the door of an undertaker, he exclaimed, "By the way, I remember I have an inquiry to make here. Wait for me two minutes." Kennedy patiently walked up and down till Maginn staggered out, too drunk to do more than tell his story. On entering the shop he had held a handkerchief before his face, sobbing out, "Let there be no expense spared; she was worthy, and I can afford it." When the usual consolation of brandy had been set before him and more than the usual amount had been consumed, the undertaker, busied with notes concerning the funeral, said, "Sir, you have not yet told me where she is to be taken to." "Taken to!" exclaimed Maginn, with a regretful glance at the empty bottle, "You may take her to hell."[30]

A more flattering account of the Doctor during these years is given by Kenealy, who was himself writing prolifically for London magazines and was an active member of the *Fraser* staff.

He is a ruin but a glorious ruin, nevertheless. He takes no care of himself. Could he be induced to do so, he would be the first man of the day in literature or in anything else. But he lives a rollicking life; and will write you one of his ablest articles while standing in his shirt or sipping brandy—so naturally do the best and wittiest thoughts flow from his pen.

Kenealy's further comment shows the Doctor as

a slight, boyish, careless figure, with a blue eye, the mildest ever seen—hair not exactly white, but of a sunned snow color—an easy, familiar smile—and a countenance, that you would be more inclined to laugh with, than feel terror from.

In 1839 Maginn succeeded in getting the editorship of the *Lancaster Herald* in Liverpool. Here for a while he charmed his employer with his learning and his anecdotes, but simultaneously drank his cellar dry and ruined his business. Doubtless Maginn's own conscience was clear in the matter. He always did a stupendous amount of writing, but he had lost the knack of persuading the public to accept his paradoxical views on politics.

In 1840, soon after he returned from Liverpool, Maginn brought out serially a collection of his own work. It may be seen today in the British Museum, a dreary little volume of forbidding print and cheap paper. At the time of its publication it was regretted by his admirers and was not bought; and instead of helping Maginn's fortunes it completed their wreck. Its publisher eventually brought suit to cover his own loss; at the beginning of 1842 Maginn was arrested for debt and thrown into the Fleet.

This time the number of pounds involved was too large to be raised by private subscription. When Lockhart and his other friends discovered the gravity of the situation they became alarmed lest the unconcerned Irishman, who had for some years been suffering from tuberculosis, should not survive imprisonment. Finally those who were influential among them succeeded in rushing through the King's Bench a plea for disability on the ground of illness, and Maginn was set at liberty in the spring of 1842. It is a monument to his extravagance that, according to Lockhart, he passed through the Insolvency Court on schedule "of just under £10,000."[31] He himself had from the beginning been bitterly opposed to intervention, and regretted that the appeal was made.

Maginn's life in the Fleet has been described by Richard Oastler, a fellow inmate. Oastler, it will be remembered, was one of the martyrs of the industrial revolution who won for himself so many enemies that the value of his articles exposing the hideous treatment of children in the factories and of other laborers was not recognized until long after his death. When one of these enemies, his former employer, secured his imprisonment for debt, he still continued to issue his indignant pamphlets under the caption of *Fleet Papers.* There was obviously much about this forthright man to appeal to Maginn. As for Oastler, his reminiscences of his companion are full of affection and admiration:

> Poor Maginn! I never think of him but I am thankful that I was consigned to prison—else I never should have known him. . . . He would tap at the door—look in—and if I was alone, he would enter, sit down, chat, read or write, just as our convenience required.

Oastler remembers Maginn's telling him about old English times, pouring forth "stores of knowledge" for his use, criticizing books, and spinning romances while they walked together in the dark Coffee Gallery.

> Often [he continues] has he sat with me at this table; he writing his "leader," and I my "Fleeter," when we passed our slips for mutual examination. How seldom would he alter a word of mine. "You have your own Oastlerian style; I cannot mend it. Perhaps you have repeated such a word too often; so and so would be as well"; and when, as it sometimes happened, I suggested the alteration of a word in his, he would instantly adopt it; and reading the passage would lay strong emphasis on that word; adding, "I thank you, Oastler; it's a great improvement." I mention this to show his great humility. . . . I am a mere babe in literature—he was a giant. . . . But the most delightful times were, when he would say, "where is your Bible?" and then request me to read the Epistle to the Hebrews, or the Romans; he would paraphrase as I read, and ask my opinion with such humility as his great friendship for me could only account for.[32]

Here is certainly one side of Maginn's life in prison. Presumably it was not the only side. James Hannay was also at that time in the Fleet, and Hannay was one of the founders of *Punch* as well as a fine man at the punch bowl. Maginn, while not a founder, was one of the first and sturdiest of its contributors, and as for his libations at the punch bowl, they were always as merry as his laudations of it. Two such valiant upholders in literature and life of bibulous jest and bibulous song probably would not forego the opportunity of mutual regalement. Hannay has left no record of a meeting, but he refers pleasantly to his fellow humorist, and a few months later at the time of Maginn's death, *Punch,* as has been stated, came out for the first time in its now famous black border.

After Maginn's liberation from prison his health was a matter of serious alarm to everyone except himself. His wife, who had remained staunchly at his side in prison, went with him and the three children to the little village of Walton-on-Thames, just outside of London. To relieve him of the burden of constant writing, his friends again circulated a subscription.[33] Peel was once more solicited and, this time purely out of the goodness of his heart, contributed once more from his personal income the sum of £100.[34] Maginn never knew of this act of singular generosity. On August 21, some four months after he left the Fleet, he died of tuberculosis, having just reached the age of forty-eight.

It was characteristic of Maginn that he was very busy even while dying. He wrote for newspapers and magazines to the last day. His favorite books were around him or in his mind: Rabelais, Shakespeare, the Bible, Homer, the folk legends of Ireland. A volume of the last, which he himself had originally helped to edit, he had asked Crofton Croker to lend him. His note to Croker is characteristic:

Dear C.,

Here I am at Walton-on-Thames, coughing my very heart up. The doctors think I am going to die. Will you lend me a copy of Smith's *Cork* and of a book on Fairy Mythology, written either by you or Keighley, or both or neither, some years ago now. I'll return them next week.

I hope all at home are well.

Faithfully yours,
William Maginn.

Walton-on-Thames,
Surrey, Aug. 11.

P.S.—A person will call to-morrow for the vols.[35]

On the Bible, which Maginn had been in the habit throughout his life of studying with his family and friends, he had put his hand just at the end, bidding his children to read it well.[36] Homer is said to have lain at his pillow, and one of the "Homeric Ballads" had not long before been dictated from his lips. Nor did he fail in his rôle of jester:

Have you ever seen my barber, Pindar? [he asked Kenealy]. Yesterday, while he shaved me, I said to him, "Pindar, there was once a celebrated poet of your name in Greece." "He was no relative of mine," says the barber. "I never heard of him before. None of my family ever went to forren parts."

"There was another, too, a namesake of yours, who relates a singular story of a man who used to sell razors that would not shave, and which were made, indeed, only to sell. He was a poet also, and his name was Peter Pindar." "That was a very knowing gentleman," replied the barber, "but I never seed him."[37]

Maginn's burial was in its way also a symbolic tableau of his life.[38] The day was one of gay sunshine and terrific thunder and lightning, of rolling clouds in a brilliant sky from which not a drop of rain descended. As the body was carried toward the grave a resounding bolt broke through the sunshine, as if the heavens in appropriate raillery welcomed the soul of the satirist.

Today Walton-on-Thames is still as sleepy and as prettily diminutive as it was when the dying humorist was taken to it. Visitors can still see the inn where he stayed with his family, a homelike house with a pleasant privacy about it, distinguished by its own trees and hedgerows. Up the street a little way is the rural church with its ancient graveyard where Maginn lies buried, and where a few years ago a Celtic cross was placed to his memory.

Maginn left his family destitute except for his host of friends, who continued loyal in their efforts. The money which was raised in his behalf was immediately turned to their use, and more was collected. Crofton Croker and Prout[39] appealed to the Royal Literary Fund Society. Lockhart was again quick to give aid. Largely through him, positions as governesses were found for the two girls and a commission in the Army was secured from Peel's government for the boy.[40] Nor did interest in the family stop after their immediate needs had been met. The affection which Maginn had awakened in the course of his abrupt life did not die quickly. Years after he had been buried in the little churchyard of Walton-on-Thames there were those who were glad to show their friendship for him by conferring a favor on some member of his family. Even the children of his brother received scholarships at St. Paul's through the efforts of the "Doctor's" well-wishers.[41]

Maginn's son when still a young man was overcome by heat during service in India. As a result his mind became slightly affected and it was necessary for him to retire. One of his daughters died young, but the other had as happy and prosperous a life as he could have wished.

CHAPTER X

ENEMIES

At the time of Maginn's death it was felt that he had done himself sharp injustice by promoting the work of others without giving thought to his own. The more emphatic his genius appeared, the more complete was the sense of its frustration. Yet though Maginn's work had fallen short of what was expected of him, the man himself had so acutely impressed his own generation that his genius remained unquestioned. And a sad shaking of heads commenced over his meager accomplishment. To those who would recall not unsympathetically the heyday of wine-whetted camaraderie Maginn became a martyr among jesters, sacrificing his rightful fame to the glory of an evening. To more exacting critics he was a spendthrift, wasting through lack of self-control powers which might have been put to brilliant use.

Both points of view were incorrect, yet both persisted till the once busy and productive editor was eventually metamorphosed by tradition into an unscrupulous prodigal of wit, wisdom, and wine. Strangely enough four men of sharply differing temperaments were chiefly responsible for the change. Above the shadows that have fallen on Maginn's memory stand the Pecksniffian figure of Samuel Carter Hall, the ample frame of Thackeray, the quizzical, mocking ghost of the Dublin Doctor himself, and the pugilistic bulk of Grantley Berkeley.

To do Thackeray justice, his share in the misinterpretation of Maginn was unconscious. There is not the slightest evidence that the author of *Pendennis* ever intended Shandon, the rake of a newspaper editor whom young Pen met in prison, to represent the powerful, if eccentric, editor of *Fraser's*. The zeal to find prototypes for Thackeray's characters has produced no theory that has run more conspicuously counter to the facts than has the alleged Shandon-Maginn analogy. To begin with, Thackeray himself quite clearly states that he had another person than Maginn in mind for his ne'er-do-well editor, a clever newspaper man of his day named Jack Sheehan. He writes to a friend, John Moreland Crawford:

You will find much to remind you of old talks and faces—of William John O'Connell, Jack Sheehan, and Andrew Archedecne—in this book. There is something of you in Warrington.[1]

Four men are mentioned here. Three of them have been accepted as undisputed originals of Thackeray's characters. Jack Sheehan alone, although accepted by Mr. O'Donoghue, the learned librarian of Dublin, in the account of the Irish journalist in the *Dictionary of National Biography,* has been generally overlooked and Maginn, entirely without sanction of the author, has been put in his place. Nor is the argument for the choice of Maginn more scholarly than the initial dropping of the name of Sheehan. It has been earnestly reasoned that since Shandon was Pen's first editor and Maginn was Thackeray's first editor, Shandon must be Maginn. The error here is fundamental. Maginn was not Thackeray's first editor, and it probably would not have occurred to the author of *Pendennis* to think of him as such. The situation would seem to have been if anything the reverse, for, it is to be remembered, Thackeray began his relations with *Fraser's* editor by being his employer, having paid some hundred or more pounds to secure his help with the *National Standard.*[2] Furthermore, Thackeray was at the start more of a journalist than a magazinist, and it was only in the latter capacity that he worked with Maginn. Other discrepancies are as conspicuous. Shandon does not support the English Church and is stated in the novel to be at swords' points in this matter with another journalist. Now Maginn, as a stout Orangeman, we have seen was valiant in his attachment to the cause of the Church, ready to champion it against dissenters, the Catholic party, or any other party, as the core of his religion and his politics. No one who knew him by either his writing or his reputation would have thought of representing him as pro-Catholic. Equally absurd would have been the idea of picturing him as the slave-driven hack of the London publishers, Colburn and Bentley. Both men had been prominent for years among the butts of *Fraser's Magazine* and were known as the particular *bêtes noires* of Maginn, who had scored them almost countless times with most high-handed savagery. Yet Colburn and Bentley are the prototypes of the rival publishers in *Pendennis.* Shandon too is made to read aloud to an admiring audience an editorial of his own composition, a pompous inflated affair which Thackeray obviously intended as a burlesque on the style of journalists who were willing to write on either side of a question. Much of the same kind of burlesque had already appeared in Maginn's "Tobias Correspondence,"[3] with which Thackeray must have been familiar and which he would scarcely have thus turned against its author. Whatever sins, moreover, might be laid to Maginn, satisfaction in his own literary achievements was not among them. He not only expressed contempt for his articles[4] but was known not to take any interest in them once they were penned.[5] Uncharacteristic of him, also, is Shandon's pathetic dependence for classical flourishes on Burton's *Anatomy of Melancholy*. As a matter of fact, Maginn is a conspicuous exception to his age in his freedom from the customary Latin tag. We look in vain in his writing for the usual application of classical unguent; yet, had he chosen to fill his work with learned allusion, so agile a scholar and translator as he would scarcely have needed even such a pleasurable source of excerpt as Burton.

In short, the more one investigates the Shandon-Maginn theory the more preposterous it becomes. Even the points which at first thought seem significant prove of little bearing. Thus we remember that Shandon's wife, like Mrs. Maginn, accompanied her beloved profligate to prison, only to notice that Thackeray's good lady is an exact replica of his own gentle little Mary in *The Great Hoggarty Diamond,* which he wrote for *Fraser's* itself while Maginn was still alive. Like Mary, Mrs. Shandon not only followed her lord and master to the Fleet but prettily bargained with his creditors for his release. Thackeray indeed knew but two kinds of wives; those who wished to thrust their husbands into prison and those who would have given their lives to pull them out.

As for Shandon, although according to his author he has a prototype in Jack Sheehan, he is probably best thought of as a caricature of the journalists in general of Thackeray's day. He is Irish, as for the most part were they; he cares little about his dress and much about his whiskey, and in neither respect does he differ from them; he is bent on his own ruin, and they were not averse to theirs; he writes on both sides of a question, and they, we are given to understand, were very apt to do so.

It is on this last point that further caution needs to be given in regard to Maginn. Wherever one turns among the more recent comments on him one finds that his reputation has suffered unreasonably through the Shandon mix-up. Because Thackeray's ne'er-do-well was willing to write on either or both sides of a question according to the exigencies of his pocketbook, it has been taken for granted that in Thackeray's own opinion Maginn was unscrupulous also, and irrespective of his personal convictions was willing to put his pen to hire.

It is only fair to say that Thackeray's Shandon was not entirely responsible for this subsequent relegation of Maginn to the shadier ranks of journalism. The Irishman's own "Tobias Correspondence" was misinterpreted as a personal confession that he wrote on both sides of a subject. The danger of being a satirist has long been recognized, and it is well known that Daniel Defoe was not the only innocent man pilloried for supposing the reading public to be intelligent. Although Maginn has suffered no more than others, it is time for reason and fair play to intervene. Let it be stated definitely that his "Tobias Correspondence" is not autobiographic, and was never intended as an admission of its author's personal lack of integrity. There is a sternness and despondency about the "Correspondence" which is not usually found outside of Swift, and which makes the work one of Maginn's most incisive criticisms of his own day. He was describing the vapid machinations and lies of the newspaper world. That it was the world which he knew best did not lessen his bitterness or his scathing accuracy of discernment. In the "Correspondence" he shows, with an artful eye chiefly on Whig delinquencies, how the topics of the day, such as the Corn Laws, currency, Catholics, Dissenters, education, factories, finance, could be handled by editors to meet any political exigency which might arise, arguments and statistics under swift rephrasing being made to serve with apparently equal validity either side of the question. To construe these double-faced letters as a confession of the writer's own sins is to make them a morbid drone of intolerable length. Nor would such a confession have been in keeping with Maginn, who was almost indecently free from introspection and never showed even normal interest in his own shortcomings. Nor again would it have been in keeping with his reputation during his lifetime.

As we have seen, Maginn's political stand was as strikingly independent as it was vigorous. Since his freebooting touched on both Tory and Radical issues, he confessedly wrote for both Tory and Radical newspapers, among them that fine champion of radicalism the *True Sun*. Yet for all that, his devotion to the Conservative cause was so fervid that during his lifetime it was never questioned. Abusive of Tory leaders as he was and drastic as were his proposals that they adopt practical reforms, no one ever intimated that he was double-faced or even faint-hearted in his Toryism. Maginn had bitter opponents among the writers for the *New Monthly Magazine,* the *Westminster Review,* and other Whig and Radical publications, who would certainly have used against him, so easy and effective a weapon as the selling of his own pen, had such an accusation been possible; but we search contemporary records in vain for any hint of duplicity associated with his name. As irrefutable evidence of his loyalty to the Conservative cause it will be remembered that just before his death Sir Robert Peel, who had ample means to acquaint himself with Maginn's record and was not a man to make mistakes, contributed £100 to relieve his suffering. Since Maginn had attacked Peel personally, and was then broken and no longer to be feared, a higher tribute to his services could not have been paid.

It is possible that Samuel Carter Hall was among those who literalized the "Tobias Correspondence," regarding it as a confession of its author's guilt. In his autobiography he states that Maginn unscrupulously wrote for both the Whigs and the Tories,[6] and it is scarcely credible that he based this accusation on his personal knowledge of the Doctor, of whose Tory prejudices he had with good reason bitterly complained when he himself was editor and contributor of the *New Monthly*. Since, during his numerous clashes with Maginn, he had never accused the exasperating Irishman of literary dishonesty, we may safely infer that it had not at the time entered his head to do so. Hall's autobiography was not published till 1883, forty-one years after the death of his rival, and it may well be that in the long interval his own impressions had become confused with hearsay arising from Shandon and Tobias. The supposition is the more probable because in his earlier account of Maginn, written for the *Art Journal* in 1865, Hall had spoken of Maginn's connection with the Radical press[7] but had made no mention of any Whig association. Nor is there contemporary evidence that he ever contributed to a Whig organ.

The real trouble was that the Irish Doctor was cherished as a famous wit long after any accurate impression of the man remained, and no report of him, such as his being Shandon's prototype or his having confessed his own sins in "Tobias" was in consequence likely to fail of repetition or specious confirmation. Unfortunately, also, since he was altogether too good a contributor to *Punch* to be trusted with his own or anybody else's reputation, adverse criticism of him unduly multiplied because his witticisms were taken seriously. For instance, on being confronted with a demand for hints as to how to write for the daily press, he dodged the ponderous question with the reply, "Read the 'Tobias Correspondence.' There is the whole art and mystery of editing a newspaper." On another occasion when asked if the wine which he had purchased from an excellent house was not unduly expensive, he lightly turned aside his inquisitive mentor by gayly quoting, perhaps from Sheridan, that he "supposed something *was* put down in a book." His less agile commentator, Samuel Carter Hall, not recognizing either the source of the retort or the mood in which it was made, solemnly repeated it as a weighty instance of Maginn's irresponsibility and extravagance, and used it to illustrate the evil effects of his drunkenness.[8]

Few men were worse qualified to write on Maginn than Hall. As one of the temperance leaders of his day, he was the author of sensational little tales in verse and prose descriptive of the fate of drunkards and the abuses darkening their families.[9] His objection to liquor, conspicuous in a time when it was more customary to drink wine and beer than water, led him occasionally, in his reminiscences, to adopt a severe tone in speaking of his contemporaries, such as Carlton and Prout, and doubtless helped to fasten upon him the reputation of being the original of Dickens's Pecksniff. Certainly for one reason or another he was famous for his caustic criticisms. In the case of Maginn especially, he had fought too many battles when that hard-drinking and hard-hitting wit was alive to find amiable things to say when he was dead.

Another aged commentator on Maginn who would seem to have been influenced either directly or indirectly by the wily "Tobias Correspondence" is Dr. J. F. Clarke. His remarks are confined to one short paragraph, but they have been referred to so frequently as offering dire confirmation of Maginn's untrustworthy habits, that it might be well to let them appear for once in all their original blackness. Moreover they are interesting as showing what a famous conversationalist was like when in uncongenial company. Dr. Clarke speaks:

> Maginn, the most versatile of writers, was scarcely anything "off the stage." He had what some one called a kind of "gin-and-water face," so far as colour went, but his features were regular and his eyes expressive, his forehead broad and expanded. He would sit in company drinking his "gin-twist," no matter how many glasses. He seldom spoke, but had a habit of biting short pieces of straw by the hour together. He professed to be a Conservative, but I believe he had unsettled principles, and was of the opinion, with Chatterton, that a man "ought to be able to write as well on one side of the question as the other." At all events, he carried out this doctrine, for he would write a leader in the *Standard* one evening; answer it in the *True Sun* the following day, and abuse both in the *John Bull* on the ensuing Sunday. He was the Ensign O'Doherty of *Blackwood's* "Noctes," and at one time Editor of *Fraser's Magazine*.[10]

When one looks over this short comment which has made so long a to-do, one realizes that the quotation about being "able to write as well on one side of the question as the other" might well have had its base in the "Tobias Correspondence," here applied to its author through reference to the *Standard*, the *True Sun*, and the *Bull*, three of the organs with which he was most closely connected. The reminiscences of Dr. Clarke appeared in 1874, thirty-two years after the death of Maginn. Possibly by the time the worthy physician came to write them he had forgotten all about the burlesque "Correspondence," if indeed he had ever known of it and was not merely remembering that he had once come across some rather interesting gossip about William Maginn.

It is unfortunate that the testimony of both Hall and Clarke was delayed for the better part of half a century, and therefore till long after Maginn and his friends had died. Of all the old *Fraser* staff—Lockhart, Croker, Hook, Prout, Jerdan—who had known Maginn's individual slant on politics, not one was alive to defend him against the attacks. It is also unfortunate that the reminiscences of both Hall and Clarke were published only a comparatively few years before

Richard Garnett wrote the life of Maginn for the *Dictionary of National Biography*. Garnett mentions that all the famous editor's contemporaries, with the exception of Hall and Clarke, spoke of him with admiration and kindness; but he himself quite naturally, none the less, accepts the adverse testimony of these detractors. Their statements were too emphatic and of too recent a date for him to overlook. He gives generous credit to Maginn's brilliance both of reputation and accomplishment, but he is appalled by the Hall-Clarke references to duplicity, and regrets that a man of genius should have thrown so much discredit upon his profession.

In the same way Mrs. Oliphant's account of Maginn in her study of *Blackwood's* published in 1897 was presumably colored by the slurs of Hall and Clarke, as well as by the estimate of Richard Garnett in the *Dictionary of National Biography,* which was based upon them and was even nearer to the date of her own writing. Anything favorable which she has to say of the once voluminous *Blackwood's* correspondent is coupled with adverse comment. She admits, as has been stated, the great extent of his writing, his brilliance, his gay humor, his devotion to the publisher's children and their devotion to him;[11] but she reprobates the nature and tone of his work for the magazine. She was herself happily one of the staunchest of Victorians, and was ill at ease with the early obstreperous days of *Blackwood's.* As for Maginn, she finds him the one "who paid the penalty of the follies which they all more or less committed," "the one to whom these follies were not the wild oats of youth, but the tares that choked all the good seed."[12] His brilliant vitality counted little in her estimation because he never learned decency and good manners.

Mrs. Oliphant's criticism is occasionally not only harsh but unjust, probably because she lacked complete data. She censures Maginn, for instance, for not openly declaring himself the author of a libelous article against Professor Leslie.

> It is curious [she writes] that in the face of the danger, pecuniary and other, which Blackwood was thus involved in by his act, the active agent of the mischief remains discreetly behind his shield, too prudent to sign himself as anything more distinct than R.T.S. The most reckless even of gay Irishmen can be reticent when need is.[13]

This seems needlessly severe since the article on which the suit was based was printed not only with the full approval of Blackwood but even with emendations by him.

> It has been so far fortunate [he writes], that this month's has been kept back for the article on Captain Parry's Expedition, as it has enabled us to insert your admirable attack on Professor John, which you will see has not lost any of its points by the hands it has passed through. It was his doctrine and discoveries with regard to freezing, and not heat, which Brewster's Journal proved to be stolen from the Philosophical Transactions, and therefore your notice of his book on heat was altered. The other alterations, I have no doubt, you will approve of, and, to add to the joke, O.P. [Maginn's signature] is baptized Olinthus Petre, D.D., of T.C.D.[14]

That Blackwood himself did not blame Maginn is shown by a letter written some time afterward to Moir. "I have living with me just now," he says by way of inducing Moir to visit him, "my celebrated Cork correspondent, who pummelled Professor Leslie in such grand style."[15]

Unfortunately the two most available sources of information on Maginn have been the accounts by Mrs. Oliphant and Richard Garnett, whose pens were not unguided by Hall and Clarke, and indirectly by that fatal foe of the Doctor's own creation "Anthony Tobias," a series of mishaps which shows that no one should attempt to joke outside the company of the quick-witted, or should make an enemy of a man having both octogenarian and autobiographic propensities.

And with this reflection, the tale of Maginn's detractors should by rights close. Unluckily another aged enemy of a reminiscent turn must still be spoken of, and this time in regard to a charge so revolting and misshapen that it seems preposterous to mention it in connection with the gay and heedless Doctor. There is scarcely another reference to Maginn, the man, which does not mention his personal kindliness, even the humorous epitaph by Lockhart beginning, "Here early to bed lies kind William Maginn"; yet again, a quarter of a century after his death, he was suddenly denounced as the vilest of blackguards. The source of the belated accusation was the Honorable Grantley Berkeley, with whom, it will be remembered, he had fought the duel ending in bad blood.

As in the case of debts, common sense would seem to establish a time limit beyond which old scores should not be opened; yet in the second and third volumes of his autobiography, published in 1866, Berkeley attempts to show that L.E.L. committed a "misstep" which placed her in the power of Maginn, and that "the hoary villain" thereupon pursued his "victim" with anonymous letters, "not for love" but for money. In garish melodrama Berkeley takes the thoroughly authenticated circumstances of Letitia's life, scandalous rumors, anonymous letters, marriage with Maclean, and death in West Africa, and attempts to affix them to his enemy, William Maginn, to whom he gives the rôle of seducer, scandal-bearer, and blackmailer.

Berkeley's testimony is *ex parte,* and was from the first considered so, Richard Garnett and everyone else who went into the subject having found nothing to substantiate it. It would not, indeed, be necessary to refute the charge were it not that Mr. Michael Sadleir in his recent biography, *Bulwer and His Wife: a Panorama,* accepts Berkeley's statement; and Mr. M. H. Spielman in his earlier history of *Punch* makes the passing comment that Maginn toward the end of his life alienated his friends by his persecution of Letitia Landon.[16] As there is not the slightest hint anywhere outside of Berkeley that Maginn persecuted Letitia or alienated his friends, it becomes necessary to descend once more into the Honorable Grantley's evil and aged mind.

Even in its premise, Berkeley's position is illogical. He narrates at length how L.E.L. appealed to him, an entire stranger, for protection against Maginn, whom he alleges annoyed her with visits and claimed through blackmail the greater part of her profits from writing.[17] He explains that the potency of his name was sufficient to keep the villain from her door but not to stop the anonymous letters.[18] In addition, he mentions that the poetess's friend, Lady Blessington, warned him that Maginn would be avenged upon him for his interference and was merely biding his time.[19] Yet in spite of this alleged warning and of this whole alleged situation, Berkeley did not seek out Maginn at the time of the adverse review of his novel in *Fraser's,* but proceeded as if he had had no previous dealings with the insolent editor. This was the more unnatural because in his *Reminiscences of a Huntsman* he showed himself accustomed to the vigorous use of his fist and whip in summary punishment of those who opposed or insulted him in any way.[20] He was a practiced bruiser, and it is difficult to believe that his blows would not have fallen at once upon the writer of the offensive article had he actually had the experiences with *Fraser's* editor which he claimed.

Illogical though it was, Berkeley's position would have been stronger had he contented himself with the single account of the affair given in the second volume of his autobiography,[21] and thereafter held his peace. In his efforts to justify himself he reveals that he does not scruple to deceive. For instance, he ascribes a significance which he must have known was never intended to Mrs. Thomson's statement, "She made one false step." This remark occurs in the center of a paragraph giving the details of L.E.L.'s relation to Maclean, his estrangement from her, and their final reunion.[22] Dr. Madden in his detailed account refers to the statement as indicating Mrs. Thomson's regret that her young friend was willing to accept Maclean.[23] Berkeley, though he was familiar with Madden's account of L.E.L., disregards his comment on Mrs. Thomson's opinion as completely as he disregards the greater part of Mrs. Thomson's own paragraph in which the opinion is expressed. Isolating the sentence in question from the text, he interprets it as her admission of a moral lapse on the part of L.E.L.[24] Yet Mrs. Thomson throughout her memoir makes clear her complete faith in Letitia's purity of motive and act. She and her husband, who had been L.E.L.'s physician for years, were old and devoted friends of the poetess; both of them had watched her grow into maturity, and both had themselves a strong sense of moral rectitude.

In a similar fashion Berkeley misrepresents Samuel Carter Hall, considering "important"[25] to his case Hall's opinion that Maginn was a rascal and that L.E.L. had been "imprudent" in writing the letters which had aroused Mrs. Maginn's jealousy.[26] But Hall had from his youth been the enemy of Maginn and would in any case regret her intimacy with a married man, a confirmed drunkard, and a spendthrift. His whole article, moreover, was written in the contention that the poetess had not really become involved with Maginn or anyone else, but in spite of her unconventionality had maintained throughout her life the beauty and spirituality of her nature, her moral uprightness and fineness. He and his wife, Anna Maria Hall, the novelist, like Dr. and Mrs. Thomson, were people who had the highest personal standards and who had long been confidential friends of L.E.L. and made it entirely clear that they believed in her and defended her in spite of the rumors that had rendered her life wretched. Berkeley's remarks concluding his discussion of Hall's testimony show his anxiety to gain supporting evidence for his allegations. In speaking of the letters to which Hall had referred he writes:

> The fact is, her embarrassment had made such letters imperative. She knew herself to be in the toils of her destroyer, and for a time dared not struggle. The tender expressions that excited the jealousy of Mrs. Maginn were matters of course—equally as a matter of course, she made to her friends the best explanation of the occurrence it was in her power to produce. The indisputable fact that she rejected one or more advantageous offers of marriage that would leave her open to the persecution of her enemy, and finally accepted another she could not have listened to under happier circumstances, that apparently would remove her far from his sphere of influence, is all the confirmation I required.[27]

On examination, this answer to Hall is appalling in its distortion and its confusion of the two sets of letters. It is quite possible that L.E.L. married Maclean and went with him to West Africa to escape from the anonymous letters, but that could offer no "confirmation" of Berkeley's supposition that she went to escape from Maginn. There is nothing in Hall's article to indicate that either he or his wife dreamed of suspecting Maginn of persecuting Letitia or of having any hand in writing the anonymous letters. In regard to the endearments in that other set of letters which Mrs. Maginn discovered and sent to Forster, they might possibly have been used as proof of L.E.L.'s love of Maginn, but surely it was straining the situation to adduce them as evidence of his blackmailing her.

The same kind of falsification is involved in Berkeley's statement:

> There was nothing new in my declaration of the relations that existed between Dr. Maginn and his hapless victim. They were a matter, to a certain extent, of public notoriety and had been referred to again and again in biographical notices.[28]

To support this assertion Berkeley cites the memoirs of L.E.L. by Laman Blanchard, Madden, Mrs. Thomson, and Lady Blessington.[29]

Yet when one turns to these carefully displayed sources, one finds not one reference which could possibly imply that the writers thought Maginn had made a "hapless victim" of L.E.L. or anyone else. There is no word to suggest that the gay Irishman had ever entered the mind of Blanchard, Madden, Mrs. Thomson, or Lady Blessington in connection with the persecution of L.E.L. or the writing of the anonymous letters. Moreover, if such a thing had been, as Berkeley declares, suspected "among literary circles" it is scarcely conceivable that these close friends of L.E.L., all of whom belonged to literary London and were the persons whom Berkeley states he had in mind, should have continued on cordial terms with the "hoary villain." Lady Blessington was, as Berkeley himself says, a friend of Maginn, and entertained him at Gore House; Blanchard and Mrs. Thomson were among his ardent admirers. The young man was his personal friend, and the middle-aged biographer contributed what is on the whole the most eulogistic memoir which exists of him.[30]

A point in Berkeley's argument which is more stupid than vicious is the statement that Lockhart and his "literary confreres" condoned Maginn's persecution of Letitia.[31] In the course of his argument he remarks:

> I shall be glad to know . . . if the necessities of female authors, and their natural desire for success, have never been taken advantage of by men in a position to forward their views. The tone employed by respectable critics in dealing with an offending brother of the guild, may be seen in the burlesque epitaph on Miss Landon's murderer, written by the then editor of the "Quarterly Review."
>
> "Barring drink and the girls I ne'er knew of a sin,
> Many worse, better few than bright broken Maginn."
>
> "Barring drink and the girls" is merely euphuistic for the habitual drunkenness and debauchery that brought his existence to a close several years after the death of his victim. Mr. Lockhart must have had the worst possible opinion of his fraternity when he penned the last line of the fore-going "epitaph." He declares that there were many worse and few better than this man. God help the poor authoresses who were doomed to come within the sphere of their influence![32]

From this passage we may infer that Grantley Berkeley had no conception of John Lockhart. There is an element of comedy in the notion that the stern Scotchman should have voluntarily shielded a man who would stoop to such abuse of power. Berkeley's interpretation of "barring drink and the girls," fails to take into account that Lockhart was using the words as a stock phrase and in humorous verse. But the question of their significance is settled beyond a doubt by Lockhart's expressing in his more formal sketch of Maginn's character the opposite opinion of his friend's morals.[33] One likes to fancy how, had Lockhart been living, the old "Scorpion" of *Blackwood* days would have arisen within him, striking sharply at Berkeley's clumsy lies. How easily he could have shown the incongruity of a man's throwing to the winds two excellent jobs because he had brought unhappiness to a woman he loved, and at the same time blackmailing her for sums paltry in comparison to the income with which he so negligently parted on her account! Lockhart, with his memory of Maginn's glad love for children and incorrigible readiness to help young writers like Callahan and Griffin or old Irishmen out of work, could have pointed out that, until Berkeley wrote, there had been recorded not one instance of Maginn's cruelty but many of his genial compassion. It may be added that Lockhart's exertions to support and befriend Maginn offer strong evidence against the truth of Berkeley's accusations—for Lockhart would have been among the first in "literary circles" to have heard of persecution had it existed, and he would have been the last to condone it.

As a matter of fact the "literary circles," so far from looking upon Maginn as the persecutor of L.E.L., may even have thought of him as her champion. As late as 1852 the author of the *Critic* article on *Fraser's* famous early staff remarked that Maginn was supposed to have written the review of Grantley Berkeley's novel in retaliation for a grievance of L.E.L.[34] The report presumably sprang from idle gossip, which the mere circumstance of a mortal combat would in itself have aroused, and there doubtless was no sound reason for suspecting that L.E.L. had a grievance against Berkeley. To begin with, the review was apparently not premeditated—Maginn, heated with wine at the time, having dashed it off in the midst of the other Fraserians on the night before the magazine went to press.[35] Beyond question, also, it was less libelous than appeared on the surface, since the events alluded to in the private life of Berkeley's family were already familiar to the public through parliamentary reports and the newspapers.[36] It was certainly in keeping with the rest of Maginn's slashing criticism and, outrageous as it might seem, was almost merited by the novel's bad taste and worse morals. Yet although there was presumably no more truth in the report that Maginn championed L.E.L. in a cause against Berkeley than there was in Berkeley's own assertion that he himself protected L.E.L. from the persecution of Maginn, the statement in the *Critic* article is none the less of interest. If Maginn was thus reputed to have protected L.E.L. and Berkeley was reputed to have annoyed her, it needed no great ingenuity on Berkeley's part in the course of time to reverse the positions which he and his adversary were said to have held. In his *Reminiscences of a Huntsman* which appeared in 1854, two years after the *Critic* article, he complains that Maginn had received, and was even at that time still receiving, far more praise for his conduct in the duel than he deserved, and threatens to give his own version of what lay behind the hostile review of *Berkeley Castle* and the ensuing encounter.[37] By the time he undertakes his autobiography in 1865 and 1866 he is able to carry out this threat with comparative safety. All of Maginn's friends had long since died, and the few of L.E.L.'s who were still living, like Samuel Carter Hall, were handicapped because Berkeley dragged into his accusation every shred of melodrama in the life of the poetess, even including the earlier rumors that had surrounded her and Jerdan. Yet Hall's defense of L.E.L.[38] is strong and sincere, while Berkeley's attack, when closely examined, is found so full of distortions that it would scarcely be credited had it been written under oath.

The difficulty is that until so examined this testimony has a novelistic flow of incident which appears circumstantial. The latest harm for which it would seem responsible is Mr. Michael Sadleir's detraction of Maginn. After all, if one accepts Berkeley, there is nothing one would not believe of Maginn. When Mr. Sadleir gives his interpretation of Maginn's relation to L.E.L.,[39] he quotes a letter written by the poetess to Bulwer Lytton explaining that the anonymous letters and rumors concerning herself had been traced to the lowest quarters of the press. Those anonymous letters, Mr. Sadleir suggests, might have been written by Maginn or, more probably, by Charles Molloy Westmacott at the instigation of Maginn. Westmacott, who was the editor of the Tory *Age,* the most scandalous paper of the time, had the evil reputation of having practiced blackmail on one or two occasions. Elsewhere Mr. Sadleir suggests that Maginn might have been the chief controversialist of the *Age* from July, 1827, to the time he started *Fraser's* in February, 1830, and that as such he would have been closely associated with Westmacott, "virtually acting as co-editor."[40] As evidence he notices that between 1830 and 1833 the attacks on Bulwer Lytton in the *Age* alternated with the more serious attacks on the novelist in *Fraser's.* He also finds that the *Age* prior to 1830 had traces of the Maginnish style conspicuous in *Blackwood's* and *Fraser's,* and finally that up to 1830 it praised *Blackwood's,* but that after that date, with the establishment of *Fraser's* and the transference of Maginn's activities, it changed its attitude, centering its flattery on the young Tory rival.[41]

Yet these circumstances would have been natural, irrespective of whether or not Maginn wrote for the *Age* or was associated with Westmacott. Maginn was a popular figure of the London press and very much in vogue in the 1830's. The witty informality and scurrility of *Fraser's* would have been more in favor with Westmacott, who sought to be something of a wit himself, than the greater sobriety of *Blackwood's,* long since stripped of its early sportiveness. Nor was the *Age* by any means exceptional in its adoption of Maginn's mannerisms. Maginnishness was so much the fad of the day, affecting lighter sheets and occasionally those of greater pretension, that it is impossible to ascribe authorship to the infectious source on the ground of style. The *Age,* moreover, was not the only periodical to follow *Fraser's* lead in denouncing Bulwer. Even the neutral *Athenæum* became unfriendly. As for the Tory press, there was every reason for fairly widespread hostility in a day when politics governed criticism. Bulwer was, as we have mentioned in the chapter on criticism, an active Whig with powerful Whig connections, and for a while the editor of the chief Whig magazine, the *New Monthly.*

Several points, indeed, tell definitely against Mr. Sadleir's supposition. After 1826 Maginn was on anything but good terms with *Blackwood's Magazine* and would certainly not have been the cause for flattering mention of it in the *Age* between 1827 and 1830, his own contributions having practically ceased before 1828. Finally there exists not the slightest trace of external evidence that Maginn ever wrote for the *Age* until after he gave up the editorship of *Fraser's* and the *Standard,* and after the *Age* itself had risen somewhat from its depravity. In the first half of the nineteenth century the men of the London press still formed so small and compact a body that no secret relationship could have been maintained. Even if Maginn and Westmacott had been non-committal, and neither was so inclined by nature, the underlings of the *Age* would have been less discreet. When Maginn, in the latter part of the thirties, wrote leaders for the *Age,* his position was at once known, even though he was ashamed of it, and he was then a much less conspicuous person. At the earlier period, when he was a dynamic figure in the press world, he would have had still less chance of escaping detection had he formed such an affiliation. Moreover, there was no reason for him to have so involved himself. As we have seen, he was on confidential terms with the leading men of the press, even including the great Whig editor of *The Times,* Barnes, and he could have had access to any paper he desired. Disraeli and Lockhart, it will be remembered, considered his aid so important to John Murray's *Representative* that they allowed him to stipulate his own salary, which began nearly two months before the gigantic venture was started and continued until its failure in 1826. Early in 1827 he was associated with Giffard in projecting the *Standard* newspaper and with its first number, that for May 21, assumed his position of assistant, or practically joint editor, a post which would have ill accorded with work on the disgraceful *Age.* Westmacott did not take over the *Age* before the summer of 1827, the beginning of the particularly dark period of its history, and it is inconceivable that Maginn would at that time have risked his reputation by joining him, even if he had had the leisure to do so. Giffard depended on his spry associate to do most of the writing for the *Standard,* and the burden of conducting one of the leading evening papers must have fallen heavily upon Maginn's shoulders, especially during the first difficult years of organization, from 1827 to 1829. It is, of course, presumable that Maginn, ever an indiscriminate leader of the press, was the personal friend of Westmacott, who in the early years of his dragooning on the *Age* was prominent and strangely enough retained some degree of respectability. Westmacott's portrait was included in the *Fraser* "Gallery," May, 1834, and at the time of his beating by Charles Kemble the magazine defended him on the ground that the *Age's* review of Fanny Kemble, though harsh, had not contained the slur against her character which her father alleged.[42] Yet personal regard for Westmacott, if indeed such existed and *Fraser's* attitude was not merely a part of its customary effort for publicity, could in no case imply that Maginn contributed to the *Age*. Here again, it is to be questioned if Sir Robert Peel would have given £100 to ease Maginn's last days had the dying Irishman been smirched with blackmail.

The letter from L.E.L. to Bulwer Lytton, already mentioned as quoted by Mr. Sadleir, was written after the breaking of her engagement to Forster. This letter, Mr. Sadleir feels, would not have been penned had the poetess not at an earlier date appealed to Bulwer for protection against Maginn. The supposition here is that Maginn, on being repulsed by L.E.L. after his arrival in London at the beginning of 1824, pressed himself upon her against her will. When L.E.L. in 1827 took Bulwer into her confidence, he interfered in her behalf; and Maginn, treasuring up that interference, punished L.E.L. by instigating the anonymous letters, and punished Bulwer by attacking his books.[43] The difficulty in accepting this hypothesis is twofold. If it is correct, Maginn would scarcely have waited from 1827 to 1830 for his hostile reviews of Bulwer's novels, since the columns of the ultra-Tory *John Bull* were always open to the ready satirist. Again, had he been going to send anonymous letters to punish L.E.L., he would not have waited until into the thirties. Anonymous slander was too well known a form of cowardly reprisal to require long preparation; and Maginn was far from cowardly and was by nature impatient of delays. Nor, on the other hand, should it be supposed that L.E.L., having accepted the successful interference of Bulwer, would have allowed herself to resume relations with Maginn, writing for his *Fraser's Magazine,* receiving his contributions to her *Drawing Room Scrap Book,* and corresponding with him in a vein so intimate as to arouse the jealousy of his wife and her own lover.

It would certainly be less difficult to believe that Maginn and L.E.L.

had from the beginning been on friendly terms. Jerdan, the editor of the *Literary Gazette,* had originally brought them together; Jerdan was in almost daily contact with L.E.L. through her work for the *Gazette;* and Jerdan, in like manner, was intimate with his other contributor, William Maginn, writing of the engaging Irishman in his autobiography with, as we have seen, affection and admiration. The uninterrupted kindliness and understanding between Jerdan and Maginn becomes in a way a surety for the right relations between Maginn and L.E.L. Both men professed the deepest attachment for L.E.L.; both almost lost their minds at her death. Since no jealousy ever arose between these two admirers and collaborators of the poetess, each considerably older than herself, she presumably treated them as good companions, granting no undue favors to either. Mr. Sadleir would seem to have been mistaken in thinking that L.E.L. complained to Lady Blessington of an attempt on Maginn's part to capture and subdue her.[44] The Countess mentioned that gossip had connected the poetess's name with his, but gave no details other than to affirm her friend's innocence.[45] The sinuous statements of Grantley Berkeley could easily account for such misinterpretation.

L.E.L.'s letter to Bulwer Lytton, which we are quoting in a note,[46] is possibly susceptible of another interpretation than that given it by Mr. Sadleir. Macready's diary, quoted earlier, reveals that the actor had been taken into Forster's confidence in regard to the broken engagement and the letters between L.E.L. and Maginn which Mrs. Maginn had discovered. Probably Macready was not the only friend in whom Forster confided. Certainly L.E.L.'s letter to Forster, also previously quoted, assumed that he would give any of his friends who had known of his engagement an explanation as to why it had been broken. L.E.L. herself freely confided the whole circumstance to her own more intimate friends. It is, therefore, quite possible that someone among these two groups of people might have urged Bulwer Lytton, who was known to have influence with her, to write her begging that she reconsider her decision. Or, what is equally probable, Bulwer himself might have been among the friends to whom she confided and after his conversation with her, convinced that she was making a mistake, might have written to her on his own account. L.E.L.'s letter to him is obviously an answer to a remonstrance; it is entirely devoted to a long explanation of her reasons for feeling that she could never be happy with Forster and that the breaking of the engagement must be final.

Innocent of blackmail though Maginn was, he could not well have left the records of his life in more complete confusion. His attitudes were insufficiently explained; his satirical comments became the basis of legend and opened the way for misrepresentation by his enemies. One of the worst consequences of this distortion is that a commentator such as Mr. Sadleir, who is peculiarly fitted to write on the brilliant satirist, should have become one of his most serious defamers. Mr. Sadleir had the condemning testimony of Grantley Berkeley, though he obviously despised the man, without any authenticated life of Maginn to which to refer. He also knew that Maginn had vilely attacked Bulwer in *Fraser's*. What he could not know was that this attack, unjust as it appeared, was in keeping, as we have earlier shown, with the whole critical policy of the magazine. Nor could he know how particularly vehement was *Fraser's* warfare against political economy, and in consequence how particularly heated was its quarrel with the Whig *New Monthly*, not only during the editorship of Bulwer Lytton, but before. Its hatred was not unanswered. The *New Monthly*, although almost uniformly self-restrained, was driven under Bulwer's rule to retaliate: "Our readers may be aware that there exists a stupid, coarse, illiterate periodical published once a month, and called 'Frazer's Magazine.' " It complains of lies "from the mouth even of the obscurest liar," and promises "the unburrowing of some half a dozen of these vermin—the Mactoddies and Macgrawlers of Mr. Frazer's fœtid magazine."[47] When Bulwer resigned from the *New Monthly* and incidentally disciplined Westmacott, he was roughly handled by Maginn;[48] yet he himself at a later date on finding his *Student of Padua* unfavorably reviewed[49] was willing to attack the Irishman with equal ferocity. In this case Maginn, who had not written the offending article, was able to bring a suit for libel and was actually awarded £150 damages. When it is remembered that Bulwer was not only the editor of the *New Monthly* but the chief novelist to expound the doctrines of political economy, as well as to promote the wholesale manufacture of literature by the publishers Colburn and Bentley, it is surprising that *Fraser's* treated him no worse.

Maginn was capable of inflicting far more staggering blows than any he visited upon the author of *Pelham* and *Eugene Aram*. There is even a good deal of fairness in his estimate of Bulwer which ends the "Gallery" sketch for August, 1832. Certainly it would not have been written by a man actuated by jealousy or even by personal dislike:

> If he would give up his "affectations"—and, surely, he is now old enough to do so—and learn to believe, that to be a Garrick Club dandy is not one of the highest objects of human ambition; if he would not fancy that the authorship of some three or four flimsy, and one clever novel, is the perfection of literary fame; if he would forswear the use of such words as "liberal principles," "enlarged ideas," "progress of mind," "behind the age," and other nonsense of the kind, which could be used by a parrot with as much effect as by the rising talent of the day; if he would read something, and think a little—get to harder study and a humbler mind, there is the making of something well worth praising in Bulwer;—and when we see it, nobody will be happier to proclaim it than ourselves.

Mr. Sadleir, in commenting on this passage expresses the opinion that had Maginn lived he would have made good his promise.[50] It is indeed to the credit of Mr. Sadleir that seeing Maginn as he does under the heavy umbrage of blackmail, he should none the less recognize the basic honesty of the wayward editor's mind. Of all the Tory sharpshooters of the thirties—Hook, Lockhart, and the rest—Maginn alone, he writes, "never lost his mental integrity."[51]

CHAPTER XI

LITERARY WORK

To put any of his own essays into permanent form was a task remote from Maginn's interest or intention. At his death, the old *Fraser* staff, rallying to his memory, write sadly, he

> resembled Swift not merely in his wit, but in the utter carelessness with which he regarded the fate of the productions of his genius. If they served the purpose of the moment, whether it were to make a minister tremble or a lady smile, "the Doctor" never troubled himself further about his thunder or his jest. They might be claimed by any passer-by, for no one ever contributed more to the fame of others or so completely disregarded his own. . . . We could lay our hands on many a goodly and popular volume, the most striking points and best passages of which, have been gleaned from the private conversations and remarks of Dr. Maginn.[1]

With the exception of his translations from Homer and his papers on Shakespeare his work would seem to have held little significance for him beyond the immediate pleasure and the money which he gained from writing. For most of it he held fine scorn,[2] feeling that by its nature it set its own expedient time limit. In consequence when his friends started to collect his brightly allusive papers that had winged the English periodicals for nearly a quarter of a century, they found them almost as irrecoverable as the fluorescent wisdom of the Dublin Doctor's talk. Like his conversation his articles belonged to their own moment of utterance, and were intricately enmeshed in its ephemera.

With isolated exceptions, only the Shakespearian papers were lifted above their own time, and here the style is excellent. In these more careful essays Maginn's prose has an easy rectitude and simplicity which is unusual in his day. Without a trace of the precious, it is cultivated, carrying lightly its knowledge of diction and manners. Something of the same guarded wisdom is to be found in his *Maxims of Sir Morgan O'Doherty,* his introduction to the *Homeric Ballads,* the *Gallery of Literary Characters,* and in passages scattered through his articles. If

Maginn anticipated much that is cheap in modern writing, he also anticipated much that is best.

In addition to his *Maxims of Sir Morgan O'Doherty,* his translations of Homer and Lucian, his Shakespearian papers, and the lively *Fraser's Gallery,* four collections of his work were made: *Magazine Miscellanies* which he himself published in 1841 in the hope of defraying his debts; the *O'Doherty Papers* and *Fraserian Papers,* both edited by Dr. R. Shelton Mackenzie; and the *Miscellanies in Prose and Verse* edited by R. W. Montagu in 1885.[3] Each of these collections is almost of necessity from the wide range of subject and treatment, ill-assorted and uneven. No adequate opinion of his work can for that reason be gained outside of the files of the magazines for which it was originally written. As Professor Saintsbury points out, Maginn was too miscellaneous to be read with pleasure within the confines of a small volume. It is also only fair to add that the poorest verses in the *Miscellanies,* the "Auncient Waggonere," the feeble completion of Coleridge's *Christabel,* "Miss Pipson," the "Spermaceti Candle" were written not by Maginn but by David Moir and Robert Macnish and that "Hamlet," the most abstract of the *Shakespeare Papers,* was from the pen of Banks.[4]

Thus it is the more remarkable that Professor Saintsbury has such clear-sighted indulgence for the meteoric work of Maginn. He finds the haphazard collections of his writing, especially his verse, "characterised by a mixture of fantastic humour, adaptive wit, and rare but real pathos and melody."[5] Of Maginn's essay on the learning of Shakespeare, he writes, "With some quite astonishing slips (such as 'Nugæ Curialiæ,' which perhaps is due to carelessness in correcting his proofs), it contains probably as much sound learning, shrewd wit, and acute criticism as can be found in any single contribution to the enormous and too often worthless library of Shakespearian comment."[6] Of the essay, "Lady Macbeth," he says, "I do not know a piece of dramatic character-criticism (no, not the thousand-times-praised thing in *Wilhelm Meister*) more unerringly delicate and right."[7] Both together, he writes, and here we see the inebriate shadow of Shandon,

show that Maginn, if only he could have kept his hand from the glass, and his pen from mere gambols or worse, not only might but would have been one of the most considerable of English critics. The goodness, and the various goodness, of both is all the more remarkable because Maginn seems to have owed little or nothing to the influence of Coleridge. Almost the only fault in the first is the hectoring incivility with which Farmer himself is spoken of. . . . But the sense and learning of the paper are simply admirable.[8]

Maginn, he adds in high approval, possessed the "last critical secret" in that he knew enough not to try to show that Shakespeare was omniscient.

Saintsbury's commendation of the essay is supported by the earlier, brief statement of Furness. In his *Variorum* the editor comments that the "admirable Review" of Farmer's work "is far too little known," and quotes Maginn's contention that Shakespeare had "read Rabelais, and read him, too, in the original," adding that, although the illustration from the *Tempest* is to be questioned, the "drift of opinion in these later days is certainly towards Maginn's position, and opposed to Farmer with his proofs of Shakespeare's ignorance."[9]

Further evidence that Maginn might have won distinction as a Shakespearian scholar is found in his "Adversaria." One of his more persistent ambitions was to bring out his own edition of the plays, and it is a pity that he lacked the time, and probably the patience, for the undertaking. His few suggested textual emendations are of interest, the two in *Fraser's,* even though anonymous, having found place in annotated editions such as the "Cambridge."[10] Furness, indeed, states in some detail Maginn's conjecture that "one (or yon, indicating Calaban) thing she hid," spoken by Prospero in explanation of the sailors' having spared the life of Sycorax because she was *enceinte,* should be substituted for "one thing she did."[11]

Maginn felt that emendations in the text could be carried further than was conceded by his friend, the Shakespearian editor, Charles Knight. On this point Knight quotes a letter from Maginn, at the same time generously mentioning the latter's helpful suggestions to himself.[12] In one of the "Adversaria" Maginn made a popular plea against the theory that Shakespeare's text was to be regarded as sacred. In speaking of the errors which arose from "the utter carelessness or the gross ignorance" of folio editors, he writes: "Now, to assert that there is something impertinent in removing these, is as reasonable as it would be to complain that the man who rubbed off dark spots and specks from the lens of your telescope was an intrusive meddler, who disturbed your celestial meditations upon the glories of the heavens."[13]

Maginn's analysis of Shakespeare's characters, on which Saintsbury briefly commented in connection with the essay, "Lady Macbeth," has recently been fully treated by Augustus Ralli. After somewhat detailed summaries of the individual papers, he concludes:

> Maginn has flashes of insight into character, but is less happy in dealing with a character's reactions. His inspiration is momentary, but the moment is a precious one. Perhaps no one has said better things about Falstaff himself: his statement that disputes about Falstaff's courage are foolish, and that he was no fit antagonist for Douglas, is on a level with Maurice Morgann. But he does not convince when he says that Falstaff was conscious of his wasted life, that he jests with a sad brow, and his wit is from the head, not the heart. . . . On Jacques Maginn is entirely excellent, and although the theory of the "four periods" is a questionable one, his words incidentally divide the creator of the reflective characters of comedy and tragedy. Nor, despite some excellent modern criticism, have two better points been made about Bottom—that he was the lucky man, and that he was afterwards unaffected by the memory of Titania.

Ralli justly qualifies this praise in his final paragraph:

> Maginn's first moment is good, but he is less happy in following out the train of thought. In the seven ages the picture of the schoolboy satisfies the reader: he need not be told that the schoolboy grieves because he must go to school—or that all the characters are well cared for. We feel the same about Falstaff's "sad brow"—the fact that even Goneril and Regan intend marriage—and Lady Macbeth's "humbled tone of an inferior." While imagination upholds Maginn he speaks well, but when it fails he sinks down to prose. Perhaps it serves him longest with Lady Macbeth.[14]

Maginn's hope of editing Shakespeare alternated with that of editing Homer, a task for which he was fitted in everything except his own restless temperament. His footnotes to his translations are full of allusions and parallels which show wide and scholarly reading. His introductory essay contains a fine and bold denunciation of the theory that the great epics were compilations of separate ballads by various hands. It is no less forceful but less discourteous than his essay on Dr. Farmer. He writes tersely:

I am not ignorant of the talent, learning, and industry of Wolf; but I should as soon believe in four-and-twenty contemporary, or nearly contemporary, Homers, as in four-and-twenty contemporary Shakespeares, or Miltons, or Dantes.

This statement is amplified and then reëmphasized:

So far from the *Iliad* being a collection or miscellany of ballads, composed at fits and starts by various minstrels, and then pieced together in ages afterward, the fact is, that it is the only epic poem ever written of which the unity is perfect and complete, and in which it would be impossible to disturb the order of the several parts of the poem without marring the regular and connected sequence of the entire.

Equally explicit is the following:

I do not think his name was Homer; and I look upon the derivations of that word which we find in the Greek scholiasts, men utterly ignorant of the principles of etymology, and the pedants who followed them, as mere trash. The meaning is to be sought elsewhere. I think he wrote or spoke his great poems as wholes, in Asia, and that they came over to Hellas piece by piece, after having filled the east with their fame; and that by the great men of Athens, or Sparta, they were gathered, not in the sense of making them into poems, but of re-making them. They were, both before their importation and afterward, sung in scraps, no doubt, just as Shakespeare or Milton is quoted by us in scraps. We do not sing our great poets—the Greeks did; but "To be or not to be?" or "Hail, holy light!" indicate to us fragments of *Hamlet* or *Paradise Lost,* just in the same way as the various "headings" of the pieces sung by the Rhapsodists indicated fragments of the *Iliad* and the *Odyssey;* and it would be as wise to consider, as the original arranger of the Shakespearean or Miltonic poems in their present shape, the industrious compiler who should restore them from Readers, or Speakers, or Elegant Extracts, as to confer the honour of *making* the poems of Homer on Pisistratus. If Wolf had tried to make an epic poem out of the abundant ballads of his native land, he would have found how hard was the task assigned by him to the Athenian prince. It might not be unamusing to prove, in the manner of Wolf, that there were some dozen of Sir Walter Scotts. On Vico's principle, it would not be hard to do so. Sir Walter wove together the traditions of Scotland, and therefore the Scottish tribes *"furono questo Gualtero."*[15]

Maginn's translations of Homer are themselves less commendable than his introduction and notes. He adopted the unfortunate theory that the great epics could be most nearly represented in English by hexameters and by the ballad form—with a result which met with enthusiastic approval in his own day of much Greek and more Latin, but which is difficult to associate with Homer. Matthew Arnold, in showing "all forms of our ballad-metre unsuited to Homer," complains irritably that Maginn keeps him from remembering the original. In a more magnanimous vein he comments:

His *Homeric Ballads* are vigorous and genuine poems in their own way; they are not one continual falsetto, like the pinchbeck *Roman Ballads* of Lord Macaulay; but just because they are ballads in their manner and movement . . . they are not at all Homeric, they have not the least in the world the manner of Homer.[16]

The blank verse translations of the comedies of Lucian are more dignified, though even in their own day they were never popular. A few critics like Richard Garnett, whose commendation of Maginn is always guarded, have recognized their skill,[17] but in general they have been forgotten, partly because Lucian himself has been forgotten.

Nor has Maginn's dexterity in translating well-known English poems into Latin and Greek met in recent years with a happier fate, since for the past half century few readers have been sufficiently adept in the classics to enjoy his swift and dapper lines. Yet in this case the rollicking scholar at least during his own lifetime won merited fame. The merry interchange of languages, which he had started in *Blackwood's* with his contagious rendering of "Chevy Chase" into lively Latin, became a fad of the twenties and thirties. Even the nimble boy Praed, acknowledging his indebtedness to Maginn, whose "Persæus ex Northumbria" he had compared so often with "Chevy Chase" that he said he could scarcely tell which was the copy, wrote a series of imaginary classic originals.[18] There was from the first nothing short of an enchantment about this special form of composition, combining as it did the charm of word-puzzle, poetry, and recollection. A writer for the *Dublin Review*, February, 1843, comments on a collection of these verses, *Arundines Cami:*

Why they should possess so singular a charm we cannot tell,—perhaps it is for the rhyme, perhaps for the eccentricity,—but we never met an accomplished classical scholar who did not enjoy their perusal even much more than the most finished longs and shorts of our greatest names. We have ourselves often got a song in Greek or Latin rhyme by heart, and chanted it for hours.

Of all the men who attempted the learned juggling Maginn was recognized as the master, the most skillful of his followers paying him tribute.

Of more general interest today are the burlesques in verse, which are sufficient in quantity and fineness to place Maginn among the best parodists in the English language. The deftness and foresight of his imitations of Coleridge and of Christopher North have already been mentioned in connection with *Fraser's* criticism.[19] Some of his earlier parodies are equally good, one of them, "Don Juan Unread," being used for years to conclude the comments on the great satire printed in Murray's edition of Byron's poems. His stinging ridicule of Moore, if not able to undermine that facile poet's popularity, left no room for doubt that less sentimental writing also had its great advantages. Among the most destructive of these "Moore-ish Melodies" were "Billingsgate Music," "Rich and Rare," and the two parodies of the "Last Rose of Summer," under the inebriate titles of " 'Tis the Last Glass of Claret," and "The Last Lamp of the Alley."

As a creative writer Maginn's fame is likely to rest on his downright honesty. His songs, such as "The Pewter Quart," "The Wine-Bibber's Glory," and "A Twist-imony in Favour of Gin-Twist" do for drink what his absurd "Irishman and the Lady" does for the Irish drinker; they exaggerate to substantial truth. His satiric ballad, "The Powldoodies of Burran," has a burly realism that harks back to Swift. It shows his faith in the Irish vernacular and his control over its outer reaches of thought and sound.

More than one person probably has enjoyed Maginn's verses and short stories as they have appeared in collections without associating them with his name. "The Pewter Quart," "Bob Burke's Duel" and "The Man in the Bell" are doubtless known by those who are unaware of their author. Yet Maginn has never at any time been wholly without his admirers. His own day shouted its applause. As we have mentioned, even as grudging a critic as Byron, according to his friend Finlay, frequently repeated passages of O'Doherty's poetry and expressed "great astonishment at the ability displayed by the author."[20]

Since then isolated readers have from time to time discovered and admired the regaling Irishman. For "Bob Burke's Duel with Ensign Brady," "The Man in the Bell," and "A Story without a Tale," Professor Saintsbury has unqualified admiration; the last, especially, he says he has read "literally scores of times and never without fresh enjoyment." Of the songs, "The Pewter Quart," he writes, "is an admirable thing, the most spirited and genuine drinking song perhaps of this century, if not the most poetical."[21] More recent in praise of Maginn is Mr. Michael Monahan, whose *Nova Hibernia* contains delightful appreciations of the learned O'Doherty and his fellow Bohemian scholar, Prout.

Nor have authorities on Irish literature been less outspoken in approval. Mr. Charles L. Graves opens one of his studies with the unqualified statement, "The first of the notable humourists of Irish life was William Maginn, one of the most versatile, as well as brilliant of Irish men of letters." Sir Morgan O'Doherty, he states more explicitly, "was the undoubted ancestor of Maxwell's and Lever's hard drinking, practical joking Irish military heroes"; as he was the first to write "genuine 'Irish Melodies' to serve as an antidote to what he called the finicking Bacchanalianism of Moore."[22] Mr. D. J. O'Donoghue is fully as appreciative. He also considers Maginn the best of Irish parodists and among the most valiant of those who established "Ireland's supremacy in the literature devoted to Bacchus." "He was," he adds, "a great humorist in every way, and may be claimed as the earliest writer who showed genuine rollicking Irish humor." Mr. O'Donoghue also states emphatically that Maginn's "great service" as a pioneer critic of Irish literature should be recognized.[23] In this connection he quotes Sir Morgan O'Doherty's lively passage proving that "the stuff styled Irish, with its unutterable refrains of the 'Whack Ballaboo kind' was of undoubted English origin, topography, phraseology, rhymes, and everything else, being utterly un-Irish." Both Mr. O'Donoghue and Mr. Graves also mention Maginn's work in folklore, and notice its delicacy and insight.

The valiant O'Doherty thus stands acclaimed as one of the pioneers of various phases of modern Irish work. Nor was this position unearned by honest effort on his part. When Maginn began writing for

Blackwood's in 1819, sentimentalizing on Irish themes was the established convention, and the vogue of Thomas Moore's Irish melodies was wide and unquestioned. Their silk bindings ornamented parlor tables and their recitation pleased parlor audiences. Readers were accustomed to a saccharine interpretation of Irish life and a purely decorative use of Irish detail. For Maginn, Moore's work, charming as it often was, was an unforgivable subversion of the Irish temper, and a mendacious apology for a thing that needed no apology. With the zeal of a true propagandist he began systematically to educate the public. His initial step was to write for *Blackwood's,* sound, honest-to-Irish songs in order that he might offset the pretty sentiments of Thomas Moore. Among the best known of these are "St. Patrick," "Gathering of the Mahonys," "Cork is an Eden for You, Love, and Me." Nor did he stop with an occasional rhyme. A rattling flood of Hibernianism poured proudly over the literary borders. In the guise of his favorite pseudonym, Sir Morgan O'Doherty, Adjutant, Maginn dared to thrust into the pages of polite reading the broad, bullying head of a true Irishman. For the first time the public found itself rebuked by an Irish brogue and the specious irrationality of Irish humor. For to Maginn the ordinary blithering Irishman, with his teasing inconsistencies and exaggerations, had an art value, and needed no refinement for polite readers. So vigorously did he ridicule everything pseudo-Irish, and so popular did he make his own authentic writing that almost immediately he was followed by a host of his compatriots, from Banim and Griffin to Maxwell and Lover and O'Leary, producing Irish songs and parodies and stories. In a way Maginn's contribution to realism was greater than theirs. Not only did he anticipate them in the movement and widely champion it; from the beginning he was invariably aware, as few men have been, of the Irish mind. He understood its paradox: the succinct quality of its exaggeration, and the simplicity of its extravagance.

One of the early results of Maginn's work was the incentive which it gave to Crofton Croker, not only pointing the way to a wider expression of Irish life but creating public appreciation for that expression. Croker was the first to collect and write down the old Irish folk tales, attempting to do for the southern counties of Ireland what the

Grimm brothers, with whom he was in touch, were doing for Germany. He found a hearty supporter in Maginn, who at once enthusiastically assisted in gathering and writing the tales. Among the best of Maginn's retellings is the old fairy whimsy of Daniel O'Rourke, one of the most deft pieces of its kind that is to be found in Irish folklore collections. Maginn, according to his custom, never asked nor expected recognition for his aid. Croker, however, felt that so much of the work had been done by Maginn and others that, when the legends were first published, they appeared anonymously. Not until the collection had been greatly enlarged and in part rewritten did Croker allow his name to appear on the title page. According to Mr. O'Donoghue, Maginn probably wrote, in addition to "Daniel O'Rourke," "The Legend of Bottle Hill," "Fairies and No Fairies," and "The Legend of Knockshegowna."[24] "O'Rourke" is reprinted as Maginn's in *Irish Literature,* edited by Justin McCarthy, Douglas Hyde, and others, and also in *Humours of Irish Life,* edited by Graves. Its attribution to the young Cork pedagogue is borne out by the Rev. Charles Maginn who told the present writer that his father, the brother of William, used to read the legend to the assembled family as one of the finest examples of the Doctor's work.

An Irish tale which has often been considered Maginn's is the famous *Father Tom and the Pope,* which originally came out in *Blackwood's* in 1838. This inimitable brochure has several times been republished and has been especially popular in America. It has variously been fathered upon Sir Samuel Ferguson, John Fisher Murray, Father Prout, and Maginn. Of the four, Maginn would seem from internal evidence to have the strongest claim to authorship. Mr. O'Donoghue gives the burlesque to him, and Mr. Yeats includes it as his with a brief biographical sketch in *Representative Irish Tales.* However, an acknowledgment of the tale by Ferguson places the question of authorship beyond dispute. In a letter included in the preface to one of the editions of the satire he writes:

> It was written by me in the summer of 1838. . . . No one else had any hand in it, and like the "Forging of the Anchor," it underwent a rejection before its appearance in *Blackwood.* I am flattered by its having been ascribed to Maginn, for whose genius I entertain a high admiration. I have never made any secret of the authorship, but as

I have constantly endeavored in any literary work I have been able to do for many years back to elevate the Irish subject out of the burlesque, I have had an indisposition to place my name on the title-page of so very rollicking a piece as Father Tom.[25]

Closely connected with Maginn's Irish work in *Blackwood's* were the original *Noctes Ambrosianæ*. Centered around that swaggering Irishman Sir Morgan O'Doherty, the series represents the goodly company of *Blackwood's* contributors cap-a-pie for literary and political gossip in Ambrose's parlor, the favorite tavern of their forgatherings. The dinners had a basis in fact, since more than one member of the staff mentions them with fondness of recollection in his autobiography or letters; but the conversations as they appeared in *Blackwood's* were in great part roistering burlesques.

We are not surprised to find that it was Maginn who wrote the initial number of the famous series, and who was one of the chief contributors throughout its first three years. In the summer of 1821, after the engaging Irishman had visited Edinburgh and London, he returned to his Emerald Isle with his retentive brain alive to the chaffer of clubs and taverns, of pressmen and politicians and publishers. One result of this trip was his turning the informal gatherings at Ambrose's to literary use, for in the following March the first *Noctes* was printed —the plural, it will be noticed, was used. The imaginary colloquy showed Maginn's habit of picking up from the life around him not only his subject matter but the very form in which the subject matter was to be presented. True to life, "Maga's" contributors appear before the public with jovial intimacy, Sir Morgan commenting loquaciously on Colburn and Bentley, the London publishers, and in short on any person or thing which had happened to pique Maginn's ever prying and whimsical interest. As Mackenzie points out,[26] it is beyond question that Maginn wrote the entire first *Noctes*. Not only does it give his personal impressions of London, which he visited after he left Edinburgh; it is Irish through and through, ends with one of his Irish songs, contains a poem known to have been his, and gives critical comments on Moore which are paralleled elsewhere in his writing. It should be mentioned that Mrs. Oliphant has suggested Blackwood himself might have originated the idea of the series and quotes a letter from Lockhart which refers to the publisher's proposal to make the *Noctes* a medium for satirizing the prominent editors and publishers of the day.[27] The plan was never carried out. Moreover, although the letter is undated, it was apparently written after the series had become an established feature of the magazine since it mentions a *Noctes* contributed by Hogg as in the process of composition.

After the initial number, Maginn would seem to have thrown open authorship in the colloquies to the entire *Blackwood's* staff. Years later in *Fraser's* he gives as a partial list of its contributors: Lockhart, himself, Wilson, Hamilton, John Cay, Douglas Cheape, Hogg, and Moir.[28] Just which one of the mirthful group wrote any particular *Noctes* is difficult to say. Presumably a great part of the more roisterous fun sprang from the swift collaboration of Maginn and Lockhart, since after both men had moved to London Maginn comments pointedly: "Wilson holds . . . the office of *Noctes Ambrosianist* to Blackwood's Magazine we must believe exclusively now that ******** and ****** have ceased to have anything to do with that periodical."[29] The fourth number at least must, however, be considered Maginn's alone. It represents Lord Byron and O'Doherty discussing over wineglasses in a Pisan tavern, friends and foes, and, more intimately than either, *Don Juan.* It was on reading this *jeu d'esprit* that Byron himself is said to have made the exclamation, quoted earlier, "By Jupiter! the fellow has me down regularly in black and white."

After 1825, when Wilson became the editor of *Blackwood's* and assumed the sole use of the brotherhood's pseudonym of Christopher North, the character of the *Noctes* changed, becoming less personal, and less true to the convivial nature of Ambrose's gossip. Sir Morgan O'Doherty was dropped and an uncouth but genial caricature of James Hogg, the Ettrick Shepherd, substituted, transforming the series into a kind of pastoral burlesque of the *Sir Roger de Coverley Papers.*

These later *Noctes* of Wilson were continued over a period of so many years and were republished so many times that it has popularly been taken for granted they represent the best, if not practically the only *Noctes.* Yet the O'Doherty colloquies from 1822 to 1825 hold too significant a place in the history of *Blackwood's* to be overlooked. These original *Noctes* were sporadic outbreaks of the youthful magazine itself, a peculiarly individual way of reporting its own inquisitive and adventurous spirit. Partly by reason of the personalities which filled them they are among the most varied as well as the liveliest of its records. It is to be remembered also that they represent fully a third of the entire series and have been recognized as among the most popular work of the magazine. Like the rest of the contributions with an Irish cast, they would, indeed, probably be better known today had Mrs. Oliphant in her study of *Blackwood's* realized their value. While she appreciated their fun, they were for her too rough and too personal, and she regretted that they were revived in 1828 and 1829 by Lockhart and Maginn after Wilson had established the *Noctes* in gentler and more conventional ways.[30]

This brief revival of the O'Doherty *Noctes* gives evidence of the continued collaboration of Lockhart and Maginn during their years in London. There were, in all, three of these unregenerate *Noctes,* representing the closest "co-partnery" between the joint authors. A letter from Lockhart to Blackwood jauntily comments on the July, 1829, *Noctes:*

> The Doctor and I have dined together again at the Salopian, and made out the plan, which shall be filled up fitly and sent off by mail on Thursday next. I hope this will do. We are to give you our "Mr. Theodore" as an interlocutor and improvisatore.[31]

The sketch as it stands today is a lively concoction in which the authors evidently found much amusement. As a commentary on Hook, it is of interest since it comes from two of that famous wit's gayest and most congenial contemporaries. It also contains what on the whole are probably Maginn's most brilliant translations. One is a free treatment of Béranger's political satire "Monsieur Judas," which is scathing in its disgust at the time's duplicity aand treachery. The other is a clever rendering in London thieves' slang of Vidocq's famous ballad of the underworld, as subtle and robust a handling of roguedom as is to be found in that decade or for many years afterward.

The collaboration of Lockhart and Maginn during the late twenties was apparently not confined to *Blackwood's Magazine*. In 1827 Lockhart sent Blackwood an article for publication in "Maga." The publisher in acknowledging it replies:

> I have not been so happy for a long while as I was last Sunday when Cay called at my house and gave me the article you had been so good as to send me for "Maga." The moment he left me I sat down and

literally devoured it. I cannot tell you how much I enjoyed the admirable way in which you show up the Cockney historical romance—the satire is so keen, and the sketches are so graphic.

Blackwood then explains most tactfully that he can not allow the article to appear in "Maga" as he fears that it might be interpreted as an attack on Sir Walter Scott, since a burlesque of an imitation could easily be transferred to the original. "Among other delectable quizzes," he goes on to specify, "that might have been quoted and commented on with this view, nothing could have been more apposite than your most droll sketch of the Duke of Wellington's Address to Napoleon's stucco figure as an inimitable counterpart to Cromwell before the picture of Charles I."[32]

The burlesque was never printed in magazine form. But toward the close of 1827 Maginn published anonymously his *Whitehall: or the Days of George IV,* which contained among its mock-heroic scenes a heartbroken speech of Wellington, stricken by remorse before a stucco statue of Napoleon. Moreover, the whole novel *Whitehall* is an admirable satire of the weak historic romances of the day, thus corresponding to Blackwood's description of the work which he received. Had Lockhart not had some share in the original sketch, it is improbable that he would have sent it as his own writing to Blackwood, who was a personal friend of long standing.

Maginn is said to have begun *Whitehall* along with another novel, the manuscript of which was lost, during a brief return to France after the failure of the *Representative* in 1826. It was a period when he seems to have been trying his hand at a good many things, from research work on Hebrew in the Bibliothèque Nationale, to a circumspect study of the Paris press. In 1827, after he was again resident in London as co-editor of the *Standard,* he once more took up the story but this time apparently not without assistance, although to what extent Lockhart helped with the tale cannot be known. Since *Whitehall* was published anonymously probably neither author wished at the time to acknowledge his share in its inclusive scoffing at the chief officers of his land. When the work was finally fathered upon Maginn, he kept its monstrosities to himself and did not betray his accomplice. Nor was it necessary that he should have done so. The book overreached itself in its fun, was never widely read, and was soon forgotten. Even the authors themselves seem to have been aware of its faults. In the brief notice of it which appeared in the *Quarterly Review* and which bears the marks of having been written by the editor, Lockhart himself, the novel is spoken of as a "laudable joke spoiled by wire-drawing it to 330 pages."[33]

Today *Whitehall* cannot be dismissed with such scant comment. It shows not only the irritation which two exceedingly keen critics felt at the abuses of their own day; there is an opening of satire within satire with preposterous but medicinal buffoonery. The plot is that of an historical novel supposedly written in the year 2227 but presenting the projects and persons of 1827. In its free dealing with events and people it satirizes the conduct of political and social life, and also its own literary forms, the historical romance, the sentimentalized novel of fashionable life, and equally sentimentalized tale of crime. Like Bernard Shaw's remedial mixtures, it tumbles together governors and governed, the noble Negro, the popular poet, the sacrificial servant, the fainting maiden, in a series of fantastic juxtapositions not less true because distorted. Most of the well-known men of the period are broadly caricatured: the Duke of York, the Lord of the Admiralty, Coleridge, Sam Rogers, Wellington, who is enslaved by Harriette Wilson of demimonde fame, and the economist Huskisson, who dies easily and instantaneously at the hand of Mr. Tierney, acting as Jack Ketch.

Maginn's work for *Fraser's* need not be considered here since the political articles, critical reviews, and occasional pieces, including the swift portraits of the illustrious "Gallery," have been discussed in previous chapters. Yet it is well to remember that his real achievement does not lie in his contributions to any one type of writing —neither in his burlesques and parodies, skillful as they often are, nor in his scholarly criticism, though that in its turn deserves attention; nor even in his fine Irish work. Rather it lies in the rapid development of the periodicals to which he so abundantly contributed. Maginn was before all else a great magazinist, without question the greatest of his day. For over twenty years he was a generative force in the organs with which he was most closely connected. His incredible vitality quickened their method, and widened their interest and observation. The very ease with which he could be imitated lifted the level of the ordinary contributions. He taught the facilities of direct expression and made directness fashionable. His own work has the quality of surprise and search, a curiosity for the things of the time that had not been expressed, and above all a wholesome predilection for plain dealing.

APPENDICES

APPENDIX 1

DISPUTED POINTS ON THACKERAY

The recurrently Maginnish tone of much of *Fraser's* writing increases the need to test all work which has in previous bibliographies been suggested as Thackeray's. One important item, the satirical tale "Elizabeth Brownrigge," we have already shown in the chapter on Thackeray[1] cannot, according to such testing, retain its place in his files. It is scarcely necessary to mention that the law-court scenes, also, which came out in *Fraser's* for October, 1831, have now been rejected by Thackeray's more thoughtful bibliographers.[2] We should perhaps add that these may have been written by Edward Marlborough Fitzgerald, one of the acknowledged contributors to the early volumes of *Fraser's,* who with his friend Praed used the signature "Θ."

A third item on the pre-*Yellowplush* list, which both C. P. Johnson and Lewis Melville[3] suggest as of possible authenticity, is "High-Ways and Low-Ways: or, Ainsworth's Dictionary with Notes by Turpin," in *Fraser's* for June, 1834. Like so much of this work which is in many ways tantalizingly like Thackeray, the critique has to be rejected on the basis of evidence pertaining to the rest of *Fraser's* brilliant staff. So far from being Thackeray's, this review of Harrison Ainsworth's novel *Rookwood* is beyond question from the pen of a gay scholar and man about town, John Churchill, who was one of the more intimate contributors of *Fraser's,* or "Regina." A letter under the date of June 2, 1836, which Ainsworth himself wrote to his publisher Macrone, refers to Churchill as the author of the article and speaks of his proposal to review the new novel *Crichton,* which was then about to be brought out. The sentence reads: "A Fraser Churchill, whom you may remember wrote the original glorious notice of *Rookwood* in Regina, has written to me to offer to Fraserize *Crichton.*"[4]

A second *Fraser* review of *Rookwood,* which was written to indorse the third edition of the book, must also lose its place on the all-too-short list of Thackeray's suggested pre-*Yellowplush* contributions. It appears in April, 1836, under the caption "Another Caw from the

Rookwood–Turpin Out Again." This title, like the contents, Johnson finds to be suggestive of Thackeray. The article is, however, included in the selections from the works of William Maginn edited by Dr. Robert Shelton Mackenzie, an acquaintance of Maginn, and the brother of one of Maginn's intimate friends. Although a critique of *Hamlet,* written by Banks, was erroneously included in this edition, probably on the assumption that any study of Shakespeare's characters published in *Fraser's* would be by Maginn, for the most part Mackenzie based the selections on publishing-house lists of James Fraser,[5] which had been sent to him by E. V. Kenealy. There would thus seem no cause to question the authenticity of a long article for which payment would beyond doubt have been made.

In this connection it should be added that, suggestive of Thackeray as "Another Caw" may be, it is far more suggestive of Maginn. And here a word of explanation is due. However close the literary bonds of the Fraserians might be, there were distinctions among the brotherhood which should not be overlooked. While it is impossible to ascribe an article to any of them on the basis solely of general style, or method, or point of view, it is often necessary to deny authenticity on the score of some discrepancy. In regard to the *Rookwood* article, for instance, there are several points which, even were its origin not established beyond question by external evidence, would have told heavily against ascription to Thackeray. The sentence, "When Scipio Africanus was accused of a miscalculation in the public accounts, by some peddling Joe Hume of that remote day, how did he act?" is to be looked at with suspicion. Nowhere in his acknowledged writings does Thackeray allude to prominent statesmen with such open insult. Moreover, on the next page, we find enthusiastic praise on the "personal puff" order of Daniel Maclise, the young artist who was ultimately to win renown as painter and engraver. It is the sort of remark with which Maginn, who had recognized the ability of Maclise and had encouraged its development by giving him the opportunity to sketch the *Fraser* "Portrait Gallery," was in the habit of making in order to boost the rising fortunes of his friend. It is not, however, to be associated with Thackeray, who though he might mete out well-earned praise in criticism, had nothing of the auctioneer about him, even when speaking of those with whom he was intimate. Nor is the article's constant rapid fire of allusions in keeping with Thackeray's acknowledged work. Occasional references, often deftly introduced, are to be found in his writing, but paragraph on paragraph of closely packed and widely diversified allusions we may look for in vain. If he had worded a critique of Ainsworth's *Rookwood* ballads in the style of the following passage, it is probable he would have rested from like labors for the remainder of the article instead of filling its pages with further erudite information. The passage reads:

> Footpad poetry, or, as Horace calls it, *sermo pedestris,* would seem to have had for him ineffable charms. Every great poet has a pet topic. In vain did Anacreon attempt to sing of Cadmus and the Atreidæ; he quickly reverted to Bacchus and Bathyllus: Burns could never get beyond the *barley-bree,* or, if he did occasionally soar upwards for a lark, he soon came back into the "bonnie rigs of barley": take the "corn-laws" from Ebenezer Elliot, and you paralyze his muse—
>
> *Sine Cerere friget:*
>
> Ovid could not manage without a metamorphose: Maturin and Lewis without a monk, a maniac, or a murderer.

Now this is a typically Maginnish passage, especially when we consider that it follows similar ones in the essay. Maginn had a naturally allusive mind, and when he gave it full scope, as he did in "Another Caw," none of the other Fraserians, not even spry little Father Prout, could approach him.

A further point in connection with the *Rookwood* article must be mentioned here, although it will be necessary to refer to it later. The review is highly laudatory of Harrison Ainsworth; yet an earlier article, "Hints for a History of Highwaymen," *Fraser's,* March, 1834, which is without question from Thackeray's pen, strongly expresses disapproval of novels that retell dark deeds from the Newgate Calendar. Thackeray was later to amplify these adverse views in his subsequent well-known attacks on Ainsworth's *Jack Sheppard.* That in the interval he should contradict himself to the extent of writing a flattering notice of a highwayman novel would in itself, apart from all other evidence, have been sufficient ground for excluding "Another Caw" from Thackeray's bibliography.

A third review which Johnson suggests may be Thackeray's is "Mr.

Grant's *Great Metropolis*," *Fraser's*, December, 1836. His only reason for the attribution is that Thackeray in *Fraser's* of December, 1843, reviewed *Paris and Its People* by the same author. Since the earlier article states that its writer will never cease to attack the politics of Tom Duncombe, Thackeray's was probably not the only hand involved. The subject matter is not, however, as in the case of the *Rookwood* review, opposed to his opinions, and possibly in this slashing criticism, as in others, he was continuing the collaboration with Maginn begun in 1833. There can be no question about Maginn's authorship since, like "Another Caw from the Rookwood," the article is included by Mackenzie in *Fraserian Papers*.

Nor is it possible to regard the series of "Pluck Examination Questions" as offering more valid grounds for belief in Thackeray's authorship. Johnson suggests the attribution on the basis of subject matter and a reference to Tennyson's "Timbuctoo" rather than of any internal evidence. Even a superficial examination of the "Pluck Papers," however reveals insurmountable obstacles to the acceptance of this view. The first paper, for instance, contains an attack on Macaulay which is impossible to associate with Thackeray:

> There are to be found throughout the volumes . . . some choice specimens of Babbletongue Macaulay's juvenile oratory at a spouting-club, called the "Union." These later affairs are, of course, florid and elaborate enough: there is no want of tropes and sophistry. We can readily fancy the babbler, in another hemisphere, laughing heartily, as well at these as at his equally enlightened effusions on reform: they answered his purpose right well. He probably finds a lac of rupees can compensate for a lack of logic and honesty; and that even rhetorical figures are not half so amusing as Arabic ones, nor half so capable of skilful combinations for the purposes of Whiggery.[6]

This aspersion against Macaulay's honesty would have been far more in keeping with any of the other Fraserians than with Thackeray, who, though uninterested in political issues, was himself a Whig. In a letter to William Blackwood he defines his field of writing:

> Some years back you used to have pleasant papers in *Blackwood* called, "The World we live in." I should be glad to do something of like nature if you are disposed to accept my contributions. No politics, as much fun and satire as I can muster, literary talk and criticism of a spicy nature, and general gossip.[7]

This preference he again expresses in a letter to Thomas Longman of the *Edinburgh Review*.[8] When we remember that Thackeray's acknowledged work avoids references to politics except of the most innocuous nature, it is unreasonable to attribute to him an assault of this kind on a prominent member of his own party who was already an eminent writer.

Furthermore in a "Postscript to the Second Letter from Cambridge" we find an equally incongruous reference to Byron. After a passage describing the predatory habits of small poets comes the sentence: "Illustrate this passage from the history of contemporary writers; apply the Italian thief to Byron's conduct to Wordsworth, and shew the author of *Lalla Rookh* to be the Smallest poet in England."[9] Again this allusion would have come more appropriately from any of the other Fraserians. Thomas Moore was an old butt of Maginn, who had again and again spurred the magazine to attack him. Byron also had come in for a full share of depreciation. The notion that he had drawn unduly from Wordsworth had already been set forth on several occasions by the Fraserians.[10] Although Thackeray in his acknowledged writings bears a manly part in various Fraserian frays, neither Byron nor Moore are among the objects of his attack.

Even more decisive evidence against Thackeray's authorship of the "Pluck" series is that all three articles have the signature T.G. and are dated from St. Johns. In the following issues of the magazine two other articles appear also signed T.G.: "A Letter from Athens to Oliver Yorke," for September, 1836, and "A Scourging Soliloquy upon the Annuals," for January, 1837, again dated from St. Johns. There can be no question that these later T.G. essays are by the same hand as the "Pluck Papers." The Fraserians, however lax they might have been about borrowing material from each other, did not swap signatures. Furthermore, the articles purport to be by the author of "Pluck Papers" and both contain the same type of allusions to Cambridge as are found in the "Papers." Yet to assign either essay to Thackeray is manifestly absurd. The "Scourging Soliloquy," in spite of its title, is lenient to the annuals, and therefore contradictory to the verdict of "A Word about Annuals," December, 1838, which is almost surely by Thackeray. The "Letter from Athens" is even more definitely disqualified by Whig anathema and also by recondite information of the sort which did not interest Thackeray. The following passage, for instance, is obviously alien to anything we find in his writings:

The style of Longus, though not free from the affectations of the Sophist, has been generally praised for its vivacity and sweetness. . . . Villoison compares it to a transparent river, overshadowed by verdant woods, and Scaliger has recommended its grace and simplicity . . . and one of his learned commentators has found in his work the simplicity of Xenophon, the amatory charms of Theocritus, and the aureate richness of Moschus. . . . Yet, with all his merits, the reader never forgets that Longus was a sophist; in the midst of his happiest passages, some affected play of syllables, or some artful elegancy of style, betrays the School of Conceits.

The above passage is the type of work which is found in the contributions to *Fraser's* of the assiduous scholar Robert Avis Willmott, who, belated in taking his college course, began his connection with the magazine while he was an undergraduate at Cambridge. A series of essays on the Greek pastoral poets, assigned to him in an editorial comment, *Fraser's,* XXI, 21, is filled with passages similar in subject matter and style to the one quoted above. It is interesting to note that even these are not free from political stabs.

Still another article which, according to Johnson, might possibly have been written by Thackeray is "One or Two Words on One or Two Books," of April, 1837, a review of Landor's *A Satire on Satirists* and of Bulwer Lytton's *The Student of Padua.* A few sentences in the article, however, point unmistakably to *Fraser's* former assistant editor, John A. Heraud. Maginn himself is out of the question since he won, it will be remembered,[11] a suit for libel by proving that he was not the author. The first sentence speaks in disrespectful terms of Hazlitt's relation to Coleridge and Lamb: "As to Hazlitt, he was never much more than a sort of brain-sucker of the two others, whose conversations he carried away and cooked up into lectures." This was a theory which Heraud when in collaboration with Maginn had expressed in an earlier article in much the same words.[12] A second sentence speaks of Keats with a disparagement in keeping with the views of Maginn and Heraud but not associated with Thackeray's:

Then, as to the case of Keats, which, if we mistake not, has been usually charged against the *Quarterly,* what is the fact? Let any man read the poems left by this young author, and answer. His style was teeming with affectations, unredeemed by any great or original qualities.

The third sentence concerns a review published in the magazine nearly six years earlier, July, 1831, in which the writer expresses disapproval of an attack which Byron made in *Don Juan* on Landor, and adds, "Little did we then anticipate that we should ever have to censure a similar violation of good taste and feeling in Mr. Landor himself." The wording here would seem to imply that the writer had had full knowledge of the magazine's stand in the July, 1831, article, if indeed he had not been responsible for it. There is little doubt that Heraud and Maginn were the authors of the 1831 critique; in no case can Thackeray be associated with it since he could scarcely have been connected with *Fraser's* at that date.

With the elimination of the Landor review little indeed remains on the Melville and Johnson lists prior to *Yellowplush's* "Fashnable Fax" of 1837. Two more ghosts only, and these of very indifferent nature, are still to be laid. In his enlarged bibliography of Thackeray, published in 1910, Melville has included among the works of possible authenticity a short paraphrase from Anacreon, "When My Weary Worn-Out Eyes,"[13] which appeared in the January number for 1834.[14] Since the verses are of slight merit it is no great matter who wrote them; nor would it be easy to ascertain. Maginn, Prout, John Churchill, Robert Avis Willmott, among other Fraserians, busied themselves about the great Greek. Although the paraphrase is included by Mackenzie in Maginn's *Fraserian Papers,* such evidence is in this case inconclusive as Maginn may have been responsible for the compilation in which it occurs rather than for the poem itself. It is also doubtful if Thackeray, in spite of his own occasional vagaries, would have sanctioned the paraphrase's rhyming of *piece* with *peace, knock* with *look, shivering* with *quiver in, God* with *road, vie* with *eau de vie, etc.*

The last ghost of this suggested pre-*Yellowplush* writing is the "Jew of York," for September, 1836. The story is included in the lists of both Johnson and Melville, but it is difficult to believe that either bibliographer seriously considered the work attributable to Thackeray. The only reason given for its selection is that its title suggests the author of *Rebecca and Rowena.*[15] The two tales, however, bear no resemblance to each other. The "Jew of York" is a feeble imitation of *Ivanhoe* without satirical intent in its dull bathos. Any attempt to put it beside the cutting burlesque, *Rebecca and Rowena,* reveals its shortcomings. Even its presence in the magazine is difficult to explain, since *Fraser's* from the beginning had ruthlessly lampooned the imitators of Scott; but its attribution to one of the staff critics who shared in exposing the enormity of such scenes as those with which it ends becomes preposterous.

Thus out of the suggested pre-*Yellowplush* bibliography there remain only three reviews and one translation, "Hints for a History of Highwaymen," *Fraser's,* March, 1834; part of "A Dozen Novels," April, 1834; "Paris and the Parisians," February, 1836; and "Il était un Roi d'Yvetot," May, 1834. Although neither Johnson nor Melville has given his reasons for ascribing the reviews to Thackeray, all four works would seem to stand the test of authenticity. Concerning one of them certainly there can be no doubt. The "Il était un Roi" ballad, included in the "*Fraser* Papers" of May, 1834, Johnson discovered was rewritten under the title "The King of Brentford" for George Cruikshank's *Omnibus,* No. 8, 1841. The resemblance between the two versions establishes beyond question the identity of the *Fraser* poem.

A second item of the four may also safely be assigned to Thackeray. It is difficult to imagine any of the other *Fraser* critics taking the time to write "Hints for a History of Highwaymen," which appeared in *Fraser's* for March, 1834. They were too vehemently preoccupied with antagonisms and other *isms* to find interest in the historic art of highwaymanry; nor, had they settled down to its untimely strifes, would they have been able to exclude from their review the more urgent contentions of their own day. Nothing is so incongruous to the majority of the *Fraser* reviewers as unimpassioned observation, and therefore nothing is so suggestive of Thackeray's more neutral stand. But in addition to its subject matter a chain of circumstances practically fixes the identity of "Hints for a History of Highwaymen."

And here it is necessary to comment briefly on Thackeray's heated opposition to his friend Harrison Ainsworth, which we have already discussed in the chapter dealing with his criticism.[16] The attack we have shown was launched in the serial novel *Catherine,* a crude burlesque on Ainsworth's *Jack Sheppard,* which was running contemporaneously in *Bentley's Miscellany. Catherine's* animadversions were supported, it will be remembered, by a stinging review of *Jack Sheppard,* in *Fraser's* for February, 1840. There can be no doubt that this critique is to be ascribed to Thackeray. To begin with, no other reviewer for *Fraser's* would have been inclined to attack Ainsworth. The old guard of Maginn were unanimously in his favor; of the new recruits there is no evidence that Theodore Martin wrote criticism for the magazine and the work of Kenealy is in a different manner. Even if a hostile reviewer could be found, it is difficult to believe that he would have kept so completely clear of political allusions and that his work would have dovetailed so neatly with Thackeray's convictions. The article inveighs against the futility and brutality of punishment by hanging, which Thackeray was shortly to attack in his "On Going to See a Man Hanged." More especially, it reiterates the arguments against the crime novels of Ainsworth which Thackeray had previously urged in "Cheap Knowledge," and which he was at that very moment stressing in the final number of *Catherine.* The passages already quoted in the discussion of *Fraser's* criticism show how closely interlocked by thought and phrase were all three of these attacks on gallows' fiction. In fact, it would be possible, as we have remarked, to interchange paragraphs from the texts without altering the content. Since two of these critiques are avowedly by Thackeray, it would be unreasonable to deny the authenticity of the third, especially as no one else at the time would appear to have been interested in his theory that the details of actual existence make better fiction than a sentimentalized interpretation.

Evidence in favor of Thackeray's authorship of the *Sheppard* review becomes even stronger when we recall that he did not limit the expression of his opinions to *Fraser's.* The same arguments and much the same phrasing are found in his article on Fielding, published in the *Times* for September 2, 1840, and indeed even years later in his well-known lecture on Hogarth, Smollett, and Fielding, and in his introduction to an edition of Fielding's works.

If the *Sheppard* review is to be added to the post-*Yellowplush* bibliography, it is impossible to exclude "Hints for a History of Highwaymen" from Thackeray's pre-*Yellowplush* work. The attack on Ainsworth opens with a long citation from the end of the 1834 critique.[17] Had Thackeray not written this first review, he would scarcely have remembered the drift of its argument, since, as he himself remarked, it had appeared nearly six years before. Furthermore, although he used the editorial "we" he was evidently making a plea for the constancy of his own personal views as evidenced by the earlier article.

It thus appears that at least two of the four items remaining on the Johnson-Melville pre-*Yellowplush* list are from Thackeray's hand. The authorship of the other two, "A Dozen Novels," April, 1834, and "Paris and the Parisians," February, 1836, is not so open to proof. The former is a long series of reviews covering thirty pages of the magazine's close print. Some of these connect too intimately with Maginn's earlier work to be from the hand of another. Thus the opening critique of the *Black Watch,* harks back to previous discussion of historical novels,[18] and is full of affectionate references to the author Andrew Picken, whose death was regarded as a personal loss by the early *Fraser* confrères. Nor is it easy to think that the review of Hook's *Parson's Daughter* was not in part the work of Maginn, who with Lockhart had some years before on several occasions written the same sort of gossipy, intimate commentaries on the mutual friend.[19] A third review of the dozen was at least brushed over by the Hibernian O'Doherty. Its full discussion of Maria Edgeworth's *Helen* includes the delightfully Irish comparison of her later effete characters with the jolly bibulous squires of *Castle Rackrent* and explains with purely Irish wisdom the theory previously brought out by Maginn in 1831[20] that the novelist's father must be held accountable for this tavern realism. More in keeping also with Maginn than with Thackeray is the review of *The Young Muscovite,* which makes an irrelevant fling of some length at Lord Palmerston, "and the other men milliners," who might "spare an hour from the duties of the office and the boudoir." With the exception of these four passages, "A Dozen Novels" might easily be entirely from Thackeray's pen.

The last of the four items remaining on the Johnson-Melville pre-*Yellowplush* list is "Paris and the Parisians" for February, 1838. Here again the complete lack of adverse evidence is an indication of Thackerian authorship. Throughout its considerable length it keeps clear from political reference, which in itself is much in its favor. Furthermore, for all its sharp thrusts, it is controlled, giving no quarter, but avoiding insult.

In addition it is quite probable that the short satiric story, "The Contested Election," published as far back as January, 1833, may be Thackeray's. In this case it would have been sent in as an individual contribution while he and Maginn were still searching for a magazine and before they had begun their collaboration. The presence of the little story in the magazine is difficult to explain on any other basis than that of Thackeray's authorship. It is not easy to picture any of the politically-agitated Fraserians sitting quietly down in an unprejudiced frame of mind to write a story of a campaign in which there is not a slur against Whigs or Radicals. The tale throughout remains a gentle satire on the absurd accusations which accompany electioneering. Thackeray later in his life was to do much the same thing far more maturely and elaborately at the end of his biographical *Adventures of Philip,* the election scenes of which were avowedly based on his own experience in helping with Charles Buller's campaign. This had occurred in 1832 and, therefore, if Thackeray was the author of "The Contested Election" of *Fraser's* for January, 1833, it would have been fresh in his mind. In the early story it will be noticed that the Whig candidate is made a philanthropist and conquers by his goodness, that a slight love touch comes at the end, that the writer is quite a little inclined to preach, and that he makes reference to Rome and other places on the Continent which would have been natural to a young man recently returned. If the story is Thackeray's, as indeed it would appear to be, it is of interest as probably his first contribution to the magazine which was to receive for so many years the best of his early writing.

In addition to the translation "Il était un Roi," two other ballads may possibly be Thackeray's, "Si j'étais petit oiseau" and "Vous veillerez," appearing in the "*Fraser* Papers" for February, 1834. Both are translations from Béranger; both are regular in meter, and therefore presumably not by Prout. They are introduced by a commendatory word from Maginn after various observations on Béranger, Leigh Hunt, Byron, and Shelley, which go back to earlier Hunt-Byron discussions. Therefore they are probably not by Maginn himself.

These last short translations, the acknowledged "Il était un Roi" ballad, "The Contested Election," the reviews which Thackeray presumably wrote alone, including "Hints for a History of Highwaymen," the various compilations in which he presumably took more or less share, and finally the critical series on poetry and on fiction, written in collaboration with Maginn, would seem to comprise the pre-*Yellowplush* bibliography.

The examination of Thackeray's post-*Yellowplush* writing is less interesting because so much of it was acknowledged that comparatively few problems of authenticity remain. Fortunately Thackeray lived for seventeen years after he stopped writing for *Fraser's* and thus had opportunity himself to republish or see republished the greater bulk of this later *Fraser* work from 1837 to 1847. Only a few items have been included, even in Mr. Melville's enlarged bibliography, which were not either reprinted in Thackeray's lifetime or claimed by the well-known pseudonyms Charles Yellowplush and Michael Angelo Titmarsh. These unacknowledged items may be briefly listed: "A Word about the Annuals," December, 1837; "Our Batch of Novels for Christmas," January, 1838; "Half-a-Crown's Worth of Cheap Knowledge," February, 1838; a caricature of Sydney Smith, April, 1838; "Four German Ditties," May, 1838; "Our Annual Execution," January, 1839; "Recollections of Germany," January, 1840. "The Diary of the Late Dolly Duster," October and November, 1838, although not signed by Yellowplush, contains a paraphrase, as Johnson pointed out, which involves it so irrefutably with the productions of that gentleman that it need not be included here for further discussion.

Of the seven remaining items one at least is not from Thackeray's hand. "Recollections of Germany," January, 1840, must be assigned definitely to Robert Pearse Gillies, *Fraser's* biographer of Sir Walter Scott, as portions of it are incorporated in his personal reminiscences, published toward the end of his life.[21] A second sketch, "The Rev. Sydney Smith," is also presumably not Thackeray's. It belongs to the *Fraser* "Gallery of Literary Characters," the famous series of cartoons which, it will be remembered, was started in the magazine shortly after its commencement in February, 1830. The sketches with five exceptions, which are carefully listed by Bates, were written by William Maginn to accompany the drawings of Maclise. There is no reason to feel that the notice of Smith should be considered among the exceptions. It is thoroughly Maginnish in tone, is reminiscent of the earlier days of magazine writing, and has always been attributed to the chief author of the series. On equally doubtful footing is "Our Annual Execution," for January, 1839, a review of the gift books of the preceding Christmas. There is no doubt that Thackeray wrote an earlier critique on the Christmas books, "A Word on the Annuals," which is also listed among the seven items under consideration. In the interim, however, between 1837 and 1839, the "Scourging Soliloquy" appeared, which as has already been shown, cannot from any point of view be attributed to Thackeray and may presumably be assigned to R. A. Willmott. There is, therefore, no reason to assume that the reviews of the annuals were written by one author. As a matter of fact in the earlier numbers of the magazine one such review is ascribed to Churchill, another to Barry Cornwall, and a third is almost certainly by Maginn.[22] Furthermore, when we examine the "Annual Execution," we find no evidence of Thackeray's authorship, but at least one reference that would tell against it. Nowhere in Thackeray's acknowledged work for the magazine is there any reference to Maginn. It was not the habit of the older Fraserians, with the exception of Lockhart, to puff the enterprising first editor. With the advent of Edward Vaughan Kenealy to the staff a new note of flattery is found, culminating in the "Brallaghan," series,[23] of which O'Doherty was made a central character. There is much about the "Annual Execution" to suggest Kenealy as the author. It contains not only a highly laudatory notice of Maginn, but a long quotation from his work. The beginning of the review is also especially characteristic of Kenealy, and especially difficult to associate with Thackeray.

A fourth item on the list, "Four German Ditties," may indeed be from Thackeray's pen. The subject matter of these adaptations is so much more in keeping with Thackeray and what he would have chosen to translate than with the other Fraserians that on that score alone one is tempted to ascribe them to him. When one takes into consideration the simple yet firm handling of the lines themselves, the regularity and ease of verse form, there remains comparatively little doubt of their authenticity.

The remaining three items of the seven may be definitely assigned to Thackeray, and are of especial interest as being the only work unacknowledged by the satirist for which there is conclusive evidence. This evidence, it should be gratefully remembered, was first brought to light by Johnson. In regard to "A Word on the Annuals," he points out that a footnote to the article reads: "Our friend Mr. Yellowplush has made inquiries as to the authorship of this tale and his report is that it is universally ascribed in the higher circles to Misses Howell and James." As the first "Yellowplush" paper had appeared only the month before, it is highly improbable that any of the other Fraserians would have been sufficiently aware of the correspondence to have made a cross reference to it. In addition it should probably be stated that the review of the annuals is precisely the sort of criticism that might be expected of Thackeray. It is in line with his later reviews in the magazine and is entirely free from political or other reference which might raise a question as to its authenticity.

The second article, or rather the first three reviews included in it, stands on even firmer ground. Johnson called attention to an entry in Thackeray's notebook for January, 1838, "Twenty-four pages in *Fraser,* Yellowplush Trollope, Bulwer, Landon, and a design"; and noted that the "Yellowplush" paper for that month covered almost twelve pages and that the reviews of Trollope, Bulwer, and Landon in "Our Batch of Novels for Christmas" amounted to another twelve. This entry, therefore, establishes the identity of the first three critiques of the "Batch."

A glance at these reviews themselves confirms Johnson's discovery. The reference to the Inner Temple in the Oliver Yorke introduction is more like Thackeray than like the other Fraserians, and the freedom from abusive political reference is an even stronger indication of his authorship. This last is in marked contrast to the second half of the "Batch." No sooner had Thackeray laid down the pen than his successor commenced a tirade against O'Connell, Lord Morpeth, Lord John Russell, and Dick Sheil. This successor was almost without question Maginn, as appears from the sentence in which the writer terms himself the earliest and dearest friend of Oliver Yorke. Other details supporting his authorship are the reminiscent mention of "Our Man of

Genius," his nickname for John Churchill, and the equally reminiscent allusion to his old butt, "Omnipresence" Montgomery of the Satanic School.

The evidence for the third article is fully as sound as for that of the reviews of Trollope, Bulwer, and L.E.L. "Half-a-Crown's Worth of Cheap Knowledge," Johnson observed is referred to twice in Thackeray's notebook: under January 31, "Wrote on Penny Newspapers for Frasers"; and again, "Wrote for Fraser on Penny Press and Yellowplush, No. IV—Feb." When we turn to the article in question, which we have already had occasion to mention in connection with the Harrison Ainsworth quarrel, we find this conclusive external evidence well borne out by internal. The review covers some fifteen of the penny journals of the day and offers ample opportunity for the introduction of political gossip; yet the author, in contrast to the practices of the rest of the staff, veers sharply from political issues. It is doubtful if any of the other Fraserians would have kept hands off with such easy rectitude.

The *Fraser* bibliography of Thackeray after *Yellowplush's* "Fashnable Fax" of November, 1837, thus presumably consists, in addition to acknowledged work, of the translation, "Four German Ditties," and of at least four articles, the authenticity of which may be considered established: the review of Ainsworth's *Jack Sheppard;* "A Word on the Annuals"; the Trollope, Bulwer, and Landon reviews in "Our Batch of Novels for Christmas"; and "Half-a-Crown's Worth of Cheap Knowledge." Unquestionably these items do not cover all of the unacknowledged post-*Yellowplush* work in *Fraser's;* yet it is not easy to add appreciably to the list. "Our Club at Paris," for April, 1838, Johnson mentions in connection with the entry in Thackeray's notebook: "Yellowplush in April, Letter from Paris." Although, as he says, this is the only thing in the April number that bears any semblance to a letter, he feels that it is scarcely possible that Thackeray could have written either the "Club" for that month or its successors for May and June, and finds that the diary note is "puzzling." His decision against Thackeray's authorship of the letters is unquestionably correct. It may be, however, that the mystifying phrase, "Letter from Paris," refers to the *Yellowplush* paper for the following month, May, which was dated from Paris. In other words, the two papers may have been written at the same time and therefore recorded under the same entry, putting Thackeray a month ahead in the correspondence of the worthy butler.

Although it is impossible to accept "Our Club at Paris," as Thackeray's work, we can definitely accredit him with at least one additional review of this later period. "Horæ Catnachianæ" for April, 1839, has already been discussed in the chapter on criticism as of special interest because it is in the sequence of his attacks against the "gallows' school" of fiction, the field of criticism which Thackeray made peculiarly his own after it had ceased to interest Maginn and other early reviewers for the magazine. The essay opens with the explanation that it is the sequel to "Half-a-Crown's Worth of Cheap Knowledge." Since this last has already been given to Thackeray on the evidence of his notebook, there can be no uncertainty as to the authenticity of the "Catnach" review. The close parallels in subject matter between the two essays, of which we have already spoken, leave no chance for suspecting that any hand other than Thackeray's was involved. Not only the main point, but the subdivisions of the reviews and the whole manner of treatment are the same. It is also to be noticed that a parallel exists between the close of the "Catnach" essay and that of *Catherine,* published in February, 1840, nearly a year later. In both the author lays aside the literary device he has been using and speaks in his own right. In both he denounces the Newgate material of Dickens and Ainsworth as not true to life or presenting wholesome company in which to live. "There is no harm," Thackeray announces at the end of "Catnachianæ," "in hearing of the manners and conversation of dustmen, chimney-sweeps, thieves, and their like: they are men, and, *nihil humanum* is alien to honest readers and critics. But we may hear too much of them. We may find them, on examination, even to be sham thieves and dustmen; and the profit to be derived from the study of such characters ceases straightway."

APPENDIX 2

A QUESTION OF IDENTIFICATION—CARLYLE, HERAUD, AND MAGINN

We have mentioned in "Revolt in Criticism" that much of the philosophical writing in *Fraser's,* aside from *Sartor Resartus* and other accredited work, shows strong Carlylian trend of thought and style.[1] Theories and methods of attack which the master had made his own are repeated in articles unacknowledged by him. There is an uncanny similarity of phrase and even of impetuous sentence swing. In fact, if Carlyle did not have a hand in these essays, certainly no one else should have had.

An item which some years ago[2] I suggested might be his is the review of Cunningham's *Maid of Elvar.* In this case the attribution hinges on the author's sympathetic attitude toward Byron and on the inclusion of a passage markedly similar to well-known lines in Carlyle's *Hero as Poet.* The Fraserians' attitude toward Byron, with the exception of Carlyle's, was uniformly hostile. Although in places they admitted his genius, they heaped abuse upon him as a man and so qualified his achievement as a poet that the effect of their criticism is highly derogatory.[3] At no time would they have adopted the elegiac strain found in the Cunningham article: "Let the dumb heart break and to sorrow be given no words."[4] In regard to the passage paralleled in the *Hero as Poet* the evidence for authenticity is even stronger. The date of the *Maid of Elvar* review was 1832; that of the *Hero as Poet* not until some eight years later. Yet the lines from the review present a closer parallel to those of the famous essay than is to be found in any of Carlyle's acknowledged works. If the review was written by anyone other than Carlyle, the person must have taken notes during some conversation with the master and used them openly. Such a conspicuous case of plagiarism appears improbable when one remembers that it would have been immediately detected. Carlyle was known to have been an old friend of Cunningham; he was known to have taken shortly before a special trip to Dumfries to speak in his honor; and no one could have presumed that he would have failed to notice an article on the poet appearing in the same periodical to which he himself so largely contributed. It is, therefore, reasonably safe to assume that Carlyle was himself responsible for the passage and for the article in which it was contained.

When I first published this conclusion, I believed that Carlyle was the sole author of this review. Further examination, however, has convinced me that Heraud also had some share in the work. The first part of the essay goes unmistakably back to the discussion of the "Man of Genius," which Heraud commenced in the initial number of the magazine, February, 1830,[5] and continued at intervals for seven or eight years. The original "Man of Genius" article presumably derives whatever thought it has chiefly from Coleridge. Imagination is looked upon as the creative faculty of the mind, the faculty which the man of genius or poet possesses in common with the Divinity. The poet, according to the essay, is not a great man in whom accident or circumstance has developed one special aptitude rather than another; instead he is a man born with a special aptitude and placed in circumstances which have fostered that aptitude and not thwarted or neglected it. This last view it will be recognized is the opposite of Carlyle's theory of the hero, who was first and foremost essentially the great man, whatever rôle he might be required by the needs of his age to play. Certainly at no point does Carlyle derive his thought from Heraud's discussion of the "Man of Genius," and in any case it is improbable that he would have taken over a subject which another writer had made conspicuously his own. Since the review of the novel devotes its first three pages to an analysis of the "Man of Genius," it is, therefore, presumable that Carlyle was not its only author.

What might easily have happened is that the article was the result of an evening's conversation between Carlyle and Heraud on the subject of the new book, *The Maid of Elvar,* by their mutual friend Allan Cunningham. The Carlyles were in London during the winter of 1832, and Heraud became sufficiently intimate with them at that time to help them select their home in Cheyne Row when they subsequently returned in 1834. There was, furthermore, as we have seen, long established precedent for collaboration among the Fraserians. Various lighter series in the magazine were avowedly composites,[6] and Maginn undoubtedly in more serious effort worked in conjunction with Lockhart, Churchill, and with Heraud himself. It is, therefore, quite possible that Carlyle also might not have been averse to letting his thought earn for him an honest penny without entailing much expenditure of time or energy. Such a view of the case would explain the introduction of the sympathetic strain which the essay adopts toward Byron; it would account for the kindly and peculiarly Carlylian tone of the latter part of the work, and finally it would explain the transition which the article presents from Heraud's man of genius to Carlyle's great man. The essay begins with Heraud's notion that genius is defective since it represents an aptitude for one thing only, a development along a single line at the expense of others.[7] It then contrasts these "people with one idea" to the hypothetical "perfect man," with faculties in a "state of equilibrium," the development of one balancing that of another. In this connection occurs the passage earlier referred to, which was paralleled eight years later in the famous *Hero as Poet.* The lines are expressive of Carlyle's point of view as opposed to that affirmed by Heraud in "Poetical Genius" and are particularly prophetic of the master's later wording:

> Shakespeare and Milton! ye were almost perfect men—so were Dante and Homer. Spenser, also, and Virgil, and Tasso, were only not perfect—and are honoured for having produced works which men entomb; splendidly bound in their libraries, and never read! But it is of these works we speak, in the article of perfection, not now of the personal conduct of the writers. In them we see the most perfect humanity developed with which we are acquainted. The form of its development is the poetical—granted. But the poetical form is capable of including the whole compass of human science and art. Are not Shakespeare, Milton, and Dante, orators as well as poets? theologians also? metaphysicians? statists? musicians? fathers? actors on the great stage of the world? men of business? All! All![8]

That these lines are forerunners of Carlyle's is seen on reviewing *Heroes and Heroism,* one passage of which reads:

> I confess, I have no notion of a truly great man that could not be all sorts of men. The Poet who could merely sit on a chair, and compose stanzas, would never make a stanza worth much. He could not sing the Heroic warrior, unless he himself were at least a Heroic warrior too. I fancy there is in him the Politician, the Thinker, Legis-

lator, Philosopher;—in one or the other degree, he could have been, he is all these.[9]

The style here is better than in the *Fraser* article, but the thought is substantially the same. Heraud, with his record for prolific uncreative work, would scarcely by himself have chanced upon the brilliant interpretation of the poet-hero theme expressed in the *Fraser* paragraph. To suppose that Carlyle was indebted to Heraud for one of the important passages in his *Hero as Poet* would be as unwarrantable. He had already in his *Burns*, his *Goethe*, and various of his other early essays published before the commencement of *Fraser's*, treated the poet as the great man, the hero. His later elaborations of the idea in *Sartor Resartus* and *Hero Worship* were such intimate expressions of his own personality that it would be absurd to isolate an individual passage as traceable to a writer with the magpie propensities of Heraud. Far more reasonable would be our supposition that the *Maid of Elvar* review grew out of a talk between Carlyle and Heraud, with the understanding that the magazine's assistant editor should make for their mutual profit the best shift he could of their joint material. Only such a theory can account for the strangely hybrid character of the essay. Later when Carlyle was preparing his lecture on the *Hero as Poet* he probably looked over his notes made in previous years and came upon the passage which had in substance already been incorporated in the *Fraser* article.

If the *Maid of Elvar* review, as would appear from this evidence, was written at least in part by Carlyle, it is possible that he was also the joint author of the excellent "Cambrian Colloquy on the Decline and Fall of Poetry," December, 1834, from which passages have been quoted in the discussion of criticism.[10] The dialogue continues the discussion of poetic genius, taking the final step toward identification of the genius with Carlyle's conception of the great man.

In this case, evidence of joint authorship does not, however, rest on so solid a base as for the *Maid of Elvar* review. The author of the 1832 article could scarcely have reached his conclusion except, as has been said, from notes taken on Carlyle's conversation; the 1834 dialogue on the other hand could have been based upon remarks in *Sartor Resartus* or indeed upon the *Maid of Elvar* review itself. While in places, such as the passages we have quoted, the general cast of thought and phrase of "The Decline and Fall of Poetry" is Carlyle's, on that score alone authenticity cannot be established. Unfortunately repetition of Carlyle's thought is to be found in the treatment of subjects in which he could have had no share. In an essay "Critical Illustrations of Lord Byron's Poetry," March, 1833, there is, for instance, an elaboration of his suggestion, made in *Burns,* 1828, and elsewhere, that Byron failed to attain moral manhood, and also an elaboration of the reason given for Byron's lack of such attainment—that he could not be "both poet and man of the world."[11] Furthermore, in its allusions, its turns of expression, and its general impetus of sentence the work is often typically Carlylian. Yet this essay definitely belongs to Heraud's series on Byron. It is connected by cross reference to other members of the series,[12] it overlaps them in subject matter, and finally, like them, it continues the analysis of poetical genius[13] which Heraud began in the first number of *Fraser's.* Moreover, in spite of the philosophical approach to the subject it is difficult to imagine Carlyle as being in even the smallest degree connected with the writing of the essay. The lengthy discussion of Boyle,[14] for example, is at once too detailed, too confused, and too reminiscent of Coleridge to be associated with Carlyle; nor can one imagine Carlyle as willingly sharing in a work which from start to finish had as its sole object a harsh exposure of the moral and poetical shortcomings of Byron.

Probably of all the quasi-philosophical articles in *Fraser's* the one which is most like Carlyle and yet cannot possibly be his, is the fine essay on Blake, "The Last of the Supernaturalists," for March, 1830. A few years ago Mr. J. A. S. Barrett, as we have mentioned, attributed it to Carlyle[15] on what he considered incontestable grounds. Without qualification he states that "there can be no doubt regarding Carlyle's authorship; the internal evidence is so strong that no lengthy proof is required." He then cites the frequent use of the word "otherwise," the phrase "it had been well for him," and the inclusion of a quotation from Wordsworth's lines on Chatterton and Burns as having parallels in Carlyle's essay on Burns. He notices also the following characteristic expressions: "charnel-fuming *lips* of the *persifleur,*" "the venerable Goethe," "a truly inspired *vates,*" "ashy apples of the Asphaltic lake," "among the great ones of her metropolitan Babel," "his tender footsteps over the burning marl of mortal life," "that he may put money in his purse." Mr. Barrett further calls attention to the quotations from Milton, Burns, Dante, Hoffmann, Burton, Schiller; to the story of *Heyne;* to the biblical quotation at the end of the review which, as he points out, is also the ending of Carlyle's essay *The Life and Writing of Werner,* 1828; and to the fact that there is a citation from "German Romance, by Thomas Carlyle, Esq."

Some of this evidence is especially convincing and would under ordinary circumstances point to Carlylian authorship. Unfortunately it is equally applicable to Heraud, whose sources of quotation and allusion were, as has been said, much the same as Carlyle's, or if anything wider, and who was prone to make swift piratical excursions into the earlier essays of his famous contemporary, showing particular partiality for his *Burns.* Moreover, "The Last of the Supernaturalists" is a detailed and studied continuation of Heraud's discussion in the essay "Poetical Genius," begun the month before in the first number of the magazine. While in itself the Blake review is not especially under the influence of Coleridge, when taken into connection with this earlier essay, its remarks on the madness of genius, or the rapt state of the mind in the process of creation,[16] become highly uncharacteristic of Carlyle. Furthermore, the citation from "German Romance by Thomas Carlyle, Esq." arouses suspicion. It was not like Carlyle to make so ostentatious a reference, but it was very like Heraud or Maginn. Nor is there evidence in Carlyle's acknowledged writing that he was interested in Blake. It is also to be noticed that in this case there is no possibility of joint authorship, as the date of the essay is March, 1830, more than a year before Carlyle became acquainted with either Heraud or Maginn.

Two other essays which Mr. Barrett attributed to Carlyle[17] and which on the strength of his recommendation were added to Mr. Dyer's bibliography, are "The Dominie's Legacy; Fashionable Novels," for April, 1830, and "Mr. Edward Lytton Bulwer's Novels, and Remarks on Novel Writing," for June, 1830. The evidence for both of these essays is even less valid than for "The Last of the Supernaturalists." In an earlier treatment of the subject[18] I noted that the various expressions which Mr. Barrett selected as characteristic of Carlyle were also to be found in other *Fraser* work in which Carlyle could have had no hand;[19] that the references to Kant, Fichte, Reid, Goethe, Schelling, Locke, Stewart, Milton, and Dryden were by no means confined to his writing;[20] that the philosophical passages raised the gravest doubts as to their authenticity, and that the author's contention against "the fashionable novels" was one which was widespread and stoutly upheld by the Fraserians in general and William Maginn in particular.[21] In fact both essays strongly bear the marks of Maginn, working perhaps in collaboration with Heraud. The flippant character of the entire subject matter, as, for instance, the passage giving Dr. Eady and "his syphilitic cures" and "old bone-grubbing" Cobbett and "his mountebank lectures" as evidences, along with Thomas Babington Macaulay and others, of "the extreme gullibility of mankind," awakens suspicion, since Carlyle even in his most irascible period did not indulge to any extent in objectionable personalities. Moreover, praise of Coleridge, which in itself would have been an astonishing contradiction in Carlyle, ends with the strange statement: "The fact is, Reid had an indistinct perception of a system of philosophy which has since been perfected by Kant and Schelling in Germany, and by Stewart and Coleridge in England." Additional evidence against authenticity is found in a highly flattering comment on Heraud's long and stodgy poem *The Descent into Hell;* and in the spelling *Göthe,* used uniformly in the first volumes by Maginn, Heraud, and other Fraserians except Carlyle, in whose acknowledged work *Goethe* alone appears. The essays are from beginning to end intimately linked with the preferences and quarrels of William Maginn. The signature of Ned Culpepper and the reference to MacGrawler[22] connect the work with his redoubtable battle against the *New Monthly Magazine,* Bulwer Lytton, and Cyrus Redding, as well as with his more sober contention against a host of political leaders, including Goulburn, Mackintosh, Huskisson, Hume, and O'Connell. These last, among a host of others, are reviled in a heated article, "Place-Men, Parliament-Men, Penny-a-Liners, and Parliamentary Reporters," for October, 1830, which is also signed Ned Culpepper. The next month, under the caption "Symposiac the First," Ned Culpepper sings a rough song at the expense of Cyrus Redding. Yet all of this, which was fire in the nostrils of Maginn and the more belligerent members of his staff, could have held at this period little interest for Carlyle, or at least only that accompanied by vexation and repugnance.

It might well, in fact, have been articles of this very nature which called forth Carlyle's irritable ejaculation of "Dog's meat-tart of a magazine." For in spite of their incongruity with his own work, these essays, as has been shown, impinge upon his field of meditation, use his literary background, sun themselves in the authorities he held most high, and flaunt even scraps from his own published work before his helpless eyes.

The difficulty is that if Carlyle, Heraud, and Maginn could on occasion thus approximate one another in style, allusion, and various points of interest, proof for genuine Carlylian work is for the most part nullified, especially since Heraud was capable of appropriating Carlyle's thought in anonymous articles where such appropriation would not be too conspicuous.

In making this assertion, we should in like manner state that, on the other hand, not more than seven articles can be definitely assigned to Heraud as the sole author. Three of the seven rest on especially firm ground. The authenticity of "Notes on Byron's *Cain*," for April, 1831, is incontestable since the essay includes a long quotation from actual notes taken by the writer during one of Coleridge's Thursday evening talks.[23] Two years later Heraud repeated the quotation, and some of the comments upon it in his oration delivered at Russell Institute, on the death of Coleridge.[24] On this occasion he stated that the notes had originally been taken by himself. On the evidence of the same Russell Institute oration "Some Account of Coleridge's Philosophy," for June, 1832, is also to be ascribed to Heraud. The article clearly furnished the ground-work for the speech. In fact the latter adds nothing to the argument and very little to the illustrative material of the original commentary. Since this commentary was again and again conspicuously cited in subsequent *Fraser* work, it is not probable that Heraud in a public address would have drawn so heavily upon it had he not himself been its author. The case for the third essay, "On Poetical Genius," February, 1830, which has already been mentioned as by Heraud, rests on much the same grounds as the commentary. Although it gives no credit to Coleridge, it is none the less an application, somewhat confused and distorted, of his theories of the creative imagination of man and the creative faculty of the Deity. Like the commentary, it is frequently referred to in later articles and is occasionally found dovetailed with their thought even when it is not mentioned. Thus the review of Byron's *Cain* holds in its more elaborate interpretation of Coleridge much of the earlier "Poetical Genius." The argument of the article was, moreover, later used by Heraud in his speech delivered at the Milton Institute, in October, 1837, on the subject "Poetical Genius as a Moral Power," and subsequently published over his signature.

Of the remaining articles, a series of three essays on German poets[25] may be ascribed to Heraud on the basis of a reference in the magazine to criticisms of Schiller, Klopstock, Berger "contributed by Mr. Carlyle and Mr. Heraud."[26] Since in this case there seems slight probability of Carlyle's having any hand whatever in the criticism of Klopstock, Berger, or the other poets in the series, it is fairly safe to assume that Heraud was the author. The obituary, "Reminiscences of Coleridge," for October, 1834, the explanatory material in "Coleridgeiana," for January, 1835, and the review, "Coleridge's Table-talk," for August, 1835, are obviously, and indeed avowedly, by the same hand as the earlier "Some Account of Coleridge's Philosophy," the subject matter of which they presuppose. On the same basis the introduction to the "Monologues by the Late Samuel Taylor Coleridge," for November and December, 1835, should be ascribed to Heraud. In connection with the authenticity of all this work it should be mentioned that a gossipy account of the early *Fraser* staff refers saucily to Heraud, the author of the dignified *Descent into Hell,* as having written "transcendentalism of the Coleridgean kind occasionally, for many a long year, until the cruel Thackeray massacred him in *Punch,* and he performed the descent which one of his own epics celebrates."[27]

As this flippant comment indicates, Heraud's share in the quasi-philosophical criticisms of the magazine was doubtless not confined to the nine articles just listed. But here caution is needed. There is little trace of the influence of either Carlyle or Maginn in the articles on German poetry, on Coleridge, or on poetic genius. They have not the impetus, the alertness, or the swift allusions of Heraud's more forceful and original colleagues, and are indeed thoroughly consistent with Heraud's own Russell Institute address on "Genius as a Moral Power," and his other acknowledged work. If, therefore, the more vigorous essays of the quasi-philosophical group are also to be ascribed to him, they should be definitely recognized as out of keeping with his identified writing. Heraud lived to be an old man, and for years his contributions to the *Athenæum* and the *London Illustrated Magazine* were matter-of-fact and superficial, while his scanty acknowledged work of greater pretension was, as has been said, pedantic and so full of repetition as to lose headway.[28] That such a man should have produced unassisted the more energetic, if eccentric, articles of the group is almost incredible.

What presumably occurred, as we suggested in the discussions of *Fraser's* criticism, is that Heraud, during these *Fraser* years, felt the directing hand of Maginn, for whom proximity tempted collaboration. Paragraphs, even whole sections of articles, might readily have passed from the vivacious editor to his more plodding assistant. In any case, Heraud would have been aware of Maginn's demand for rapidity, concreteness, and informality.

If such a collaborative relation existed, Maginn, with his attention to some extent turned toward philosophical comment, might easily have himself written that strange medley of criticism, politics, and metaphysics which has earlier been discussed, "Mr. Edward Lytton Bulwer's Novels, and Remarks on Novel Writing." Heraud, on his side, might have produced the greater part of the concrete and appealing interpretation of Blake, "The Last of the Supernaturalists," as well as explosive criticisms like "Lord Byron's Juvenile Poems," for September, 1832, "Critical Illustrations of Lord Byron's Poetry," for March, 1833, "The Book of Enoch," for November, 1833; condescending answers to atheism like "Godwin's *Thoughts on Man,*" for June, 1831; and direct denunciations like the "Bridgewater Treatises," chiefly against Whewell and Chalmers, for July, 1833, and October, 1835. These essays and others of the singular group are literary anomalies difficult to explain on any other basis than collaboration. They are as unlike Heraud's normal writing as they are unlike Maginn's.

Indeed the participation of Maginn and Carlyle in these articles is in somewhat the same case. There is evidence that both collaborated with Heraud in at least one or two essays. It is presumably that their collaboration was extended to other articles as well, but it is also presumable that in every instance it was limited to comparatively few paragraphs or even possibly to notes which Heraud used as an incentive to his own contribution.

Informal and uneven collaboration of this sort, for which there was ample precedent among Maginn's staff, would explain how it happened that Heraud's writing for *Fraser's* was so often kept well above that hard-working metaphysician's own level. Since such collaboration would at least to some extent have augmented the earnings of Maginn and Carlyle, it would also throw light on a reference in Carlyle's *Reminiscences*. On looking back over the lean months of 1834-1836, when he was in the throes of the *French Revolution,* he mentions receiving some "trifling increments from *Fraser's Magazine,* perhaps," and then adds in parenthesis, "Diamond Necklace, etc. were probably of those years."[29] Yet the first installment of the *Diamond Necklace* was not published till January, 1837, and between August, 1834, and that date, no acknowledged work of Carlyle appeared in the periodical with the exception of the brief obituary notice of his friend Edward Irving. Moreover, no acknowledged work appeared in any other periodical. It is, therefore, possible (providing, indeed, there were increments and Carlyle's memory was not playing him false) that he had in mind articles for *Fraser's* which were of too ephemeral a nature to be acknowledged. The only evidence against this explanation is a remark in his *Journal,* under February 7, 1835:

> . . . it is now some three-and-twenty months since I have earned one penny by the craft of literature. Be this recorded as a fact and document for the literary history of this time. I have been ready to work, I am abler than ever to work, know no fault that I have committed; and yet so it stands.[30]

Since Carlyle obviously was here thinking of the prevailing inhospitality of magazines toward work of literary merit, it is improbable that among his earnings "by the craft of literature" he would have included sums received for potboiler reviews which periodicals were only too ready to accept.

Collaboration would also explain why Heraud, though he lived to be an old man and far beyond the time when Browning became famous, never claimed the brilliant review of *Paracelsus,* included in the *Fraser* series "Asinarii Senici."[31] The series belongs to the pseudo-philosophical group,[32] and had Heraud been its sole author, it is probable that he would not have allowed such an almost clairvoyant instance of accurate and creative criticism to remain unacknowledged. Had the authorship been divided with another, however, it is not likely that either writer would have claimed the review. In this case it is probable that the hypothetical second author was Maginn, for although Carlyle liked Browning personally, he had no especial taste for his early poetry.

It would be pleasant to think that Carlyle's hand could be found in the article, "The Doctrine of St. Simon," which came out in the magazine for July, 1832. The subject was one in which both Heraud and Carlyle were deeply interested and which they might easily have discussed together.[33] Somewhat earlier, in the series on German poetry, Heraud had announced that he hoped to secure the aid of Carlyle.[34] Although there is no indication in the concluding number of the series that he was successful, it is to be noticed that the essay on Saint-Simon appeared shortly afterward. The authorship of the article must, however, like most questions concerning this puzzling *Fraser* work, remain conjectural.

One essay at least of the pseudo-philosophical group we have already indicated would appear to be from the pen of Carlyle alone. In my earlier article on the identification of this work, I pointed out that in regard to the review of Cunningham's *Life of Burns* there could at least be no question of Heraud's authorship, nor yet of Maginn's since its writer at some length acclaims his own Scotch parentage and describes the peasant home in which he was brought up.[35] The review contains a brief reference to the "Man of Genius" and was therefore presumably not contributed by an outsider; moreover, its interests are those of Carlyle. Its chief aim is to show that Burns by following the "meagre Arminianism," or New-Light, lost the moral support of the old faith. The point was one which Carlyle had introduced into his essay on Burns, 1828, but had developed only scantily. Since the *Fraser* review is detailed in treatment, it affords an interesting supplement to the more famous essay, corresponding as it does even with Carlyle's estimate of the biographies by Currie, Walker, and Lockhart. Further evidence for the identification of the review is that among the magazine's contributors who were of Scotch peasant birth, Carlyle alone shared with its author the boyhood experience of being obliged to run into the field to read in secret.[36] In this connection it should be noted that although Carlyle's brother John had earlier written for *Fraser's*, he had at the time the article was published in 1834 already been abroad for nearly three years as physician to the Countess Clare, and would seem never to have resumed his connection with the magazine. A minor point perhaps, but one not to be overlooked, is the resemblance between the review and sections of Carlyle's sketch of his father, Thomas Carlyle, which was written shortly after 1830 although not published until included in the *Reminiscences*. There are no parallel passages, but there is much about the impromptu essay which suggests the more analytical account of the hardy old Scotchman who dominated the Teufelsdröckh home. In both, religion is at some length shown to be the basis of the peasant's education, that which kept mind alert and self-respect strong. Carlyle's memorable comment on his father: "Man's face he did not fear; God he always feared," finds an echo in the review's statement that the peasants, accustomed "to commune with their Creator," "feared not to lift an independent brow in the presence of any fellow creature." All told, the essay on Cunningham's *Burns* offers more evidence of Carlyle's authorship than is to be found in any of the other unacknowledged work in *Fraser's*.

APPENDIX 3

GENERAL BIBLIOGRAPHY OF FRASER'S MAGAZINE

POSTHUMOUS WORK FIRST PUBLISHED IN FRASER'S

Byron. Verses on Sam Rogers, VII, 82; Verses on the Rev. Dr. Nott, VII, 341.

Coleridge. See p. 281.

Cowley. Letters included in The Familiar Letters of Cowley, with Notices of His Life, and Sketches of Some of His Friends and Contemporaries, XIII, 395; XIV, 234.

Hogg, James. See p. 285.

Picken, Andrew. See p. 292.

Saint Lawrence, Rev. Thomas. Paraphrases of the Twenty-third and Forty-sixth Psalms, VIII, 175.

Shelley. To *****, VI, 599; To A. B., with a Guitar, VII, 79; The Wandering Jew [in collaboration with Thomas Medwin, see pp. 290 f.], III, 666.

KEY TO PSEUDONYMS AND INITIALS

Apprentice of the Law	Percival Weldon Banks
J. B.	Bryan Waller Procter
J. Bethel	Bryan Waller Procter
Blondel-Cumulo-Stratus	Sir Theodore Martin
Blue Friar	George Wightwick
Bombardinio	Col. John Mitchell
Bon Gaultier	Sir Theodore Martin
T. C. C.	Thomas Crofton Croker
Candidus (after 1839)	Edward Vaughan Kenealy, LL.D.
Barry Cornwall	Bryan Waller Procter
Alfred Croquis	Daniel Maclise
Delta (or Δ)	Dr. David Macbeth Moir
Dominie	Andrew Picken
Dolly Duster	William Makepeace Thackeray
Ettrick Shepherd	James Hogg
George Fitz-Boodle	William Makepeace Thackeray
T. G.	Robert Avis Willmott
J. A. H.	John Abraham Heraud
Harrovian	Robert Avis Willmott
Hermes	Isaac Cullimore

Hermogenes	Isaac Cullimore
J. M. K.	William Maginn, LL.D.
Baron Kalchenvogel	Robert Pearse Gillies
L. E. L.	Letitia Elizabeth Landon
Layman of the Church of England	R. B. Seeley
B. F. Locke	George Wightwick
M.	William Maginn, LL.D.
W. M.	William Maginn, LL.D.
Man of Genius	John Churchill
Man o' War's Man	John Howell
Modern Pythagorean	Dr. Robert Macnish
Monthly Nurse	Mrs. Harriet Downing
Newspaper Editor	Gibbons Merle
Nimrod	Charles Apperley
Sir Morgan O'Doherty	William Maginn, LL.D.
Ensign Cornelius O'Donoghue	Thomas Crofton Croker
Brother Peregrine	Octavian Blewitt
Pilpay Junior	Thomas Carlyle
Father Prout	Rev. Francis Mahony
Pierce Pungent	Lockhart and Maginn
Quaffypunchovicz	John Churchill and collaborators
Captain Orlando Sabertash	Col. John Mitchell
Selwyn	Caroline Bowles
Ikey Solomons	William Makepeace Thackeray
Templar	Edward Vaughan Kenealy, LL.D.
Michael Angelo Titmarsh	William Makepeace Thackeray
Tydus-pooh-pooh	John Churchill
W.	Robert Avis Willmott
Charles Yellowplush	William Makepeace Thackeray
You Know Who	William Makepeace Thackeray

THE TWENTY-SEVEN FRASERIANS OF MACLISE'S ETCHING

[See Frontispiece.]

In the center, Dr. Maginn; then, circling the table from left to right, as named by the Rev. Francis Mahony in his preface to *The Reliques of Father Prout:* "Barry Cornwall (Procter), Robert Southey, Percival Banks, Thackeray, Churchill, Serjeant Murphy, Macnish, Ainsworth, Coleridge, Hogg, Galt, Dunlop, and Jerdan. Fraser is croupier, having on his right Crofton Croker, Lockhart, Theodore Hook, Sir David Brewster, Dr. Moir (Delta), Tom Carlyle, Count D'Orsay (talking to Allan Cunningham), Sir Egerton Brydges, Rev. G. R. Gleig, chaplain of Chelsea Hospital, Rev. F. Mahony, Rev. Edward Irving."

IDENTIFIED CONTRIBUTORS AND WORK

The following contributors are mentioned among the Fraserians of January, 1835, or listed in *Fraser's* Parliamentary Report for January, 1836, or otherwise identified as belonging to the staff. The Parliamentary Report is not by itself conclusive evidence since it includes well-known enemies of the magazine, as A. A. Watts, and "immortals," as the "ghost of Goethe" and the "ghost of Mendelssohn."

Titles have often been omitted or given in part. Only the initial page of each reference has been indicated.

AINSWORTH, WILLIAM HARRISON. Probably contributed stories and occasional squibs. It has been possible to identify only two items.

La Guglielmina of Milan [signed W*; suggested as Ainsworth's by S. M. Ellis, *William Harrison Ainsworth and His Friends* (1911), I, 229], X, 173. One Foot in the Stirrup [ballad, identified through introductory remarks by Maginn and included by Ainsworth in subsequent editions of *Rookwood*], XI, 23.

AIRD, THOMAS. Scotch poet.

The Scarlet Witch [Macnish in a letter to Moir, published in *The Modern Pythagorean: a Series of Tales, Essays, and Sketches by the Late Robert Macnish, LL.D.* (London, 1838), I, 238, mentions sending to *Fraser's* this story by Aird.], VII, 85.

APPERLEY, CHARLES. Signature: Nimrod [acknowledged]. Popular light essayist, an authority on sports; gave new life to the *Sporting Magazine*. Chief works: *Northern Tour; Jorrock's Jaunts and Jollities; Diary of a Huntsman.*

Memorabilia Bacchanalia [signed], XII, 522; XIII, 225, 727; XIV, 273. Ciberia Memorabilia [signed], XV, 371, 434. Anatomy of Gaming [signed], XVI, 9, 368, 748; XVII, 269, 538. My Life and Times [signed], XXV, 9, 127, 288, 409, 503, 674; XXVI, 159, 321, 420, 668.

BAILLIE, JOANNA. Prolific poet and dramatist. Produced three volumes of *Plays on the Passions; Miscellaneous Plays;* and three volumes of poetry.

Letter [signed], XIV, 748.

BANKS, PERCIVAL WELDON. Signatures [acknowledged]: Morgan Rattler; An Apprentice of the Law; Morgan Rattler, Esq., M.A., an Apprentice of the Law. See *Fraser's,* XXXI, 253; also present text, p. 35.

Essays, stories, letters [signed], III, 73; VII, 507, 682; VIII, 125, 339; IX, 586, 654; X, 106, 505; XI, 530; XII, 32, 551; XIII, 177; XIV, 1; XX, 513; XXI, 212; XXII, 60, 320, 613; XXIII, 295; XXIV, 401; XXV, 81, 470, 645; XXVI, 29, 121, 142; XXVII, 225; XXIX, 496, 655; XXX, 436, 537. Banks continued to write intermittently for *Fraser's* until 1850, the year of his death.

BAYLEY, F. W. N. Called Omnibus Bayley from having edited a cheap periodical by that name; a prolific scribbler of light verse and prose; accompanied his soldier father to the West Indies, publishing, in 1830, *Four Years' Residence in the West Indies;* probably wrote several articles on the West Indies for *Fraser's* as well as occasional verse squibs.

BAYLY, THOMAS HAYNES. Imitator of Praed; reduced the drawing room ballad to its lowest level.

Verse [signed], I, 216, 483.

BLEWITT, OCTAVIAN. Signature: Brother Peregrine [identified by Cushing]. For years the secretary of the Royal Literary Fund; in 1872 created a Knight of the Order of Leopold by the King of the Belgians. Author of *A Panorama of Torquay* and of various guide books.

Essays [signed], XXI, 90, 319, 649; XXII, 81, 560, 684.

BOWLES, CAROLINE. Signature: Selwyn [acknowledged. Some of the *Fraser* work signed Selwyn was republished in *Selwyn in Search of a Daughter and Other Tales.*]. Popular poetess, often ranked with Mrs. Hemans and L. E. L.; in 1839 married Robert Southey.

Rencontres on the Road [signed; several sketches reprinted in *Selwyn in Search of a Daughter and Other Tales*], IV, 585; V, 35, 229, 567; VI, 431; VII, 349, 425. The Dead Alive [story, reprinted in *Selwyn in Search of a Daughter*], IX, 411.

BOWLES, WILLIAM LISLE.

Letter [signed], XIII, 498.

Sonnet [attributed in text], XIII, 738.

BOYTON, REV. CHARLES. Professor at Trinity College, Dublin University; was associated with the Rev. Mortimer O'Sullivan in gathering statistics and writing articles on the English Church; listed as a contributor in *Fraser's* Parliamentary Report for January, 1836.

BREWSTER, SIR DAVID. Eminent scientist; for years the editor and chief contributor of the *Edinburgh Encyclopedia.* He filled the chair of Natural Philosophy in Edinburgh University. Like Faraday, he took all the medals of the Royal Society of London. As he is mentioned as one of the staff in The Fraserians, 1835, and appears in Maclise's etching, he may have contributed scientific or biographic articles to the magazine. It has been possible, however, to identify nothing beyond the two short items mentioned as his in the *Fraser* text.

Letter to James Hogg, Esq. [signed], VII, 16. On the Universality of Goethe's Genius, XI, 11.

BROCKEDON, WILLIAM.

Selections from the Diary of a Traveller in the Alps [identified through the statement, XIX, 348, that the author contributed the sketches for Beattie's *Valdenses.* These sketches are signed Brockedon.], XIX, 221, 329.

BRYDGES, SIR SAMUEL EGERTON. A querulous man of letters, well thought of by his contemporaries; genealogist, bibliographer, and editor of rare Elizabethan texts and other work.

Essays, reviews, letters [signed], VIII, 291; X, 33, 423, 725; XIII, 673; XIV, 596, 695; XV, 581.

Sonnets [signed or attributed by editor], XIII, 255; XV, 30, 169, 803.

BULWER, MRS. EDWARD LYTTON (Lady Rosina Bulwer-Lytton).

Artaphernes, the Platonist [signed], XVII, 513.

CARLYLE, DR. JOHN. Thomas Carlyle mentions under September 9, 1830 [Note Books, p. 170], that he had received a bundle of *Fraser's Magazines* containing "two little papers by my Brother." Earlier, in August, 1829, he had written to John Carlyle, "Let me hope you . . . are now busy with your *Animal Magnetism.*" It has not been possible to identify this work with any certainty.

CHAPMAN, M. J. Trinity College, Cambridge.

Ode to the Coming Year [signed], XI, 79. Hebrew Idyls [signed], XII, 642; XIII, 121, 154, 324, 440, 665; XIV, 18.

CHURCHILL, JOHN. Signature: Man of Genius [identified by Maginn, *Fraser's,* XIII, 76]. Edited, with a preface signed J. C., Maginn's *Homeric Ballads* (1850), helped edit *Fraser's Literary Chronicle* and the *Carlton Chronicle,* probably contributing work signed W. J. See present text, pp. 20, 35.

Wallenstein's Camp [translation from Schiller, attributed to him in *Fraser's,* XXI, 21; see also Mackenzie, "Memoir" prefacing *Fraserian Papers,* p. lxxi], II, 641. High-Ways and Low-Ways, or Ainsworth's Dictionary with Notes by Turpin [see present text, p. 247], IX, 724. Judgment of the Annuals [attributed in text and signed Man of Genius], X, 610. Punch Song, from the German [first published in *Fraser's Literary Chronicle,* March 5, 1836, over the signature W. J.], XX, 16.

Work in collaboration with Maginn assisted by others: The Magyars *versus* Dr. Bowring [given in *Fraser's* to the Man of Genius; see present text, p. 20 and note 3], I, 433. Kisfaludy's Meeting of the Similes [continuation of The Magyars *versus* Dr. Bowring], I, 601. Unpublished Poems and Other Misfortunes of a Man of Genius, II, 267. The Poetry of the Sandwich Islands [attributed in text to the Man of Genius], III, 334. The Poems of Quaffypunchovicz, done into English by Tydus-pooh-pooh, our Man of Genius, XIII, 593. Resurrectional Recreations [caption used in *Carlton Chronicle,* August.

1836, p. 1140], V. 85. The Fraser Papers [with Thackeray. Churchill is named as Maginn's assistant by Kenealy, *Dublin University Magazine,* XXIII, 89.], VII, 240, 367, 498, 620; VIII, 376, 499, 742; IX, 240, 371, 615; X, 365; XV, 528, 654. For other probable collaboration, see Bibliography of Maginn, items followed by "presumably with others."

COLERIDGE, SAMUEL TAYLOR.

Two Round Spaces on the Tombstone: being an Epitaph on the Late Sir James Mackintosh by S. T. Coleridge, VII, 176. Epitaph on S. T. Coleridge, Esq., by Himself, VII, 177. Association of Ideas: By Likeness; Association by Contrast; Association by Time, XI, 54. Three Sorts of Friends, XI, 54. Letter to Gillman, XI, 54. Extract from a Letter to Pringle, XI, 56. Monologues by the Late Samuel Taylor Coleridge [reported by Heraud], Life: Growth, Motion, Sensation, XII, 493; The Science and System of Logic, XII, 619. The squibs, What is an Irish Orator? V, 721; and An Irish Orator's Booze, V, 721, are signed by his name, but were presumably written by Maginn.

COLLINGRIDGE, A.

Three Years of My Life [identified through the advertisement on the reverse of the Table of Contents for May, 1838, Vol. XVII: " 'A Night near Windsor or Port Royal Annals and A Tale of the Turf' by A. Collingridge, Esq., author of 'Rough Sketches Afloat,' and 'Three Years of My Life,' &c., &c." The book was published in 1838 by James Fraser.], XV, 487. Rough Sketches Afloat, XVI, 33, 242; XIX, 35, 425.

CROKER, THOMAS CROFTON. The article on Croker in the *Dublin University Magazine,* XXXIV, 202-16, the material for which was supplied by Croker himself, speaks of him as an active and regular contributor to *Fraser's Magazine.* See present text, pp. 36 f.

Specimens of Irish Minstrelsy [signed], I, 191, 314, 580; II, 41; VIII, 127. The Nameless Fountain [verse signed T.C.C.], II, 221.

Ensign O'Donoghue's stories and letters [for identification see present text, p. 36], IV, 79; VI, 341; VIII, 156; IX, 32, 147, 375, 711; X, 409; XI, 137, 630; XIII, 645, 657; XIV, 168, 474; XV, 339, 662, 663; XVII, 432; XVIII, 86, 140. The signature is found occasionally after 1840.

CULLIMORE, ISAAC. Signature: Hermogenes. Egyptologist, one of the first Orientalists to use astronomy in determining dates; his work was chiefly published in the *Proceedings of the Royal Society of Literature.*

On the Periods of the Erection of the Theban Temple of Ammon [see *Dictionary of National Biography*], VIII, 637. Archæographia [signed Hermogenes; identified by the reference, XIV, 461 n., to the article on the temple of Ammon as the first of the series to which it belongs], XIV, 461.

Other articles signed Hermogenes, IX, 288, 629; XIII, 579; XVI, 401, 627, 736; XX, 1, 200, 326.

CUNNINGHAM, ALLAN.

Verse [signed], I, 399; III, 687.

Lay Sermons, by the Ettrick Shepherd [identified by reference in the first paragraph to a scene the writer had witnessed twenty years before on paying a visit of homage to Hogg. Cunningham, who was born in 1784, made such a visit when eighteen years of age.], X, 1.

D'ORSAY, COUNT ALFRED. See present text, p. 33. He may have helped with the lighter work of the magazine and possibly contributed translations from the French.

DOWNING, MRS. HARRIET. Signature: The Monthly Nurse.

The long series, Remembrances of a Monthly Nurse, began in XIV, 398 (October, 1836), continued for a little over a year, and were republished by Mrs. Downing.

Verse [signed by "the author of the Remembrances of a Monthly Nurse"], XVI, 451, 732.

DUNLOP, DR. WILLIAM. "A compound of a bear and a gentleman." He served in the army in Canada and India as an intrepid physician who often took an active part in the fighting. Later he returned to India, edited a paper, and became famous for tiger hunting, earning the name "the Tiger." During a period of recuperation from jungle fever he lectured on medical jurisprudence in Edinburgh University and later became an active Bohemian in London, founding the club, "The Pig and Whistle." In 1826 he accepted, according to Maginn, the post of "Warden of the Black Forest" in Galt's Canadian Company. Until his death in 1848 he remained in Canada, distinguishing himself as a member of the Provincial Parliament and the projector of public enterprises. Chief work: *Recollections of the American War.* Contributions to *Blackwood's,* signed Colin Ballantyne, R.N. See Maginn's bibliographical notice opening the review of Dunlop's *Statistical Sketches of Upper Canada, for the Use of Emigrants,* V, 635; and the Gallery sketch, The Tiger, VII, 436.

The following work in *Fraser's* would seem to be his: Authentic Narrative of Facts which Occurred during a March in India, XII, 664. Sketches of Savage Life, XIII, 169, 316, 499.

FITZGERALD, EDWARD MARLBOROUGH. Trinity College, Cambridge; friend and imitator of Praed, using with him the signature Θ. Mentioned in early volumes of *Fraser's* as belonging to the *Fraser* fellowship; listed as a contributor to the Parliamentary Report for January, 1836, XIII, 4.

Scenes in the Law Courts [signed Θ], IV, 308.

FRASER, HUGH. One of the projectors of *Fraser's*. He probably now and then assisted Maginn and may have written the verse signed H.F., I, 426; IV, 112.

GALT, JOHN. See present text, p. 29. All of Galt's articles, sketches, and stories except An Autumn in the North are identified by his signature or by the title of one of his books. An Autumn in the North may be identified from a reference in Macnish's letter to Leitch, dated December 3, and published in *The Modern Pythagorean: a Series of Tales, Essays, and Sketches, by the Late Robert Macnish, LL.D.* (London, 1838), I, 333. Galt was in Scotland in the latter half of 1834 in order to recover his health. He was still in the North in January of 1835, according to Maginn's comment, XI, 9.

The Hurons, I, 90. The Bell of St. Regis, I, 268. American Traditions, II, 321; IV, 96; V, 275. Letters on West Indian Slavery, II, 440, 556, 706. Guelph in Upper Canada, II, 456. Pot versus Kettle, II, 533. Means of Lessening the West Indian Distress, III, 346. The Ancient Commerce of England, IV, 403. Letters on Free Trade, VI, 593; VII, 106. The Whole West India Question, VIII, 81. The Joke, VIII, 279. My Father's House, VIII, 495. The Gudewife, VIII, 651. The Mem, or Schoolmistress, X, 157. An Autumn in the North, X, 488, 573, 682; XI, 66, 170. Anonymous Publications, XI, 549. Metropolitan Emigrant, XII, 291. On the Sea-Fed Engine, XIII, 494. The Statesman, XIV, 657. Letter from Galt, XVI, 24.

GILLIES, ROBERT PEARSE. Signature: Baron Kalchenvogel. Editor for some years of the *Foreign Quarterly Review*. Early German studies in *Blackwood's* place him among the pioneers of the movement to acquaint English readers with German literature.

Recollections of Sir Walter Scott [republished by Gillies], XII, 249, 502, 687; XIII, 104. O'Hanlon and His Wife [signed W. F. from Maidstone, acknowledged in Gillies's *Memoirs of a Literary Veteran,* II, 219], XIV, 184. Humours of the North [reprinted in part in *Memoirs of a Literary Veteran*], XV, 20, 161, 355, 591; XVI, 323; XIX, 50; XXII, 658. Respectability: a Sketch by the Author of O'Hanlon and His Wife [signed W. F. from Maidstone], XVI, 417. John Bull's Castle: a Sketch by the Author of O'Hanlon and His Wife, XX, 152. Some Recollections of James Hogg [signed by the author of Humours of the North; reprinted in part in *Memoirs of a Literary Veteran,* II, 240 ff.], XX, 414. Recollections of Germany [reprinted in part in *Memoirs of a Literary Veteran,* II, Chap. 13], XXI, 53.

GLEIG, REV. GEORGE ROBERT. Referred to as "The Subaltern." An army officer who served in the Peninsula campaigns and the American War of 1812, received the B.A. and M.A. degrees from Oxford, entered the Church in 1820, was appointed chaplain of Chelsea Hospital, 1834, and Chaplain General of the Army, 1844. Best known works: *The Subaltern; The Chronicles of Waltham; The History of India; Lives of the Military Commanders; Personal Reminiscences of the First Duke of Wellington* [posthumous].

Annals of the Peninsular Campaign [review of Hamilton; attributed by Mackenzie in "Memoir" prefacing *Fraserian Papers,* p. lxv], I, 100. Lord Brougham on Natural Theology [reprinted in Gleig's *Essays*], XII, 375. The Maidschenstein: a Tradition of the Saxon Swiss [reprinted in Gleig's *Essays*], XVIII, 574.

GRAHAM, JOHN.

Verse [signed], XVIII, 443.

HEMANS, MRS. FELICIA.

Verse [signed], III, 603.

HERAUD, JOHN ABAHAM. See present text, pp. 33, 89-93, and Appendix 2.

Poetry [signed J.A.H. or John Abraham Heraud, or attributed in the text], I, 24, 271, 489; II, 341; IV, 44, 713; V, 166; XI, 58, 735; XII, 601; XIII, 726; XV, 533.

Work identified in present text [see pp. 270 f.]: On Poetical Genius I, 56. Grant's Notes on Byron's *Cain,* III, 285. German Poetry, IV, 167, 540; V, 280. Some Account of Coleridge's Philosophy, V, 585. Reminiscences of Coleridge, Biographical, Philosophical, Poetical, and Critical, X, 379. Coleridgeiana, XI, 50. Coleridge's *Table-Talk,* XII, 123.

Work presumably by Heraud alone: On Human Perfectibility, I, 147. Oliver Yorke at Home, IV, 113, 361; V, 22. French, German, and English Philosophy, IV, 428. Historical Romances, V, 6, 207, 670. Turner's *Sacred History of the World,* VI, 329. Wordsworth's Poetical Works, VI, 607. Fanaticism and the Natural History of Enthusiasm, IX, 159. Odd Thoughts on Strange Subjects by Mordaunt Couplet, Esq., XI, 330. Wordsworth's New Volume of Poetry, XI, 689. The Last Portrait of Coleridge [verse], XIV, 179. Ion and the Provost of Bruges, XIV, 218. Isaac Taylor's Physical Theory of Another Life, XIV, 407. Oliver Yorke at Paris, XIV, 662; XVI, 25. One or Two Words on One or Two Books [reviews of Landor and Bulwer], XV, 498. The Rev. W. J. Irons on Final Causes, XVI, 254. The Poetry of Shelley, XVII, 653.

Work probably by Heraud in collaboration with Maginn: Poetry of the Magyars [review of Bowring], I, 155. The Last of the Supernaturalists [see present text, pp. 267 f.], I, 217. The Dominie's Legacy [see present text, pp. 268 f.], I, 318. Mr. Edward Lytton Bulwer's Novels and Remarks on Novel-Writing [signed Ned Culpepper, the Tomahawk; see present text, pp. 268 ff.], I, 509. Place-Men, Parliament-Men, Penny-a-Liners, and Parliamentary Reporters [signed Ned Culpepper; see present text, pp. 269 f.], II, 282. Galt's Life of Byron, II, 347. Mr. Godwin's Novels, II, 381. Southey's Life of Bunyan, III, 54. The Wandering Jew: a New Poem by P. B. Shelley, III, 529. Godwin's Thoughts on Man, III, 569. Landor's Poems, III, 736. Lord Byron's Juvenile Poems, VI, 183. Asinarii Scenici, VII, 96; XIII, 362. Critical Illustrations of Lord Byron's Poetry, VII, 303. The Bridgewater Treatises, VIII, 65, 259; XII, 415; XVI, 719. The Book of Enoch, VIII, 511. Lord Byron's Dramas, X, 699.

Work probably in collaboration with Carlyle: Allan Cunningham's *Maid of Elvar* [see present text, pp. 263-66], V, 659. Letter on the Doctrine of St. Simon [see present text, p. 274], V, 666. A Cambrian Colloquy on the Decline and Fall of Poetry [see present text, pp. 266 f.], X, 646.

HOGG, JAMES. Signature: The Ettrick Shepherd.

Verse [signed], I, 308, 398, 654; II, 31; III, 39, 567; IV, 422; V, 20, 84, 234; VI, 359; VII, 68; X, 403, 556, 639; XI, 9, 357, 516, 666; XII, 281. Also poems included in Maginn's article, VIII, 49.

Stories and comments [signed], II, 171, 526; III, 174, 720; IV, 529; VII, 16, 147; IX, 97, 273; XI, 103, 226; XIII, 609; [posthumous] XIV, 430.

HOOK, THEODORE EDWARD. See present text, pp. 23, 32 f.

Verse [attributed by Maginn in *Fraser's* text]: The Improvisatore's Speech, II, 502. Of Dutch Low or High, XI, 12. April Fools [Hook suggested as joint author with Maginn by E. V. Kenealy, *Dublin University Magazine,* XXIII, 89], XI, 369.

HOWELL, JOHN. Signatures: S.: Man-o'-War's Man.

Stories [signed], II, 295, 431.

HOWITT, RICHARD.

Verse [signed], XV, 535; XVI, 164.

Letter [signed], XV, 535.

HOWITT, WILLIAM.

Story [signed], II, 215.

Verse [signed], III, 171.

IRVING, REV. EDWARD. See present text, pp. 33 f.

Recollections and Observations of a Scottish Clergyman [mentioned as his, XI, 99], I, 443. Facts Connected with the Recent Manifestations of Spiritual Gifts [signed], IV, 754; V, 198, 316.

JERDAN, WILLIAM. For many years the tyrannical editor of the *Literary Gazette*. He helped to found the Royal Society of Literature, was one of the original members of the Camden Society, and was on the Council of the Percy Society.

Mephistopheles Politicus [Jerdan is addressed as Mephistopheles, *Fraser's,* XI, 10.], VIII, 733.

JESSE, EDWARD. Author of guides, light essays, and studies of nature. Chief work: *Gleanings in Natural History; An Angler's Rambles; Favourite Haunts and Rural Studies.*

Thames Fishing [signed by Author of Gleanings in Natural History; reprinted in *An Angler's Rambles*], IX, 88.

JESSE, JOHN HENEAGE. Son of Edward Jesse [see above]; a voluminous historical writer. Chief works: *George Selwyn and his Contemporaries; Literary and Historical Memorials of London; Memoirs of Richard III; Memoirs of the Life and Reign of George III.* Although only a boy of fifteen when *Fraser's* was started, he was a prime favorite of Maginn and the inner staff and is presented in the magazine's symposia as playing a lively part, on several occasions telling anecdotes and singing songs. He may have helped with the composition of The Election of Editor, I, 496, 738; II, 238, and of similar work. He is listed as a contributor in the Parliamentary Report, January, 1836, XIII, 4.

JEWSBURY, GERALDINE. A young friend of Mrs. Carlyle; won brief popularity through *Zoe* and other novels.

Verse [signed], I, 720.

KENEALY, EDWARD VAUGHAN, LL.D. Signature: A Templar. An accomplished linguist and scholar, biographer and intimate friend of Maginn, later to become prominent as a lawyer.

Acknowledged work: A Letther from Mr. Barney Brallaghan, Piper at the Paddy's Goose Public-House, Ratcliffe Highway [republished by Kenealy], XXV, 65, 160. The Love Epistles of Aristænetus: edited by a Templar, XXVI, 76, 176, 360, 487, 609, 661; XXVII, 578. Introduction to Maginn's The Last of the Homeric Ballads, XXVI, 439.

Work possibly attributable to Kenealy: Specimens of Persian Poetry, XVIII, 348, 637; XIX, 486; XX, 127; XXI, 414. Our Annual Execution [see present text, p. 259], XIX, 57. Sinners and Saints in Far Cathay, XIX, 105. Cheveley: or the Man of Honour [a review of Lady Bulwer-Lytton], XIX, 618. My Irish Tutorship, by a Trinity Bachelor, XX, 667; XXI, 33, 274. A Chapter about Boutiques and Gin Palaces, by Candidus, XX, 697. A Budget of Bards, XX, 752. What's What, XXI, 442. Here and There [by the author of What's What, see introduction], XXII, 43. Wightwickism, by Candidus, XXII, 359. A Codicil to a Chapter about Boutiques, by Candidus, XXIII, 328.

LANDON, LETITIA ELIZABETH. Signature: L. E. L.

Verse [signed]: I, 606, 643.

LOCKHART, JOHN G. See present text, pp. 34 f.

The Standard Bearer: a Ballad from the Spanish [attributed by Mackenzie in "Memoir" prefacing *Fraserian Papers,* p. lxv], I, 38. Gallery sketch of Maginn, The Doctor [attributed by Mackenzie, p. lxx], II, 716.

Work probably in collaboration with Maginn [see present text, pp. 35, 63 f.]: Ars Ridendi: or Hook and Hood—on Laughter, III, 154. Elizabeth Brownrigge, VI, 67, 131. Articles and poems signed Pierce Pungent: James Hogg, I, 291. The Bard of Hope [Thomas Campbell], I, 563. Thoughts on the Wellington Administration, I, 729. Mr. Wordsworth, III, 557. Men and Manners: a Series of Satires by Pierce Pungent, IX, 111, 171, 348, 638; X, 11, 164, 283, 416, 530, 692.

MACLISE, DANIEL. Signature: Alfred Croquis. *Fraser's* famous young artist, later to win national renown. See present text, pp. 20 f.

Sketches in the Gallery of Illustrious Literary Characters [acknowledged; see below, Maclise and Maginn].

Our Fathers' Swords [verse, attributed by Maginn in text], XI, 17. Christmas Revels [verse, signed Alfred Croquis], XVII, 635.

MACLISE AND MAGINN (with Carlyle, Lockhart, and Prout).

Gallery of Illustrious Literary Characters [republished by William Bates]:

1. William Jerdan, Esq., Editor of the *Literary Gazette,* I, 605.
2. Thomas Campbell, Esq., Editor of the *New Monthly,* I, 714.
3. John Gibson Lockhart, Esq., Editor of *The Quarterly,* II, 77.
4. Samuel Rogers, Esq., Author of the *Pleasures of Memory,* II, 237.
5. Thomas Moore, Esq., Author of *Lalla Rookh,* II, 266.
6. Sir Walter Scott, II, 412.
7. John Galt, II, 555.
8. The Doctor [William Maginn], II, 716. [By Lockhart. See above.]
9. Crofton Croker, III, 67.
10. Mrs. Norton, III, 222.
11. John Wilson, Esq., III, 364.
12. Mary Russell Mitford, III, 410.
13. Don Telesforo de Trueba y Cozio, III, 613.
14. The Earl of Munster, III, 686.
15. Lord John Russell, IV, 65.
16. Right Hon. John Wilson Croker, IV, 240.
17. Tydus-pooh-pooh, IV, 333.
18. Washington Irving, IV, 435.
19. The Lord Brougham and Vaux, IV, 609.

20. Robert Montgomery, IV, 672.
21. James Hogg, V, 97.
22. The Baron von Goethe, V, 206. [By Carlyle. See Bibliography of Carlyle, p. 299.]
23. Israel [Isaac] D'Israeli, Esq., V, 321.
24. The Antiquaries, V, 475.
25. Louis Eustache Ude, V, 584.
26. Reverend Dr. Lardner, V, 696.
27. Edward Lytton Bulwer, Esq., VI, 112.
28. Allan Cunningham, Esq., VI, 249.
29. William Wordsworth, Esq., VI, 313.
30. Sir David Brewster, K.H., VI, 416.
31. William Roscoe, Esq., VI, 685.
32. Prince de Talleyrand, VII, 80.
33. James Morier, Esq., VII, 159.
34. Countess of Blessington, VII, 267.
35. The Tiger [Dr. William Dunlop], VII, 436.
36. Benjamin D'Israeli, Esq., VII, 602.
37. Thomas Carlyle, Esq., VII, 706.
38. Samuel Taylor Coleridge, Esq., VIII, 64.
39. George Cruikshank, Esq., VIII, 190.
40. Doctor Moir, VIII, 290.
41. Miss Landon, VIII, 433. [By Prout. See Mahony.]
42. Miss Harriet Martineau, VIII, 576.
43. Grant Thorburn, The Original Lawrie Todd, VIII, 700.
44. Captain Ross, IX, 64.
45. Sir Egerton Brydges, IX, 146.
46. Daniel O'Connell, Esq., and Richard Lalor Sheil, Esq., IX, 300.
47. Theodore E. Hook, Esq., IX, 435.
48. Charles Molloy Westmacott, Esq., IX, 536.
49. Leigh Hunt, Esq., IX, 644.
50. W. H. Ainsworth, Esq., X, 48.
51. Thomas Hill, Esq., X, 172.
52. The Rev. George Robert Gleig, X, 282.
53. William Godwin, Esq., X, 463.
54. James Smith, Esq., X, 538.
55. Comte D'Orsay, X, 645.
56. The Fraserians: or the Commencement of the Year Thirty-Five, XI, 1.
57. Charles Lamb, Esq., XI, 136.
58. Pierre-Jean de Béranger, XI, 300. [By Prout. See Mahony.]
59. Miss Jane Porter, XI, 404.
60. Lady Morgan, XI, 529.

61. Mr. Alaric Attila Watts, XI, 652.
62. Lord Francis Egerton, XII, 43.
63. Henry O'Brien, A.B., XII, 154. [By Prout. See Mahony.]
64. Michael Thomas Sadler, Esq., XII, 280.
65. William Cobbett, M.P. for Oldham, XII, 430.
66. Earl of Mulgrave, XII, 540.
67. Robert Macnish, Esq., XII, 650.
68. Regina's Maids of Honour, XIII, 80.
69. Michael Faraday, XIII, 224.
70. Rev. William Lisle Bowles, XIII, 300.
71. Francis Place, Esq., XIII, 427.
72. Sir John Hobhouse, XIII, 568.
73. Mrs. S. C. Hall, XIII, 718.
74. Mr. Sergeant Talford, XIV, 68.
75. Sir John Soane, XIV, 202.
76. Sheridan Knowles, Esq., XIV, 272.
77. Lord Lyndhurst, XIV, 457.
78. Edmund Lodge, XIV, 595.
79. John Baldwin Buckstone, XIV, 720.
80. Sir William Molesworth, XVII, 338.
81. Rev. Sydney Smith, XVII, 468.

MACNISH, ROBERT, LL.D. Signature: The Modern Pythagorean.

Verse [signed], III, 623; IV, 401; V, 227; VI, 160, 376, 575; VII, 231; VIII, 63, 382; X, 49.

Stories, familiar essays [signed], III, 350, 411; IV, 329; V, 52; VI, 236; VIII, 302; XI, 33.

The Books of Aphorisms, by an Oriental Author, with a running commentary by Sir Morgan O'Doherty, VI, 712.

Work acknowledged in Macnish's letters to Moir [see *The Modern Pythagorean: a Series of Tales, Essays, and Sketches by the Late Robert Macnish, LL.D.* (London, 1838), I, 200, 236-38.] Miss Pipson [reprinted in *The Modern Pythagorean,* I, 247], V, 708. Parody of T. H. Bayly's Susan Sutton, VI, 631. Ye Ladies Fair of Timbuctoo, VI, 632. Monsieur de Papillon, VI, 632. On a Pimple [parody of Wordsworth], VI, 632. Epitaphs from Lerwick, VI, 633. A Self-Laudatory Ode, VI, 636. The Spermaceti Candle [also attributed to Macnish by Maginn, *Fraser's,* XIII, 59], VI, 686. Quiz on the Ettrick Shepherd, VII, 248. Bacchanalian Song, VII, 249.

MAHONY, REV. FRANCIS. Signature: Father Prout. See present text, pp. 30 ff.

Prout Papers, IX, 487, 537, 679; X, 18, 194, 310, 464, 587, 666; XI, 83, 121, 259, 441, 559; XII, 89, 192, 313, 448; XIV, 87, 203, 360, 484, 641.

Gallery sketches [given to him by William Bates, learned editor of the Gallery of Illustrious Literary Characters, and by Charles Kent, *Works of Father Prout,* p. xxii]: L.E.L., VIII, 433. Béranger, XI, 300. Henry O'Brien, XII, 154.

Reliques of Father Prout [a witty and erudite review of his own book; acknowledged in text], XIII, 333. Crichton [a review of Ainsworth; given to Prout by Ellis in *Harrison Ainsworth and His Friends,* I, 323], XIV, 733.

Verse: Stabat Mater [mentioned as Prout's in *Fraser's Literary Chronicle,* April 2, 1836, p. 280b], XIII, 497. Epiphany, a Fragment [signed], XV, 92.

MARTIN, SIR THEODORE. Signature: Bon Gaultier. A considerable amount of his early work appeared in *Fraser's Literary Chronicle,* later the *Carlton Chronicle,* over the signatures E.N.; Martinus Scriblerus; I.G.; Invisible Gentleman. A small part of this was republished in Martin's *Disputation between the Body and the Soul by T.M. with Other Poems by the Same Author* [probably printed,1838; a copy in the British Museum].

Early acknowledged work signed Bon Gaultier: Who Are You? or the Modern Salathiel [the first tale to bear this signature, which later became well known as the joint pen name of Martin and Aytoun], XXI, 487. The Dead Alive: an Inn Story, XXVI, 85. My Namesake, XXVI, 649.

Work possibly by Martin [selected for resemblances to his *Carlton Chronicle* contributions]: McVicar's Balaam Box, XII, 63; XIII, 289. The Possums of Aristophanes, XIV, 285. The Highland Sergeant, XVI, 294. A Rigmarole on Taverns and Things in General, by Rory Rattlebrain, XVIII, 102. The City of Temptations: a Dramatic Sketch [verse], XVIII, 694. The Poetry of Guy's Arithmetic, XIX, 17. The Raven, or the Power of Conscience: an Old Border Legend [verse], XIX, 284. Robyn Hode and Kynge Richarde, XIX, 593. The Devil's Diary, or Temptations, XIX, 653. The Last Eve of St. John: A Lay of the Scottish Mist, by Blondel-Cumulo-Stratus [verse], XX, 505.

MEDWIN, THOMAS.

The Wandering Jew [in collaboration with Shelley; acknowledged by Medwin in *Memoir of Shelley,* 1833, pp. 8 f.], III, 666.

Translations from the Greek dramatists [signed]: The Choëphori, VI, 511. The Persians, VII, 17. Seven before Thebes, VII, 437. The Eumenides, IX, 553. Prometheus Bound, XVI, 209. Agamemnon, XVIII, 505.

Hazlitt in Switzerland: a Conversation [signed], XIX, 278. Canova Leaves from the Autobiography of an Amateur [signed], XX, 370.

MERLE, GIBBONS. Editor of the *Courier* and later of the *Globe.*

A Newspaper Editor's Reminiscences [for identification see present work, p. 28], XX, 588; XXII, 336, 415.

MITCHELL, JOHN. Colonel; later Major General. Signatures: Bombardinio; Captain Orlando Sabertash. Chief works: *Life of Wellington; Fall of Napoleon.* All of his essays for *Fraser's* were republished except his Reminiscences of Men and Things, by One Who Has a Good Memory. See present text, pp. 27 f.

Essays signed Bombardinio, VIII, 311; X, 97, 226; XII, 137, 356, 477, 709; XIV, 441.

Essays signed Captain Orlando Sabertash, XVII, 291; XIX, 68; XX, 189; XXI, 425; XXIII, 53; XXV, 144; XXVIII, 127, XXIX, 580.

Tableaux of the Most Eminent Soldiers of the Eighteenth Century, XXII, 159; XXIII, 187, 284, 486.

Military Tableaux: or Scenes from the Wars of Napoleon, by Captain Orlando Sabertash, XXVIII, 695; XXIX, 103, 302, 487; XXX, 176, 550.

Reminiscences of Men and Things, by One Who Has a Good Memory [for identification see present text, pp. 27 f.], XXVI, 347, 730; XXVII, 99, 145, 289, 454, 609, 687; XXVIII, 60, 169, 278, 379, 539, 647; XXIX, 1, 219, 331.

MOIR, DR. DAVID MACBETH. Signature: Delta, Δ. Best work: *Mansie Wauch.*

The Wounded Spirit [story, signed by Moir], I, 417, 663. Letter to the Learned Profession [signed Gabriel Cowitch, mentioned as Moir's in Macnish's letter to Moir, *The Modern Pythagorean: a Series of Tales, Essays, and Sketches, by the Late Robert Macnish* (1838), I, 219], V, 238. Horæ Sinicæ [No. III signed Δ], IX, 675; X, 222; XI, 542; XVII, 259. Casa Wappy [verse, signed], XVII, 535. Occult Science [Author refers to writing Horæ Sinicæ.], XXII, 1.

MURPHY, FRANCIS STACK; well known as Serjeant Murphy. Collaborated with Prout in translating modern verse into Greek; probably also contributed other verse and stories.

O'SULLIVAN, REV. MORTIMER. His chief works were defenses of the Protestant Church in Ireland and statistics in regard to Catholicism. Since he is mentioned in the *Dictionary of National Biography* as a regular contributor to *Fraser's* and is also included in the Parliamentary Report for January, 1836, XIII, 4, he was presumably the author of at least some of the articles on the Church in Ireland.

PANIZZI, ANTONIO. Political fugitive from Italy; critic and translator of Italian work. He filled the chair of Italian literature at London University, and became a member of the staff of the British Museum library and later its head, establishing much of the present system. Maginn gives an interesting account of Panizzi in Poetry of the Italians, III, 598, and a briefer notice in the Parliamentary Report for January, 1836, XIII, 73. Since Panizzi is listed as a contributor in the Report, he may have written some of the Italian translations in the magazine or have helped Maginn and other members of the staff.

PICKEN, ANDREW. Referred to as the Dominie. Edited the *Club Book,* 1831. Chief work: *The Dominie's Legacy; Emigration to the Canadas* [in collaboration with Dunlop and Galt]; *Traditionary Stories of Old Families; The Black Watch.* According to an editorial comment, *Fraser's,* XXI, 21, he contributed the Scotch dialect stories in the early numbers of the magazine.

A Legend of MacAlister More [attributed by Mackenzie in "Memoir" prefacing *Fraserian Papers,* p. lxv], I, 46. Mrs. M'Crie, I, 353. The Only Daughter, III, 44. Posthumous stories [given to him in the text], XI, 275; XII, 12, 496, 629.

PORTER, ANNA MARIA.

Verse [signed], II, 603.

PROCTER, BRYAN WALLER. Signatures: Barry Cornwall; J.B. [see *Fraser's,* I, 728 n.]; J. Bethel.

Poems [signed], I, 286, 366, 450, 540, 600, 727; II, 110.

The Man Hunter [story signed J. Bethel; reprinted in Procter's *Tales in Prose*], II, 153. Judgment of the Annuals [given to him in the text], X, 605.

PROUT, FATHER. See MAHONY, REV. FRANCIS.

SEELEY, ROBERT BENTON. Signature: A Layman of the Church of England. Publisher, author, philanthropist; supported the factory reform bills; helped to found the Church Pastoral Aid Society (1837), and the Society for Improving the Condition of the Labouring Classes (1844). Chief works: a long and authoritative biography of Michael Sadler; *Essays on the Church, by a Layman,* 1834, which went through many editions; *The Church of Christ in the Middle Ages,* 1845; *The Life of William Cowper,* 1855. Seeley would seem to have contributed to *Fraser's* many of the articles on the Church. He is listed in the Parliamentary Report for 1836, XIII, 4, and is also mentioned as a contributor in the *Dictionary of National Biography.* In the preface to his second edition of *Essays on the Church by a Layman,* he states that the essays were republished from magazine articles. Only one of the *Fraser* articles is signed.

Political Conduct of the Clergy [signed A Layman of the Church of England], IV, 641.

SHEPHERD, LADY MARY.

Lady Mary Shepherd's Metaphysics [signed], V, 697.

SOUTHEY, ROBERT. Poet laureate.

Poem [signed], I, 255, 560, 651.

STAUNTON, A. AYLMER.

Scenes in the Desert [signed], XXI, 346, 473; XXII, 521, 736.

THORBURN, GRANT. The original of John Galt's Lawrie Todd.

Autobiographical comments [attributed to him in the text], VII, 668; VIII, 55. Letter to Mr. and Mrs. H–, from Grant Thorburn, XV, 531.

TOWNSHEND. Signature: Senex [identified as Mr. Townshend of Cork by Mackenzie in his edition of *Noctes Ambrosianæ,* p. 13].

The Present State of Ireland, XIII, 181.

WEBBE, EGERTON.

The Diver: a ballad translated from the German of Schiller [signed], XV, 229.

WIGHTWICK, GEORGE. Signatures: Blue Friar; B. F. Locke. An architect of repute.

My Acquaintance with the Late Charles Mathews [attributed to Wightwick in the *Dictionary of National Biography*], XIII, 343.

Blue Friar Pleasantries [At the beginning of the opening number the author acknowledges writing My Acquaintance with the Late Charles Mathews.], XV, 223. The Blue Friar series is continued with intermissions until the latter half of the 1840's.

A Word or Two on Candidus's Article, "Wightwickism," by Wightwick himself, XXII, 751.

WILLIAMS, ROBERT FOLKESTONE.

Poems [given to Williams, *Fraser's,* VIII, 662 b]: A Song of Greece, IV, 274. Thoughts on the Sea, VI, 219.

WILLMOTT, ROBERT AVIS. Signatures: The Harrovian; W. [see Willmott's *The Harrovian*]. Author, editor, later ordained priest.

Critical articles and squibs: The Minor Greek Poets [signed The Harrovian], I, 608; II, 53. Lord Broughan and the Court of Chancery [signed W.], IV, 301. The Greek Pastoral Poets [attributed to him in *Fraser's,* XXI, 21], XII, 222, 541; XIII, 92. *The Greek Pastoral Poets* [review of Chapman; identified through the author's reference to having just completed the *Fraser articles* on the Greek pastoral poets, XIII, 601], XIII, 600. Greek Comedy [attributed to him in *Fraser's,* XXI, 21], XV, 285; XVIII, 127, 317; XIX, 639; XX, 379.

Other articles presumably by Willmott: Introductory comments in The Familiar Letters of Cowley, XIII, 395; XIV, 234. Morning Musings with Favourite Old Poets, XIII, 416. A Letter from Cambridge to Oliver Yorke, about the Art of Plucking [signed T. G.; for identification of all of the articles signed T. G. see present text, pp. 250 ff.], XIII, 707. A Second Letter from Cambridge to Oliver Yorke, Esq. [signed T. G.], XIV, 117. A Postscript to the Second Letter from Cambridge [signed T. G.], XIV, 180. A Letter from Athens to Oliver Yorke [signed T. G.], XIV, 349. A Scourging Soliloquy about the Annuals [signed T. G.], XV, 33. One or Two Guesses at One or Two Truths, XIX, 529.

Verse [signed]: Corinna and her Pupil, II, 320. Song, IV, 460. Love and the Myrtle-Leaf, IV, 660. The Contrast: from the French of Tristan l'Hermite, VI, 449.

WRIGHT, THOMAS.

Essays [reprinted with omissions and other changes in Wright's *Essays on Subjects Connected with the Literature, Popular Superstitions, and History of England in the Middle Ages*]: Old English Political Songs, VIII, 717. The National Fairy Mythology of England, X, 51. Europe during the Middle Ages [not reprinted but acknowledged in On Anglo-Saxon Poetry, XII, 76a], XI, 28. Popular Superstitions of Modern Greece, XI, 218. On Anglo-Saxon Poetry, XII, 76. On Ker's Nursery Rhymes and Proverbs [reprinted as the last half of "Proverbs and Popular Sayings"], XII, 283. Conquest of Ireland by the Anglo-Normans, XIII, 269. On Anglo-Norman Poetry, XIV, 55. The Story of Eustace the Monk, XV, 75.

WYATT, CHARLES PERCY.

The Banished Angel [translation from Béranger, reprinted in Wyatt's *Poems Original and Translated*], XIII, 65.

Probably the following from the Parliamentary Report for January, 1836, should also be listed among *Fraser's* contributors: R. Alexander, Rev. F. Barham, Leigh Hunt (a friend of Heraud), Washington Irving, Dr. J. Leitch, W. M. Praed, James Wilson (intimate friend of Maginn, a zoologist and traveler, the brother of John Wilson [*Blackwood's* Christopher North]). R. Alexander may have contributed The Schoolmaster's Experience in Newgate and other articles [see present text, pp. 135, 313, n. 20]. The Schoolmaster's Experience was republished as *Old Bailey Experience* (London, 1833), and is attributed to Wontner in Cushing's *Anonyms*. It is improbable that Thomas Wontner, the Governor of Newgate, wrote the series, as the author not only occasionally speaks of Wontner in flattering terms, but mentions differing from him in opinion. See *Fraser's*, V, 521.

APPENDIX 4

BIBLIOGRAPHY OF THACKERAY

WORK OF ESTABLISHED AUTHENTICITY

Hints for a History of Highwaymen [a review of C. Whitehead's *Lives and Exploits of English Highwaymen*], IX, 279.

Il était un Roi d'Yvetot, IX, 617.

The Yellowplush Correspondence: Fashnable Fax and Polite Annygoats [a review of J. H. Skelton's *My Book, or, The Anatomy of Conduct*], XVI, 644; Mrs. Shum's Husband, XVII, 39; Dimond Cut Dimond, XVII, 243; Skimmings from "The Dairy of George IV" [a review of Lady Charlotte Bury's *Diary Illustrative of the Times of George the Fourth*], XVII, 353; Foring Parts, XVII, 404; Mr. Deucease at Paris, XVII, 616, 734; the end of Mr. Deucease's History, XVIII, 59; Mr. Yellowplush's Ajew, XVIII, 195.

A Word on the Annuals [a review of *The Keepsake* and of other annuals for 1838], XVI, 757.

Our Batch of Novels for Christmas, 1837 [in collaboration with Maginn. The three reviews following are Thackeray's: Mrs. Trollope's *The Vicar of Wrexhill,* Bulwer's *Ernest Maltravers,* Letitia Landon's *Ethel Churchill.*], XVII, 79-103.

Half-a-Crown's Worth of Cheap Knowledge [a review of *The Poor Man's Friend* and of other penny and twopenny papers], XVII, 279.

Strictures on Pictures: a Letter from Michael Angelo Titmarsh, XVII, 758.

Passages from the Diary of the Late Dolly Duster, XVIII, 471, 597.

Horæ Catnachianæ: a Dissertation on Ballads, XIX, 407.

Catherine: a Story, XIX, 604, 694; XX, 98, 224, 531; XXI, 106, 200.

Paris Pastimes for the Month of May [signed You Know Who], XIX, 710.

A Second Lecture on the Fine Arts, by Michael Angelo Titmarsh, XIX, 743.

The Paris Rebels of the Twelfth of May [signed You Know Who], XX, 212.

The Fêtes of July [signed You Know Who], XX, 348.

The French Plutarch: I, Cartouche; II, Poinsinet, XX, 447.

On the French School of Painting: With Appropriate Anecdotes, Illustrations, and Philosophical Disputations. In a Letter from Mr. Michael Angelo Titmarsh to Mr. MacGilp of London [signed M.A.T.], XX, 679.

The Great Cossack Epic of Demetrius Rigmarolovicz, XX, 715.

Epistles to the Literati, No. XIII. Ch–s Y–ll–wpl–sh, Esq. to Sir Edward Lytton Bulwer, Bart. John Thomas Smith, Esq. to C–s Y–h, Esq., XXI, 71.

William Ainsworth and Jack Sheppard, XXI, 227.

A Shabby-Genteel Story, XXI, 677; XXII, 90, 226, 399.

A Pictorial Rhapsody, by Michael Angelo Titmarsh, with an Introductory Letter to Mr. Yorke, XXI, 720. A Pictorial Rhapsody: Concluded, and Followed by a Remarkable Statement of Facts by Mrs. Barbara, XXII, 112.

Going to See a Man Hanged [signed W.M.T.], XXII, 150.

Memorials of Gormandising. In a Letter to Oliver Yorke, Esq., by M. A. Titmarsh, XXIII, 710.

On Men and Pictures: *à propos* of a Walk in the Louvre, Paris, June, 1841, XXIV, 98.

Men and Coats, XXIV, 208.

The History of Samuel Titmarsh and the Great Hoggarty Diamond. Edited and Illustrated by Sam's Cousin, Michael Angelo, XXIV, 324, 389, 594, 717.

Dickens in France, XXV, 342.

Fitz-Boodle's Confessions, XXV, 707; XXVI, 395.

Professions by George Fitz-Boodle, XXVI, 43.

Confessions of George Fitz-Boodle. Dorothea, XXVII, 76. Ottilia, XXVII, 214. Men's Wives: Mr. and Mrs. Frank Berry, XXVII, 349. Men's Wives, No. II, The Ravenswing, XXVII, 465, 597, 723; XXVIII, 188, 321. Men's Wives, No. III, Dennis Haggarty's Wife, XXVIII, 494. Men's Wives, No. IV, The——'s Wife, XXVIII, 581.

Jérôme Paturot: with Considerations on Novels in General. In a Letter from M. A. Titmarsh [a review of Reybaud's *Jérôme Paturot a la recherche d'une position sociale*], XXVIII, 349.

Bluebeard's Ghost, by M. A. Titmarsh, XXVIII, 413.

Grant in Paris, by Fitz-Boodle [a review of James Grant's *Paris and Its People*], XXVIII, 702.

The Luck of Barry Lyndon: a Romance of the Last Century, by Fitz-Boodle, XXIX, 35, 187, 318, 391, 548, 723; XXX, 93, 227, 353, 584, 666.

A Box of Novels [signed M.A.T.; reviews of Charles Lever's *Tom Burke of Ours;* Samuel Lover's *L.S.D., or, Accounts of Irish Heirs;* Charles Dickens's *A Christmas Carol,* and others], XXIX, 153.

Titmarsh's Carmen Lilliense [signed M.A.T.], XXIX, 361.

Little Travels and Road-Side Sketches, by Titmarsh, XXIX, 517; XXX. 465; XXXI, 94.

May Gambols: or Titmarsh in the Picture Galleries, XXIX, 700.
Picture Gossip. In a Letter from Michael Angelo Titmarsh, XXXI, 713.
Barmecide Banquets with Joseph Bregion and Anne Miller. George Savage Fitz-Boodle, Esquire, to the Rev. Lionel Gaster, XXXII, 584.
About a Christmas Book. In a Letter from Michael Angelo Titmarsh to Oliver Yorke, Esq. [a review of *Poems and Pictures: A Collection of Ballads, etc.*], XXXII, 744.
Ronsard to his Mistress [signed Michael Angelo Titmarsh], XXXIII, 120.
A Brother of the Press on the History of a Literary Man, Laman Blanchard, and the Chances of the Literary Profession. In a Letter to the Reverend Francis Sylvester at Rome, from Michael Angelo Titmarsh, Esq., XXXIII, 332.
On Some Illustrated Children's Books, by Michael Angelo Titmarsh, XXXIII, 495.
Proposals for a Continuation of *Ivanhoe*. In a Letter to Monsieur Alexandre Dumas, by Monsieur Michael Angelo Titmarsh, XXXIV, 237, 359.
A Grumble about the Christmas Books, by Michael Angelo Titmarsh, XXXV, 111.

WORK PROBABLY ATTRIBUTABLE TO THACKERAY ALONE

The Contested Election [see present text, p. 257], VII, 65.
Paris and the Parisians in 1835 [a review of Mrs. Trollope's *Paris and the Parisians*], XIII, 209.
Si j'étais petit oiseau. Vous veillerez [paraphrases of Béranger; see present text, p. 257], IX, 248.
Four German Ditties [translations from Adelbert von Chamisso and others], XVII, 577.

WORK PROBABLY ATTRIBUTABLE TO THACKERAY AND MAGINN IN COLLABORATION

The Fraser Papers [in collaboration with Churchill and probably others], VII, 240, 367, 498, 620; VIII, 118, 376, 499, 742; IX, 240, 371, 615; X, 365; XV, 528, 654.
The Poets of the Day, VII, 658; VIII, 360, 658; X, 338; XI, 708.
New Edition of *Rejected Addresses* [review], VIII, 36.
Boaden's *Memoirs of Mrs. Inchbald* [review], VIII, 536.
Lady Morgan's *Dramatic Scenes* [review], VIII, 613.
Allan Cunningham's *Fifty Years* [review], IX, 224.
A Dozen of Novels [reviews, among others, of Andrew Picken's *The Black Watch;* G. R. Gleig's *Allan Breck;* Theodore Hook's *The Par-*

son's Daughter and *Love and Pride;* Maria Edgeworth's *Helen*], IX, 456.

Life and Correspondence of Mrs. Hannah More [a review of William Robert's *Memoirs of the Life and Correspondence of Mrs. Hannah More*], X, 448.

France, Social, Literary, Political [review of Henry Lytton Bulwer's book by that title], XI, 59.

A Quintette of Novels [reviews, among others, of Lady Blessington's *Two Friends,* and Letitia Elizabeth Landon's *Francesca Carrara*], XI, 465.

A Decade of Novels and Nouvellettes [reviews, among others, of Hood's "Housekeeper's Tale" in the *Comic Annual* and *Tylney Hall;* James Hogg's *Wars of Montrose;* Mrs. Shelley's *Lodore*], XI, 586.

Washington Irving's *Miscellanies* [review], XII, 409.

Mr. Grant's *Great Metropolis* [review], XIV, 710.

APPENDIX 5

BIBLIOGRAPHY OF CARLYLE

ADDITIONS TO BIBLIOGRAPHY

Allan Cunningham's *Maid of Elvar* [in collaboration with Heraud, see present text, pp. 263-66], V, 659.

Cunningham's Life of Burns [see present text, pp. 92, 274 f.], IX, 400.

For other work in which Carlyle may have shared, see General Bibliography of *Fraser's* under Heraud, pp. 284f.

ACKNOWLEDGED WORK

Jean Paul Friedrich Richter's Review of Madame de Staël's *Allemagne,* I, 28, 407.

Cui Bono? Four Fables by Pilpay Junior, II, 178.

Thoughts on History, II, 413.

Cruthers and Jonson: or the Outskirts of Life, a True Story, II, 691.

Luther's Psalm, II, 743.

Peter Nimmo, III, 12.

The Beetle, III, 72.

Schiller, III, 127.

The Sower's Song, III, 390.

Tragedy of the Night-Moth, IV, 64.

Schiller, Goethe, and Madame de Staël, V, 171.

The Baron von Goethe [Gallery sketch], V, 206.

Biography, V, 253.

Boswell's Life of Johnson, V, 379.

The Tale, by Goethe, VI, 257.

Fragment, by Goethe, VI, 383.

Quæ Cogitavit, VII, 585.

Count Cagliostro: in Two Flights, VIII, 19, 132.

Sartor Resartus, VIII, 581, 669 [second page by that number in the volume]; IX, 177, 301, 443, 664; X, 77, 182.

Death of the Rev. Edward Irving, XI, 101.

The Diamond Necklace, XV, 1, 172.

Epistles to the Literati, No. XI, Thomas Carlyle, Esq., to Oliver Yorke, Esq., on the Sinking of the Vengeur, XX, 76.

An Election to the Long Parliament, XXX, 379.

APPENDIX 6

BIBLIOGRAPHY OF MAGINN

[Titles are often given only in part or merely briefly indicated.]

ACKNOWLEDGED WORK

Sonnets [signed by O'Doherty], XIII, 394, 520, 760; XIV, 256, 514, 640, 750; XV, 144, 284, 554, 680, 804; XVI, 136, 266, 400, 526, 656, 776; XVIII, 126; XIX, 126, 638, 758; XX, 512, 766; XXI, 125, 254, 380, 505; XXII, 382, 636, 768.

Translations from Homer [republished by Mackenzie in Maginn's *Homeric Ballads and Comedies of Lucian*]: The Visit of Helen to the Scæan Gate [signed M.], XI, 582. Homeric Ballads, XVII, 1, 251, 359, 506, 648, 728; XVIII, 71, 209, 367, 489, 621, 739; XXII, 383; XXV, 521; XXVI, 61, 439.

Comedies of Lucian [republished by Mackenzie in Maginn's *Homeric Ballads and Comedies of Lucian*], XIX, 89, 215, 470, 630, 732; XX, 300; XXI, 32.

Other poetry [signed by O'Doherty unless otherwise identified]: Song—Idem Latine Redditum [a Latin paraphrase of Herrick's "Gather Ye Rose-Buds"; reprinted by Maginn in *Magazine Miscellanies* and by Mackenzie in *Fraserian Papers*], I, 335. Horace in Other Shapes [signature of O'Doherty among others; reprinted in *Fraserian Papers*], I, 414. Specimens of a Translation into Latin of *The Beggar's Opera* [given in text to Maginn and others, reprinted in *Fraserian Papers*], I, 432. Song of a Sceptic [reprinted in *Magazine Miscellanies*], III, 712. Song of the Shirtless, VII, 125. All-Hallow-Eve, VII, 628. End of May and Grey, IX, 744. Dinner to Earl Grey: The Eating of Edinburgh, X, 481. A Ballad by a Bystander, X, 624. The Wind-Up of the Year, X, 736. Quatrain on the Queen, XX, 376. Stanza on Seeing the Poniatowski Gems, XXV, 747.

Gallery of Illustrious Literary Characters [republished by Bates; see below under Collected Work and Novels. Individual portraits are listed in General Bibliography of *Fraser's* under Maclise and Maginn.].

Stories [reprinted by Maginn in his *Magazine Miscellanies*]: The First Foot [signed M.], VI, 302. The Mask: or Part of a Story, XI, 552. A Father's Confession, XI, 576. The Spear-Head, XIV, 637.

Articles, letters, and squibs: Letter from Sir Morgan O'Doherty, Bart., I, 685. Review of the Reproof of Brutus [According to editorial note, this is one of the contributions acknowledged in the Letter listed immediately above.], I, 688. A Dozen Nuisances of London [signed by O'Doherty], II, 450. Ruminations Round a Punch Bowl [signed by O'Doherty], II, 638*. Rumbling Murmurs of an Old Tory [signed by O'Doherty], III, 648. A Growl at the Lords [signed by O'Doherty], V, 630. Canada by Tiger, Galt, Picken [reviews of William Dunlop's *Statistical Sketches of Upper Canada* and John Galt's and Andrew Picken's *The Canadas;* acknowledged by Maginn in the Gallery sketch of Dunlop, VII, 436], V, 635. Letter to the Primate of Ireland on the State of the Irish Church [signed by O'Doherty], VI, 124. Running commentary on Macnish's The Books of Aphorisms [see General Bibliography of *Fraser's,* p. 289, under Macnish], VI, 712. Meditations for May-Day [signed by O'Doherty], VII, 615. The Triumph of Humbug: a Homily for July [signed by O'Doherty], VIII, 113. A Letter to Oliver Yorke, and Notes on Military Promotion by Bombardinio [Col. John Mitchell; see General Bibliography of *Fraser's,* p. 291] [signed by O'Doherty], VIII, 311. On Manners, Fashions, and Things in General by Bombardinio, with Notes by Sir Morgan O'Doherty, Bart., X, 105, 237. Mr. Grantley Berkeley and His Novel [acknowledged by Maginn before his duel with Grantley Berkeley], XIV, 242. Defence of *Fraser's* Magazine in the Berkeley Affair [signed William Maginn, Esq., LL.D.], XV, 137. Mitchell's *Life of Wallenstein* [reprinted in *Magazine Miscellanies*], XVII, 484. Familiar Epistle to the Hereditary Grand Duke of Russia [signed by O'Doherty], XIX, 738. Epistles to the Literati: Dr. Maginn to Oliver Yorke, Esq., XX, 253. Dr. Farmer's Essay on the Learning of Shakespeare, Considered by William Maginn, Esq., XX, 254, 476, 647. Did Hannibal Know the Use of Gunpowder? Adversaria No. I [reprinted in *Magazine Miscellanies*], XXI, 608. A Few Notes upon Shakespeare: Adversaria No. II [signed M.; see Adversaria No. I above], XXI, 740. Darley's Edition of Beaumont and Fletcher: Adversaria, No. III [see Adversaria No. I above], XXII, 189.

OTHER WORK OF ESTABLISHED AUTHENTICITY

Our Confession of Faith [given by Mackenzie in "Memoir" prefacing *Fraserian Papers,* p. lxv], I, 1. Mr. Robert Montgomery's *Satan* [given to Maginn by Mackenzie, *op. cit.,* p. lxv], I, 95. Moore's Life of Byron [given to Maginn by Mackenzie, *op. cit.,* p. lxv], I, 129; III, 238. The Election of Editor [presumably with others; republished in *Fraserian Papers*], I, 496, 738; II, 238. The Edinburgh Review [reprinted in *Fraserian Papers* as Maginn on Macaulay], I, 584. The Hon. Mrs. Norton's *Undying One* [opening pages republished in *Fraserian Papers* as "The Sheridan Family"], II, 180. Ars Ridendi: or Hook and Hood on Laughter [in all probability with Lockhart, see

General Bibliography of *Fraser's,* under Lockhard, p. 287. Opening paragraphs republished in *Fraserian Papers* as "Philosophy of Laughter."], III, 154. On Our National Prospects and Political History, by W. Holmes, Esq. [republished in *Fraserian Papers* as "The Politics of 1831"], III, 252. The Poetry of the Sandwich Islands [with Churchill; see General Bibliography of *Fraser's,* under Churchill, p. 281 f. One of its poems, The Lay of the Dismal Camp, was republished in *Fraserian Papers.*], III, 334. Elegy on the Demise of Napoleon [republished as "The Death of Napoleon" in *Fraserian Papers*], IV, 36. Poetical Plagiaries: Thomas Moore [republished in *Fraserian Papers*], IV, 45, 566. Barney Moore: a Vision of Covent Garden and St. Giles's [republished in *Fraserian Papers*], IV, 253. The Great and Celebrated Hogg Dinner [attributed by Mackenzie, *op. cit.,* p. lxxiii], V, 113. The Death of Sir Walter Scott [republished in *Fraserian Papers*], VI, 380. Introductory comments in Lord Byron's Verses on Sam Rogers, VII, 81, and in Coleridge's Two Round Spaces on the Tombstone, VII, 175 [both attributed by Kenealy, *Dublin University Magazine,* XXIII, 89]. The Fraser Papers [with Churchill and probably Thackeray and others. Maginn is mentioned by Kenealy as the responsible writer, *Dublin University Magazine,* XXIII, 89.], VII, 240, 367, 498, 620; VIII, 376, 499, 742; IX, 240, 371, 615; X, 365; XV, 528, 654. Let the Spirit of the Murphies [verse squib republished in *Fraserian Papers* as "Nonsense Verses"], VIII, 121. An Irishman's Lament upon Apsley House [written in Gaelic and translated; republished in *Fraserian Papers*], VIII, 503. The Miller Correspondence [given to Maginn by Mackenzie, *op. cit.,* p. lxxiii], VIII, 624. When My Weary, Worn-Out Eyes [paraphrase of Anacreon; see present text, p. 253], IX, 121. Domestic Manners of Sir Walter Scott, by James Hogg [review of Hogg; given to Maginn by Lockhart in a letter to William Blackwood: Margaret Oliphant, *Annals of a Publishing House,* II, 123], X, 125. Of Ireland in 1834 by an Officer in the Marching Regiment [pp. 197-99 reprinted in *Fraserian Papers* as "Irish Genius"], XI, 193, 342. April Fools, or One Hundred Matrimonial Letters [given to Maginn by Kenealy (*op. cit.,* p. 89), who suggests Hook, see General Bibliography of *Fraser's,* p. 285, as a possible collaborator; also attributed by Mackenzie, *op. cit.,* p. lxxiii], XI, 369. Parliamentary Report of the Proceedings Instituted at the Close of the Last Session, to Inquire into the Conduct and to Regulate the Future Management of *Fraser's Magazine* [probably with others; attributed to Maginn by Kenealy, *op. cit.,* p. 89, and by Mackenzie, *op. cit.,* p. lxxiii], XIII, 1. Willis's Pencillings [reprinted in *Fraserian Papers*], XIII, 195. Another Caw from the Rookwood [reprinted in *Fraserian Papers;* see present text, pp. 247 ff.], XIII,

488. Sabbath Joy [a poem, republished in *Fraserian Papers*], XIII, 597. Agnewidos [republished in *Fraserian Papers*], XIII, 639. The Statesman [review of Sir Henry Taylor's *The Statesman;* reprinted in *Fraserian Papers*], XIV, 393. Mr. Grant's *Great Metropolis* [probably in collaboration with Thackeray; reprinted in *Fraserian Papers*], XIV, 710. The Doctor [article identifying Southey's work; given to Maginn by Kenealy, *op. cit.,* p. 91], XVI, 657; XVII, 106, 310. Epaminondas Grubb, or Fenimore Cooper *versus* the Memory of Sir Walter Scott [reprinted in *Fraserian Papers*], XIX, 371. De Re Vehiculari [The *Aberdeen Journal* for July 13, 1842, contains the comment: "*Fraser's* is buoyant with the curious learning and refined humour of Maginn, in the 'Homeric Ballads' and 'De Re Vehiculari.'" This comment with other tributes to the publisher, Nickisson, is reprinted on the reverse of the cover of *Fraser's*], XXV, 584; XXVI, 15.

WORK IN ALL PROBABILITY BY MAGINN

Donovan the Intoxicator, I, 209. On the Civil Disabilities of British Jews, I, 541. The Desperate System, Poverty, Crime, and Emigration, I, 635. Webster's *Travels through the Crimea and Egypt* and Bruckhardt's *Arabic Proverbs,* I, 695. An Expostulation with the Law of Divorce, I, 427. Dr. Kennedy and Lord Byron, II, 1. Lardner's Cabinet, II, 58. Machinery and the Manufacturing System, II, 419. Burnings in Kent, and the State of the Labouring Classes, II, 572. The Downfall of the Wellington Administration, II, 592. Dr. Phillpott, the Bishop, II, 687. Boaden's Life of Mrs. Jordan, II, 736. Some Passages from the Diary of the Late Mr. St. John Long, II, 739. The Novels of the Season, III, 95. *The Siamese Twins* [review of Bulwer Lytton's satirical poem], III, 195. Mr. Sadler and the *Edinburgh Review,* III, 209. Symposiac the Second [presumably with others], III, 255. Montgomery's *Oxford,* III, 280. Bits of Classicality [presumably with others], III, 284; IV, 727; V, 520. Visit from Mr. Saint John Long, III, 365. On Quackery, Twaddle, and Other Offences, III, 368. To Petrus Maximus, III, 391. The Metropolitan: a 'Prospect'ive Puff of a New Periodical, III, 493. Nicholas and Palgrave, III, 522. The Quarterly Review on Reform, III, 525. National Song of Ireland, III, 537. Romantic Poetry of the Italians [includes a long review of Panizzi], III, 598. Autobiography of Edward Lytton Bulwer, III, 713. Landor's Poems [presumably with Heraud], III, 736. An Apology for a Preface, IV, 1. Novels of the Season—Batch the Second, IV, 8. Bubble and Squeak [presumably with others], IV, 33, 347. On the Metropolitan English Lexicon, IV, 41. Lays of the Twaddle School, IV, 52. Sketches of Irish Character [review of Mrs. Hall], IV, 100.

Peter Robertson *versus* the Edinburgh Review, IV, 180. Coronation Coronal [presumably with others], IV, 375. Lays of the Twaddle School: No. II [presumably with others], IV, 433. The Briareus of the Press, IV, 490. Oliver Yorke's Levee [presumably with others], IV. 495. Epistles to the Literati: No. I, to E. L. Bulwer [signed Robin Roughhead; authorship practically admitted, p. 525], IV, 520. Bits of Classicality, No. II [presumably with others], IV, 727. A Brief Good-Morrow to the New Leap-Year, IV, 762. A Good Tale, Badly Told [review of Bulwer's *Eugene Aram*], V, 107. Trollope and Paulding on America [reviews of *Domestic Manners of the Americans,* by Mrs. Trollope, and of *The Dutchman's Fireside,* by James Kirke Paulding], V, 336. The American Chesterfield [a review of *The American Chesterfield,* by John Grigg], V, 515. Lays of the Twaddle School: No. III [presumably with others], V, 583. A Cool Dialogue on Passing Events, between Oliver Yorke and His Chum, V, 621. Elizabeth Brownrigge: a Tale [presumably with Lockhart; see present text, pp. 62 ff.], VI, 67, 131. On National Economy, VI, 113, 239, 403; VII, 282, 377, 603; VIII, 103, 222, 604; IX, 356. The Late Sir James Mackintosh and the Law Magazine, VI, 307. Archbishop Whateley's Secondary Punishments Dissected [The author acknowledges writing the series On National Economy.], VI, 566. The Departed of XXXII, VI, 751. New-Year's Day Address to Contributors and Readers, VII, 1. Reconstruction of the Tory Party, VII, 223. Piozziana, VII, 471. Introductory comments on The Shepherd's Noctes and the Reason Why They Do Not Appear in *Fraser's Magazine* [reminiscent remarks reveal authorship], VIII, 49. Babbage on Machinery and Manufactures, VIII, 167. Specimens of the Art of Governing by Commission, VIII, 470. The Last News with Three Cheers for the Earl of Durham as a Tail-Piece, VIII, 740. The State and Prospects of Toryism, IX, 1, 364. Notes Written on the Last Day of the Year Thirty-Three, IX, 117. Bridlegoose Brougham, IX, 501. Report on the Poor Laws, IX, 507. Mr. Duncombe and Mr. Fraser, X, 494. Politics of the Month, XI, 234. The Book of the Season [presumably with others], XI, 414. Letter to Francis Baring, Esq., Joint Secretary to the Treasury by an Old Whipper-in [signed W.H. (William Holmes); the letter is a burlesque on Holmes], XI, 617. Martial Elegies of Tyrtæus, XI, 621. Cobbett, XII, 207. Stray Reflections [presumably with others], XIII, 254. The Book of Blunders [review of James Grant's *Random Recollections of the House of Commons*], XIII, 747. Prior's Life of Goldsmith [a review], XV, 387. Cooper's *England,* XVI, 233. Murphy, the Meteorological Quack, XVII, 378. Poor Lingo's Petition to Their High Mightinesses, the Poor-Law Commissioners, XVII, 467. Comments on Peter Plymley's Letter on the

Catholics [completes the Gallery sketch of Sydney Smith], XVII, 470. Mitchell's *Thoughts on Tactics,* XVII, 602. Nisbet's Sweepings of Exeter Hall, XIX, 23. Talleyrand, XIX, 127, 287. Croker's *Popular Songs of Ireland,* XIX, 678. Sydney Smith, John Styles, and Grantley Berkeley, XX, 233. New Educational Gems: or a Brace of Scripture Perversions, XX, 310. See also General Bibliography of *Fraser's,* under Churchill, pp. 301 f.; Heraud, pp. 284 f.; and Lockhart, p. 287.

COLLECTED ESSAYS AND POETRY

[The following are republished chiefly from *Blackwood's* and *Fraser's.*]

Magazine Miscellanies (selected by Maginn, London, 1841).

Maxims of Sir Morgan O'Doherty, Bart. (W. Blackwood and Sons, Edinburgh, 1849).

Homeric Ballads (preface signed J.C. [John Churchill], London, 1850).

Noctes Ambrosianæ, by John Wilson, William Maginn, J. G. Lockhart, James Hogg and Others, edited by R. Shelton Mackenzie, LL.D. (New York, 1854). Of the various existing editions of the Noctes, Mackenzie's is the most authoritative for the work of Maginn.

Miscellaneous Writings of the Late Dr. Maginn, edited by R. Shelton Mackenzie, LL.D. (New York, 1855-57): Vols. I and II, The O'Doherty Papers; Vol. III, Shakespeare Papers; Vol. IV, Homeric Ballads and Comedies of Lucian; Vol. V, Fraserian Papers.

Shakspeare Papers: Pictures Grave and Gay (Bentley, London, 1859).

Shakspeare Papers by William Maginn, LL.D. (new ed., Bentley, London, 1860).

A Gallery of Illustrious Literary Characters, 1830-38, Drawn by the Late Daniel Maclise, and Accompanied by Notices, Chiefly by Maginn, edited by W. Bates, with preface and notes (London, 1873).

Miscellanies in Prose and Verse, edited by R. W. Montagu (London, 1885).

NOVELS

Whitehall: or the Days of George IV (London, preface dated 1827). [Presumably with Lockhart, see present text, pp. 241 ff.]

John Manesty (London, 1844). [Probably at least outlined by Maginn since published posthumously by his widow.]

SOME WORK IN BLACKWOOD'S AND FRASER'S ERRONEOUSLY ATTRIBUTED TO MAGINN

Rime of the Auncient Waggonere [by O'Doherty. Hamilton, and apparently Moir, had used the pseudonym before Maginn adopted it.], *Blackwood's,* IV, 571. David Moir acknowledges writing this parody of Coleridge's *Ancient Mariner:* Thomas Aird's "Memoir" prefacing *Poetical Works of D. M. Moir* (London, 1860), I, 11.

Christabel, Part III, *Blackwood's,* V, 286. This is referred to as Maginn's in one of Coleridge's "Conversations": *Letters, Conversations, and Recollections,* edited by T. Allsop (New York, 1836), p. 64. Moir in speaking of Coleridge's attributing the verses to Maginn acknowledges writing them himself: *The Modern Pythagorean: a Series of Tales, Essays, and Sketches by the Late Robert Macnish, LL.D.* (London, 1838), I, 392 n. Kenealy, presumably on the basis of Coleridge's statement, attributes them to Maginn, *Dublin University Magazine,* XXIII, 77.

Miss Pipson, *Fraser's,* V, 708. This squib was included by Mackenzie in Maginn's *Fraserian Papers.* It is, however, acknowledged by Macnish in a letter to Moir, and reprinted as his in *The Modern Pythagorean.* See General Bibliography of *Fraser's* under Macnish, p. 289.

The Spermaceti Candle, *Fraser's,* VI, 686. These verses were also included by Mackenzie in Maginn's *Fraserian Papers,* but were acknowledged by Macnish, and mentioned as his by Maginn. See General Bibliography of *Fraser's* under Macnish, p. 289.

Of Hamlet, *Fraser's,* XIV, 1. This essay was reprinted by Mackenzie in Maginn's *Fraserian Papers* under the caption "The Character of Hamlet," with the explanation that it should have been included in the earlier edition of Maginn's *Shakespeare Papers.* It also appears in Bentley's *Shakspeare Papers* by William Maginn, (1860). It was unquestionably written by Banks, as it is included in his series on Books on My Table, and signed by his pseudonym, Morgan Rattler. See present text, p. 248; also General Bibliography of *Fraser's* under Banks, p. 278.

Father Tom and the Pope, *Blackwood's,* XLIII, 607. See discussion of Maginn's literary work, present text, pp. 238 ff.

NOTES

PART ONE: THE ROUND TABLE

I. *Fraser's and the 1830's*

[1] Percival Weldon Banks speaks of "our illustrious friend and fellow collegian, the editor of *Regina*." *Fraser's*, III, 82(a).

[2] Preface (signed Frank Mahony and dated Paris, 1859) to *The Reliques of Father Prout* (London, 1866), p. vii.

[3] The last number of *Fraser's* to appear with James Fraser's name was that for March, 1842. The first number with John Parker's name was that for July, 1847. Parker, the well-known publisher for the Broad Church group, and himself one of its members, was his own editor for a few years until James Anthony Froude began his long editorship in January, 1861. In July, 1879, Principal Tulloch became editor.

[4] Quoted in "Our Past and Our Present," *Fraser's*, New Series XX, 11, from the issue of January, 1849 (XXXIX, 2).

[5] See General Bibliography of *Fraser's*, p. 281.

[6] Robert Pearse Gillies states that Wilson and Lockhart wrote thirty-two columns as an ordinary day's work, which left margin for other things. *Memoirs of a Literary Veteran* (London, 1851), II, 236 f.

[7] R. S. Mackenzie, "Memoir of William Maginn," prefacing Vol. V (*Fraserian Papers*) of Maginn's *Miscellaneous Writings* (New York, 1855-57), p. lxxi; see also E. V. Kenealy, *Dublin University Magazine*, XXIII, 79.

[8] *Fraser's*, III, 260.

[9] Michael Sadleir, *Bulwer and His Wife: a Panorama* (London, 1933), pp. 242 f.

[10] *Fraser's*, XI, 2 f.

[11] For the full list, see General Bibliography of *Fraser's*, p. 277.

[12] Quotations taken from *Fraser's*, III, 365.

II. *Magazine Miscellanies*

[1] *Fraser's*, III, 154(a). Reprinted in *Fraserian Papers* under the caption "Philosophy of Laughter."

[2] For complete list of "Portraits" see General Bibliography of *Fraser's*, under Maclise and Maginn, pp. 287-89.

[3] *Fraser's*, IV, 498.

[4] *A Gallery of Illustrious Characters, 1830-1838*, edited by W. Bates (London, 1873).

[5] G. S. Layard, *A Great "Punch" Editor* (London, 1907), p. 28.

[6] *Fraser's*, XX, 590 f.

[7] See the recent study, *John Galt*, by Robert K. Gorden.

[8] An interesting interpretation of Letitia Landon is given by D. E. Enfield, *L.E.L.: a Mystery of the Thirties* (London, 1928).

[9] A detailed study of Ainsworth has been made by S. M. Ellis, *William Harrison Ainsworth and His Friends* (London, 1911).

[10] The *Carlton Chronicle* (edited by the Fraserian, Percival Weldon Banks), for Oct. 1, 1836, speaks of Oliver Yorke as of late being "generally described as Proutian."

[11] Browning has left reminiscences of Prout which are included in Blanchard Jerrold's biographical introduction to his edition of the *Final Reliques of Father Prout* (London, 1876), pp. 62 ff.
[12] *Ibid.*, p. 147.
[13] William Allingham, *Diary* (London, 1907), pp. 77 f.
[14] *Fraser's*, X, 194-210.
[15] *Ibid.*, IX, 549-52.
[16] C. A. Read, *The Cabinet of Irish Literature*, III, 48, 52.
[17] M. F. Brightfield, *Theodore Hook and His Novels* (Harvard University Press, 1928), p. 163.
[18] *Fraser's*, IX, 477(a).
[19] *Ibid.*, III, 423-28.
[20] *Ibid.*, XI, 3.
[21] *Ibid.*, XI, 3-5, 99-101. See also the appreciations, XVI, 195; XVII, 350 f.
[22] Preface to *The Reliques of Father Prout*, signed Frank Mahony, p. vii.
[23] *Fraser's*, IV, 754.
[24] *Ibid.*, XI, 99. See General Bibliography of *Fraser's*, p. 285.
[25] According to the writer of the article on the Fraserians in *The Critic, London Literary Journal*, XI, No. 265 (April 15, 1852), Lockhart saw in *Fraser's* "a famous opportunity for scarifying men whom he did not care, or did not like, to attack in the *Quarterly*."
[26] *Fraser's*, I, 291-300, 563-71; III, 557-66.
[27] Theodore Martin, himself a well-known translator, writes to the editor of Bentley's *Miscellany*, "I was disappointed at not finding a Rabelaisian paper in *The Miscellany* this month. It would be none the worse, don't you think, for a lift from a man of mettle like Banks?" S. M. Ellis, *William Harrison Ainsworth and His Friends* (London, 1911), I, 383, n.
[28] *The Critic, London Literary Journal*, XI, 202.
[29] The first O'Donoghue story appeared in *Fraser's*, Aug., 1831 (IV, 79). The last appearance of O'Donoghue is in Oct., 1844 (XXX, 412).
[30] *Ibid.*, XXII, 320(a).
[31] *Dublin University Magazine*, XXXIV, 210.
[32] Quoted by his son, T. F. Dillon Croker, in the memoir prefacing Thomas Wright's edition of the *Fairy Legends* (1859), pp. vii f.
[33] *Fraser's*, reverse of the Table of Contents, April, 1830.
[34] *Ibid.*, V, 3.
[35] *Ibid.*, IV, 380.
[36] *Ibid.*, III, 259.
[37] *Ibid.*, IX, 372.
[38] *Ibid.*, XI, 421(b) f.
[39] *Ibid.*, XI, 420(b).
[40] *Ibid.*, IV, 40.
[41] *Ibid.*, X, 366.
[42] *Ibid.*, VIII, 751.
[43] *Ibid.*, I, 503 f.
[44] *Ibid.*, XIII, 22.

[45] *Fraser's,* II, 244.

[46] *Ibid.,* II, 246 f.

[47] *Ibid.,* II, 638*-40*.

[48] *Ibid.,* II, 245 f.

[49] William Fraser was the editor of the *Foreign Review,* a popular man, and reputed something of a dandy.

[50] *Fraser's,* I, 749 f.

[51] *Ibid.,* VII, 81-84.

[52] *Ibid.,* VIII, 743 f.

[53] *Ibid.,* VII, 176 f.

[54] *Ibid.,* VII, 367.

[55] *Ibid.,* XIII, 132-42; XV, 100-36. See also the statement by Maginn which follows, XV, 137-43.

PART TWO: REVOLT IN CRITICISM

III. *Thackeray*

[1] Lewis Benjamin (pseudonym, Lewis Melville), *William Makepeace Thackeray* (London, 1910), I, 130.

[2] James Grant Wilson, *Thackeray in the United States* (London, 1904), II, 133.

[3] C. P. Johnson, *The Early Writings of William Makepeace Thackeray* (London, 1888), p. 39.

[4] *Final Reliques of Father Prout,* ed. by Blanchard Jerrold (London, 1876), pp. 141 ff.

[5] Lewis Benjamin, *The Life of William Makepeace Thackeray* (London, 1899), I, 70 f.

[6] Thackeray's stepfather, Major Carmichael-Smyth, is said to have procured the *National Standard* for Thackeray. Lewis Benjamin, *William Makepeace Thackeray* (1910 ed.), I, 92.

[7] Parts of the "Adversaria" series in *Fraser's Literary Chronicle* and in the *Carlton Chronicle* were later used by Maginn. For instance, the greater part of No. XVI in the opening issue of the *Carlton Chronicle,* for June 11, 1836, was incorporated in "A Few Notes upon Shakespeare: Adversaria, No. II," *Fraser's,* XXI, 740-42. For assigning the *Fraser* "Adversaria" to Maginn, see Bibliography of Maginn, p. 301.

[8] R. S. Mackenzie, "Memoir of William Maginn," prefacing Vol. V *(Fraserian Papers)* of Maginn's *Miscellaneous Writings* (New York, 1855-57), p. lxxii.

[9] J. G. Wilson, *op. cit.,* II, 134.

[10] Lewis Benjamin, *William Makepeace Thackeray* (1910 ed.), I, 137.

[11] *Fraser's,* VII, 240-50, 367-76, 498-506, 620-31; VIII, 499-510, 742-54; IX, 240-52, 371-78, 615-28; X, 365-78; XV, 528-53, 654-79.

[12] *North British Review,* XL, 216-19.

[13] Letter to R. H. Shepherd, quoted in *Sultan Stork and Other Stories* (London, 1837), p. vii.

[14] Reprinted by R. H. Shepherd, *op. cit.,* and included in his bibliography appended to that volume. Anderson also includes it in his bibliography in the edition of Thackeray by Merivale and Marzials (London, 1891).

[15] Charles Whibley, *William Makepeace Thackeray* (Modern English Writers: Edinburgh, 1903), p. 28.

[16] C. P. Johnson, *op. cit.,* p. 41.

[17] "Thackeray's 'Stray papers,'" *Bookman,* May, 1901, XIII, 239.

[18] Lewis Benjamin (1910 ed.), I, 133 f.
[19] *Fraser's,* I, 528(b) ff.; III, 714(a). An interesting note follows the Table of Contents for January, 1832: "Liston Bulwer has just hit upon a new line of business. His '*fancy flash*' having proved an unmarketable commodity, he has discovered that his genius lies one degree lower; and therefore, most prudently has he resolved upon doing the NEWGATE CALENDAR into a series of '*fashionable novels.*'" This was followed before the year was up by the burlesque "Elizabeth Brownrigge."
[20] *Fraser's,* XVI, 757.
[21] *Life of Edward Bulwer, First Lord Lytton,* by his grandson the Earl of Lytton (London, 1913), I, 81.
[22] *Fraser's,* XVII, 85.
[23] *Life of Edward Bulwer,* I, 548.
[24] Michael Sadleir, *Bulwer and His Wife: a Panorama* (London, 1933), pp. 248-66.
[25] *Ibid.,* pp. 178-80.
[26] R. H. Shepherd, *Memoirs of The Life and Writings of Thomas Carlyle* (London, 1881), I, 80.
[27] Michael Sadleir, *op. cit.,* pp. 195, 280 f.
[28] Bulwer's interest in the movement is summed up by Mr. Sadleir: *op. cit.,* pp. 166-68.
[29] *Ibid.,* pp. 283-85.
[30] *Ibid.,* p. 253. Maginn's review appeared in *Fraser's,* V, 107-13.
[31] *Life of Edward Bulwer,* I, 548.
[32] *Fraser's,* XIII, 488-93.
[33] *Ibid.,* XI, 23 f. This ballad was included by Ainsworth in subsequent editions of *Rookwood.*
[34] S. M. Ellis, *William Harrison Ainsworth and His Friends* (London, 1911), I, 359, 371 ff., 376.
[35] *Ibid.,* I, 377.
[36] *Ibid.,* I, 375.
[37] *Fraser's,* XXI, 238 f.
[38] *Ibid.,* XIX, 408(b) f.
[39] *Ibid.,* XIX, 423(a).
[40] *Ibid.,* XIX, 408(a) f.
[41] *Ibid.,* XXI, 210 ff.

IV. *The Critical Workshop*

[1] *Fraser's,* V, 27.
[2] *Ibid.,* X, 364(b).
[3] *Ibid.,* III, 96(a).
[4] *Whitehall; or the Days of George IV,* pp. 302-23.
[5] *Fraser's,* IV, 9(b).
[6] *Ibid.,* III, 99(b) f.
[7] *Ibid.,* I, 319(a), 320(a).
[8] *Ibid.,* III, 97(a) f.
[9] Harriet Martineau, *Autobiography,* Period IV, Sec. IV. (Boston, 1877), I, 399-403.
[10] S. C. Hall, *Memories of Great Men and Women of the Age* (London, 1871), p. 284.

[11] Wm. Jerdan, *Autobiography* (London, 1853), Appendix B, IV, 392.
[12] For a serious statement of its position, see *Fraser's,* II, 745 f.
[13] *Ibid.,* VIII, 662-67; XVI, 190-94.
[14] *Ibid.,* IX, 460-68.
[15] *Ibid.,* IX, 476(b)-80.
[16] *Ibid.,* X, 516(b) f.
[17] *Ibid.,* XII, 409(a).
[18] *Ibid.,* XIV, 87.
[19] One of the most contemptible attacks in the magazine is the "Gallery" sketch of Harriet Martineau, *Fraser's,* VIII, 576. Her economic theories are derided in political articles. One of her novels is insultingly reviewed by Maginn, *Fraser's,* VI, 403-13.
[20] *Ibid.,* I, 433(a); the quotations following are taken from I, 434-42.
[21] *Ibid.,* IV, 17(b).
[22] *Ibid.,* III, 285-304; VIII, 65-80; 259-78; XII, 415-29; XIV, 407-24; XVI, 719-31.
[23] C. E. Vaughan, "Carlyle and His German Masters" ("Essays and Studies by Members of the English Association," Vol. I, Article VII); Margaret Storrs, *The Relation of Carlyle to Kant and Fichte* (Bryn Mawr, 1929).
[24] *Fraser's,* X, 649(b), 651(a), 655 (b).
[25] *Ibid.,* X, 649 ff. The idea that fate played a large part in determining Byron's fame had been previously brought out, *Fraser's,* I, 130(a).
[26] *Publications of the Modern Language Association,* XXXIX, 919-31.
[27] Recent studies of Coleridge's philosophy have been made by S. F. Gingerich, *Essays in the Romantic Poets* (New York, 1924); and by J. H. Muirhead, *Coleridge as Philosopher* (New York, 1930).
[28] *Fraser's,* IV, 434.
[29] *Ibid.,* XVII, 653-76.
[30] *Ibid.,* XIII, 255(a).
[31] *Ibid.,* VIII, 64.
[32] *Ibid.,* I, 497 f.
[33] *Ibid.,* XIII, 363-74.
[34] *Ibid.,* VIII, 669(b).
[35] *Ibid.,* XVI, 85-104. Passages quoted are from 88(a), 93(a) f.
[36] *Ibid.,* XI, 728(b).
[37] *Ibid.,* I, 159.
[38] *Ibid.,* I, 129-43. Passages quoted are from 130(a), 135 (a).
[39] *Ibid.,* III, 161(b).
[40] *Ibid.,* XIII, 255(a).
[41] *Ibid.,* X, 651(b).
[42] *Ibid.,* I, 95-99. Passages quoted are from 95(a), 97(b), 96(b).
[43] *Ibid.,* II, 493.
[44] *Ibid.,* VIII, 747.
[45] *Ibid.,* XI, 708(a).
[46] *Ibid.,* X, 341(a).
[47] *Ibid.,* X, 343.
[48] *Ibid.,* X, 352-56.
[49] *Ibid.,* II, 185(b).

[50] *Fraser's*, XI, 426(b) f.
[51] *Ibid.*, III, 338.
[52] *Ibid.*, IV, 386.
[53] *Ibid.*, IV, 378.
[54] *Ibid.*, IV, 383.
[55] *Ibid.*, IV, 498.
[56] *Ibid.*, IV, 52.
[57] *Ibid.*, IV, 255.
[58] *Ibid.*, III, 107(b) f.
[59] *Ibid.*, IV, 16(b).
[60] *Ibid.*, IX, 477(b) f.
[61] *Ibid.*, XI, 586-93. Passages quoted are from 591 f.
[62] *Ibid.*, IV, 520-28. Passages quoted are from 520(a).
[63] *Ibid.*, III, 714(a).
[64] *Ibid.*, III, 96(b); IX, 483.
[65] *Ibid.*, IV, 36 f.; III, 73-84.
[66] *Ibid.*, IV, 11-15. Passages quoted are from 12(b), 15(b).
[67] *Ibid.*, XI, 472 f.
[68] *Ibid.*, XIV, 117(a).
[69] *Ibid.*, XIII, 374(b).

PART THREE: REVOLT IN POLITICS

v. *Four Leaders*

[1] Monypenny and Buckle, *Life of Benjamin Disraeli* (new and rev. ed., New York, 1929), I, 215 f.
[2] *Ibid.*, I, 271.
[3] *Ibid.*, I, 233.
[4] The popular nature of *Fraser's* articles indicates that the influence of Coleridge's thought as expressed in simplified and very much modified form was probably widely felt. Excellent studies of Coleridge's views as found in *Church and State* and other writings bearing on political, economic, and theological questions have recently been made by Dr. Alfred Cobban in *Edmund Burke, A Study of the Political and Social Thinking of Burke, Wordsworth, Coleridge, and Southey;* and by Professor John H. Muirhead in the chapter "Political Philosophy" of his *Coleridge as Philosopher.*
[5] Emery Neff, *Carlyle and Mill* (New York, 1926), pp. 208-21; *Carlyle* (New York, 1932), pp. 116-26.
[6] See, for instance, "The March of Intellect and Universal Education," *Fraser's*, II, 161; "A Visit to the National Schools," I, 607.
[7] R. P. Gillies, *Memoirs of a Literary Veteran* (London, 1851), III, 150.
[8] Among the most insolent of *Fraser's* libels is a letter addressed "To the Most Reverend Father in God, Richard, Archbishop of Dublin, Bishop of Glandelagh, Primate of Ireland, and Chancellor of the Illustrious Order of Saint Patrick," VI, 124.
[9] *Ibid.*, XVII, 393.

vi. *Denunciation of Political Economists*

[1] Practically all articles on political, economic, or social conditions have as their basis hatred of political economy. Especially clear statements of the opening of Maginn's

attack may be found in the following: "Suicide of a Financier and Thoughts on Education," *Fraser's*, I, 242; "The Desperate System—Poverty, Crime, and Emigration," I, 635; "The Death of Mr. Huskisson and the Approaching Parliament," II, 255-58, especially; "The March of Intellect and Universal Education," II, 161; "Machinery and the Manufacturing System," II, 419; "Mr. Sadler and the Edinburgh Review," III, 209; "The Althorp Budget," III, 236; "Senior on the Introduction of Poor-Laws into Ireland," IV, 554.

[2] *Ibid.*, VI, 438(a).

[3] *Ibid.*, IX, 322(a).

[4] *Ibid.*, VI, 626.

[5] *Ibid.*, I, 245(a) f.

[6] In his opposition to Malthus Maginn may have been influenced by Michael Sadler. One of the strongest articles in the magazine is that written in defense of Sadler's long refutation of the Malthusian theory. *Ibid.*, III, 209-21.

[7] *Ibid.*, I, 638(a).

[8] *Ibid.*, VII, 282(a).

[9] *Ibid.*, VI, 404(b).

[10] *Ibid.*, VI, 408(b).

[11] *Ibid.*, IX, 516*(a) f.

[12] *Ibid.*, IX, 520(b).

[13] For Maginn's interest in the poor, see also present text, pp. 127, 164.

[14] *Fraser's*, I, 638(a).

[15] *Ibid.*, I, 639(a).

[16] *Ibid.*, II, 573-76.

[17] *Ibid.*, I, 637(a).

[18] *Ibid.*, II, 666-72.

[19] *Ibid.*, XXII, 150-58.

[20] *Ibid.*, V, 521-33, 736-49; VI, 12-23, 285-301, 460-98.

[21] *Ibid.*, V, 529(a).

[22] *Ibid.*, V, 526(a).

[23] *Ibid.*, V, 727 f.; VI, 12.

[24] *Ibid.*, "The Present Condition of the People," IX, 72, 574.

[25] *Ibid.*, VII, 377-92, 707-15; VIII, 470-78.

[26] Sadler's first proposals for relieving the children in the factory were much more extensive than those finally embodied in his Ten Hour Bill. He wished both to forbid the employment of children under nine and to provide six hours on one day a week for their education. Since, however, he felt it imperative that a factory bill in some form should be passed as soon as possible, he limited his demands to those embodied in the Ten Hour Bill. According to this bill no person under twenty-one years of age was to work more than eight hours on Saturday, or more than ten hours on any other day, and was never to be employed at night between the hours of 7 P.M. and 6 A.M. Among other provisions the bill required the fencing off of machinery and adequate supervision of factories. This bill was presented but failed of passage until further modified.

[27] *Fraser's*, VII, 380(b).

[28] *Ibid.*, VIII, 477(b).

[29] *Fraser's,* VII, 391(a).
[30] *Ibid.,* II, 581; III, 9(a); VII, 284-91.
[31] *Ibid.,* VII, 283(a).
[32] *Ibid.,* II, 578(a).
[33] *Ibid.,* IX, 514*(a) f.
[34] *Ibid.,* II, 425(a) f.
[35] *Ibid.,* IX, 507-22. For passages quoted see pp. 513-14.
[36] *Ibid.,* VI, 405(b).
[37] *Ibid.,* VI, 437-45.
[38] *Ibid.,* VI, 445. For the quoted passages which follow see again 445; 437, 444.
[39] *Ibid.,* VI, 406(a) f. Other articles on free trade are the series by John Galt, VI, 593; VII, 106; and Maginn's studies on the relation of free trade and labor, V, 322, 577; VIII, 604; IX, 33; X, 294; XII, 155.
[40] *Ibid.,* VII, 283(a) f.
[41] *Ibid.,* VIII, 104(b).
[42] *Ibid.,* VI, 364(b).
[43] *Ibid.,* VI, 439(b).
[44] The comparatively humane treatment of the slaves was contrasted with the brutal punishments inflicted upon men in the British Army and Navy. *Ibid.,* III, 114-17. An especially revolting and needless torture of one of the guards is instanced as inflicted under the command of the Duke of Wellington, who was zealous in supporting the antislavery movement, III, 116(a).
[45] See, for instance, *ibid.,* VII, 709(a).
[46] *Ibid.,* VII, 392(b).
[47] *Ibid.,* I, 6.

VII. *Progressive Toryism*

[1] Some of the worst onslaughts against Wellington and Peel are in the following: "Thoughts on the Wellington Administration," *Fraser's,* I, 729-37; "The Dead Parliament," II, 115-18; "The Prospects of the Ministry," II, 190; "Place-men, Parliament-men, Penny-a-liners," II, 282; "Downfall of the Wellington Administration," II, 592; "Ruminations Round a Punch Bowl," II, 646; "L'Envoy—Ourselves, the Grey Administration," II, 745; "Repeal of the Union," III, 1.
[2] *Ibid.,* III, 512(a) f.
[3] *Ibid.,* I, 732(a).
[4] *Ibid.,* I, 733(a) f.
[5] *Ibid.,* III, 11(a) f.
[6] *Ibid.,* III, 6(a).
[7] *Ibid.,* III, 1-11. Passages quoted are from pp. 7(b), 5(b), 3(a) f.
[8] *Ibid.,* VII, 752.
[9] *Ibid.,* I, 729(b).
[10] *Ibid.,* I, 730(b).
[11] *Ibid.,* III, 3(b).
[12] *Ibid.,* III, 515(a) f.
[13] Some of the clearest statements in favor of parliamentary reform are in the following: "Parliamentary Reform," *ibid.,* II, 612; "Parliamentary Reform and Vote by Ballot," II, 717; III, 269; "Unrepresented London," III, 69-72; "Moral and Political

State of the British Empire," III, 223; "The Quarterly Review on Reform," III, 231; "Dissolution of Parliament," III, 509; "The Honourable House of the Reform Debate," III, 604.

[14] *Ibid.*, II, 746.

[15] *Ibid.*, II, 117(b) f.

[16] *Ibid.*, III, 275(b).

[17] *Ibid.*, IX, 11(a).

[18] *Ibid.*, VII, 8.

[19] *Ibid.*, VII, 751.

[20] *Ibid.*, V, 505(a).

[21] *Ibid.*, III, 515(b).

[22] *Ibid.*, IX, 628.

[23] *Ibid.*, XII, 310(a).

[24] *Ibid.*, XII, 301(a).

[25] *Ibid.*, IX, 324(a).

[26] *Ibid.*, IX, 314(a).

[27] *Ibid.*, IX, 370(b).

[28] *Ibid.*, XII, 308(b).

[29] *Ibid.*, XII, 309(b).

[30] *Ibid.*, XII, 309(b).

[31] *Ibid.*, XII, 311(b) f.

[32] *Ibid.*, VII, 376.

PART FOUR: WILLIAM MAGINN

VIII. *The Growth of an Editor*

[1] A prominent Fraserian, Rev. George Robert Gleig, chaplain-general of the British forces, writes frankly: "Maginn was one of those brilliant men of genius whom it was impossible effectively to serve . . . such was his reckless extravagance that he went about in constant fear of arrest, and was repeatedly bailed by his friends out of a sponging house." *Personal Reminiscences of the Duke of Wellington* (Edinburgh, 1904), p. 227. Rev. Charles Maginn, the nephew of William Maginn, and Miss Elizabeth Maginn, the niece, both mentioned to the present writer the thoughtless generosity with which their uncle signed bonds and disposed of his possessions.

[2] Gerald Griffin, for instance, writes to his brother that Maginn "attacked Campbell's Ritter Bann most happily and at the same time most cuttingly, and afterward wanted Jerdan to get up a dinner and bring Campbell and him together." Quoted in the *Irish Quarterly Review* for Sept., 1852, II, 612.

[3] R. W. Montagu, Memoir prefacing *Miscellanies* of William Maginn (London, 1885), I, xvii.

[4] In regard to Maginn's knowledge at first hand of the poor, his early biographers are explicit: E. V. Kenealy, *Dublin University Magazine,* XXIII, 92 f.; R. S. Mackenzie, Memoir prefacing Vol. V *(Fraserian Papers)* of Maginn's *Miscellaneous Writings* (New York, 1855-57), pp. lvi f.

[5] Maginn: "Sir John Falstaff," in *Shakspeare Papers* (London, 1860), p. 50.

[6] Autobiography included in *Memoirs of Edward Vaughan Kenealy,* by Arabella Kenealy (London, 1908), p. 98 f.

[7] The date of Maginn's birth is sometimes incorrectly given as 1793. According to Cork records, it is July 10, 1794. This date has been placed on the stone cross recently erected to his memory in the churchyard of Walton-on-Thames by his grandchildren and others interested in his work and life.

[8] When one of the girls, Mary, was later living with William in London and Paris, Theodore Hook on meeting her exclaimed, "She's Maginn in petticoats." [Narrated to the present writer by Miss Elizabeth Maginn, the niece.]

[9] Maginn's friend, E. V. Kenealy, testifies in regard to the extent of his theological knowledge: *Brallaghan: or, The Deipnosophists* (London, 1845), p. 336. R. P. Gillies also speaks of the ease with which Maginn could cite from memory the early Christian fathers, such as Gregory, Basil, and Thomas Aquinas: *Memoirs of a Literary Veteran* (London, 1851), III, 150 f. A friend of Maginn whose brothers were educated at his school told Mackenzie that occasionally while sitting in the family circle and off and on joining in the conversation he used to dash off a sermon for a clergyman who distrusted his own abilities.

[10] This story was narrated to the present writer by Miss Elizabeth Maginn.

[11] Miss Elizabeth Maginn also explained that before Maginn could talk his mother used to ask him to hand her the various letters of the alphabet, merely saying, "Billy, give me *M*," or some other letter.

[12] Rev. Charles Maginn, the nephew of William Maginn, has kindly sent the following extract from the matriculation roll of Trinity College, Dublin University:

Date of entrance	Christian name	Surname	Rank	Father's name	Father's profession	Tutor
Jan. 6, 1806	William	Maginn	Pens	John	Schoolmaster	Dr. Kyle

Rev. Charles Maginn also contributes the story told by his own father that the University examiners on first seeing small William, exclaimed, "Take that child back to his nursery," but ended by giving him first place and a Hebrew prize. It will be noticed that according to this account the ranking of the boy is first and not tenth.

[13] R. S. Mackenzie, "Memoir," p. xiii.

[14] *Catalogue of the Graduates of the University of Dublin.*

[15] *Irish Quarterly Review,* II, 598. This article is anonymous, but gives evidence that its writer was accurately informed and intimate with Maginn.

[16] Stories have come down in Maginn's family of his delightful relations with his youngest brother Charles, the baby of the household, and later of his devotion to his own children and those of his friends. Even Mrs. Oliphant emphasizes his fondness for young people and his ability to fill a house in which they were with laughter. *Annals of a Publishing House* (Edinburgh, 1897), I, 385. Even during the last weeks of his life when he was dying at Walton-on-Thames, a little boy used to come daily to his bedside to read Greek with him and to take his dictation of the "Homeric Ballads." R. S. Mackenzie, "Memoir," p. cv.

[17] *Catalogue of the Graduates of the University of Dublin.*

[18] S. C. Hall, *Retrospect of a Long Life* (New York, 1883), p. 68.

[19] William Jerdan, *Autobiography* (London, 1853), III, 82 f.

[20] Margaret Oliphant, *Annals of a Publishing House,* I, 207.

[21] E. V. Kenealy, *Dublin University Magazine,* XXIII, 83.

[22] E. V. Kenealy, *Dublin University Magazine,* XXIII, 83.

[23] Margaret Oliphant, *op. cit.,* I, 364.

[24] *Ibid.,* I, 299.

[25] *Ibid.,* I, 208.

[26] *Ibid.,* I, 218.

[27] *Ibid.,* I, 210.

[28] *Ibid.,* I, 225.

[29] *Dublin University Magazine,* XXIII, 81.

[30] Well-known examples are Samuel Rogers, whose devotion to poetry injured his reputation as a banker; W. B. Procter, who at one time felt it necessary to substitute for his familiar pseudonym Barry Cornwall the unknown J. Bethel; Sir John Skelton, who for years cautiously retained his pen name of Shirley.

[31] The direct quotations have been extracted from the account given in the *Irish Quarterly Review,* II, 599.

[32] Richard Edgcumbe, *Byron: the Last Phase* (London, 1909), p. 150.

[33] Margaret Oliphant, *op. cit.,* I, 398 f.

[34] *Ibid.,* I, 397.

[35] *Ibid.,* I, 396.

[36] J. G. Lockhart, *Theodore Hook, a Sketch* (London, 1852), p. 60 f.; first published in the *Quarterly Review* for May, 1843, LXXII, 86.

[37] Rev. Charles Maginn has kindly contributed the following testimony, the original of which is in his possession: "I certify that William Maginn, Doctor of Laws, and Ellen Bullen were married by me (by permission) this 31st day of January, 1824.

[signed] Wm Colburn

Witness my hand this
27th day of Feb'y, 1895."

[38] *Memoir of John Wilson,* by his daughter Mary Gordon (New York, 1863), p. 271.

[39] *Ibid.,* p. 273.

[40] R. H. D. Barham, *The Life and Remains of Theodore Edward Hook* (London, 1849), I, 225.

[41] Walter Scott, *Familiar Letters* (Boston, 1894), II, 411.

[42] *Memoir of John Wilson,* p. 293.

[43] S. C. Hall, *Retrospect of a Long Life,* p. 73.

[44] S. C. Hall, *Book of Memories* (London, 1871), p. 237.

[45] *Memoir of John Wilson,* p. 289.

[46] Walter Jerrold, *Douglas Jerrold, Dramatist and Wit* (London, 1914), I, 132-34.

[47] Margaret Oliphant, *op. cit.,* II, 123.

[48] See present text, p. 56. Probably this is the basis of the report mentioned by James Hannay and others that Thackeray gave £500 to relieve the straitened circumstances of Maginn.

[49] Andrew Lang, *Life and Letters of John Gibson Lockhart* (London, 1897), II, 210.

[50] *Correspondence and Diaries of the Right Honourable John Wilson Croker,* edited by L. J. Jennings (London, 1884), II, 258.

[51] On January 29 Peel wrote to Croker, "I have done what you suggested as to Maginn." *Ibid.,* II, 262.

[52] An account of Maginn's shocking condition is given by K. B. Thomson, *Recollections of Literary Characters and Celebrated Places* (London, 1854), I, 5.

[53] Malcolm Elwin, *Thackeray: a Personality* (London, 1932), p. 48.
[54] Carlyle, *Two Note Books from 1822 to 1832* (Grolier Club, New York, 1898), p. 258.
[55] J. A. Froude, *Thomas Carlyle: a History of the First Forty Years of His Life* (New York, 1882), II, 212.
[56] Carlyle, *op. cit.,* p. 246.
[57] "Portrait Gallery" sketch of Maginn, *Fraser's,* II, 716.
[58] E. V. Kenealy, chapter on Maginn included in *Brallaghan,* p. 333.
[59] K. B. Thomson, *op. cit.,* I, 2 f.
[60] Rev. Charles Maginn has kindly contributed this evidence from a manuscript by Dr. J. S. Crone, which is in his possession.
[61] *Literary Souvenir* for 1883.

IX. *The Story of L.E.L.*

[1] E. V. Kenealy makes this statement on what he feels to be good authority, though he does not give the name of his informant: *Dublin University Review,* XXIII, 90. It is, however, denied by William Jerdan: *Autobiography,* III, 184.
[2] S. C. Hall, *Book of Memories,* p. 284.
[3] Emma Roberts, Memoir prefacing posthumous edition of *Zenana and Other Poems,* pp. 14 f.; K. B. Thomson, *op. cit.,* II, 79.
[4] S. C. Hall and Mrs. Hall, "Memories of Authors: Miss Landon," *Atlantic Monthly,* March, 1865, XV, 334(a); published contemporaneously in the *Art Journal* for March, 1865, New Series, IV; republished in *Book of Memories.*
[5] K. B. Thomson, *op. cit.,* II, 80.
[6] Emma Roberts, Memoir, *op. cit.,* pp. 17 f.
[7] *Art Journal,* New Series IV, 90(b) f.
[8] Watts was an old enemy of the Fraserians. See present text, p. 51.
[9] *Diaries of William Charles Macready, 1833-1851,* edited by William Toynbee (London, 1912), I, 262.
[10] S. Laman Blanchard, *Life and Literary Remains of L.E.L.* (Philadelphia, 1841), I, 111 f. R. Renton has expressed the opinion that Forster was never actually engaged to L.E.L. In view of the passage quoted from Macready's diary and of L.E.L.'s letter it is difficult to accept this view. It is also to be remembered that Charles Kent, Forster's old friend, states that they were engaged: life of Forster in the *Dictionary of National Biography.*
[11] D. E. Enfield, *L.E.L.: a Mystery of the Thirties* (London, 1928), pp. 110 f.
[12] Autobiography included in *Memoirs of Edward Vaughan Kenealy,* p. 94.
[13] *Dublin University Magazine,* XXIII, 74 (also, n.).
[14] James Grant Wilson, *Thackeray in the United States* (London, 1904), II, 134.
[15] See present text, p. 51 f.
[16] A detailed account of the assault was given during the trial of Berkeley. This description is quoted in full in *Fraser's,* XV, 100-04. Maginn's comments on the affair, *Fraser's,* XV, 137-43, show that he had by no means been intimidated by his duel with Berkeley or stood in awe of the titles and positions held by the young nobleman. "I do not imagine that birth, dignity, or office command of themselves respect. The holder of these advantages should not abuse them to their dishonour. If ruffian and cowardly violence is a qualification for a magistrate, I recommend Lord John Russell by all means to retain Mr. Grantley Berkeley in the commission of the peace.

If striking an unarmed man, with all the advantage of strength and numbers, be fitting for an officer under his majesty's colours, Lord Fitzroy Somerset ought to deem Mr. Grantley Berkeley an ornament to any mess table to which he is attached; and if exhibitions of stupidity and violence are qualifications for the reformed parliament, I wish the intelligent and independent electors of West Gloucestershire joy of their representative."

[17] Maginn's narrow escape from his own bullet's plowing the ground a short distance from his foot is recorded by Berkeley, who also mentions his adversary's not firing another shot in its stead. For his account of the duel see *My Life and Recollections* (London, 1865-66), II, 64-67.

[18] The brief depositions of George Maclean, the servant Emily Bayley, and the fort's physician, which were obtained from the secretary of the Western African Company by L.E.L.'s brother, W. H. Landon, are given in full by S. Laman Blanchard, *op. cit.*, I, 177-80.

[19] R. R. Madden, *The Literary Life and Correspondence of the Countess of Blessington* (London, 1855), II, 278.

[20] *Ibid.*, II, 277.

[21] These statements were made by the brother of L.E.L. in a letter to the Colonial Secretary, Lord John Russell, quoted by S. Laman Blanchard, *op. cit.*, I, 199 ff.

[22] These reports are described in a letter by Lady Blessington. R. R. Madden, *op. cit.*, II, 298.

[23] *Ibid.*, III, 516. The full account of his investigation is given in Vol. II, Chaps. XXVI, XXVII, with supplementary details in Vol. III, Appendix XIV, pp. 511-32.

[24] K. B. Thomson, *op. cit.*, II, 93.

[25] *Ibid.*, II, 88.

[26] R. R. Madden, *op. cit.*, II, 275. See also Brodie Cruikshank, *Eighteen Years on the Gold Coast of Africa* (London, 1873).

[27] K. B. Thomson, *op. cit.*, II, 87.

[28] See the letter written by the secretary to Lord John Russell in reply to W. H. Landon: S. Laman Blanchard, *op. cit.*, I, 201.

[29] Margaret Oliphant, *op. cit.*, II, 334.

[30] S. C. Hall, *Retrospect of a Long Life*, pp. 68-70.

[31] Andrew Lang, *op. cit.*, II, 210.

[32] *Dublin University Magazine*, XXIII, 95 f.

[33] Andrew Lang, *op. cit.*, II, 78, 209.

[34] John Lockhart, *Theodore Hook: a Sketch* (third ed., London, 1852), p. 62, n.

[35] Rev. Precentor Webster, *Cork Historical and Archaeological Society*, XXIII, 44.

[36] Related to the present writer by Miss Elizabeth Maginn.

[37] Autobiography included in *Memoirs of Edward Vaughan Kenealy*, pp. 99 f.

[38] E. V. Kenealy has given three descriptions of Maginn's last days and funeral: *Fraser's*, Jan., 1843, XXVII, 21; *Dublin University Magazine*, XXIII, 99-101; *Brallaghan*, pp. 331 f.

[39] Rev. Precentor Webster, *Cork Historical and Archaeological Society*, XXIII, 45 f.

[40] Andrew Lang, *op. cit.*, II, 209 f.

[41] Information kindly given to the present writer by Rev. Charles Maginn and by Miss Elizabeth Maginn.

x. *Enemies*

[1] From a letter to George Moreland Crawford, Paris correspondent for the *Daily News,* quoted in the *Critic* (New York), Dec. 26, 1885, New Series, IV, 306(b).

[2] *Final Reliques of Father Prout,* ed. by Blanchard Jerrold (London, 1876), p. 143. See above, earlier discussion of Thackeray's acquaintance with Maginn, pp. 56 f.

[3] "The Tobias Correspondence" appeared in *Blackwood's Magazine* for July and Aug., 1840, XLVIII, 52-63, 205-14.

[4] According to Robert Pearse Gillies, Maginn had an "almost irresistible impulse" to throw into the fire his writing dashed off for magazines and newspapers, and used to refer to himself as a "mere scrap writer." *Memoirs of a Literary Veteran,* III, 152.

[5] His habitual attitude is commented on in the obituary notice in *Fraser's* for Sept., 1842, XXVI, 377.

[6] *Retrospect of a Long Life,* p. 68.

[7] S. C. Hall, *Art Journal* for April, 1865, New Series IV, 109. Later included in his *Book of Memories,* p. 159.

[8] *Book of Memories,* p. 159. It is to be noted that this anecdote is given as an instance of Maginn's wit by R. H. D. Barham, *op. cit.,* p. 225, n.

[9] *The Trials of Sir Jasper: a Temperance Tale in Verse* (London, 1873?); *An Old Story: a Temperance Tale in Verse* (London, 1876).

[10] J. F. Clarke, *Autobiographical Recollections of the Medical Profession* (London, 1874), p. 112.

[11] Margaret Oliphant, *op. cit.,* I, 364, 385.

[12] *Ibid.,* I, 404.

[13] *Ibid.,* I, 373.

[14] *Dublin University Magazine,* XXIII, 81. For Maginn's article on Leslie, see *Blackwood's Magazine,* VIII, 207-09.

[15] *Ibid.,* XXIII, 82.

[16] M. H. Spielmann, *The History of "Punch"* (London, 1895), p. 307.

[17] Grantley Berkeley, *op. cit.,* II, 43-51.

[18] *Ibid.,* III, 188.

[19] *Ibid.,* II, 51.

[20] Of his numerous frays, see, for instance, that described on page 61 of the edition by Leech and Jalland (London, 1897).

[21] Grantley Berkeley, *op. cit.,* II, 43-77.

[22] K. B. Thomson, *op. cit.,* II, 86.

[23] R. R. Madden, *op. cit.,* III, 511.

[24] Grantley Berkeley, *op. cit.,* III, 187.

[25] *Ibid.,* III, 193.

[26] S. C. Hall and Mrs. Hall, "Memories of Authors: Miss Landon," *Art Journal,* New Series IV, p. 92(b), n.

[27] Grantley Berkeley, *op. cit.,* III, 197 f.

[28] *Ibid.,* III, 187.

[29] S. Laman Blanchard, *op. cit.,* I; R. R. Madden, *op. cit.,* II, Chaps. XXVI and XXVII; Appendix XIV; K. B. Thomson, *op. cit.,* II, 71-98.

[30] K. B. Thomson, *op. cit.,* I, 1-12. This account was originally published as an anony-

mous article, "A Literary Retrospect by a Middle-Aged Man," *Bentley's Miscellany,* XVIII, 587.

[31] Grantley Berkeley, *op. cit.,* III, 199.

[32] *Ibid.,* III, 199.

[33] Lockhart's "Gallery" sketch of Maginn. *Fraser's,* II, 716.

[34] *The Critic, London Literary Journal* for April, 1852, XI, No. 265, p. 201(a).

[35] E. V. Kenealy, *Dublin University Magazine,* XXIII, 90.

[36] An unsuccessful attempt had been made to establish before the House of Lords the legality of Earl Berkeley's marriage in 1785 to Mary Cole, thereby making legitimate his first four sons. After he had been formally married in 1796 two other sons, of whom Grantley Berkeley was the younger, were born.

[37] *Reminiscences of a Huntsman* (ed. by Leech and Jollard, London, 1897), p. 315.

[38] S. C. Hall and Mrs. Hall, "Memories of Authors: Miss Landon."

[39] Michael Sadleir, *Bulwer and His Wife: a Panorama* (London, 1933), pp. 421-26; see also pp. 249 f.

[40] *Ibid.,* pp. 341, 245 f., 255-66.

[41] *Ibid.,* p. 341 n.

[42] *Fraser's,* II, 466.

[43] Michael Sadleir, *op. cit.,* pp. 425 f.; see also p. 250.

[44] *Ibid.,* p. 249 f.

[45] R. R. Madden, *op. cit.,* II, 295 f.

[46] L.E.L.'s letter is undated, but was probably written toward the end of 1835, rather than in 1834, the date given by Mr. Sadleir. The notice in Macready's diary, it will be remembered, was under Nov., 1835, and obviously refers to events which had just occurred. This later date is in keeping with statements in the biographies of Maginn, which refer to his estrangement from his wife in 1836. The letter is quoted from Michael Sadleir, *op. cit.,* pp. 425 f.

L.E.L. to Bulwer.

I prefer writing to speaking. When I speak I become ashamed and confused and never say precisely what I mean. Misunderstanding there certainly is, if you suppose that I wish all connection between myself and Mr. Forster at an end on account merely of the steps he has taken in the late most miserable business. . . .

From all I can learn, the cruel scandal was old; was well known to have originated in the very lowest portion of the press; was put down by the kindly countenance of friends—and, I may add, by the whole tenor of my life. It was forgotten by most and scorned by all. . . . I will not admit that Mr. Forster *vindicated* my conduct, inasmuch as there was nothing to vindicate. Still holding as I do this opinion, I should not consider it a sufficient justification of my resolve that the gentleman can never be to me more than a friend. Mr. Forster states that he will not consider me as bound to him if I can prove that he mentioned the report to any to whom it was previously unknown! Yet there was one person it was utterly unknown to—one person to whom, if he had any common feeling or delicacy he could not have named it—and that is myself. If his future protection is to harass and humiliate me as much as the present—God keep me from it. . . . I cannot get over the entire want of delicacy to me which could repeat such a slander to myself. The whole of his late conduct to me personally has left behind almost dislike—certainly fear of his imperious and overbearing temper. I am sure we never could be happy together. He is clever, honourable, kind; but he is quite deficient in the sensitiveness to the feelings of another which is to me an indispensable requisite. I bitterly regret what has passed and any pain my determination may inflict upon him; but we are quite unsuited to each other and the proof is the very first question of opinion—feeling—that arises between us. How differently do we view it!

I must repeat my thanks for your kindness. I cannot say what I owe to your friendship on this occasion—its delicacy, its generosity, and its patience can never be forgotten. I am grateful, most earnestly, deeply grateful.

[47] *New Monthly Magazine,* XXXII, 577.

[48] *Fraser's,* VIII, 479-82.

[49] *Ibid.,* XV, 505-14.

[50] Michael Sadleir, *op. cit.,* p. 282.

[51] *Ibid.,* p. 247; see also p. 281.

XI. *Literary Work*

[1] Obituary notice of Maginn in *Fraser's,* XXVI, 377.

[2] R. P. Gillies, *op. cit.,* III, 153 f. This is in keeping with Maginn's comment, "The task of the satirist appears to me lowest in which talent can be employed." Since the greater part of his own creative work was satire the remark reveals his frame of mind.

[3] See Appendix 6, under "Collected Essays and Poetry."

[4] See Appendix 6, under "Work Erroneously Attributed to Maginn."

[5] *A History of Nineteenth Century Literature* (New York, 1910), p. 204.

[6] George Saintsbury, "Three Humourists," in *Essays in English Literature,* Second Series (New York, 1895), p. 297.

[7] *A History of Criticism and Literary Taste in Europe* (New York, 1917), III, 489.

[8] *Ibid.,* III, 488.

[9] *A New Variorum Edition of Shakespeare* (Philadelphia, 1892). See note for *The Tempest,* Act I, scene 1, line 43.

[10] *Ibid.* See note for *Henry VI,* Part I, Act I, scene 1, line 56; and for *The Tempest,* Act I, scene 2, line 266.

[11] *Ibid.* See note for *The Tempest,* Act I, scene 2, line 315.

[12] *Passages of a Working Life during Half a Century* (London, 1864-65), II, 290 f.

[13] *Fraser's,* XXI, 741(a).

[14] *A History of Shakespearian Criticism* (Oxford University Press, 1932), I, 193-97.

[15] *Fraser's,* XVII, 1-5.

[16] *On Translating Homer* (New York, 1883), pp. 187 f.

[17] Article on Maginn in the *Dictionary of National Biography.*

[18] W. M. Praed, "Musæ O'Connorianæ," in *The Etonian* (London, 1822), I, 351.

[19] See present text, pp. 96 f., 106 f.

[20] Richard Edgcumbe, *Byron: the Last Phase* (London, 1909), p. 100.

[21] *Essays in English Literature,* pp. 298 f.

[22] C. L. Graves, Introduction to *Humours of Irish Life* (Every Irishman's Library Series, London, 191-), pp. i-ii.

[23] D. J. O'Donoghue, "Irish Wit and Humour," in *Irish Literature,* edited by Justin McCarthy and others (Philadelphia, 1904), VI, xiv-xvi.

[24] D. J. Donoghue, article on Maginn in *The Poets of Ireland* (London, 1912).

[25] See "Ante-Preface" to the edition by Moorhead, Simpson and Bond (New York, 1868), p. vii.
[26] R. S. Mackenzie, "Memoir," p. liv.
[27] Margaret Oliphant, *op. cit.,* I, 202 f.
[28] *Fraser's,* VIII, 45.
[29] *Ibid.,* III, 95.
[30] Margaret Oliphant, *op. cit.,* I, 403 f.
[31] *Ibid.,* I, 243.
[32] *Ibid.,* I, 244 f.
[33] *Quarterly Review,* XXXVII, 87.

APPENDIX 1: DISPUTED POINTS ON THACKERAY

[1] See present text, pp. 62-64.
[2] The first to reject the series was Johnson: *The Early Writings of William Makepeace Thackeray* (London, 1888), p. 41.
[3] *Ibid.,* p. 41.
[4] S. M. Ellis, *William Harrison Ainsworth and His Friends* (London, 1911), I, 294.
[5] R. S. Mackenzie says that a list of Maginn's writings had been sent to him in America by E. V. Kenealy after the latter had decided not to attempt bringing out an edition in England: "Memoir" prefacing Vol. V *(Fraserian Papers)* of Maginn's *Miscellaneous Writings* (New York, 1855-57), p. x. Kenealy explains that he secured his list of Maginn's contributions to *Fraser's* from Mr. Nickisson, the successor to the publisher James Fraser: *Dublin University Magazine,* XXIII, 89.
[6] *Fraser's,* XIII, 714(b).
[7] Margaret Oliphant, *Annals of a Publishing House* (Edinburgh, 1897), II, 240.
[8] Quoted from a letter now in the British Museum: Lewis Benjamin, *William Makepeace Thackeray* (London, 1910), I, 138.
[9] *Fraser's,* XIV, 181(b)
[10] Only a few months earlier the statement had been made that "Byron bore away the palm from Wordsworth and Shelley, though his best thoughts were stolen from them." *Ibid.,* XIII, 255(a).
[11] See present text, p. 227.
[12] *Ibid.,* I, 504.
[13] Lewis Benjamin, *op. cit.,* II, 154.
[14] *Fraser's,* IX, 121 f.
[15] C. P. Johnson, *The Early Writings of William Makepeace Thackeray* (London, 1888), p. 41.
[16] See present text, pp. 71-77
[17] *Fraser's,* XXI, 227 f.
[18] See, for instance, *ibid.,* I, 521(b) f.
[19] "Portrait Gallery" sketch of Hook, *ibid.,* IX, 455; *Noctes Ambrosianæ,* No. 45, *Blackwood's Magazine* for July, 1829; and also a later collaboration by Lockhart and Maginn, *Fraser's,* III, 156(a) ff.
[20] *Fraser's,* III, 96(b).
[21] R. P. Gillies, *Memoirs of a Literary Veteran* (London, 1851), Vol. II, Chap. XIII.
[22] In the introduction to "Two Articles on the Annuals," in *Fraser's* for November, 1834, Maginn attributes the first article to Barry Cornwall and the second to Our

Man of Geinus (John Churchill). Maginn's own article appeared in *Fraser's,* II, 543-54.

[23] See, for instance, "A Rigmarole on Taverns and Things in General," *Fraser's,* XVIII, 115(a); and "A Budget of Bards," *Fraser's,* XX, 765(a) f. "Brallaghan" was commenced in *Fraser's,* Jan., 1842, XXV, 65-80.

APPENDIX 2: A QUESTION OF IDENTIFICATION—CARLYLE, HERAUD, AND MAGINN

[1] See present text, pp. 89-93.

[2] "A Phase of Carlyle's Relation to *Fraser's Magazine,*" *P.M.L.A.,* Vol. XXXIX, No. 4, pp. 923-25.

[3] *Fraser's,* I, 159(a) f., 130(a), 135(a); III, 161 (b); VII, 317; XIII, 255(a).

[4] *Ibid.,* V, 659.

[5] *Ibid.,* I, 56-63.

[6] See, for instance: the "Election of Editor," *ibid.,* I, 738-57; II, 238-50; and the various "Symposiacs" and "Fraser Papers," beginning in *ibid.,* II, 487-504.

[7] *Ibid.,* V, 659(a).

[8] *Ibid.,* V, 660(a).

[9] *Works* (Centenary ed.), V, 78.

[10] See present text, pp. 90 f.

[11] *Fraser's,* VII, 309.

[12] In addition to various overlappings of thought, the last paragraph of the essay, *Fraser's,* VII, 317(b), states that the author wrote an earlier article on Byron's youth, "Lord Byron's Juvenile Poems," *Fraser's,* VI, 183-204.

[13] *Ibid.,* VII, 309(b).

[14] *Ibid.,* VII, 303-07.

[15] *Times Literary Supplement* (London), April 26, 1928.

[16] Heraud had discussed in some detail the alleged madness of genius, or the rapt state of mind in the process of creation: "On Poetical Genius," *Fraser's,* I, 60(a) ff.

[17] *Times Literary Supplement* (London), Jan. 20, 1927.

[18] *Modern Language Notes,* May, 1931, pp. 316-21.

[19] *Fraser's,* II, 162(a); III, 199(b); 713(a); I, 5, 303-08, 636-42.

[20] *Ibid.,* I, 60(b) f.; 595(a); II, 394(a); V, 590 ff., 22 f.; I, 273(a), 588; II, 84 f.

[21] *Ibid.,* I, 695 f., 751; III, 195-204, 713-19; V, 107-13, 125.

[22] The MacGrawler reference, *Fraser's,* I, 526(b), was to Bulwer Lytton's caricature of Scotch reviewers. In the quarrel between the *New Monthly* and *Fraser's* it was obviously considered to include Maginn, who had been prominent on *Blackwood's* staff. See *New Monthly,* XXXII, 577.

[23] *Fraser's,* III, 292 ff.

[24] *Oration on the Death of Coleridge* (2d ed., London, 1834), pp. 6 ff.

[25] *Fraser's,* IV, 167-79, 540-53; V, 280-94.

[26] *Ibid.,* VII, 532.

[27] *The Critic, London Literary Journal,* Vol. XI, No. 265, p. 201(a).

[28] See his prize essay *Expediency and Means of Elevating the Profession of the Educator in the Public Estimation,* 1839 (reprinted by Bronson Alcott as No. 3 in *Human Culture*); *Shakespeare: His Inner Life as Intimated in His Works,* 1865.

[29] *Reminiscences* (Froude's ed., Scribner's, 1881), p. 411.

[30] J. A. Froude: *Thomas Carlyle: a History of His Life in London* (New York, 1884), I, 16.

[31] *Fraser's,* XIII, 363-74.
[32] The opening of this "Asinarii Senici," as well as that of the previous one, *Fraser's,* VII, 96-106, is concerned with the often-repeated discussion of genius.
[33] Professor Emery Neff gives a significant treatment of Carlyle's interest in Saint-Simon's doctrines: *Carlyle* (New York, 1932), pp. 116-21.
[34] *Fraser's,* III, 169(b).
[35] *P.M.L.A.,* Vol. XXXIX, No. 4, p. 926.
[36] M. D. Conway, *Thomas Carlyle* (New York, 1881), pp. 31 f.

INDEX